State Corporate Control in Transition

Piotr Kozarzewski

State Corporate Control in Transition

Poland in a Comparative Perspective

palgrave
macmillan

Piotr Kozarzewski
Faculty of Economics
Maria Curie-Skłodowska University
Lublin, Poland

ISBN 978-3-030-78561-1 ISBN 978-3-030-78562-8 (eBook)
https://doi.org/10.1007/978-3-030-78562-8

This Palgrave Macmillan imprint is published by the registered company Springer Nature Switzerland AG
The registered company address is: Gewerbestrasse 11, 6330 Cham, Switzerland

Acknowledgments

This work was supported by the National Science Centre of Poland under Grant no. 2017/25/B/HS4/01103 "The Phenomenon of 'The Return of State-Owned Enterprises' in Contemporary Economy: Identification, Characteristics, and Consequences for the Economic Theory and for the Theory of Economic Policy." I would like to express my gratitude to all my friends and colleagues, who directly or indirectly helped me write this book. In particular, I am extremely grateful to Maciej Bałtowski from Maria Curie-Skłodowska University for always being the first person with whom I discussed my ideas, as well as an exceptionally insightful reader of everything I have written. For fruitful discussions and generating new ideas, I am grateful to Barbara Błaszczyk from the Institute of Economics of the Polish Academy of Sciences, as well as to my numerous Hungarian colleagues, Miklós Szanyi and Eva Voszka from the Hungarian Academy of Sciences, and Beáta Farkas from Szeged University—to name but few. I am also grateful to my former doctoral student Aliaksandr Papko from Centre for East European Studies, University of Warsaw and Belsat TV for very fruitful discussions and for guiding me to interesting literature. And, traditionally, to my Moscow friend Irina Sinitsina from the Russian Academy of Sciences, for her kindness combined with the role of the devil's advocate, which helped me to clarify many ideas used in this book. Last but not least, I'm thankful to two anonymous reviewers of my publishing proposal to Palgrave Macmillan, who helped me to improve the structure of the book as well as gave me better understanding of the place of my research in the current literature.

Contents

List of Figures

List of Tables

CHAPTER 1

Introduction

After the global financial crisis of 2008–2009, we see the growing interest among policymakers towards the more active role of the state in the enterprise sector. Under the pressure of the new challenges set up by globalization processes, after several decades of neoliberal policies, many governments in developed economies started appreciating more active attitude towards enterprises as crisis management and development support tools, which includes wider use of state ownership. The response of many governments in market economies to the challenges posed by the COVID-19 pandemic in the form of the wide-scale support for businesses including bailouts, expanding (at least temporarily) the scope of state ownership, seems to confirm that active ownership policy has become a persistent element of the updated paradigm of the role of the state in the economy.

At the same time, we witness the growing importance of emerging economies, a significant number of them regarding state-owned enterprises (SOEs) as vehicles of their economic development, such as China, Brazil, India, Indonesia, Egypt or Thailand. Also, in several post-communist countries, even such former leaders of transition as Poland and Hungary, as well as in Russia and some other former USSR republics, growing statism in their economic policies can be seen, including the privatization reversal, i.e., expansion of the state-owned enterprise sector through nationalizations and large-scale governmental investments.

P. Kozarzewski, *State Corporate Control in Transition*,
https://doi.org/10.1007/978-3-030-78562-8_1

The widespread character of these statist trends (often referred as state capitalism—Bremmer 2010; Kurlantzick 2016) was noticed by researches and even the term "the return of state-owned enterprises" (Flores-Macias and Musacchio 2009) has been coined. However, the existing knowledge on this subject still has important gaps. SOEs and the state as an owner and investor became a subject of growing number of literature, grounding these subjects in modern economic theories and in real economic practice—including the seminal Routledge handbook (Bernier et al. 2020). But so far, the literature on state ownership and state corporate control concentrated mostly on the developed economies and on selected emerging economies, first of all Russia and China, with very few (and fragmentary) publications devoted to other regions, including countries of the former Eastern Bloc (Daiser et al. 2017).[1]

* * *

There are several reasons, why concentrating on studying the state corporate control in transition countries may be important—and I try to fill the relevant knowledge gaps in my book.

The first and the most obvious reason is that it would increase the volume of knowledge on the post-communist transition, where ownership issues were of crucial, systemic importance and meant a radical change of a policy towards the enterprise sector. It was pre-determined by the essence of transition from the administrative economy, where state ownership dominated, towards a market one, based on private property with governments performing corporate control over enterprises only when it is really essential: where market mechanisms fail or when it's the state owner and investor who is the best in meeting some goals very important for the nation.

For the time being, the post-communist transition as a process of change in both the economic (market reforms) and political dimension (transforming the authoritarian regimes into democratic ones) seems to be over. For many years we see no progress here, and in several post-communist countries we even witness the increasing state interventionism and growing elements of authoritarianism. But the transition is not fully over, even for its leaders, in the sense of achieving the goal of building a Western-type capitalist system based on market and democracy. The problem is not solely that in most of the post-communist countries market mechanisms are still not mature compared with the developed marked economies and democracy is to a larger or smaller extent flawed compared to the best performers of the Western world. The similar lack of excellence can be found in many other capitalist countries, for example in a number of Latin American or South European ones. But the main deficiencies in the emerging capitalist systems in the post-communist world more often than not are direct or indirect remnants of their past, and it is too early for placing them on the same varieties of capitalism (VoC) shelf together with formally similar countries with no communist past. The key peculiarities lay, among others, in the structural and institutional setup of the last, decaying stage of the communist system which has not been fully overcome, and in the dysfunctions which were created by the transition process itself. In the economic dimension, the most prominent area of this unfinished transition is the role of the state in the enterprise sector: the state corporate control still goes beyond the scope determined by the market economy paradigm—regardless the version of capitalism being built in a given post-communist country.

At the same time, despite the post-communist transition seemingly has been studied in every possible way, it still has gaps in the area of the state corporate control: through the years, researchers concentrated predominantly on privatization of state-owned enterprises (SOEs) which resulted in a significant number of valuable studies (to name but few: Boycko et al. 1996; Estrin et al. 2009; Iwasaki and Mizobata 2018), while largely neglecting the remaining SOE sector. Those few publications that exist in English concentrate at most on its quantitative (Matuszak and Szarzec 2019) or institutional (Besnik 2017) characteristics and usually omit the problems of the state policy towards this sector. A number of detailed studies on some countries in national languages exist, but they are not available for an international reader.

The reformist governments used to neglect this sector as well and generally failed to re-define the role of SOEs in the new economic system. Among decision makers in the countries that have embarked on market reforms a view prevailed that the existing SOE sector was predominantly just an intermediate phase on the road towards the economy based on private property. But in practice, mainly due to non-economic reasons, this sector has survived and has become a permanent feature of many post-communist economies. This "attention gap" led to numerous dysfunctions in the SOE sector and its impact on the national economies. It may be argued that this is the area where the institutional weaknesses of post-communist economies manifested themselves most strongly, with the phenomena of rent-seeking, corruption, and oligarchization, which led to destructive economic and even political consequences.

Secondly, our understanding of the causes of the recent statist trends in the world which have not omitted a number of post-communist countries, including Poland, should be improved. The economic (and political) systems of many transition countries are already similar enough with the rest of the capitalist world to experience common problems and to look for common solutions. So, the statist turn accompanied with deteriorating democratic mechanisms in several transition countries may have more universal grounds. On the other hand, the emerging populist-nationalist regimes, especially in Poland and Hungary, may offer a potential blueprint for a regime conversion towards authoritarianism in countries outside the post-communist region.

Whereas the revival of state corporate control in developed economies has been studied quite well (OECD 2005a; Mazzucato 2013; Musacchio and Lazzarini 2014, etc.), in the literature on transition countries, despite the growing number of publications, substantial knowledge gaps remain, especially in studies on the ownership policy of the state. Among others, the understudied issues include the roots and driving forces of the statist change which took place in several countries and whether it really addressed the previously neglected challenges of the state corporate control over enterprises. Here, at least two crucial questions remained unanswered and I discuss them in detail in this book:

1. to what extent these statist trends have universal grounds or they are rather contextual; in other words, what is the role of exogenous and endogenous factors: whether these trends have been provoked predominantly by some external factors or they originate from regularities of these countries' development;
2. to what extent these statist trends are a response to the development challenges and are intended to make SOEs a more effective tool for correcting market imperfections and meeting other vital public goals, or they are rather an outcome of private interest groups' efforts to expand their sources of rent.

Thirdly, the applicability of different research perspectives to studies of the role of the state in the enterprise sector in transition economies needs being improved; so far, they usually do not appreciate enough this are of study, or at least its specificity comparing with developed or other emerging economies. The transitology perspective seems to be one of the most applicable here, but, surprisingly, whereas a lot of attention was directed by these studies at ownership issues, they were focused almost exclusively on privatization, leaving the policy towards enterprises which remain under state control virtually unnoticed. Similarly, economic policy research largely omits the ownership policy of the state or at most concentrates on privatization, and not on the policy towards enterprises that stay under the state control. Economic systems research has several promising perspectives, but the role of the state in the economy or their applicability to transition countries is only recently started being appreciated. Institutionalism studies represent valuable approaches as well, especially public choice perspective, mainly through providing a set of analytical tools but so far, they were used less often for the study of the state corporate control in transition countries than they deserved.

Besides an inadequate elaboration of state corporate control issues, these perspectives function mostly independently, using their own concepts, methodology and terminology. Therefore, apart from filling the existing knowledge gaps, there is a need to at least to try establishing a certain level of coordination between these approaches, making an attempt in creating missing linkages among them. However, this book does not aim to create a universal approach unifying the existing perspectives; its intentions in this area are much more modest: to make the existing research tools more applicable to the subject under the study.

Fourthly, deficiency in in-depth studies on state corporate control in transition economies together with growing interest of policy makes towards more active role of the state in the national economy and its enterprise sector creates theoretical and methodological vacuum for practitioners both at the national and supra-national (e.g., European Union) levels. Thus, they have no appropriate access to the relevant knowledge on existing and possible approaches within the state's ownership policy from the point of view of the ability to contribute to the country's social and economic development and may be not aware of the risks of dysfunctions their decisions may create. This supply of knowledge must go beyond a technical advice "do this and don't do that" aimed at creation of some idealized model of the state corporate control. We already have a lot of knowledge about what technically could be done in order to achieve it the goals of state ownership policy—numerous recommendations on corporate governance in SOEs elaborated by international organizations exist

(OECD 2005b, 2010, 2015, 2018; World Bank 2014). The problem is how to introduce this knowledge to the economic policy.

Apart from organizational difficulties in creation of efficient and smoothly running machinery of the state corporate control (with all the problems of distribution of responsibilities among its elements, coordination, monitoring, etc.), important institutional issues must be resolved. The governments act in conditions of contradictory interests, expectations and behavior of various social groups that are engaged in creation and implementation of the social and economic policy. The interplay of contradictory interests, especially the behavior of powerful interest groups which extract rents from the economic policy of the state, may severely undermine or even fully block the reforms—the experience of transition countries being very meaningful here (Hellman 1998). There is still no answer in the literature and the decision-making practice, how governments can efficiently function in such unfavorable institutional conditions. The main knowledge gaps here are both in the in-depth analysis of these institutional conditions and in the lack of known feasible ways of overcoming the decision-making barriers that have institutional origin.

* * *

Poland seems to be one of the most appropriate cases to be studied because this country has exhibited the most prominent turn from being the leader of post-communist system change which included both economic and political transition (becoming one of the most reformed post-communist economies with developed market and democratic institutions), towards state capitalism and deteriorating democracy. In this respect, the emerging authoritarian regime in Poland which combines statism and populism may demonstrate patterns of possible transition from democracy to authoritarianism in other countries in Europe, even outside of the post-communist economies. Other two post-communist countries which also have experienced the statist turn, even earlier than Poland, i.e., Hungary and Russia, do not provide a researcher with such a multifaceted material to study. Developments in Hungary in many respects are quite similar to those in Poland, but Poland is distinct in the role of the state sector in the economy, which creates more possibilities in studying state interventionism that uses corporate control tools. Russia, where since the beginning of the twenty-first century we also witness even more significant expansion of the state in the enterprise sector and much deeper deterioration of democracy rule than in Poland, despite having some successes in post-communist transition, has never been a model for economic and political reforms.

But there's still the need to distinguish what is typical from what is unique in the Polish experience, so it should be studied in a comparative perspective of other transition countries, first of all those where the role of the state-controlled sector is very significant and/or increasing. Apart from the most obvious choices of Hungary and Russia with their clear statization trends, albeit following quite different patterns, I've chosen one more country as a certain kind of a benchmark of statism in a post-communist economy: Belarus. This country represents as a special case of "reluctant transition," being the reform outcast, where the state still keeps corporate control over the majority of the enterprise sector and gradually loosens it only under the threat of collapse of the inefficient economic system. In this country, the state plays (or at least tries to play) a role of the main vehicle of economic development, SOEs being among the major tools of it. At the same time, it is not a planned, administrative economy any more, and in conducting its economic policy, the government has to deal with the existence of market mechanisms, albeit highly flawed.

* * *

Summing up, this book addresses the role of the government in transition economies in direct management of enterprises and businesses based on control rights resulting from state ownership of firms. It consists of eight chapters. Chapter 2 is an extensive literature review that serves two objectives: to study the existing volume of knowledge on the subject and to critically asses the existing theoretical perspectives which are used (or may be used) in a study on the state corporate control in transition economies. Chapter 3 is mostly of a theoretical and methodological character dealing with the radical change of the state corporate control which had to take place in the course of the post-communist transition, its objectives and the manner of exercising the property rights which created a broad set of conceptual and practical challenges. Chapter 4 shows the evolution of the state corporate control in Poland during the transition divided into subsequent stages which were identified according to policy objectives, directions and tools of implementation, and changes in the institution setup. Chapter 5 discusses the outcomes of the evolution of the state corporate control policy in Poland in two dimensions: from the perspective of achieving the goals of this policy and the quantitative perspective analyzing the scale, extent and importance of SOEs in the Polish economy. Chapter 6 analyzes the key factors that may have influenced the course and effects of Polish state corporate control policy, its specific combination of the elements of continuity and change, along two dichotomies: action of decision-makers in the general public interest vs. the realization of specific group interests and the role of internal factors vs. the role of external factors. Chapter 7 is a comparative one: it is devoted to the origins, evolution and effects of corporate control policy in Hungary, Russia and Belarus vis-à-vis the Polish experience using a uniform research approach which makes possible to identify the role of common and contextual factors in these policies. The concluding Chapter 8 contains a stylized summary of the findings, a discussion on still existing knowledge gaps, suggestions on directions of future research and an attempt to look at the current clientelistic equilibrium in the state corporate control from the perspective of its stability and possible ways of its overcoming.

The book is based on a very diversified sources of knowledge. Apart from published ones, such as legal regulations of the respective countries, statistical data, theoretical and empirical publications, etc., I made extensive use of my own research and advisory experience gained over the last more than thirty years in Poland and a number of other post-communist countries. A significant part of the results of these projects, especially those of an advisory nature carried out within development assistance programs, for various reasons were not published. Therefore, some important information is provided without reference to the source or in a way that makes it impossible to precisely identify people and countries. My personal impressions based on my entire experience were also used, which also makes it impossible to refer to any particular source of knowledge.

Note

1. See more in Chapter 2.

References

Bernier, Luc, Massimo Florio, and Philippe Bance, eds. 2020. *The Routledge Handbook of State-Owned Enterprises*. New York: Routledge.

Besnik, Pula. 2017. Whither State Ownership? The Persistence of State-Owned Industry in Postsocialist Central and Eastern Europe. *Journal of East-West Business* 23 (4): 309–336. https://doi.org/10.1080/10669868.2017.1340388.

Boycko, Maxim, Andrei Shleifer, and Robert Vishny. 1996. "A Theory of Privatization." *The Economic Journal* 106 (435): 309–319.

Bremmer, Ian. 2010. "The End of the Free Market: Who Wins the War between States and Corporations?" *European View* 9: 249–252.

Daiser, Peter, Tamyko Ysa, and Daniel Schmitt. 2017. "Corporate Governance of State-owned Enterprises: A Systematic Analysis of Empirical Literature." *International Journal of Public Sector Management* 30 (5): 447–466.

Estrin, Saul, Jan Hanousek, Evžen Kočenda, and Jan Svejnar. 2009. "The Effects of Privatization and Ownership in Transition Economies." *Journal of Economic Literature* 47 (3): 699–728.

Flores-Macias, Francisco, and Aldo Musacchio. 2009. "The Return of State-owned Enterprises. Should We Be Afraid?" *Harvard International Review*. http://hir.harvard.edu/2009/04/the-return-of-state-owned-enterprises/. Accessed January 20, 2020.

Hellman, Joel S. 1998. "Winners Take All: The Politics of Partial Reform in Postcommunist Transition," *World Politics* 50 (2):203–234.

Iwasaki, Ichiro, and Satoshi Mizobata. 2018. "Post-privatization Ownership and Firm Performance: A Large Meta-analysis of the Transition Literature." *Annals of Public and Cooperative Economics* 89 (2): 263–322.

Kurlantzick, Joshua. 2016. *State Capitalism: How the Return of Statism is Transforming the World*. New York: Oxford University Press.

Matuszak, Piotr, and Katarzyna Szarzec. 2019. "The Scale and Financial Performance of State-owned Enterprises in the CEE Region." *Acta Oeconomica* 69 (4): 549–570.

Mazzucato, Mariana. 2013. *The Entrepreneurial State: Debunking Public vs. Private Sector Myths*. London: Anthem Press.

Musacchio, Aldo, and Sergio G. Lazzarini. 2014. *Reinventing State Capitalism: Leviathan in Business, Brazil and Beyond*. Cambridge: Harvard University Press.

OECD. 2005a. *Corporate Governance of State-owned Enterprises: A Survey of OECD Countries*. Paris: OECD Publishing.

OECD. 2005b. *Guidelines on Corporate Governance of State-owned Enterprises*. Paris: OECD Publishing.

OECD. 2010. *Accountability and Transparency: A Guide for State Ownership*. Paris: OECD Publishing.

OECD. 2015. *OECD Guidelines on Corporate Governance of State-owned Enterprises*. 2015 edition. Paris: OECD Publishing.

OECD. 2018. *Ownership and Governance of State-owned Enterprises. A Compendium of National Practices*. Paris: OECD Publishing.
World Bank. 2014. *Corporate Governance of State-owned Enterprises: A Toolkit*. Washington: The World Bank.

CHAPTER 2

State Corporate Control in Transition: Research Perspectives

In this chapter, I will try to critically assess the present state of knowledge on the state corporate control in transition countries, including Poland, within the existing research perspectives, and identify the existing knowledge gaps and possibilities of using these approaches in further research.

From the very start, I've encountered two major challenges here. Firstly, state corporate control is not a clearly distinguishable area of research which lays at the intersection of several research streams. A manifestation of this is the scattering of the existing studies on this subject among numerous perspectives, very often interweaved; many authors were interdisciplinary, if not to say eclectic in their approach and used tools taken from different disciplines of knowledge—not only from economics (and mixing approaches there as well), but also from sociology, political science, etc. This could reflect both the complexity of the object under study (first of all its complex relationships with other elements of economic reality) and the lack of a unified "theory of everything" which would provide a universal framework for such studies. Or at least clear "bridges" between these research perspectives. The second challenge is that, despite the diversity of approaches, the state of knowledge on the subject is still very fragmentary and very uneven across the research streams.

P. Kozarzewski, *State Corporate Control in Transition*, https://doi.org/10.1007/978-3-030-78562-8_2

The fact that these research streams are to a great extent interconnected and quite often one stream provides analytic tools for another, and it is not easy to separate them; therefore, a certain degree of arbitrariness was needed. In this chapter, I will discuss the research streams and perspectives that I find the most promising for studying state corporate control in Poland in a comparative perspective of selected other transition economies. Firstly, these are research streams important from the point of view of the objects they study. The first two, transition research and economic policy research, I will discuss quite briefly because I will pay more attention to them in Chapter 3. The third one includes various streams of economic systems studies which are important because the post-communist transition means a change of the economic system—thus, this perspective is important in analyzing the assumptions and the outcomes of the transition. Finally, I will discuss selected approaches within the institutional perspective which is important for two reasons. Firstly, because post-communist transition and the economic policy in this period is to a large extent about institutional change (Douarin and Mickiewicz 2017), a process of the creation of new, necessary institutions from scratch, while reforming and or eliminating the old ones. Secondly, institutional approach, highly diversified among numerous theories and research perspectives, has a very strong explanatory potential in analyzing the real trajectories and outcomes of the evolution of the state corporate control, and the factors which lay behind the changes.

2.1 Transition Research

The first and the most obvious stream of the studies on state corporate control in post-communist transition could be transitology studies. They may mean either just a body of literature dedicated to systemic transitions, in our case from communism to capitalism, or it may be a research perspective, defined as studying regime change (Gans-Morse 2004), with its specific approach and tools.

The term transitology was initially used in political studies as applied to processes of change from one political system to another and was perceived mostly as studies on democratization. Later, after the collapse of the communist regimes, transitology studies started to treat transition as a complex multidimensional process, where system change includes both political and economic change (Przeworski 1991). Thus, we can distinguish two pillars of post-communist transition: political transition and economic transition. In both areas, the transition is much more than just reforms (although reforms are the key tools of transition policies): it is a radical paradigm change, break in continuity, creation of a new political and economic system. In its economic dimension, it is, generally speaking, transition from command (administrative, centrally planned) economy towards a market one. This transition can be studied from two perspectives which reflect its dual character. On the one hand, this is a process of systemic change; on the other hand, it is a policy, a project implemented by the authorities aimed at introducing this change—both perspectives being important in this book.

The first perspective puts transition in the framework, among others, of the theory of economic systems, which is in its turn a branch of economics which according to Kornai (1971) exists just because economic systems are not something given, but can be transformed into other systems. The main features of an economic system are allocation mechanisms an ownership structure of the economy (Prybyla 1969). In the communist economy, allocation is performed through the state planning mechanisms and the state is the owner of almost all means of production; in the capitalist economy, the allocation is mostly market-based and the ownership structure is dominated by private entities. Therefore, post-communist transition includes both changes in allocation and ownership. Within this perspective, the theory of transition functions within positive economics and tries first of all to increase the volume of knowledge on specific phenomena and processes in these areas, including changes in their major parts as privatization, creation of market institutions and infrastructure, stabilization and deregulation of the economy, etc.

The second perspective focuses on introduction of these changes and treats transition as a branch of economic policy within normative economics approach. Here, the goals of transition and the ways of their achieving, and the economic, social, political and other conditions of the reforms gain crucial importance. Within this perspective, the ultimate model of the economic system is created which has to ensure high effectiveness of allocation and property mechanisms. It would set the direction of the reforms and plays the role of a benchmark for their implementation. When talking about the transition from communism to capitalism, in the allocation sphere these reforms would lead to withdrawing of the state from direct regulation of the economy via administrative tools and support for creation of market mechanisms and institutions, as well as of mechanisms of their protection. In the ownership sphere, it means the withdrawal of the state from ownership of the most part of enterprises and creation of favorable conditions for the private sector development. Within this perspective, the choice of the ultimate model and the tools of achieving it were crucial—both had no one best solution, because the models of capitalism to which reformers long may vary (as the real ones vary), and the same goal could be achieved by different means, which is also confirmed by practice. At the same time, the transition process itself was complex with interrelated policy steps that had no previous precedent and best practice. Therefore the process was inevitably patchwork-like and flawed with many contradictions and inconsistencies. The process of transition is also not immediate, it takes years, so one can speak about a lengthy transition period which requires special policies aimed both at achieving the ultimate state of the economic system and withstanding the challenges of the transition process itself. Among others, it means the necessity of a sound ownership policy of the state which deals with both radical institutional change (privatization) and corporate control over enterprises which remain the state property (which, by the way, also must undergo a deep change comparing with the communist times).

It may be argued that the transitology approach, at least towards economic transition, and especially when the research has normative and postulative elements, can hardly be isolated from other research perspectives if an attempt is made to describe the transition using not only the question "how," but also "why." Therefore the literature on the post-communist transition is usually intrinsically multidisciplinary. That's why it is hard to set an exact border between the transition literature and the rest of the literature which tackles the problems related to the post-communist transition. Here, I just use a practical criterion: in the transition literature, the post-communist transition must be the protagonist.

Even when the literature on transitology is treated in such a broad way, from the perspective of studies on the state corporate control, its content is quite disappointing. The literature on the post-communist transition itself is abundant. Due to the fact that one of its fundamental elements was ownership change, certain aspects of the state's ownership policy were inevitably in the field of view of researchers. Obviously, this concerned mainly privatization, which is by now an area of research that has been really well studied, while corporate control policy towards of SOEs was usually omitted, just as it was underestimated in the practice of economic policy of the transition countries, including Poland. It was only in 2010s when researchers became increasingly interested in this topic, although the existing studies on state corporate control practically still do not consider it as one of the areas of the post-communist transition.

For example, Anders Åslund (2002) in his seminal book on the transition paid almost no attention to the problems of enterprises under state control, mentioning them only when discussing the reform of the state apparatus. Five years later (Åslund 2007a), his focus was still on privatization, but the re-statization of Russia's economic policy after Vladimir Putin came to power drew the author's attention towards nationalization and politicization of SOEs. However, only a few sentences were devoted to these issues. Five more years later, a second edition of this book was published under a slightly revised title (Åslund 2013), the mentioning of state corporate policy was just a little expanded to include crisis management measures, especially in the banking sector.

Among the transition researchers from the post-communist countries, analysis of the state corporate control within the transition discourse also was not popular; this apparently comes from the underestimation of this problem which was common both among the academia and the decision makers. Perhaps the only major publication on the post-communist economic transition, where the reform of the state corporate control enjoyed closer attention, was a monograph by Bałtowski and Miszewski (2007). In his book on the post-communist transition in Poland, Miszewski (2012) included a short analysis of selected problems of the state corporate control in this country such as the lack of precisely and comprehensively formulated goals, and the lack of effective implementation mechanisms. The idea that the state corporate control is one of the key, albeit neglected areas of post-communist reforms was further developed by Bałtowski and Kozarzewski (2014) on the case Poland. Kozarzewski (2019) conducted an extensive research on the corporate control of the Polish government as a part of state ownership policy in transition pointing at its dysfunctional character and capture by private interest groups. Apart from being devoted mostly to only one post-communist country, these books were published in Polish only, which put them outside the world literature debate.

Since the second half of the 2010s, fuelled by the increasing statist trends in economic policy of several post-communist countries, and first of all Poland and Hungary, the issue of SOEs in the former Eastern bloc, their corporate governance and performance, gained popularity among the researchers, although few of them put their studies into the context of post-communist transition. Nevertheless, the notion of the U-turn in the enterprise sector reform started to appear, of a radical change of a transition development path from based on private ownership and foreign direct investments (FDI) to the one based on increased state interventionism (Szanyi 2016a; Błaszczyk 2017a; Kozarzewski and Bałtowski 2017). The statist turn in the policy of the enterprise sector policy of the Russian also has attracted the attention of researchers (e.g., Chernykh 2011; Radygin et al. 2019). However, generally speaking so far the transition research perspective hasn't contributed much neither to valuable ideas and tools, nor research in the field of the state policy in the enterprise sector.

2.2 Economic Policy Research

Economic policy as a branch of science studies the state's influence on the economy and at the same time creates the theoretical basis for economic practice. The literature on economic policy, especially within neoclassical and liberal approach, generally underestimates ownership policy of the state. In the giant economic encyclopedia *The New Palgrave Dictionary of Economics* (2018), there are no articles devoted to issues of the state sector in the economy. Most well-known textbooks on economics also either ignored or gave extremely marginal treatment to issues of state ownership policy, including issues of state corporate control. Greg Mankiw (2015), as well as Paul Krugman and Robin Wells (2015) quite briefly discussed the SOE sector only in the context of monopolies; Paul Samuelson and William Nordhaus (2015) merely mentioned it a few times without any deeper analysis.

Comprehensive studies devoted specifically to the SOE sector and the state policy towards it (and towards the whole enterprise sector as well) were not numerous, especially before the 2008–2009 global crisis. This was perhaps due to the fact that in the developed countries of the West, especially Anglo-Saxon ones, where both economic theory and economic policy theory have been formed, ownership policy did not play an important role because of the limited size of the state sector, especially after the wave of privatization in the 1980s and 1990s and was collateral compared, for example, to regulatory policy, or even industrial policy. However, there are countries where the state ownership was and still is relatively large and, for example, in Norway, Italy, Austria, France, and partly in Sweden and Germany. In these countries, the ownership policy has its important and established place in the palette of tools of state influence on the economy. In addition, most developed capitalist countries used the tools of ownership policy as one of the means to overcome the global financial crisis of 2008–2009 supporting important enterprises or even through rescue nationalizations.

Generally speaking, the modern theory and practice of active economic policy is based on Keynesian economics. However, Keynes (1936) ignored such a policy's ownership dimension. He envisaged state investment in optimal economic policy, but he did not discussed state ownership control policy, assuming state perfection, and immunity from wrong decision-making for political reasons, the actions of interest groups, etc. Such a position was generally taken by Keynes' continuators until modern times in both the practical and theoretical dimensions of economic policy.

Liberal economists did not pay much attention to state corporate control either, seeing more threats than chances in the state involvement in the enterprise sector. Vino Tanzi (2011) in his comprehensive monograph on the role of the state in the market economy devoted little space, just two and a half pages, to the ownership functions of the state. Briefly discussing the objectives and effects of the state functioning as the owner, he emphasizes that the state is able to provide funding for public policies in this way. At the same time, he argues, too much state ownership may not allow the state to realize the maximum possible profit (in the social sense) from the capital it owns; it is also a powerful tool for distributing resources among privileged social groups (Tanzi 2011, p. 219).

General lack of interest of liberal researchers in the active role of the state as an owner, in studying the factors of its efficiency comes from the conviction that the key function of the state should be involvement in the effective monitoring of economic processes and regulation, and not in the production of goods and services that can be produced by the private sector or imported; most natural monopolies do not make sense to exist.

Before recently, perhaps there was only important Western publication (at least within mainstream economics) which paid a fair amount of attention to the SOE sector, a volume of a textbook character by Joseph Stiglitz (2000) devoted to the public sector. The author discusses the rationale for the existence of state-owned enterprises (control over natural monopolies and realization of social interest) with a detailed analysis of the threats posed by state ownership and the ways to overcome them. Stiglitz advocates a "minimalist" design of the state sector, limiting its existence to cases where it is not possible for private companies to function (including those subject to special regulations to safeguard social interest) and when competition does not work. Despite a certain evolution of Stiglitz's views caused by the global financial crisis of 2008–2009, which led him to perceive a greater importance of state regulation (Stiglitz 2009), his attitude towards the role of the state in the production of goods seems not to have changed. The relevant parts of latest edition of his monograph on the public sector (Stiglitz and Rosengard 2015, pp. 199–229) were just transferred from the previous edition without significant changes.

The theses presented by Stiglitz are mainly a set of principles that should be followed by the state in relation to the public sector, state-owned enterprises being treated as its part. The monograph contains practically no proposals for overcoming existing barriers and contradictions related to the performance of ownership functions by the state. There is also no illustrative material showing applied solutions in this area. Moreover, the book is written with the developed capitalist economies in mind and illustrated with such examples (first of all, the economy of the USA, where the scope of state-owned enterprises is extremely low, even on a world scale). Consequently, it does not take into account the specific conditions and challenges of post-socialist countries—including the need to reform state corporate governance and pursue a large-scale ownership transformation policy.

The crisis of 2008–2009 became a catalyst for interest in the role of state-owned enterprises in the economy and their use as a tool of economic policy, which Musacchio and Flores-Macias (2009) called "the return of state-owned enterprises." There is a growing body of literature in this area: i.e., Bremmer (2010), Victor et al. (2012), Musacchio and Lazzarini (2014), Detter and Fölster (2015), Mühlenkamp (2015), Karolyi and Liao (2017), but it is still typically quite fragmented at most passingly covering post-communist economies with their specific problems inherited from the communist past.

Experts working for international organizations and consultancy firms were among the first, who since mid-2000s started to appreciate the importance of an effective policy towards the enterprise sector (at least in the developed economies), their activity in this field boosting after the global financial crisis which led to increasing state interventionism in the enterprise sector. It became a catalyst for interest in the role of SOEs in the economy and their use as a tool of economic policy—although the issues of state ownership policy as a whole were still on the periphery of interest of economists.

The greatest activity has been characterized by the Organization for Economic Co-operation and Development (OECD 2005a, b, 2010, 2015, 2018), there have also been valuable publications on this topic by the World Bank (2014) and the global consulting firm PwC (2015). Apart from increasing volume of knowledge on the SOE sector and the corporate governance of the state, these reports included analysis of the effectiveness of various policies and tools of the state corporate control, as well as recommendations. This, together with the efforts of economic policy practitioners, has resulted in the fact that state corporate governance in developed market economies is now a fairly well-recognized and codified area.

Until recently, post-communist countries were mostly outside of the field of view of these organizations. The European Commission (2016) report on the SOE sector after the global financial crisis of 2008–2009 was perhaps the first study, where at least a part of former Eastern bloc economies (new EU member states) was analyzed as a separate group. It allowed its authors to distinguish the specific features if these countries, such as high share of state ownership and inferior performance and management of SOEs comparing with private companies. The joint study performed by the International Monetary Fund and the European Bank for Reconstruction and Development (IMF 2019) on the SOE sector in the countries Central, Eastern and Southeastern Europe draws attention to the widespread drawbacks of the state corporate control which leads to SOEs underperformance. The authors conclude that generally speaking, large SOE sector in post-communist countries rather cannot be used as a vehicle of economic growth and convergence.

Literature devoted to economic policy in specific post-communist countries, including Poland, usually completely omits the policy of the state towards SOEs or treats it very marginally, mainly from the organizational perspective. Even publications devoted to ownership policy usually concentrate only one of its pillars—privatization. (Another problem is that a great deal of such literature is published only in national languages.) After the statist turns in different time experienced by Poland, Hungary, and Russia, studies on the re-growing involvement of the state in these countries started to appear, pointing first of all at nationalizations—that is, processes of re-enlargement of state ownership, while paying much less attention (if any) to the control processes associated with the existence of "old" state ownership: e.g., Chernykh (2011), Błaszczyk (2017b), Voszka (2018). (More references are provided in the relevant parts of this book.) In the case of studies on Poland so far perhaps only above-mentioned monographs in Polish by Bałtowski and Kozarzewski (2014) and Kozarzewski (2019) analyze in detail state corporate control policy as a part of economic policy. The author of this book does not know similarly comprehensive publications devoted to the three countries discussed in Chapter 7.

2.3 Economic Systems Research

There is no a single approach within studies on economic systems, it is a number of different research perspectives with often quite fuzzy borders between them and between such studies and other research streams, such as economic policy research or institutional research. Among the existing perspectives, two devoted to studies of capitalism seem to be especially important for the analysis resented in this book (varieties of capitalism—VoC and state capitalism—SC); there is also a potentially valuable perspective rather unknown to the wider research community which claims that in several post-communist countries the new system cannot be studied as a capitalist on (theories of resource and distributive economy).

2.3.1 Varieties of Capitalism

Formerly, post-communist countries were usually regarded as an institutionally separate category of analysis "by default:" assuming that they had common features which distinguished them from the rest of the world (developed and developing economies)—which probably originates from transitology studies, the monographs by Åslund (2002, 2007a, 2013) being notable examples. This group of countries was very internally diversified though, and since the early years of the transition they were divided in analyses into several subgroups, starting from just two (World Bank 2002): Commonwealth of the Independent States (CIS—former Soviet republics without three Baltic states) and the rest of the European post-communist countries. Division into more subgroups was also used, for example, in my earlier publications, as three or five subgroups: one or three for CIS countries and Mongolia (countries with advanced reforms, with less advanced reforms and reform outsiders) and two for the rest of European post-communist countries (Central-East European and South-East European) (Kozarzewski 2016).

It was reasonable to expect that as the post-communist transition proceeded, the historical factors inherited from the communist past would gradually lose their importance because there would be a convergence towards a fairly obvious pattern, which since the beginning of the transition has been the developed countries of Western Europe. Therefore the transition countries would be more and more similar to other countries with a comparable level of socio-economic and institutional development. Post-communist countries thus started being included in the studies on market economies without separating them in a special group or groups. Such approach was applied, e.g., in reports by international organizations, including those tackling the issues of the state corporate control (World Bank 2014; OECD 2018).

There was growing confidence among the researchers that post-communist countries, especially the new EU member states, did not need anymore a special research perspective, such as transitology, and they could be included in general studies on contemporary capitalism. And the VoC approach, which started gaining popularity in the early 2000s, seemed to be suitable as such a "more general" perspective and as a development of this perspective, because initially it applied only to developed market economies (Hall and Soskice 2001; Amable 2003). So far, the research shows that even post-communist economies of Central and Eastern Europe still represent a special type of capitalism which cannot be just placed between two extremes: coordinated market economies (CMEs) and liberal market economies (LME). Neither had they fit the existing plural classifications such as proposed by Amable (2003). Basing on Amable's choice of factors, Farkas (2016) distinguishes a special Central and Eastern European cluster (with several internal sub-divisions) which represents post-communist countries. Being generally quite close to the modes that describe the countries of "old" Europe, it has its specificity that first of all lies in the high role of foreign direct investments, but also in the way the product and labor markets, as well as social protections are functioning. Rapacki and Czerniak (2018) also came to the conclusion that Central and East European post-communist countries represent a special model of capitalism which they call "patchwork capitalism." In all but two areas (product market competition and financial intermediation) it is substantially different than that of the developed European economies.

The idea that at least some post-communist countries may represent a special model of capitalism seems to gain in popularity after the statist turn which took place in Hungary and contributed to the emergence of new theories which so far seem to be too specialized on the experience predominantly of only this country. Magyar (2016) puts forward a concept of mafia state which is characteristic, in his view, for Hungary, Russia and some other post-communist countries (although he studies only Hungarian experience). This is a form of organization of the ruling elite which is bound by very close, mafia-type relationships and has captured the state. Sallai and Schnyder (2018) put forward the concept of colonization of the quite strong developmental state created in Hungary at earlier stages of the transition by a new narrow elite which aims at the emergence of the new model—a clan state which differs from other forms of capitalism, including state capitalism (discussed below). They argue than within the latter, the state must have been an autonomous entity which at list partially serves public interest, and not almost solely private interests of a small elite, as in the case of clan state.

For a person who studies post-communist economies the idea that post-communist countries, even before the statist shifts, may represent special models of capitalism, looks intuitively correct; the reason is not solely that in most of the post-communist countries market and political mechanisms are still underdeveloped compared with the most developed market economies, and democracy is to a larger or smaller extent flawed compared to the best performers of the Western world. The similar lack of excellence can be found in many other capitalist countries, for example, in a number of Latin American or South European ones. The key peculiarities lay, among others, in the structural and institutional setup of the last, decaying stage of the communist system which has not been fully overcome, and in the dysfunctions which were created by the transition process itself which in my view is not over in the sense of meeting its goals. In the economic dimension, the most prominent area of this unfinished transition is the role of the state in the enterprise sector.

From this perspective, the existing studies may have a significant gap resulted to sticking to the tools used in the "mainstream" VoC approach which do not take into account this very specificity of the transition countries. It is not only the size of the SOE sector, i.e., the share of SOEs in the enterprise sector, but also their specific function in the economy which goes beyond that of the CME, which is more often than not highly politicized, being an important tool of the economic policy including in distributing resources for the ruling political elite and its allies. It has a strong impact on the political and economic setup in these countries and their development paradigm (Magyar 2016; Åslund 2017; Błaszczyk 2017b; Kozarzewski 2019).

2.3.2 State Capitalism

This gap in describing the economic systems of the transition countries may be filled through fine-tuning the VoC approach, among others through extending of the set of indicators used. Another option is using an existing approach which would be more suitable for the economies in question. One of the possible options is state capitalism perspective which is, generally speaking, about the structural and institutional relationships between the government and the economy.

The exact place of SC among the approaches which construct models of market economies and economic policies is not fully clear. It may be treated as a stand-alone type based on a unique set of features; it may be a part of some another research perspective which tries classifying capitalism into different types, such as oligarchic capitalism, state-guided capitalism, big-firm capitalism, and entrepreneurial capitalism (Baumol et al. 2012); it may be regarded as a possible extension of the VoC approach: either an extreme form of the coordinated market economy, or as some another separate type. Some approaches within state capitalism studies may be even classified as economic policy rather than economic systems research.

Problems with placing the SC concept within capitalism studies at least partly originate from the ambiguity of the term: there is still no commonly agreed definition on what the term "state capitalism" really means. It is used in many different meanings and researchers applied a number of different perspectives: not only institutional, but also, e.g., transaction costs economics or agency theory (Grosman et al. 2016; Allen et al. 2021); some authors even altering their approach in their subsequent papers. Perhaps creation of a single common and functional definition of state capitalism is even impossible due to a much diversified subject to be defined and the variety of research perspectives that could be applied. The existing definitions may be divided into broad and narrow ones. In the broad approach, SC is regarded as a market economic system where the state intervention in the economy is much higher than in developed capitalist countries and plays a key role in meeting political and developmental goals (Bremmer 2010; Spechler et al. 2017). There is also an extreme view that SC just means state domination in the economy and essentially equals planned socialist system (Mises 2009; Fabry 2019). In the narrow approach, SC is a set of policies, where the government has an active impact on the corporate sector, which goes beyond the contextual standards, mainly by means of ownership or quasi-ownership tools rather than, as is the case of the developed economies' model, regulatory ones (Musacchio and Lazzarini 2014; Kurlantzick 2016).

From the point of view of the goals of this book, the SC perspective, especially its narrow variant, seems promising; it also makes sense to added a condition (often overlooked by SC researchers) that it is not the scope but the arbitrariness of the government that is a decisive characteristic that distinguishes state capitalism from interventionist versions of the "regular" capitalism (Bałtowski et al. 2021). However, one "side effect" of the lack of common definition of SC is lack of consensus among the researchers on whether SC is just some variant of the capitalist system and/or state economic policy within it, or this term is applicable only to dysfunctional (from a certain perspective) forms of the state's involvement in the economy.

Another problem with the SC approach critically important for its usefulness for post-communist studies, including studies on ownership policy of the state, is that till recently, it was applied mostly to developed economies. Only China and Russia used to be an exception, towards which some version of this perspective was applied (e.g., Lane 2008; Bremmer 2010). Recently, two studies on Belarus (Papko and Kozarzewski 2020; Rudy 2020) have been published. But perhaps only in the recent very extensive volume on state capitalism which is treated as the direct influence of the state on the economy and behavior of enterprises (Wright et al. 2021) for the first time the notion of state capitalism was extended on all economies throughout the world. Another valuable novelty in this publication was an attempt to get closer to a universal conceptualization of state capitalism and strongly manifested assumption that one of its basic features are specific relations between the state and the enterprise sector, especially SOEs.

However, in quite a lot of publications devoted to other transition countries, first of all Poland and Hungary, one can find elements of state capitalism analysis, both in the broad and the narrow sense, although this term usually was not used (the detailed literature review can be found in Bałtowski et al. 2021). For example, Szélenyi (2017) draws the attention to certain re-convergence of regimes in Hungary,

Russia and China as being socially conservative, with inadequate separation of powers and security of private ownership. Szanyi (2019) argues that Poland and Hungary serve as an example of resignation from the neoliberal FDI-led development path which is being replaced by the emergence of the patronage economic system. Jasiecki (2017) argues that the statist economic course pursued by the Polish government since mid-2010s was intended to overcome the limitations of the dependent market economy (DME) model through changing it to state capitalism development model, where the state-owned sector aspire to stimulate innovation and becomes the core investor in the economy. In the recent years, the growing body of literature is devoted to statist changes in the economic policy of selected post-communist countries which include the enterprise sector and issues of the state corporate control, first of all in Poland, Hungary, and Russia (e.g., Pula 2017; Kozarzewski and Bałtowski 2017; Radygin et al. 2019).

One more problem is that lack of consensus on what state capitalism is and inadequate body of knowledge on manifestations of state capitalism (however defined) in practice in many regions of the world, including the territory of the former Eastern bloc, makes it difficult to answer a question on whether the state capitalism approach may treat all countries in the same way, assuming a high level of unification of SC manifestations, or one can talk about "varieties of state capitalism." Till recently, the latter term was mostly used to indicate different tools the economic policy of a state (Musacchio et al. 2015). Nowadays researchers find more and more evidence that state capitalism has several different patterns in different countries which, among others, may require using different sets of indicators in studying them. Analyzing the reaction of governments on the global economic crisis of 2008–2009 from the perspective of using state interventionism tools, Szanyi (2018) distinguishes two such patterns. The first one was typical for the countries with developed economies and democratic institutions, where state interventionism was briefly used as a crisis management tools (e.g., nationalizations) which was followed by withdrawing the state from the enterprises sector. The second one was typical for other economies, including post-communist and emerging ones, where the state did not withdraw from the economy after the crisis and pursued a wide range of goals from developmental ones to rent-seeking.

Bałtowski et al. (2021) share the view about diversity of state capitalism and generally treat state capitalism as state interventionism of dysfunctional kind. Studying Polish and Hungarian cases, they made an attempt to conceptualize "state capitalism with populist characteristics" which according to them may be typical for post-communist countries in general. They formulated six basic features of this variety of capitalism, each having specific goals, tools and core groups of beneficiaries who are chosen by the government (in market capitalism, the main beneficiaries are set by market mechanisms):

1. politicization of SOEs: the government and political elite use the state-controlled enterprise sector as a source of rents;
2. politicization of SOEs *à rebours*: the state-controlled enterprise sector (their staff, executives and affiliated trade unions, among others) is the main rent-seeker itself;
3. cronyism: the main beneficiaries of SC are private agents from outside the public sector;
4. oligarchy (a consolidated form of cronyism): powerful private agents have a very significant influence on economic policy;
5. economic populism (clientelism): a patronage system where the political elite transfers goods to clients in chosen social groups expecting their political support in return;
6. economic nationalism: the state exerts an impact on the economy the declared objective of which is to enhance, in the long run, the state's political capacity, military power or international importance. The state itself may be treated here as the major beneficiary.

State capitalism with populist characteristics is also characterized by a set of tools of interventionism, such as impact through enterprises fully or partly belonging to the state, restricting ownership rights of private entities, regulatory tools and persuasion (pressure, threats) measures.

2.3.3 Resource/Distributive Economy

There are also studies on economic systems which go beyond the capitalism paradigm; they are largely unknown to the international academia because until recently (Kordonsky 2016) the studies were published in Russian only. This approach draws attention to the peculiar non-market, resource-based and redistributive character of the economic systems which have formed in such post-communist countries as Russia (which was the main subject of the research) and most of the other former USSR republics. According to Bessonova (2006), who calls this system a "distributive economy," it originates from the USSR and is characterized by lack of full property rights and developed market, and by specific relationships between the state and economic agents, where the former distributes resources in return for "contributions," i.e., goods and services produced by the economic agents to meet the needs of the state.

Kordonsky (2007) describes a quite similar model of a "resource-based state." Its economy is not based on the market exchange, but on the centralized accumulation of resources from population and economic agents with their redistribution according to the government's political and economic priorities which are mostly related to the stability of the authoritarian state. From enterprises' point of view, efficiency is based not on profit, but on the ability to get resources from the state and to process them. It does not mean that such a system is devoid of market mechanisms; at the beginning of the transition, they may even dominate the economy because the centralized redistribution system collapsed. However, the logic of the system would squeeze out market relationships and restore up-down coordination mechanisms. The system is also characterized by lack of rule of law and omnipotence of informal institutions.

These theories are not (and did not meant to be) universal, being devoted to a quite specific institutional setup. However, they may be useful not only for the analysis of Russia and Belarus in this book, but also for Poland and Hungary because of the dysfunctional elements of their ownership policies based on distribution of resources.

2.4 Public Choice Approach

2.4.1 Public Choice Approach as a Part of the Institutional Perspective

In this book, I treat the institutional perspective first of all as a set of tools that allow me to explain the nature and driving forces of shaping up and evolution of the state corporate control as a part of the system change. This perspective is generally about the written and unwritten rules of the game in a society (North 1990). Studies on institutions which influence economic policy of the state, particularly with regard to its principles and outcomes, are extremely popular nowadays. The expression "institutions matter" became a kind of common knowledge and one of the most probable conclusions of many studies on socio-economic and political issues. Institutional economics is a constantly developing branch of knowledge; new concepts arise which are meant to help to fine-tune the research tools to the analyzed reality. One of the recent achievements on this field is the seminal work by Acemoğlu and Robinson (2012) which has introduced dichotomist categories of inclusive ("good") and extractive ("bad") institutions. They were created on the basis of observations of developing economies, but may be very useful for studying transition economies as well. Inclusive institutions protect property rights, create a level playing field for all participants in economic activity, stimulate free games of economic exchange, and encourage technological innovation. As a result, they provide access to the generation of national wealth for an increasing proportion of the population. Extractive institutions focus on the concentration of economic resources in the hands of elite social groups and the alienation in their favor of the results of labor of the rest of the population. Therefore, they do not protect the property rights of the members of the society in general and do not create effective incentives for economic activity.

Among numerous approaches within institutionalism, for the purposes of my book i find the public choice perspective especially promising. It uses the tools and methodological assumptions of economics to analyze human behavior in politically motivated activities and other areas of the public sphere. The main assumption is that people are motivated by their own self-interest. One of the areas of the public choice studies is corruption understood as a special kind of relations between the society and the state when transaction between actors from private and public sectors take place which involve illegitimate conversion of public resources into private ones (Heidenheimer et al. 1989; Amundsen 1999). After Fukuyama (2018), corruption may be divided into two types: creation and extraction of rents, and patronage or clientelism.

2.4.2 *Rent-Seeking and Interest Groups*

The basics of the concept of rent-seeking in the sense used in this book were created by Tullock (1967) and Krueger (1974). Here, the term "rent" is used in its Smithsonian economic sense, as increasing one's wealth through non-productive redistribution, and not via profit or wage;

another feature of rents is that they do not serve common good and are costs for the society. These costs are, among others, negative impact on economic growth because existence of rents reduces the incentives for value creation (Olson 2000).

Possibilities of receiving such rents exist, firstly, because of the so-called Tullock paradox (Tullock 1980) when costs of rent-seeking are much smaller than gains from it. Secondly, because of the scarcity of the resources redistributed which gives those who dispose them a privileged position towards those who needs these resources (Sørensen 2000).

Slightly changing the definition by Thomas (2020), interest group is an association of individuals or organizations, formal or informal, which based on common interest and attempts to influence public policy in its favor. One of the objectives of this influence may be rent-seeking in the sense described above. Such groups are also called "private interest groups" or "special interest groups" to stress that their objective is satisfying interests of a particular group at the expense of the society. More often than not, rent-seeking groups are informal and try to keep their activity low profile. But in certain circumstances such as weak democratic institutions, they may use ignorance of voters and shield their redistributive actions claiming that they act in the interest of the society (Olson 2000).

The rent-seeking and private interest groups perspective is extremely popular in transition studies—as an autonomous approach or a part of wider studies which try to explain the logic of events and path dependencies in the post-communist world.

Within the latter approach Hellman (1998) coined a term "partial reform equilibrium trap" which explained the common trajectory of post-communist transition (fast start and then stalling of the reforms) with interplay of three major interest groups. The first one was "reform advocates" who consistently supported transition because they benefited from its progress (pro-reform politicians and new entrants to the market). The second group was "transformation losers" (mainly from the SOEs sector) whose interests were jeopardized by the reforms (e.g., lifting of state support and exposing to competition on the market). The third group was "initial winners," a loose coalition which extracts rents from the unfinished reform process when liberalization of the economy which granted them access to various types of resources had not yet been accompanied by consolidation of the reform process which would stop the misuse of these resources. Therefore this group (which controlled the state assets at the beginning of transition) supported the initial stages of the reforms which expanded sources of the rents and opposed their continuation which would limit these sources or even eliminate them. Using this concept, Mitra and Selowsky (2002) show the key role of the latter group in the transition process the situation, when reform supporters are still weak and transformation losers are still strong enough.

The main advantage of this approach was in proposing a plausible explanation for post-communist transition dynamics and showing that market reforms were not a purely technical tasks. Kozarzewski and Woodward (2006) argue, that each reform, apart from being technically sound, must take into account all the major interests affected by it. It is especially important in microeconomic reforms, which are intrinsically of participatory character, i.e., their success depends on the readiness of all actors involved to behave according to the expectations of the reform authors. The reform of the ownership policy and state corporate control during the transition undoubtedly belongs to this type.

Although this approach proved to be very fruitful in explaining the dynamics of the post-communist transition and stressed the role of the state assets as a source of rents, it treated both the main actors and the rents in a too general way. A large body of literature has emerged devoted to selected interest groups and mechanisms of rent-seeking. At the beginning, publications were devoted mostly to various new rich which gained their wealth (and many of them political power as well) though privileged access to national resources and protection from competition in former Soviet republics, first of all Russia (Åslund 2007b; Braguinsky 2009), followed by growing interest towards this group in Hungary (Becker 2017; Mihályi and Szelényi 2017). Poland was not the subject of these studies, because in this country there were no institutional conditions for oligarchy to emerge (Schoenman 2014; Bałtowski and Sękowski 2020)—it is discussed in more detail in Sects. 6.1.3 and 6.2.2.

A bit later studies started to appear which analyzed rent-seeking within the state structures, where only the government and SOEs were involved, without tunneling public assets to the private sector, or at least when its scale was moderate and did not create fortunes and politically influential tycoons. They show that the state ownership policy became one of the major sources of rent created by the government's economic policy and analyze mechanisms of rent-seeking (Radygin et al. 2015; Senderski 2015; Szarzec et al. 2020). Kozarzewski (2019) even argues that in Poland, unlike in many other post-communist countries, it's state corporate control, and not privatization, is the main source of rents. These studies also show that rent-seeking and interest groups play in the SOE sector of several transition countries go far beyond just extracting rent by incumbent individuals. They contribute to creation of powerful institutional arrangements which influence the economic policy of the governments and even, as in the case of Hungary and Poland, affect its paradigm (Szanyi 2016b; Kozarzewski and Bałtowski 2017).

2.4.3 Clientelism

Clientelism may be defined in a broad and a narrow sense. In a broad sense, it involves patron-client relationship where the former, having higher status and power, gives favors to the latter, who reciprocates with loyalty and political support (Fukuyama 2018). In a narrow sense, it's just an exchange of material goods for electoral support (Stokes 2011). This relationship may be described as patronage; although several researchers distinguish between clientelism and patronage. Fukuyama (2018) mentions definitions of patronage as a kind of a small-scale clientelism which involves direct contacts between patrons and clients, whereas clientelism is large-scale exchange which usually requires intermediaries. For Stokes (2011) patronage is one of two subtypes of clientelism (providing public resources to certain groups in exchange for their electoral support), another being vote buying from individual persons.

The literature on clientelism in transition countries is not extensive: it is mostly fragmentary (devoted to selected issues and/or group of countries—e.g., Stefes 2006) and rarely tackles ownership policy of the state. In some publications clientelism is tackled only passingly, as just one of the features of the object of the study. The latter goes for, e.g., the seminal study by Magyar and Madlovics (2020) which creates a conceptual framework to describe post-communist regimes. Within limited-access type of social order called by the authors "patronal autocracy" (typical for Hungary, Russia, and Kazakhstan—and perhaps for Belarus as well) patron-client relationships, while still formally staying voluntary on both sides, lead to the emergence of large social groups becoming dependent on supply of resources from patrons. Magyar and Madlovics call them clientage; their autonomy is de facto limited, and these groups are kept subordinated to the ruling elite under the threat of withdrawing the resources.

For other researchers, cronyism and patronage are among the key characteristics of regimes that were shaping up in selected post-communist countries. Schoenman (2014) puts forward a concept of patronage state where lack of strong networks among enterprises makes them dependent on good relations with their political patrons. For him, Romania was an example of such a regime, although he identified elements of patron-client relationships in other post-communist countries as well, including Poland. It must be noted that this book was published before the populist political coalition came to power in 2015 in this country. A few years later, Szanyi (2019) included Poland in the category of patronage state, as well as Hungary, and identified manifestations of such a regime in several other post-communist countries of Eastern and Central Europe such as Rumania, Bulgaria, and Czech Republic. Unlike Schoenman, Szanyi refers to competition rather than networks: in these countries, the patronage state to a large extent demolished market institutions, protecting clientelist economic agents from foreign and domestic competitors and this made them dependent on the patrons. Besides, at least in the case of Poland and Hungary, development of the patronage state is for Szanyi not an evolution of the regimes shaping up during transition, but the radical change of path, resignation from the FDI-led development model.

So far, from the perspective of this book studies on clientelism still have a gap being generally speaking common for the whole institutional studies, but perhaps even more pronounced: it is a rather passing view on SOEs and, broader, ownership policy of the state, not treating them as one of the core elements of post-communist economies. Even when clientelism was mentioned as being systemically linked to the SOE sector (Bałtowski et al. 2021), it was not elaborated in more detail.

References

Acemoğlu, Daron, and James A. Robinson. 2012. *Why Nations Fail: The Origins of Power, Prosperity, and Poverty.* New York: Crown Publishers.

Allen, Matthew M.C., Geoffrey T. Wood, and Matthew R. Keller. 2021. "State Capitalism: Means and Dimensions." In *Oxford Handbook on State Capitalism and the Firm*, edited by Mike Wright, Geoffrey Wood, Alvaro Cuervo-Cazurra, Pei Sun, Ilya Okhmatovskiy, and Anna Grosman. Oxford: Oxford University Press (forthcoming).

Amable, Bruno. 2003. *The Diversity of Modern Capitalism.* London: Oxford University Press.

Amundsen, Inge. 1999. Political Corruption: An Introduction to the Issues. CMI Working Paper WP 7, Chr. Michelsen Institute, Bergen.

Åslund, Anders. 2002. *Building Capitalism. The Transformation of the Former Soviet Bloc*. New York: Cambridge University Press.

Åslund, Anders. 2007a. *How Capitalism Was Built: The Transformation of Central and Eastern Europe, Russia, and Central Asia*. New York: Cambridge University Press.

Åslund, Anders. 2007b. "Comparative Oligarchy: Russia, Ukraine, and the United States." In *Europe after Enlargement*, edited by Anders Åslund and Marek Dąbrowski, 143–164. Cambridge: Cambridge University Press.

Åslund, Anders. 2013. *How Capitalism Was Built: The Transformation of Central and Eastern Europe, Russia, the Caucasus, and Central Asia*. 2nd ed. New York: Cambridge University Press.

Åslund, Anders. 2017. Russia's Crony Capitalism: Stagnant but Stable. mBank—CASE Seminar Proceedings 148. mBank and CASE—Center for Social and Economic Research, Warsaw.

Bałtowski, Maciej, and Maciej Miszewski. 2007. *Transformacja gospodarcza w Polsce*. Warsaw: PWN.

Bałtowski, Maciej, and Piotr Kozarzewski. 2014. *Zmiana własnościowa polskiej gospodarki 1989–2013*. Warsaw: PWE.

Bałtowski, Maciej, Piotr Kozarzewski, and Tomasz Mickiewicz. 2021. "State Capitalism in Poland and Hungary: Populist Varieties." In *Oxford Handbook on State Capitalism and the Firm*, edited by Mike Wright, Geoffrey Wood, Alvaro Cuervo-Cazurra, Pei Sun, Ilya Okhmatovskiy, and Anna Grosman. Oxford: Oxford University Press (forthcoming).

Bałtowski, Maciej, and Stefan Sękowski. 2020. "Oligarchia w Polsce – dlaczego jej nie ma?" *Sprawy Międzynarodowe* 73 (4): 20–38.

Baumol, William J., Robert E. Litan, and Carl J. Schramm. 2012. "The Four Types of Capitalism, Innovation, and Economic Growth." In *The Oxford Handbook of Capitalism*, edited by Dennis C. Mueller, 115–128. New York: Oxford University Press.

Becker, András. 2017. "The Circulation of Oligarchs." In *Twenty-Five Sides of a Post-Communist Mafia State*, edited by Balint Magyar and Júlia Vásárhelyi, 111–128. Budapest: CEU Press.

Bessonova, Olga. 2006. *Razdatochnaya ekonomika Rossii: evolyutsiya cherez transformatsii* [Russian Redistributive Economy: Evolution through Transformations]. Moscow: ROSSPEN. http://razdatok.narod.ru/BESSONOVA/b2006/Bessonova_RER_2006.pdf. Accessed December 23, 2020.

Błaszczyk, Barbara. 2017a. "Privatization Reversal and Crowding Out the Private Business. Polish Examples." Paper presented at the 3rd SVOC International Conference "The Role of State in Varieties of Capitalism" organized by Hungarian Academy of Sciences and CEU, Budapest, December 1.

Błaszczyk, Barbara. 2017b. "Zmiany w systemie instytucjonalnym polskiej gospodarki. Wypieranie własności prywatnej, rynku i konkurencji przez państwo w ramach dobrej zmiany." In *Perspektywy dla Polski. Polska gospodarka w latach 2015–2017 na tle lat wcześniejszych i prognozy na przyszłość*, 203–248. Warsaw: FOR.

Braguinsky, Serguey. 2009. "Postcommunist Oligarchs in Russia: Quantitative Analysis." *The Journal of Law and Economics* 52 (2): 307–349.

Bremmer, Ian. 2010. *The End of the Free Market: Who Wins the War Between States and Corporations?* New York: Penguin.

Chernykh, Lucy. 2011. "Profit or Politics? Understanding Renationalizations in Russia." *Journal of Corporate Finance* 17 (5): 1237–1253.

Detter, Dag, and Stefen Fölster. 2015. *The Public Wealth of Nations*. New York: Palgrave Macmillan.

Douarin, Elodie, and Tomasz Mickiewicz. 2017. *Economics of Institutional Change: Central and Eastern Europe Revisited*. Cham: Palgrave Macmillan.

European Commission. 2016. State-Owned Enterprises in the EU: Lessons Learnt and Ways Forward in a Post-Crisis Context, Institutional Paper 031. Publications Office of the European Union, Luxembourg. https://ec.europa.eu/info/sites/info/files/file_import/ip031_en_2.pdf. Accessed March 31, 2021.

Fabry, Adam. 2019. *The Political Economy of Hungary: From State Capitalism to Authoritarian Neoliberalism*. Cham: Palgrave Macmillan.

Farkas, Beáta. 2016. *Models of Capitalism in the European Union. Post-crisis Perspectives*. London: Palgrave Macmillan.

Fukuyama, Francis. 2018. "Corruption as a Political Phenomenon." In *Institutions, Governance and the Control of Corruption*, edited by Kaushik Basu, and Tito Cordella, 51–73. Cham: Palgrave Macmillan.

Gans-Morse, Jordan. 2004. "Searching for Transitologists: Contemporary Theories of Post-communist Transitions and the Myth of a Dominant Paradigm." *Post-Soviet Affairs* 20 (4): 320–349.

Grosman, Anna, Ilya Okhmatovskiy, and Mike Wright. 2016. "State Control and Corporate Governance in Transition Economies: 25 Years on from 1989." *Corporate Governance: An International Review* 24 (3): 200–221.

Hall, Peter, and David Soskice, eds. 2001. *Varieties of Capitalism: The Institutional Foundations of Comparative Advantage*. Oxford: Oxford University Press.

Heidenheimer, Arnold J., Michael Johnston, and Victor T. LeVine, eds. 1989. *Political Corruption: A Handbook*. New Brunswick, NJ: Transaction Books.

Hellman, Joel S. 1998. "Winners Take All: The Politics of Partial Reform in Postcommunist Transition." *World Politics* 50 (2): 203–234.

IMF. 2019. *Reassessing the Role of State-Owned Enterprises in Central, Eastern, and Southeastern Europe*. Washington: International Monetary Fund.

Jasiecki, Krzysztof. 2017. "The Nature of Capitalism in Poland. Controversy over the Economy since the End of 2015: The Prospects of Business Elite and Employer Associations." *Corvinus Journal of Sociology and Social Policy* 8 (3): 171–193.

Karolyi, G. Andrew, and Rose C. Liao. 2017. "State Capitalism's Global Reach: Evidence from Foreign Acquisitions by State-Owned Companies." *Journal of Corporate Finance* 42 (C): 367–391.

Keynes, John Maynard. 1936. *The General Theory of Employment, Interest and Money*. London: Macmillan.

Kordonsky, Simon. 2007. *Resursnoe gosudarstvo* [Resource State]. Moscow: Regnum. https://www.litmir.me/br/?b=415429. Accessed December 23, 2020.

Kordonsky, Simon. 2016. *Socio-Economic Foundations of the Russian Post-Soviet Regime: The Resource-Based Economy and Estate-Based Social Structure of Contemporary Russia*. Stuttgart: Ibidem-Verlag.

Kornai, János. 1971. "Economic Systems Theory and General Equilibrium Theory." *Acta Oeconomica* 6 (4): 297–317.

Kozarzewski, Piotr. 2016. "Przekształcenia własnościowe w państwach postsocjalistycznych: cele, strategie, wyniki." *Rocznik Instytutu Europy Środkowo-Wschodniej* 14 (5): 23–48.

Kozarzewski, Piotr. 2019. *Polityka właścicielska państwa w okresie transformacji systemowej. Próba syntezy*. Lublin: Wydawnictwo Uniwersytetu Marii Curie-Skłodowskiej.

Kozarzewski, Piotr, and Maciej Bałtowski. 2017. "Change in the Ownership Policy Paradigm in Poland: State Control vs. Privatisation." *Acta Oeconomica* 67 (1): 1–20.

Kozarzewski, Piotr, and Richard Woodward. 2006. "The Reform Process in Post-Communist Transition: Understanding Reform in Eastern and Central Europe and the Commonwealth of Independent States." In *Understanding Market Reforms, Vol. 2, Motivation, Implementation and Sustainability*, edited by José MariaFanelli and Gary McMahon, 141–192. New York: Palgrave Macmillan.

Krueger, Anne O. 1974. "The Political Economy of the Rent-Seeking Society." *The American Economic Review* 64 (3): 291–303.

Krugman, Paul, and Robin Wells. 2015. *Economics*. 4th ed. New York: Worth Publishers.

Kurlantzick, Joshua. 2016. *State Capitalism: How the Return of Statism Is Transforming the World*. New York: Oxford University Press.

Lane, David. 2008. "From Chaotic to State-Led Capitalism." *New Political Economy* 13 (2): 177–184.

Magyar, Balint. 2016. *Post-Communist Mafia State: The Case of Hungary*. Budapest: CEU Press.

Magyar, Bálint, and Bálint Madlovics. 2020. *The Anatomy of Post-Communist Regimes: A Conceptual Framework*. Budapest: CEU Press.

Mankiw, N. Gregory. 2015. *Principles of Economics*. 7th ed. Florence, KY: Cengage Learning.

Mihályi, Peter, and Iván Szelényi. 2017. "The Role of Rents in the Transition from Socialist Redistributive Economies to Market Capitalism." *Comparative Sociology* 16: 13–38.

Mises, Ludwig. 2009. *Socialism: An Economic and Sociological Analysis*. Auburn, AL: The Ludwig von Mises Institute.

Miszewski, Maciej. 2012. *Polska transformacja gospodarcza i jej uwarunkowania*. Katowice: UE w Katowicach.

Mitra, Pradeep K., and Marcelo Selowsky. 2002. "Lessons from Decade of Transition in Eastern Europe and the Former Soviet Union." *Finance and Development* 39 (2). https://www.imf.org/external/pubs/ft/fandd/2002/06/mitra.htm. Accessed February 18, 2021.

Mühlenkamp, Hogler. 2015. "From State to Market Revisited: A Reassessment of the Empirical Evidence on the Efficiency of Public (and Privately-Owned) Enterprises." *Annals of Public and Cooperative Economics* 86 (4): 535–557.

Musacchio, Aldo, and Francisco Flores-Macias. 2009. "The Return of State-Owned Enterprises." *Harvard International Review*, April 4. https://www.hbs.edu/faculty/Pages/item.aspx?num=36235. Accessed February 9, 2021.

Musacchio, Aldo, and Sergio G. Lazzarini. 2014. *Reinventing State Capitalism: Leviathan in Business, Brazil and Beyond*. Cambridge: Harvard University Press.

Musacchio, Aldo, Sergio G. Lazzarini, and Ruth V. Aguilera. 2015. "New Varieties of State Capitalism: Strategic and Governance Implications." *The Academy of Management Perspectives* 29 (1): 115–131.

North, Douglas C. 1990. *Institutions, Institutional Change and Economic Performance*. Cambridge: Cambridge University Press.

OECD. 2005a. *Corporate Governance of State-Owned Enterprises: A Survey of OECD Countries*. Paris: OECD Publishing.

OECD. 2005b. *Guidelines on Corporate Governance of State-Owned Enterprises*. Paris: OECD Publishing.

OECD. 2010. *Accountability and Transparency: A Guide for State Ownership*. Paris: OECD Publishing.

OECD. 2015. *OECD Guidelines on Corporate Governance of State-Owned Enterprises*. 2015 ed. Paris: OECD Publishing.

OECD. 2018. *Ownership and Governance of State-Owned Enterprises. A Compendium of National Practices*. Paris: OECD Publishing.

Olson, Mancur. 2000. *Power and Prosperity. Outgrowing Communist and Capitalist Dictatorships*. New York: Basic Books.

Papko, Aliaksandr, and Piotr Kozarzewski. 2020. The Evolution of Belarusian Public Sector: From Command Economy to State Capitalism? CASE Working Papers 12(136). CASE—Center for Social and Economic Research, Warsaw. https://www.case-research.eu/files/?id_plik=6381. Accessed December 10, 2020.

Prybyla, Jan S. 1969. "Meaning and Classification of Economic Systems: An Outline." In *Comparative Economic Systems*, edited by Jan S. Prybyla, 9–18. New York: Appleton-Century-Crofts.

Przeworski, Andam. 1991. *Democracy and the Market: Political and Economic Reforms in Eastern Europe and Latin America*. New York: Cambridge University Press.

Pula, Besnik. 2017. "Whither State Ownership? The Persistence of State-Owned Industry in Postsocialist Central and Eastern Europe." *Journal of East–West Business* 23 (4): 309–336.

PwC. 2015. *State-Owned Enterprises: Catalysts for Public Value Creation?* Arlington: PwC.

Radygin, Alexander, Revold Entov, Alexander Abramov, Mariya Chernova, and Georgiy Malginov. 2019. *Privatizatsiya 30 let spustya. Masshtaby i effektovnost' gosudarstvennogo sektora* [Privatization 30 Years Later: Scale and Efficiency of the Public Sector]. Moscow: Delo.

Radygin, Alexander, Yury Simachev, and Revold Entov. 2015. "The State-Owned Company: 'State Failure' or 'Market Failure'?" *Russian Journal of Economics* 1: 55–80.

Rapacki, Ryszard, and Adam Czerniak. 2018. "Emerging Models of Patchwork Capitalism in Central and Eastern Europe: Empirical Results of Subspace Clustering." *International Journal of Management and Economics* 54 (4): 251–268.

Rudy, Kiryl. 2020. "State Capitalism in Belarus: Behind Economic Anemia." In *Public Sector Crisis Management*, edited by Edited by Alexander Rozanov, Alexander Barannikov, and Olga Belyaeva. London: IntechOpen. https://www.intechopen.com/chapters/73192. Accessed August 4, 2021.

Sallai, Dorottya, and Gerhard Schnyder. 2018. The Transformation of Post-Socialist Capitalism—From Developmental State to Clan State? Greenwich Papers in Political Economy 57. https://ssrn.com/abstract=3100775. Accessed February 26, 2021.

Samuelson, Paul A., and William D. Nordhaus. 2015. *Economics*. 19th ed. London: McGraw-Hill.

Schoenman, Roger. 2014. *Networks and Institutions in Europe's Emerging Markets*. Cambridge: Cambridge University Press.

Senderski, Marcin. 2015. "Inhibited Privatization: A Hurdle Race over Vested Interests." *European Journal of Government and Economics* 4 (1): 46–66.

Sørensen, Aage B. 2000. "Toward a Sounder Basis for Class Analysis." *American Journal of Sociology* 105 (6): 1523–1558.
Spechler, Martin C., Joachim Ahrens, and Herman W. Hoen. 2017. *State Capitalism in Eurasia.* Singapore: World Scientific.
Stefes, Christoph H. 2006. *Understanding Post-Soviet Transitions: Corruption, Collusion and Clientelism.* New York: Palgrave Macmillan.
Stiglitz, Joseph E. 2000. *Economics of the Public Sector*. 3rd ed. New York: W. W. Norton.
Stiglitz, Joseph E. 2009. "Regulation and Failure." In *New Perspectives on Regulation*, edited by David Moss, and John Cisternino, 11–23. Cambridge, MA: The Tobin Project.
Stiglitz, Joseph E., and Jay K. Rosengard. 2015. *Economics of the Public Sector*, 4th ed. New York: W.W. Norton Company.
Stokes, Susan. 2011. "Political Clientelism." In *The Oxford Handbook of Political Science*, edited by Robert E. Goodin, 648–672. Oxford: Oxford University Press.
Szanyi, Miklós. 2016a. "The Reversal of the Privatisation Logic in Central European Transition Economies (An Essay)." *Acta Oeconomica* 66 (1): 33–65.
Szanyi, Miklós. 2016b. The FDI-Led Development Model Revisited? The Case of Hungary. IWE Working Papers 220. Centre for Economic and Regional Studies HAS, Budapest.
Szanyi, Miklós. 2018. "Varieties of State Capitalism." *Global Economic Observer* 6 (2): 140–146.
Szanyi, Miklós. 2019. "The Emergence of Patronage and Changing Forms of Rent-seeking in East Central Europe." *Post-Communist Economies.* https://doi.org/10.1080/14631377.2019.1693738.
Szarzec, Katarzyna, Bartosz Totleben, and Dawid Piątek. 2020. "How Do Politicians Capture a State? Evidence from State-Owned Enterprises." *East European Politics and Societies.* https://journals.sagepub.com/doi/10.1177/0888325420953485. Accessed September 22, 2020.
Szélenyi, Iván. 2017. "Capitalism after Communism." In *Twenty-Five Sides of a Post-Communist Mafia State*, edited by Balint Magyar and Júlia Vásárhelyi, 637–649. Budapest: CEU Press.
Tanzi, Vino. 2011. *Government Versus Markets: The Changing Economic Role of the State.* New York: Cambridge University Press.
The New Palgrave Dictionary of Economics. 2018. London: Palgrave Macmillan.
Thomas, Clive S. 2020. "Interest Group." In *Encyclopedia Britannica.* https://www.britannica.com/topic/interest-group. Accessed February 16, 2021.
Tullock, Gordon. 1967. "The Welfare Cost of Tariffs, Monopolies, and Theft." *Western Economic Journal* 5 (3): 224–232.

Tullock, Gordon. 1980. "Efficient Rent-Seeking." In *Toward a Theory of the Rent-Seeking Society*, edited by James Buchanan, Robert Tollison, and Gordon Tullock, 97–112. College Station, TX: Texas A&M University Press.

Victor, David G., David R. Hults, and Mark C. Thurber, eds. 2012. *Oil and Governance: State-Owned Enterprises and the World Energy Supply*. Cambridge: Cambridge University Press.

Voszka, Éva. 2018. "Nationalisation in Hungary in the Post-Crisis Years: A Specific Twist on a European Trend." *Europe Asia Studies* 70 (8): 1–22.

World Bank. 2002. *Transition, the First Ten Years: Analysis and Lessons for Eastern Europe and the Former Soviet Union*. Washington: The World Bank.

World Bank. 2014. *Corporate Governance of State-owned Enterprises: A Toolkit*. Washington: The World Bank.

Wright, Mike, Geoffrey Wood, Alvaro Cuervo-Cazurra, Pei Sun, Ilya Okhmatovskiy, and Anna Grosman, eds. 2021. *Oxford Handbook on State Capitalism and the Firm*. Oxford: Oxford University Press (forthcoming).

CHAPTER 3

State Corporate Control in Transition: Challenges and Goals

3.1 The "Heritage" of the Planned Economy

3.1.1 Failed Marxian Hopes

The challenges faced by the state's ownership policy during the post-communist transition resulted from the specificity of the previous system: its assumptions, practical implementation and their consequences for the enterprise sector and the entire economy.

The communist economic system, otherwise known as the command economy or centrally planned economy, was based on a strict centralization of all economic processes, in particular decision-making and control processes. Central planning was to eliminate the existing and alleged deficiencies of market mechanisms, such as "the contradiction between socialised production and capitalistic appropriation" and the "anarchy in production" (Engels 2010, pp. 259, 261). Contrary to the expectations of Engels, who was against the state ownership of enterprises in favor of some forms of the socialization of the means of production (Engels 1951, p. 136), the real central planning system could not function without the concentration of rights for the production assets in the hands of the state. In order to have both a mandate to manage the assets and a real possibility to perform this function, the state had to be the owner of the vast majority of the means of production; state ownership becoming the second pillar of the communist system after central planning. The Soviet lawyer Anatoly Venediktov (1948) has formulated the principle of the

P. Kozarzewski, *State Corporate Control in Transition*,
https://doi.org/10.1007/978-3-030-78562-8_3

functioning of property rights in socialism, based on the unity of the state authority in fulfilling the function of a regulator and an owner of the means of production.

However, state ownership in planned economy differed much from that of in market economies. Firstly, it was incomplete in the understanding of contemporary property rights theories, because it did not provide a complete set of rights for its owner. The right to earn income was distorted by centralized price setting. The transfer of ownership did not exist at all, while the right to use the assets of the state enterprise was dispersed between the state bureaucracy and the management of enterprises. As Janos Kornai (1992) put it, state ownership in the planned economy was completely depersonalized. Secondly, it was "the mystification of property" (Bałtowski and Kozarzewski 2014, Chapter 2.1), i.e., the fact that the state did not exercise its power over state enterprises in a rational and fair manner and in fact instead of representing the interests of the whole society, it represented the interests of bureaucracy which had captured the state.

After the initial successes associated with the concentration of production potential in the hands of the state (both through the nationalization of private enterprises and through the forceful industrialization), the capabilities for ensuring socio-economic development through administrative mobilization began to rapidly deplete. The efficiency of the command economy began to fall dramatically, macroeconomic and social disproportions were growing, deviant (in relation to the then binding political and economic doctrine) behavior of the main actors became more and more common. It forced the authorities of all communist countries to make numerous attempts to modernize the system in various ways: from trying to strengthen the administrative mobilization, through introducing some degree of Marxist socialization of industrial relationships to re-introducing of some elements of the market.

3.1.2 SOEs' Self-Management Reform in Poland

In this respect, Poland was the country where the range of these attempts was probably the widest, and in the declining phase of the communist system in this country, i.e., in the 1980s, their main direction became generally liberalizing and marked-oriented. These reforms have created a peculiar system of corporate governance of SOEs which pre-determined the initial conditions for post-communist reforms and their implementation, especially in relation to enterprises that stayed under the state control.

Reforms of the enterprise sector in the 1980s tackled mainly the issues of the corporate control within formally the state ownership. Only by the end of the decade both the researchers and policymakers started appreciating the need of privatization, at least partial. However, all the attempts still were aimed at improvement of the existing economic system (predominance of at least formally state ownership and some form of central control) and the political regime (the communist party rule and the alliance with the USSR). This happened for at least several reasons. Firstly, the belief in the existence of a large, untapped development potential of socialism was still strong enough. Secondly, a kind of political pragmatism existed, i.e., the conviction that there were internal (communist party power) and external (Soviet Union existence) limits to the degree of how radical the reforms could be. Thirdly, the society's expectations were not anti-socialist at all; the population rather wanted the political elite to fulfill their paternalistic and egalitarian promises of socialism. This was particularly evident in the main slogan of the August 1980 strikes (which eventually led to the creation of the Solidarity trade unions) which was "Socialism yes, deviations no!" Fourthly, the rather positive experience of reforming the "real socialism" in Hungary and especially in Yugoslavia existed, based, among other things, on the decentralization of corporate control and on employee participation, without violating the principles of communist party leadership and the primacy of state property. All this led to a certain consensus among the government, intellectuals and the opposition that in the given circumstances the best possible solution was to relieve the grip of the central planning system on the SOEs and give them more autonomy.

The two acts: Act on State-owned Enterprises and Act on Self-Management of the Employees of State-owned Enterprises from 25 September 1981 transformed SOEs into autonomous, self-managing and self-financing entities which managed the separate piece of state property. Autonomy was understood as independence from the state and party administration (including the abolition of imposing production tasks on enterprises); self-management meant employee participation (going beyond the operational management and entering quite clearly into the ownership rights); self-financing was the introduction of an economic account and (at least formally) full separation of the enterprise from the state budget. According to the Act of 26 February 1982 on the Financial Management of State-owned Enterprises, SOEs gained the right to independently decide on their finances, e.g., on distribution of a part of their profits, getting the sources of financing, and setting salaries. The Act of 26 February 1982 on Social and Economic Planning had abolished the directive planning by the government. It was replaced with economic tools for indirect influencing enterprises, e.g., through the government procurement system and regulation of prices. The state administration retained the direct tools (albeit in a reduced form) only towards enterprises of particular importance to the national economy.

The crucial innovation from the perspective of this study was the new structure and methods of appointing SOEs bodies. They were constructed as equivalents of bodies in a corporation, i.e., a typical private enterprise. The new bodies were the general meeting of employees (which had functions and powers similar to those of a general meeting of shareholders) and the employee council (which performed supervisory functions, just like supervisory boards in companies in the Continental model of corporate governance). The director was elected by the council and not appointed by a relevant branch ministry anymore; thus, the system of party nomenclature typical for communist planned economies has been abandoned.

However, the system of corporate control in SOEs established by the two acts of September 1981 differed substantially from that of private corporations. It could have implied that, de facto, the company was to belong to the employees. However, firstly, this was not the legislator's intention who instead of Marxian socialization of enterprises was aiming at just creating a mobilization tool for the workforce to increase labor productivity (Stypułkowski 1986, pp. 101–102). Secondly, the employees did not receive a full bundle of property rights: they did not have the right to transfer ownership. Despite the introduction of the legal possibility to liquidate an unprofitable SOE, in practice the right to use the property meant only gaining profits from it, while losses were still covered by the state through soft budgetary restrictions and special government's investment schemes. So, in practice the state kept inefficient enterprises alive. What is more, in subsequent amendments to the acts, the powers of the state bodies were gradually extended, while those of the employee self-management were more and more limited.

At the same time the state was not a full-fledged SOEs owner as well. There was no representative of the state owner in the SOEs bodies.

State authorities in charge of ownership supervision of SOEs (so-called founding bodies which usually were branch ministers) had only limited powers of interfering into SOEs functioning, the only significant tool being the possibility to influence the appointment of the director.

It should be also noted that the reformed SOE did not become a corporation even formally. It still was a special legal form of an enterprise and functioned under the special legislation, and not under the general corporate law (which in a reduced form had survived in communist Poland). There were just a few state-controlled firms in Poland before the transition, which were corporations (joint-stock companies).

Despite the fact that the 1981 acts were not intended to overthrow the communist system, they have deeply modified the economic system of the People's Republic of Poland by introducing a permanent (and these regulations are still in force) and fundamental change in the relationship between the state as the owner and the SOE as an object of ownership. Firstly, these relations have been given a formalized, law-based character. Secondly, they radically reduced the ownership functions of the state: they distributed the control rights over SOEs between the government and the employees. What is more, the acts meant a revolution in the functioning of the command economy, abolishing the de facto the directive character of central planning, the hierarchical structure of the economy, and the principle of uniform state ownership (Bałtowski 2009, p. 259).

The enterprise reform of the early 1980s (which was accompanied with some changes in price regulation and tax policies) ended in failure and the Polish economy did not succeed in restoring its development capabilities. This pushed the government and economists to look for deeper reforms, including more radical changes of the state policy towards the enterprise sector. There was also a stimulating factor of a positive kind, i.e., coming to power in the USSR of the reformist wing of the Communist Party headed by Mikhail Gorbachev who started the deepest ever reforms aimed at "improving" socialism in this country. In several aspects, such as freedom of speech, they placed the USSR far ahead of other countries of the Eastern bloc, even those with relatively less oppressed rule, as Poland and Hungary. Besides, the USSR proclaimed the policy of non-interference into the affairs of other countries of the Eastern bloc. All this created a favorable geopolitical situation for the supporters of more radical reforms in Poland. Last but not least, contacts with the West were gradually expanding in Poland and more and more people both among intellectuals and governmental and party circles, who had the occasion to get Western education or just have more experience with capitalism, got a much better understanding how Western economic and political processes work.

Closer to the end of the 1980s the government decided to introduce deeper reforms which went beyond the attempts to "repair" the command economy. The Act of 28 January 1987 on Counteracting Monopoly Practices in the National Economy served to counteract the dominance of the state sector on the market. In November 1988, the Council of Ministers adopted the extensive Plan of Consolidation of the National Economy for 1989–1990. The key to its implementation in the area of the policy towards the enterprise sector was the Act of 23 December 1988 on Economic Activity which introduced real mechanisms ensuring economic freedom. Firstly, through equal treatment of all forms of ownership (in terms of employment, taxes, etc.). Secondly, by introducing the core principle of market economies: all economic activities are permitted except those prohibited by law. The Act of 23 December 1988 on Economic Activity with the Participation of Foreign Entities lifted restrictions on foreign direct investments (FDI) in the Polish economy and introduced incentives for FDI inflow.

It's worth noting that despite the extensive reforms started being introduced during the last years of the communist rule (which also included, among others, banking reform, liberalization of use of foreign currency and deregulation of consumer prices), nothing has been done to improve the effectiveness of the state corporate control (apart from certain restrictions on the rights of employee self-management). The governmental 1988 Plan of Consolidation of the National Economy only promised to create the Treasury which would take over the property rights over SOEs from the founding bodies with the possibility of privatization of SOEs. However, nothing was said neither done about the incomplete character of property rights of the state, and the state's inability to properly perform its ownership functions.

Apart from this, despite all the relative radicalism of the reforms in 1987–1989, they still did not cover certain important areas of the functioning of the economy: the rationing of basic resources for enterprises was maintained, as well as the non-market, arbitrarily decreed exchange rates. SOEs still enjoyed soft budgetary constraints and, regardless the formal introduction of economic freedom and equal treatment of all ownership forms, SOEs were to maintain the leading role of the state sector in the economy, leaving room for the private sector only where, in the opinion of the authorities, state ownership could not function effectively enough, which meant mainly small business (Bałtowski 2009, p. 291; Kaliński 2015). The reforms of the last communist government were still in the corset of communist ideological principles.

All this created the situation, when at the final, decaying stage of command economy in Poland it was still formally based on state ownership of means of production. The state domain consisted of state-owned enterprises and cooperatives and at the end of the communist era was huge. Over 95% of all the enterprises belonged to the state. In the non-agricultural sector (excluding cooperatives) the state employed 66% of the country's workforce, SOEs' share in total sales was over 70% (Table 3.1).

At the same time the state had no strong legal or even just conceptual grounds to perform its ownership functions. Mechanisms of centralized control of the SOE sector were essentially eliminated in the early 1980s, while other, comprehensive and effective mechanisms of state corporate control were not established. It is puzzling that the issue of effective state ownership in the late 1980s did not exist in the public discourse. It seems that practically nobody (at least nobody who could influence the economic policy) saw the need for such a policy. The concept of independent state-owned enterprises gained an absolute advantage, and all ideas for overcoming the accumulated dysfunctions of the state sector followed

Table 3.1 Sales and employment in the state domain (excluding agriculture and cooperatives) in the main sectors of the Polish economy at the end of 1989

	Sales		*Employment*	
	in PLZ trillion[a]	*share in total, %*	*persons in thousands*	*share in total, %*
Industry	86.1	83.8	3521.1	70.9
Construction	10.8	74.5	769.9	62.6
Transport and communications	8.9	91.9	854.5	92.2
Trade	18.6	40.4	396.2	27.3
Municipal	2.4	77.9	309.9	70.1
Total	126.8	71.2	5541.7	66.2

[a]1 USD = PLZ 9500. PLZ was Polish złoty before denomination in 1995 at the rate 1000:1. The new złoty's code is PLN

Source Bałtowski and Kozarzewski (2014, Table 8.1)

this decentralization stance. The supporters of strengthening the state's role towards SOEs were virtually inaudible.

3.1.3 Decline and Fall of Socialism

The end of the 1980s was marked with the deep, catastrophic economic crisis (Bałtowski and Kozarzewski 2014, Chapter 3.1.1). The GDP growth rate in 1989 dropped practically to zero; shortages caused by low productivity of Polish enterprises and the irrational pricing policy maintaining artificially low prices of "socially important" goods were paramount on investment and consumption markets; the bottom-up pressure to raise wages led to a loss of control over their growth. This led to shortageflation, i.e., the co-occurrence of market shortages and inflation (Kołodko and McMahon 1987). The budget deficit increased in the absence of effective mechanisms for its financing. Foreign trade was characterized by too high share of low-processed products, as well as those which were uncompetitive on Western markets (so demand existed mainly on the Comecon market). The total foreign debt reached the level of five-year export income and was practically unpayable. The backwardness of agriculture, especially its state sector, resulted in chronic shortages and the introduction of rationing of selected articles.

The question arises, whether this catastrophe could be prevented. Among others, whether the reform of the state's policy towards the SOEs aimed at restoring the corporate control over them, if implemented in the given circumstances, could be effective. The same goes to other attempts to repair the decaying economy without applying a radical change, which eventually has been done after the political collapse of the communist regime in Poland in 1989.

More than 100 years ago Karl Hampe coined a maxim *Die Geschichte kennt kein Wenn* (Demandt 2011, p. 17) which means "The history does not know the word if." However it is tempting to find an answer to the question "Was it possible to do better?" which is a hard task in the economic history especially when we do not have a relevant example of success: all the countries of the former Eastern bloc failed to overcome the crisis of the command economy without a systemic change, and those which started comprehensive market reforms nowadays show much more success in their social and economic development than those reluctant to introduce radical reforms.

This it's quite possible that the answer to the question whether the catastrophe could be prevented is no and the Polish experience provides this point of view with a number of arguments. Poland was the first country in the Eastern bloc to embark on systemic reforms and has shown that there was a possibility of a peaceful transition from the command economy and the omnipotent rule of a communist party towards market economy and democratic rule. At the same time, it showed that a number of factors existed which made impossible to overcome the crisis of the command economy while preserving its main paradigms and resting on the existing institutional system and the social forces embedded in the political and economic system. The command economy proved ineffective not only because it was based on unrealistic assumptions (including the decision-making and control effectiveness of the omnipotent state), but also because it was rigid, unable to adapt quickly to changes in economic conditions, and thus not susceptible to restructuring and introduction of necessary innovations.

Due to the lack of an efficient owner, autonomy and competition, state-owned enterprises were not interested in minimizing costs, including the use of resources, and maximizing profits. Rather the other way around: their modus vivendi was formed by maximizing the funds they received from the central resource allocation while minimizing production plans, which increased the system's anti-efficiency potential and created a quasi-market for tenders between companies and the state administration. At the level of enterprises, this led to low labor and capital productivity, inefficient use of production capacity and a deepening of the technological backwardness. The economic system lacked an effective flow of information, especially the feedback from enterprises to the government.

A closed system has been formed, based on the struggle for sources of rents between the various interest groups which captured the state: SOEs, members of various types of bureaucratic hierarchies, etc. (Hausner and Wojtyna 1993; Shleifer and Vishny 1994). Such a system sought to preserve the status quo to which all participants in the economic life were accustomed, while the role of the state boiled down to the function of a central distributer of rents from the highest levels of state administration and party apparatus to individual enterprises. The system therefore rejected all technological and social changes, seriously limiting or even eliminating not only political but also economic competition. Moreover, as a result of the blocked flow of information it was deprived of an effective "early warning" system (Kozarzewski 2006, pp. 26–27).

The system began to lose its relative stability (ability to survive in the medium term) when, firstly, the possibilities for extensive growth, driven by state-controlled industrialization using the resources of the agricultural sector, were exhausted (Gaidar 1997). Secondly, which to a large extent results from the above, the deepening economic collapse worsened the possibilities of satisfying the needs of basic social groups, and therefore the mechanisms for reconciling social interests, defined by Rychard (1993) as "pragmatic stabilizers," being quite weak in the past, ceased to work completely. The economic crisis of the command economy at the end of the eighties depleted the possibility of ensuring a sufficient level of income for the main social groups, regardless of whether such income was based on value creation or on rent-seeking. Enterprises (and more broadly, enterprise-related interest groups) were dissatisfied with the drying up resources in the hands of the state and began to seek rescue on their own. In turn, bureaucrats, who began to rapidly lose profits from their position as resource distributors, began to look for new sources of income. In the society as a whole, dissatisfaction with the system began to grow and the population began, individually and in groups, the search for ways out. This marked the beginning of a phase of accelerated disintegration of the system, when initially more than just a modest institutional, political and economic capacity for adaptation was dramatically weakened.

Paradoxically, the crisis and disintegration of the command system was further accelerated by the attempts to repair it. A coherence of the system has been broken: partial and often contradictory reforms have not created a "critical mass" for fundamental changes, but have gradually expanded the possibilities to behave contrary to the logic of the system. New elements, woven into the authoritarian structure of the state, instead of helping, only blew it apart from the inside. The economy of the late People's Republic of Poland was partly planned, partly market-driven, with very ineffective control over macroeconomic processes and enterprises often not interested in increasing profits and improving efficiency. The loosening of the administrative control over state-owned enterprises, increasing their autonomy, led to the "privatization of profits," with the losses on the enterprises' operations still being covered by the society.

This new situation created better conditions for the widespread defensive measures in society and its elites which had been triggered by the economic crisis. The nature of these measures depended on the resources held by particular social groups. Bureaucrats and the members of the political and economic elites started a massive "conversion" of the opportunities they had holding their positions in the command economy into another form: money and property. This way they tried to keep their broadly understood profits under the conditions of the disappearance of traditional sources of rents.

In the area of ownership and quasi-ownership relations, the new possibilities created by the disintegrating economic system and the attempts to repair it took the form of the transfer of SOEs' assets to private firms set up by their directors. Apart from asset stripping and tunneling, such firms helped avoiding of a tax on excessive remuneration, which was applicable to SOEs only. Since these companies were set up by the management of state-owned enterprises, they were baptized in the press as nomenklatura companies and the transfer of state assets to these companies as nomenklatura privatization or nomenklatura enfranchisement—although the term "nomenklatura" at that time did not already reflect the essence of the mechanism of appointment of directors of state-owned enterprises, who were mostly elected by employee self-management. This procedure was very common: according to estimations, by September 1989 12.6 thousand nomenklatura companies were established, half of the directors of SOEs being involved (Gruszecki 1990, p. 8). I encountered a typical nomenklatura company even among my family: my rather distant relative, the director of a SOE in the construction sector, established a company with his chief accountant, leased equipment from this SOE and captured its clients.

It should be noted however that the new opportunities rather facilitated such actions than initiated them. The behavior of officials, party dignitaries, and directors of enterprises resulted mainly from pragmatic motivations of the necessity to fulfil their needs in changing external conditions. It was just a part of the process of disintegration of the command economy system. At the same time, no efforts were made to improve the state corporate control; no one (both in governmental and opposition circles) seemed to even notice the problem of lack of proper corporate control tools in the hands of the state. The concept of independent state-owned enterprises had no real competition. Despite falling performance of SOEs, the solutions were looked for everywhere (in strengthening their independence, their privatization, deregulation and liberalization of the economy, etc.), but not in the deep and comprehensive reform of the state corporate control.

Eventually the political elites resigned from further attempts to repair the system because they came to the same conclusion, as many economists in Poland and other countries of the Eastern Bloc, about the inherent non-reformability of the command economy (Bałtowski 2009, Chapter 8). So, in spring 1989, after the extensive Round Table negotiations with the representatives of the political opposition and the Catholic Church, the Polish communist elites agreed to participate in conducting the necessary economic and political reforms of the systemic kind. It was a sign of their pragmatism, as they became aware that building market economy and democratization had no reasonable alternative. They have also realized that they lack the political, social and economic resources to make the systemic change. In this situation, a peaceful transfer of political power was initiated and permission was given to future governing teams to carry out comprehensive reforms. Apart from the unquestionable benefits for the country as a whole, such a solution saved the departing elites from alienation, both political and, perhaps even more important, economic, and gave them the opportunity to participate, on new terms, in the functioning of the new emerging economic and political order. Alas, the Round Table agreements essentially omitted the problem of the state corporate control only mentioning, in quite general words (Zespół "Okrągłego Stołu" ds. Gospodarki i Polityki Społecznej 1989), the need to transfer state ownership rights to a centralized body and at the same time declaring extension of employee self-management role in SOEs.

Despite this negligence it seems that, from the perspective of the past three decades, the overall pragmatism of the political elite of those times deserves appreciation. The notions on the advantages of the command economy and the regime which restricts civil liberties for the nation's benefit have disappeared from public discourse for good; the former communists have become social democrats who did not proclaim the need to return to the previous system. And the need for this return was never claimed by any major political force in Poland. In this respect, this country differs from many other post-communist countries, especially most of the former Soviet republics, where the myth of a good, only inappropriately built communist system with planned economy and authoritarian political rule is still very popular. However, as the recent years show, the Polish society proved not to be fully vaccinated against the attempts to re-introduce the "leading role" of the state in the economy and elements of making democracy "illiberal."

3.2 Conceptual Challenges of the State Corporate Control in the Course of Post-Communist Transition

3.2.1 *Unprecedented Character of the Tasks and Challenges*

The reform of the role of the state in the enterprise sector was one of the pillars of the post-communist transition due to the fact that it is one of the main determinants of the economic system and this role is fundamentally different in the command economy and the market economy. It was not only about the fundamental difference in the ownership structure between these economies, but also (and perhaps most importantly) about the need to radically change the paradigm of the state ownership policy: from omnipotence, basing the economy on state property, to the ownership role of the state realized in the conditions of a mostly private economy, in a selective way, in order to achieve specific social and economic goals. At the same time, a huge challenge was to carry out the transformation in the area of ownership relations, which included the choice of the target model of capitalism and elaborating the ways to build it.

This was an extremely difficult task. First of all, the scale of the challenges was enormous and resulted not only from the fundamental differences between the initial and target systems, which determined the scope of changes that had to be introduced and the need to ensure their comprehensiveness taking into account a gigantic number of various mutually dependent factors. On the brink of the transition, almost all command economies were in a state of deep crisis, so the reformist governments had to take anti-crisis measures in addition to the tasks of implementing the systemic transformation. In this respect the reform of ownership policy could also play a useful role improving the functioning of the enterprise sector through better governance of SOEs and through privatization policy.

Secondly, the scope of the tasks was unprecedented; therefore, the possibilities of using the experience of other countries were very limited. In market economies, there were no radical reforms in the corporate control of the SOEs, and the logic of creating the state sector was completely different; SOEs themselves did not create such a burden for economic policy, such a pile-up of dysfunctions in relations between the state and enterprises. Another pillar of the ownership policy, i.e., privatization of state-owned enterprises was indeed used in market economies as a tool of economic policy, but not on such a mass scale and in completely different economic and institutional conditions which made simple replication impossible.

Three decades of the transition show that this not only made it difficult to make choices or resolve dilemmas, but also sometimes did not allow for identification of the existing challenges and dilemmas, which resulted in a suboptimal effectiveness of the reform policy. Various "side effects" have appeared which increased the costs of the transition or even jeopardized achievement of some of its goals. Nowadays, I am in a much more comfortable position than the authors of post-communist reforms, as their course and results are already known. And I have the opportunity, when writing about the choices and dilemmas of reforms of the state corporate control, to do it relying on both the discussions and literature of the time and the knowledge accumulated over the past thirty years.

3.2.2 *Corporate Policy of the State as a Part of the Ownership Policy*

As already mentioned above, ownership policy of the state consists of two main areas (pillars). The first is the policy of ownership transformation, which deals with changes in ownership structure of the economy. According to the logic of post-communist transition, this was to consist mainly in privatization in the narrow sense, i.e., transfer of state assets into non-state hands, although it may also cover other areas, such as supporting the creation and development of new private entities or even, as practice shows, initiating and supporting changes in the opposite direction: increasing the state share in the economy. The second area (pillar) is the state corporate control policy which deals with the assets remaining in the hands of the state in a shorter (until privatization) or longer time horizon (when the state keeps the assets for strategic reasons). The corporate control policy covers the state's impact on enterprises of which it is the owner (also partial) in order to ensure their proper functioning, consistent with the objectives set by the government for these enterprises.

The two pillars of state ownership policy are in a way a mirror image of each other and at the same time a system of connected vessels: the withdrawal of the state from its ownership functions reduces the area of supervision and increases the scope of the private sector. Conversely, the tendency to increase the role of the state as an investor and owner, either directly (nationalization) or indirectly (increasing the share of the state sector in the economy, increasing the regulatory burden on the private sector, etc.) limits this sector. However, this symmetry is not complete: the state was (and is) not only the owner, but also the regulator, moreover, the policy of ownership transformation (both privatization and nationalization) is in fact a temporary policy and is to be completed once its quantitative and structural objectives have been achieved. Whereas the state's corporate governance policy will continue to exist as long as the state possesses a substantial amount of assets.

Besides, the policy of ownership transformation is always (not only during post-communist transition) a response to extraordinary challenges, a tool for overcoming an unfavorable situation, even a crisis. Whereas state corporate control policy is inherent to economic policy, resulting from the fact that the existence of a larger or smaller state sector in a market economy is inevitable, and does not just a comes out of the need to face certain dysfunctions. Although in crisis situations, to which the state often reacts by increasing the state involvement in the economy, the state's corporate control policy may also take the form of emergency measures. Also, post-communist transition may be regarded as a crisis management project, albeit on a much larger scale than anti-crisis measures which are applied in marked economies. Until the transition ends, this policy has mostly extraordinary character, where even the "regular" tasks resulting from the state's role in the economy are the subject of a radical change.

3.2.3 Creating the Concept

3.2.3.1 Choosing the Right Model of Capitalism

First of all, there was a need for making at least a very general choice of the shape of the economic system to be created as a result of the transition, because it conditioned the ways of achieving it. Due to the variety of existing and imaginable varieties of capitalism, in the period immediately preceding the beginning of the transition, there were, simplifying, several basic options that could be considered on two levels: ideological and pragmatic. These perspectives were not entirely separate and concepts and solutions usually combined elements of both perspectives.

The ideological perspective meant choosing a model of the new economic system based on a certain system of values and beliefs. Extreme approaches can be conventionally described here as liberal and social—but their common idea was that the new system must be some form of capitalism, i.e., predominantly based on market mechanisms of regulation and private property. These approaches differed primarily in their perception of the optimal role of the state in the economy. Despite being driven by ideological considerations, these concepts usually did not appear out of the intellectual blue, but most often than not were more or less based on the real systems which much later were described as liberal and coordinated market economies by the founders of the Varieties of Capitalism research approach (Hall and Soskice 2001).

The liberal option was based on the concept of state failure (or government failure), which postulated maximum use of market self-regulation (Coase 1964; Goodman 2015). In this approach, the state was to be mainly concerned with the protection of market relations, and thus also to give up its ownership functions to the maximum extent possible. The improvement of the living conditions of the population was in a way to be automatically ensured by economic growth, while social inequalities were perceived as a natural result of the members of this society acting on their own account and responsibility for their own fate.

The social option was based on the conviction of market failure (Bator 1958), which is characterized by a number of immanent dysfunctions, primarily tendencies towards monopolization, negative externalities and the inability to deliver public goods (Friedman 1990, Chapter 18). Its partisans stressed that the main goal and subject of economic policy is to be man. The state should therefore interfere in economic processes also in order to ensure the achievement of social goals, including those based on the ideas of equality and justice (Kowalik 1995). This meant, among other things, the need for an extensive sector of state-controlled enterprises. The extreme manifestation of this approach is represented by theories of democratic socialism (Prychitko 2002).

In a way outside this dichotomic dispute there were supporters of a "third way": a multi-sectoral economy of a hybrid nature, within which the private sector and the extensive unreformed state sector were to coexist for a long time. This view was mainly based on the belief that there was no systemic advantage of the private sector over the state-controlled one. It referred to pseudo-liberal arguments such as the need to preserve and use the potential of existing SOEs (that might be destroyed by privatization) and that the decisions on the competitive advantage of any form of ownership should left to the market (Sadowski 1991; Borisov 2005).

The ideological assumptions of the target system predetermined the postulated ways of its introduction. The liberal option assumed the rapid creation of an institutional and legal infrastructure, so the productive forces liberated from the statist oppression would fill in market niches. Creation of the market infrastructure should be accompanied by an appropriate economic policy, which would create hard budget constraints for already operating businesses, primarily the state-owned ones, and reduce entry costs for newly established companies (Fischer and Gelb 1991). Ownership transformation was of key importance: without a fundamental reduction of the state domain, it would not have been possible to introduce an effectively functioning market mechanism (Lipowski 1988). In this perspective, the post-communist transformation was primarily a technical task, while the state ownership policy was almost completely reduced to privatization.

In the social option, the main factor in getting the country out of the crisis and at the same time the condition for effective systemic transformation was not so much the rapid creation of an institutional framework for rational economic behavior, but the unleashing creativity of the population which had been suppressed in the previous system. The implementation of this goal would be ensured by a relatively broad state interventionism, minimizing the social costs of reforms by, among other things, keeping the "strategic" areas of the economy under the state control, securing the interests of employees and guaranteeing the society the largest possible share in distribution of state property (through management-employee buyouts, mass privatization, etc.) (Kowalik 1995).

The "third way" option assumed de facto limiting the reform of the ownership policy of the state to eliminating barriers for creation of new private firms and limited privatization of predominantly small enterprises of lesser importance for the economy.

What is striking from the today's perspective, all three options neglected the necessity of making corporate control of the state more effective, to address its inability to achieve its objectives regardless whether the system of control over SOEs in the late command economy era was still fully centralized (like, e.g., in Eastern Germany, Romania, and Czechoslovakia) or deeply decentralized (like in Poland, Hungary, and Yugoslavia). Apparently for the "liberals" this issue was of secondary importance, as the state-controlled enterprise sector was to dramatically shrink and lose its importance. But the implementation of both the social and "hybrid" options was obviously to be based on efficient corporate governance of the state. The proponents of these approaches, however, did not pay any attention to this problem as well, tacitly assuming the capacity of the state to perform the extensive ownership and regulatory functions not only to efficiently manage large assets, but also to effectively overcome the conflict of its ownership and regulatory functions. Among others, it included the ability not to be prone to the pressure of interest groups connected with SOEs. This was rather an unrealistic assumption, especially in light of the exceptional institutional weakness of the state as an owner during the declining stage of the communist system.

The second perspective for the choice of the target model of the economic system can be described as pragmatic. It reflects the division of the authors of post-communist reforms into supporters of building a new system based on solutions already existing in other countries and supporters of building a system not having a direct equivalent among modern developed market economies.

The argumentation in favor of the first approach, which can be described as imitative, was based on a very simple assumption: a system based on market economy and parliamentary democracy is probably not perfect, but it was the only one to confirm its effectiveness and stability in many countries in the long-term. Therefore, the most sensible solution would be to copy this system in one of its versions. There was an extensive choice of them from more liberal ones to more socially oriented ones, or to the model of the developmental state (Evans 1995), characteristic of emerging Asian economies, such as South Korea and Taiwan. In these countries, the state played the role of a "substitute entrepreneur" in the absence of a national bourgeoisie and was the main driving force behind industrialization (Morawski 2001, pp. 153–154).

What is more, discussions at the turn of the 1980s and 1990s (which unfortunately have left almost no traces in printed form) also considered the possibility of carrying out market reforms without creation of institutions of political democracy referring to Augusto Pinochet's reforms in Chile and the Chinese experience. The attractiveness of the Chilean road was seen in the reduction of political risks for reformers when implementing rapid liberal reforms: the lack of democratic control mechanisms was to prevent the society (which was tired of the costs of the reforms) from depriving the reformers of power prematurely. The Chinese road, on the other hand, was attractive to the elites of the collapsing communist system because it promised to preserve their political power. The ideas of a more efficient authoritarian state lost their popularity only later, when extensive studies have shown that democratic institutions which activate civil society provide better prospects for economic development (Przeworski et al. 2000).

The supporters of the imitative approach were not concentrated only on the choice of the appropriate ultimate model of the new system. They also studied the experience in the implementation of reforms in other countries, including West Germany and Japan after the Second World War, regarding these reforms as "constructivist," i.e., being a "government-controlled, far-reaching systemic change," and being utterly successful (Kowalik 2005, p. 288).

The argumentation under the second approach, which could be called innovative, was that the need to reform the decaying system provided a unique opportunity to go beyond the popular system solutions and to build a system that could have many features in common with existing market systems, but without their drawbacks: e.g., without social inequalities or alienation of labor being an inherent feature of modern capitalism. In Poland, such a "third way" was considered to be primarily a system based on participation: first of all, in the form of employee self-management, but also of local self-government. This was probably due to the popularity of participatory ideas in Poland, especially in the declining period of the communist system. The main novelty was the location of participation in the general paradigm of capitalism and market economy which, among other things, made it incomparable with the Yugoslavian model and this model was not regarded as a plausible solution for transition in Poland.

The system of participatory market economy did not exist anywhere in the world, so an attempt to build it would be a socio-economic innovation. Nevertheless, the supporters of the participatory economy referred to experience of developed economies, such as Employee Stock Ownership Plans (ESOP) in the USA as well as Spanish Mondragon, Israeli kibbutzim and other employee ownership solutions (Bar 1995; Gilbert 1995). The fact that in developed Western countries employee ownership was (and still is) a fairly exotic margin of the economy and its share in total industrial ownership did not exceed 1% (Błaszczyk 1995), thus not being a systemic pillar, was ignored.

The post-communist transition in Poland was ultimately carried out according to imitative recipes, combining a liberal approach (inspired by the ideas of the Washington Consensus) with elements of a social market economy (the latter in 1997 became a constitutional norm). Nevertheless, participatory solutions paved the way for the state ownership policy, but only through various forms of employee participation in privatization of SOEs. The views of the adepts of participation probably also contributed to the rapid reconstruction of local self-governments, in my view perhaps the most successful reform in post-communist Poland (but the continuation of this thread goes beyond the thematic framework of this book).

3.2.3.2 Goals and Tasks of the Corporate Control of the State

Determining the optimal scope of the ownership role of the state is a highly complex task: because of the "varieties of capitalism," the adopted model of the state's role in the economy, as well as of other factors such as the challenges of socio-economic development, the specificity of formal and informal institutional setup, social expectations, etc. These factors may change over time, the latest example being the global financial crisis of 2008–2009 which forced many governments in developed economies to temporarily increase the state's interventionism as a part of their crisis management policy. Among others, it included rescue nationalizations of corporations too important to fail; when the crisis had receded, they were re-privatized.

The ideas on the optimal scope of the state's ownership function and the shape of the sector of SOEs depend primarily on how the optimal role of the state in the economy is perceived. There is no single right model of the state's role in the economy; the specific scope of this role is determined not only pragmatically, but also politically or even ideologically. The choice of the set of functions that the state should perform in the economy determines the scope and nature of the state's ownership functions.

Here, the important question is whether the state is to limit itself to correcting market failures by producing socially important goods which are not worth producing for the private sector. Or should it also, as Mariana Mazzucato (2013) claims, be a "super entrepreneur" investing in new, prospective and important areas for social and economic development, aimed at improving the competitiveness of national economies, and bearing a high investment risk. Finally, should the state use SOEs to perform also some other tasks, e.g., of social or political nature.

In general, the dominant view in the literature on the subject is that nowadays the role of the state should not be limited to correcting market imperfections. There are many different classifications of the role and tasks of the state in the economy, but from the point of view of the state's ownership function they can be reduced to four areas:

- ensuring stability in the functioning of the economy,
- improving the standard of living of citizens,
- creating public goods and socially important private goods,
- stimulating social and economic development.

Depending on the specific variant of capitalism, these tasks may differ in content and meaning, and some may not exist at all. In a country undergoing post-communist transition, market reforms, including ownership transformation, should be added to these tasks. The aim of the reforms is, among other things, to ensure the effectiveness of the implementation of all other functions of the state; the comprehensive nature of the necessary reforms, the need to create a specialized institutional and organizational environment and the limited time horizon of the reforms require a clear separation of ownership functions of the state from the other functions.

OECD (2015, p. 17) experts point out that ownership functions of the state in the economy must be subject to a comprehensive policy in this respect. It should include a justification of the existence of the state ownership, definition of its objectives and ways to achieve them—including clearly defined responsibilities of public administration. According to Putniņš (2020) the rationale in engaging SOEs in correcting widely understood market failures (monopolies, negative externalities and lack of provision of public goods) exists only under two conditions. Firstly, these failures are essential for social welfare and other ways of addressing them are unfeasible (through regulations, taxation, subsidies, or private provision of goods). Secondly, the direct provision of goods by the government through SOEs would bring more profits than losses incurred from this intervention (such as technical and allocative inefficiency and rent-seeking).

The appropriate goal setting was particularly important in post-communist transition countries because of the place ownership policy of the state had in the shaping up the new economic system, and this significantly broadens the scope of challenges compared to ownership policy of the state in developed market economies.

One of the main challenges here is to create appropriate corporate governance mechanisms. In the private sector, these mechanisms (within the existing legal, institutional and economic conditions) to a large extent shape up spontaneously, according to the goals and needs of stakeholders. Here, state interference boils down to attempts to eliminate economically and socially significant dysfunctions. Whereas in the state sector these mechanisms must be created in a controlled manner in order to prevent the emergence of numerous dysfunctions and ensure effective implementation of the state's objectives as an owner. State-owned enterprises have to deal with a much wider range of barriers and challenges than private ones.

The World Bank's research on both developed and emerging economies allows identifying six areas that pose the greatest problems in the implementation of the state's ownership function (World Bank 2014, pp. 13–15):

- the agency problem, due to multiple principals (whose functions are performed by many state actors usually with not very precisely formulated roles);
- the multiplicity of goals objectives, often conflicting (economic and non-economic, openly formulated or hidden);
- protection from competition (privileged position of SOEs over other market players, including soft budget constraints);
- politicization of management (concerning both nominations on the boards and decision-making);
- low transparency and accountability (weakness of control mechanisms, which puts at risk efficiency and encourages corruption);
- weak shareholder and stakeholder protection: the state may abuse minority investors and have problems with balancing interests of powerful stakeholders such as employees, consumers, creditors, local authorities, etc.

During the post-communist transition, the importance of shaping proper corporate control of the state becomes particularly high because of the need to overcome the model of relations between the state and its enterprises which was formed in the declining period of command economy and which would be totally unacceptable in a market economy.

3.2.3.3 *The Scope of State Ownership and Control*

The problem of the scope of the ownership role of the state was particularly important and difficult to solve during the post-communist transition, when the system built on the absolute domination of the state sector was to be transformed into a system where any form of ownership would take its proper place resulting from the advantage in the realization of important economic and social functions.

The pro-market nature of the post-communist transition, regardless of the target shape of the system being built, meant a significant change in the ownership structure towards denationalization, achieving the advantage of the economy based on private ownership while retaining the state's ownership control in specific, justified cases: when it was more desirable than private ownership according to some criteria. So, the problem of the proper role of the state as the owner of the means of production (enterprises) may be regarded as a kind of mirror image of the effectiveness of the private sector. It may be argued that as the general rule the state should play the role of an owner and investor where the expected effects are not achievable by the private sector. And to avoid involvement in areas where the private sector is, in a broad sense, more efficient than the public sector.

Despite the simplicity of this general principle, making a really reasonable, as less ideology driven as possible assessment of what is to be private and what is to remain state is, for many reasons, an extremely complicated matter; in the early years of transition it was rather an impossible task. Even for practical reasons, it made no sense to apply a "symmetrical" approach by reviewing the entire sector of enterprises and stating for each sector or even individual enterprise what form of ownership suits them best. So, some general rules had to be applied based on certain general assumptions. One of the main seems to be the need to justify leaving a company or a sector under state control, rather than its privatization (or keeping in private hands).

At least three reasons stay behind this "minimalistic" approach, all related to a widely understood cost of the state corporate control. Firstly, in light of numerous theoretical concepts (with the school of property rights at the forefront) generally confirmed by empirical research (which will be discussed in detail later in the book), state ownership is generally less effective in microeconomic terms. The latter results, among other things, from the inherent conflict between the roles of the state as a regulator and owner. Secondly, the use of state-owned enterprises for the implementation of state economic policy objectives may entail various costs for the entire economy, such as distorting the functioning of market mechanisms, e.g., related to the restriction of competition, politicization of SOEs functioning, as well as the multiplicity of objectives pursued by individual state-owned enterprises (as opposed to private enterprises whose primary objective is only to maximize profit and/or the value of the company). The multiplicity of objectives makes it difficult to manage such an enterprise and may reduce its efficiency (broadly understood, not only economic). Thirdly, there are also direct costs generated in the state administration: the costs (financial and human) of managing the state-controlled assets. The state does not have unlimited resources, especially in the period of transition, when to the "ordinary" tasks of the state those related to the need to manage large-scale socio-economic reforms are added. At the same time, especially at the beginning of transition, a post-communist state suffers a significant deficit of qualified officials capable of effectively implementing the state's policy, in this case the ownership policy. Thus, even if the state owner was as microeconomically effective as the private owner, keeping the company in the state domain without any other reasons would have induced additional costs and the rationality of this decision may seem dubious.

Besides, it is worth noting that exercising ownership control is not the only way for the state to control microeconomic behavior of enterprises and possible extraction of its resources. To a certain extent, these objectives can also be achieved through regulations, e.g., through those defining the functioning of monopolies, or the tax system. Regulatory solutions may in many cases turn out to be more effective than ownership solutions, e.g., because they involve fewer resources of the state bureaucracy. Additionally, there would be no conflict between the ownership and regulatory functions of the state.

Therefore, it seems logical that the "minimalistic" approach to the scope of the state ownership is reflected in the law and practice of many developed market economies, where the state can be the owner of enterprises only if the given objectives cannot be achieved in any other way, and the need to maintain state ownership is to be periodically verified (Böwer 2017; OECD 2018; Bałtowski and Kwiatkowski 2018, Chapter 3). This is in line with the OECD recommendations (2015, pp. 17, 29), according to which the state ownership of enterprises requires justification and the reasons for maintaining it are to be constantly monitored, including an analysis of alternatives in the form of management of these enterprises by a private owner or an appropriate tax system that stimulates the desired behavior of enterprises.

A potential drawback of applying such an approach in the conditions of post-communist transition was the threat of privatizing enterprises which, due to the objectives of state policy, should have remained under its control. This is what the authors of the statist turn in Polish economic policy, which took place in the middle of the 2010s, accused their predecessors of. In practice, however, as numerous studies have shown, and as will be shown later in this book, such a threat did not exist in Poland (and perhaps in no other post-communist country). The problem was usually of the opposite kind: a lack of justification for maintaining too large a state-controlled enterprise sector.

3.2.4 State Corporate Control of What Exactly? The Boundaries of the SOE Sector

The first and most important problem is to establish a borderline between what belongs to the state and what is not due to the multitude of ambiguous, undefined situations where ownership rights (sometimes difficult to identify) are partly in the hands of the state and partly in private hands. While in early capitalist and in communist economies there was a fairly clear division in this respect, by the end of the twentieth century this division was increasingly blurred in market economies, as well as in transition economies; in the latter, privatization processes have created numerous cases of ownership structures difficult to be unequivocally classified as state-owned or private.

According to Bałtowski and Kwiatkowski (2018, Chapter 2.2.1) there are at least three reasons for that:

- mass creation of public–private companies;
- expansion of sophisticated ownership structures, often opaque, including cascade ownership, when formally private enterprises are de facto controlled by the state;
- the increasing use of regulatory mechanisms allowing the state to control companies even without any share in their ownership.

The need for setting as precise as possible border between SOEs and private enterprises is not a purely scholastic task. As it is shown in the next chapters of this book, the fuzziness of this border leads to underestimation of the state-controlled sector of the economy and has negative impact on the effectiveness of the ownership policy of the state up to emergence of outright dysfunctions. Among others, this is using public, state-controlled assets in a way covered from public control and not in the public interest.

The boundary between the two forms of ownership can be attempted to define from its "private" or "state" side, according to the principle "everything that is not state owned is private" or vice versa. Here, the term "private" is used in a broad sense—as assets that do not belong directly or indirectly to the state (i.e., are not controlled by public administration at all levels, including local governments), which also includes companies whose shares are publicly traded and to which the term "public company" is sometimes used, as opposed to "private companies," i.e., wholly owned by a narrow group of owners. I treat both these types of companies as private.

It seems that, at least in the case of the countries undergoing transformation, it is more fruitful to analyze this problem from the "state" side, since it was the state ownership that formed the foundations of the previous system and it was supposed to be the subject of reforms in the first place (through privatization or at least deep restructuring performed by the state owner). An additional argument is that in practice (which will be discussed in detail later in this book), it is the state, and not private owners, which creates most of the ownership identification problems through the use of a wide array of ownership and non-ownership tools.

However, it is not possible to develop a universal criterion for delimitation, as in many cases it is volatile and contextual even for the same enterprise. The boundary must therefore be set by a researcher arbitrarily in one way or another depending on the objectives and area of research. Such researcher has to consider the multiplicity of ways in which the state influences enterprises and the different strength and scope of this influence, as illustrated in Fig. 3.1.

Generally speaking, the forms of the state's control can be divided into corporate and non-corporate. Corporate control means the use by the state of tools of direct influence on the decisions of companies through participation in the formation and functioning of their bodies, and participation in decision-making processes. The "classic" set of control tools is based on ownership; it is about influencing the decisions of the General

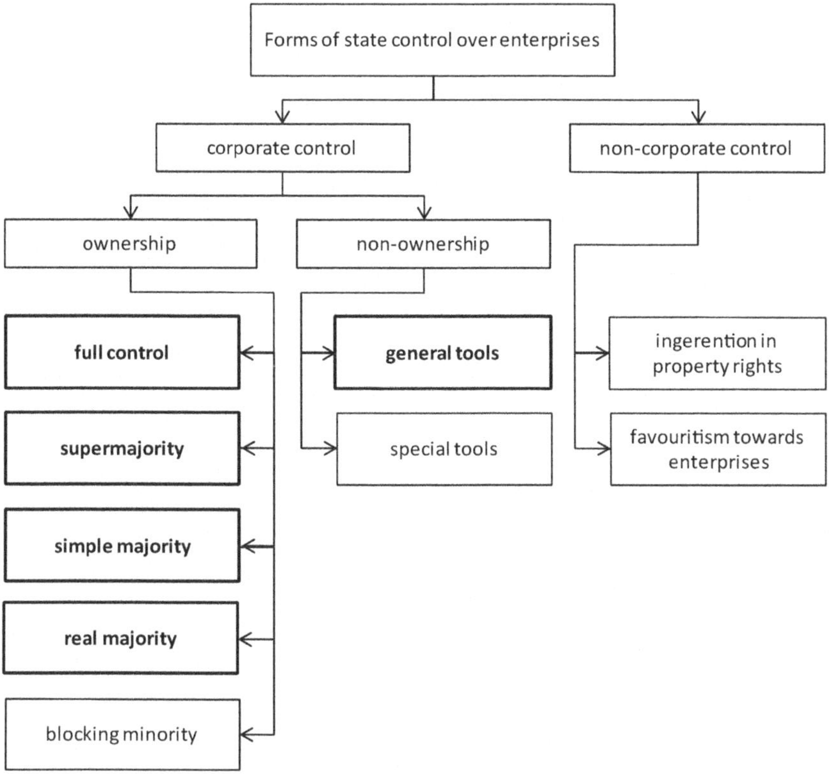

Fig. 3.1 Forms of state control over enterprises (*Source* Own study. *Note* Bold elements show the scope of the state-controlled sector of enterprises defined by me for the purpose of the study)

Meeting of Shareholders in proportion of number of shares held by the state. Such corporate control is graded:

- the strongest with 100% state ownership;
- slightly weaker (because it is limited by the requirements related to functioning on the capital market) with shares giving a supermajority;
- even weaker with only a simple majority (formally over 50% of votes), because minority investors still can block certain decisions;

- the weakest (but still important in certain situations) minority ownership which allows the state to block certain decisions on the most important issues (in Fig. 3.1: blocking minority).

In reality, boundaries between these levels of control are fuzzy and depend on the ownership structure of the company, as well as on certain specific regulations, e.g., in the companies' charters. If other owners are dispersed, even a relatively small block of shares, e.g., 20% (and sometimes even less), may give the state the possibility to control, and thus effectively manage the company (in Fig. 3.1: real majority). It is even more difficult to determine the real influence of the state as the owner in case of cascade holding structures. The complexity of the matter therefore forces to apply certain model simplifications.

Defining a state entity through state ownership does not take into account the increasingly widespread non-ownership forms of corporate control by the state. This is the case where the state has more corporate powers than would result from the number of shares it holds. The state therefore enjoys a privileged position over other investors. Such situations are particularly common in countries where there is strong state interventionism and ownership rights are not defined precisely enough (Bałtowski and Kozarzewski 2016).

The first group of non-ownership tools of state control (in Fig. 3.1 marked as general tools) includes primarily all possible provisions in the companies' charters that give the state more votes at the General Meeting of Shareholders than it results from the size of the state's portfolio. This may be, for example, introduction of a voting cap for non-state investors, or introduction of preference shares which give the state more than one vote per share. Although such actions are within the limits of the law, international organizations do not recommend them, pointing to numerous threats, e.g., violation of the interests of other investors, reduction of investors' confidence in securities issued by such companies which may negatively affect their performance and development prospects (World Bank 2014). Therefore, it is advisable for the state to comply with the principle of equal treatment of all owners of the company (OECD 2015).

The second group of non-ownership tools (in Fig. 3.1. marked as special tools) includes special corporate rights of the state in companies where it has only a minority stake or no shares at all. These rights are granted by special regulations, e.g., in France the state has the right to appoint managers in selected companies (Chadeau 2000). This practice has often taken the form of the so-called golden share, a set of rights to take (or block) particularly important decisions within a company, usually on appointments to company boards or major transactions. In the European Union, the use of the "golden share" is now banned as violating the fundamental principles of freedom of entrepreneurship and free movement of capital, although, as will be shown later in this book, it has not blocked other possibilities to legally guarantee the state's privileged position in corporate control.

It should be noted that the state may influence (and, as numerous studies confirm, really influences) enterprises also indirectly, not through the mechanisms of corporate control, but through various types of regulations that create privileges or restrictions for different types of business activity or even individual enterprises (marked as non-corporate control in Fig. 3.1).

In general, there are two types of such control. In the literature one can find the term state-favored companies (Bremmer 2010), which describes both state-owned and private companies for some reason enjoying special care from the state. It may be supporting "locomotives of growth" or protecting domestic companies against foreign competition, etc. The forms of support are most varied: preferences in access to public procurement and credit, creating barriers to competition, etc. The state may also interfere into private property rights, e.g., by introducing, as in Poland, control over selling large blocks of shares of companies considered particularly important for the national economy, even fully private ones (see Sect. 4.3). Preferences, and especially restrictions, are a way of making companies dependent on the state.

One of the consequences of the lack of clear border between state and private enterprises is the lack of precise and commonly accepted definition of a state-owned enterprise. Apart from creating problems with more precise design and implementation of the state's ownership policy and its evaluation, it negatively affects studies of this sector, especially in an international comparative perspective (Christiansen 2011). Additional problem is that in the literature and in political and business practice a lot of different terms are used to define the same category of enterprises owned by the state (apart from calling them state-owned enterprises, they may be called state companies, state-controlled enterprises, public enterprises, public sector enterprises, public corporations, public companies, government companies, government-controlled companies, crown enterprises, etc.).

Usually in the literature one can find either a general definition according to which a SOE is an enterprise controlled by the state, or more often than not, no definition at all, using this term implicitly. However, a few more precise definitions exist, referring to different degrees and nature of control of the state. For example, according to the OECD (2010), a SOE is a business entity in which the state, directly or indirectly, holds 100% or the majority of shares; categories of fully owned and partially owned SOEs are introduced, later (OECD 2017) being renamed into majority and minority sate-owned enterprises. Matuszak and Szarzec (2019) modified the latter category: in their research, it consists of the enterprises with minority state shareholdings, but the rest of ownership structure must be dispersed. It gives the government real possibilities to exert control over these enterprises. Musacchio and Lazzarini (2014) distinguish between full, majority and minority state ownership (Leviathan as an entrepreneur, a majority investor, and a minority investor). Bałtowski and Kozarzewski (2016) tried to take into account both ownership and non-ownership forms of corporate control of the state and proposed the general term state enterprise (SE) for all forms of such control. Next, they distinguish between state-owned enterprises—SOEs (controlled by the government through ownership tools) and state-controlled enterprises—SCEs (controlled through non-ownership means). In their empirical analysis however, they moved enterprises with government's stakes between 25 and 50% from SOEs to SCEs.

Summing up the considerations on the definition problems, I must admit that I failed to create a precise definition of a SOE because of the contextuality and often graded nature of state control. Therefore, most of the time I use the general term "state-owned enterprise" in the way the OECD (2007, p. 630) uses it—as enterprises which "are entirely, or mainly, owned and/or controlled by the public authorities." I include in this category enterprises that are controlled by the state by means of corporate control mechanisms by holding a real majority of votes resulting either from the number of shares held or from provisions in the statutes under the applicable general corporate law (shown in thick boxes in Fig. 3.1). When there is a need to take into account the gradation of control or its specific type, I will refer to the notions of majority, minority, strategic investors, controlling stock, etc.

Apart from setting the border between what belongs to the state and what is not, and finding the right words to name it, one more border should be defined: what entity can be perceived as an enterprise and what is not an enterprise, i.e., it's the need to separate business activities from other economic activities of the state. In different sources one can encounter lack of clear distinction in this regard. For example, the creators of Amadeus and Orbis databases included ZUS, the Polish state social insurance agency, and Warsaw University as one of the largest enterprises in this country. In the book, I follow the approach proposed by Acharoni (1986, p. 20) and Musacchio and Lazzarini (2014, p. 297) which emphasizes the commercial nature of enterprises, i.e., the sale of goods and services (even if the main objectives of such an enterprise are non-commercial), unlike other state entities which provide public services. One must, of course, be aware of the imperfection of the "separating" function of this approach: a state entity may simultaneously engage in commercial activities and provide public services, and the provision of these services may be to a certain extent commercialized.

3.3 Policy Challenges and Goals of the State Corporate Control in Transition Economies

3.3.1 Place of State Corporate Control Policy in Post-Communist Transition

As it was mentioned in Sect. 3.2.3 of this chapter, in the course of transition the state corporate control had to be not only a tool for managing state property, but also a tool of systemic reforms. In developed marked economies, the objectives of the state corporate control policy may be described through the objectives of state-owned enterprises. In transition economies, corporate control policy of the state, as a part of the ownership policy of the state, inevitably becomes a part of the policy of transition, a set of economic reforms with a wide set of goals which has to support the systemic change in at least five areas (Kozarzewski 2019, pp. 123–125).

The first was the system area. The task of the ownership policy of the state was to contribute to the creation of a new socio-economic order based on private property and market mechanisms. From the structural point of view, it meant the necessity of wide-scale privatization of SOEs and support for creation of new private entities, but it did not mean that the state-controlled enterprise sector had to disappear. However, SOEs had to perform a radically different function compared to that in the command system. They had to cease being the basis of the economic system and to become functioning only in niches where they provided the economy and society with goods and resources what the market and private sector for various reasons could not provide. From the regulatory perspective, the state had to move away from the command economy principles in favor of being in charge of shaping the general conditions of economic activity, i.e., the "rules of the game" and their enforcement. It included changes in scope and instruments of the state corporate control which had to move from command-style steering of the enterprise sector towards control over selected enterprises with a differentiated set of tools which would take into account the SOEs objectives and their market environment.

The second area was the economic one. It consisted of two parts: micro and macro. At the micro-level, the goal was to radically improve the effectiveness of enterprises and generally their ability to shape effective market strategies. Within ownership policy of the state, this goal had to be met mainly through privatization; due to the multitude of objectives of a state-owned enterprise in a market economy, the improvement of microeconomic efficiency may not have been the primary objective of the state's corporate control and the implementation of their main objectives could have taken place at the cost of a certain reduction in their financial efficiency. But efficiency improvement would have been conducive to these objectives indeed. Besides, it was important to take care of microeconomic efficiency in sectors where state-owned enterprises held a dominant position and were therefore not sufficiently subject to market rigors. At the macro-level, the main goal was to contribute to fast, balanced and sustainable economic development. It was to be ensured by achieving the objectives at the micro-level and, within concepts of a strong developmental state, also through the active policy of the state corporate control making SOEs and state investments a catalyst for economic development.

The third area covered fiscal issues, i.e., the influence of the state corporate control policy on the situation of public finances. Within the ownership policy of the state the leading role here could be played by privatization as the largest source of budget revenues and a tool of lifting from the state the financial burden of keeping enterprises alive. But the proper policy of state corporate control could have had also a significant positive impact on public finances, both in increasing revenues and limiting state budget expenditures, and both in short- and long-term perspectives. First of all, state-owned enterprises could be attractive from a fiscal point of view as they would be providing the state budget not only with taxes but also dividends. The increase in the microeconomic efficiency of SOEs would therefore mean an increase in these revenues; besides, it would also lead to a reduction in expenditures to cover the costs of goods generated by these enterprises, including covering losses.

The fourth area was social issues. The ownership policy of the state in transition could achieve social goals of different kind, from restoring social justice in various ways, to social problems of individual enterprises and wider groups of the society. Here, a much broader range of such goals could be pursued by the state's corporate control policy than the ownership transformation policy (both privatization and nationalization), since most of the goals of state-owned enterprises carry a certain social element: production of public goods, improvement of labor relations, increase of accessibility of public services, providing financial resources for social policy reform, etc.

The fifth area concerned political issues. It consisted of two groups of tasks. The first one was de-politicization of the economy in line with the goals of the systemic transition, which had to be partly provided by privatization, taking from state tutelage of most of the enterprise sector. To a large extent it would be provided by a structural change within the realization of the systemic goals. But also de-politicization and deep reform of the state corporate control was necessary, making SOEs pursue general social interest in its activities. Its reform had to contribute to depoliticizing the system of managing state-owned enterprises, blocking group interests related to the functioning of this sector. The second one was creating a social and political base for the new system, which among others would help block the political influence of interests connected with the previous system and generally all private interest groups.

3.3.2 The Need of Special Attention towards SOEs

The main driver ensuring the introduction of market relations was to be the emerging sector of private enterprises, both privatized and newly established. But, regardless of the target vision of the reformed economy, the importance of the state sector was and remains important, and at the beginning of the transition the role of the state-owned enterprises was especially big, and in most areas of the economy even absolutely decisive. This situation could not be changed overnight; it was not possible to carry out privatization of state-owned enterprises on the target scale in an instant. Therefore, for some extensive period of time, the reformist governments were "doomed" to dealing with the state sector which was much bigger than in the target economic system.

The reform programs of practically all the countries of the former Eastern bloc assumed that most of state-owned enterprises would be more or less subject to the rigors of the market, which, among other things, would force them to change their behavior, discipline them, force market rationality on them. (In Poland, as well as in the majority of the Central and Eastern European countries, the desired scope of marketization of the functioning of state-owned enterprises was particularly high.) Given the fact that SOEs were to become, at least for some time, one of the main players in the market that was just being formed, they had to be not only an object of market influence, but also inevitably would influence the development of market relations. Taking into account the different objectives of state and private enterprises, the baggage of experience and ways of behavior of SOEs accumulated in the previous system, as well as the fact that SOEs could still expect special treatment from their owner, it could be expected that the participation of SOEs in reforming the economic system, creating market economy institutions would not always produce a desirable outcome. Pursuing their own interests, state-owned enterprises could be expected to claim for special relaxed treatment from the state (soft budget constraints) and other types of non-market support, like protecting them from competition. This way they would spread patterns of behavior of dysfunctional or even pathological nature. Nota bene, such behavior could also include dysfunctional attitudes towards privatization of these enterprises in the form of resistance against being transferred to private hands or pressure to carry out privatization in the most beneficial way for certain interest groups, primarily insiders.

The state as owner had to take account of this threat and create mechanisms to discipline the SOEs so that they would be (with the exception of justified cases) subject to market rigors on an equal footing with private companies, to make SOEs act in line with public interests. To achieve this, the government had also to discipline itself to prevent the conflict between the functions of the state as the regulator and the state as the owner, to create the set of goals for SOEs functioning and effective mechanisms for their realization and monitoring. All this meant that from the very start of the transition, there was no place for laissez-faire approach, it was necessary to create a coherent and comprehensive policy of state corporate control. The complex nature of tasks and challenges for the SOE sector (also discussed in the further parts of this chapter), operating in a complicated, often distorted institutional environment, as well as the susceptibility of state-owned enterprises to excessive politicization of their operations, created particularly high requirements for the accuracy and effectiveness of shaping the foundations of state corporate control.

3.3.3 *The Quest for the Right Solutions: Was Knowledge Import Possible?*

But how these foundations could be created, with the use of what sources of knowledge? The communist times have provided rather only negative experience in this respect, both on the systemic role of the state ownership and organizational solutions. But unlike post-communist privatization with its unprecedented scale and set of objectives which made possible to rely on the experience of developed economies only on a very limited scale, the experience of the state corporate control in these economies could be more useful. Over the past several decades, capitalist countries have accumulated extensive experience in this area. What is particularly important, those countries gathered a lot of positive experience which can be seen, among others, in generally good financial condition of SOEs in Western economies. However, this experience has not been easy to apply.

Firstly, the post-communist countries which started the transition were structurally and institutionally fundamentally different from the developed Western countries, making it difficult to draw on this experience and in general to develop and implement a new approach towards the role of the state sector in the economy. Among the main factors is that post-communist countries had a legacy of enterprise sectors absolutely dominated by the state. Moreover, SOEs operated under the conditions of a command economy and an authoritarian political system, with a minimal impact of market incentives and social control over the government, which created a specific set of objectives, motivations and behavior. The task of radically changing all this was inevitably complicated not only because of its scale and depth (in technical and institutional terms). It assumed a radical change in thinking, behavior, in the way various interests are satisfied, especially those involved in complex arrangements between the enterprises and the bureaucracy. An additional complicating factor was the limited political, organizational and intellectual resources of the new post-communist government which had to cope with the huge task of reforming the enterprise sector and withstand the resistance of numerous social groups which were losing their sources of rents. It should be added that in post-communist countries there was usually no public consensus on the role of the state in the enterprise sector; in Poland, 30 years after the transition started, there are still disputes about "the amount of the state in the economy" and how the state ownership is to be managed. The real state corporate policy is not a model of stability either.

Secondly, the possibility of applying the experience of developed capitalist countries was also limited by a very deep redefinition of the state's ownership functions in many of them. From the end of the Second World War, and at least until the end of the 1970s, the state domain in many of these economies was expanding to support economic development through the activity of the state as an investor, although private ownership still maintained dominant positions. This trend began to be reversed only in the 1980s, the most spectacular example of which was the policy of privatizing the British economy pursued by the government of Margaret Thatcher, which privatized several dozen large enterprises in industry and infrastructure. It proved to be an effective remedy for their low efficiency and huge public expenditure on keeping these enterprises alive (Moore 1992). In the 1990s, the redefinition of the tasks of the state as the owner (with their serious reduction) gained popularity, which was reflected, among others, in the growing pace of privatization (Mahboobi 2002). However, the de-statization of developed Western economies was not accompanied by a deeper reflection (among decision-makers and researchers) on what the optimal role of state ownership in the economy should look like, what are its objectives and mechanisms of implementation.

It was only at the beginning of the new century that awareness about this issue grew, together with a growing conviction in expert and decision-making circles that the state sector is still an important resource for achieving social and economic goals. The OECD has conducted an extensive research on corporate governance of the state in developed market economies (OECD 2005a), which in 2005 resulted in the set of recommendations (OECD 2005b), in 2015 being refined and extended (OECD 2015). Similar studies which included very specific recommendations were also carried out in the same period by the World Bank (2014). This means that at the beginning of the transition Poland and other countries of the former Eastern Bloc did not have access to a well-ordered knowledge on the role and functions of the state as an owner in developed market economies.

However, the experience of developed capitalist countries still gave very valuable information on what the target system could look like, what legal, organizational and technical solutions could be pursued and what was to be avoided. Such an experience has gained importance especially nowadays, as the knowledge on overcoming the global financial crisis with the help of the state's microeconomic involvement is already available, and the economies of a number of post-communist countries, including Poland, have become largely similar to developed market economies throughout the world. It means a high level of unification of problems of state corporate control and possible solutions.

3.3.4 Objectives of SOEs: Setting and Monitoring

To be efficient, the state-controlled enterprise sector must have a clear set of objectives. They can be described as objectives to be pursued by state-owned enterprises which make use of their advantage over the private sector in specific areas of economic policy. The existing literature does not provide clear answers as to the optimal set of such objectives. An additional difficulty is that researchers often use a normative and positive approach together, i.e., mixing an analysis of what they think should be, with an analysis of what is. Or they just limit themselves to describing the existing situation.

According to the OECD which generally follows a normative perspective, the primary objective of a state-owned enterprise should be to maximize the value creation for society through an efficient allocation of resources. This new value may take form of achieving public policy or fiscal goals (OECD 2015, pp. 29–30). The objectives and priorities of SOEs may be commercial or non-commercial, but both types of objectives must be balanced, and all functions beyond those typical of "regular" enterprises in a given economy should be anchored in regulations (Christiansen 2013).

Mühlenkamp (2015) proposes to evaluate the objectives of state-owned enterprises in selected areas in a mainly positive way, using two perspectives. The first is the "welfare approach," i.e., the ability of the public sector to provide welfare when market mechanisms fail and therefore profit-oriented private companies fail, for example in the case of natural monopolies or negative externalities. The second is the "public choice approach," when the existence of state-owned enterprises is politically justified: they are able to produce resources which are not available in the private sector and which are essential for the state to implement a specific policy or to get rent for certain interest groups. Although the rent-seeking is generally detrimental to the economy and society as a whole, it would be a serious mistake not to take this phenomenon into account when designing and implementing the policy of state corporate control.

The range of resources generated by the state sector may be very wide, e.g., in the report of the consulting company PwC (2015, p. 14), on the basis of the analysis of developed and transforming economies, the following were mentioned:

- production of public goods and socially important private goods;
- improvement of labor relations, especially in "strategic" sectors;
- reducing the role of private and foreign investors in the national economy;
- generation of public funds from the profits of SOEs;
- increasing the availability of public services by providing them below cost;
- stimulating economic development and industrialization by supporting selected sectors of the economy, launching production in emerging sectors of the economy and controlling the functioning of declining sectors.

It should be noted that this list is created from the normative perspective and valid first of all for the developed countries with healthy and stable institutional systems. In practice, especially in transition and emerging economies, the real list of SOEs objectives defined as goods they produce and/or distribute may look somewhat incomplete. For example, in the case of Poland and at least some other post-communist countries (I will discuss it in Chapters 4 and 7) one more entry should be added: conducting by SOEs of more or less hidden redistribution of resources to selected social groups—in the form of rents, but not only. This could be, for example, the hidden financing of state policy in specific areas (transferring certain tasks usually financed from the state budget to state-owned enterprises). During the post-communist transition, there may have been additional objectives which would facilitate its implementation, especially in the short- or medium-term perspective: for example, increasing the attractiveness of SOEs for potential buyers and increasing its competitiveness after their privatization.

It is also important to note that within one economy, groups of state-owned enterprises or even individual SOEs may have different sets of objectives. The diversity of specific sets may be very large; in the literature (Kankaanpää et al. 2014) one can find their division into two large categories:

- enterprises that pursue mainly commercial objectives (where economic efficiency is the main concern);
- enterprises that pursue mostly non-commercial goals (mainly social objectives).

As is the case with the functions of the state in the economy, there is no, and cannot be, "the one and only" set of objectives for a state-owned enterprise. The specific set of objectives and their detailed definition depends very much on the context: the specific role of the state in a given economic system, the goals of social and economic policy, and existing formal and informal institutional arrangements. Besides, usually a SOE has much more than one objective, so they have to be put in some form of hierarchical order. At the same time, the objectives specific to private companies (like profit and value maximization) are usually not of primary importance for SOEs. And more often than not they just cannot have them at the top of the hierarchy, as the achievement of most the SOEs objectives may rather take place at the expense of their financial efficiency. An exception may be made for situations where the state is primarily concerned about the high profitability and/or value of the SOE, when its main task is to provide financial resources or be attractive to a potential buyer. It should be noted however that multiplicity and inconsistence of SOEs objectives are not the only factor that may reduce its economic performance. Other factors (also specific usually only to SOEs) include limitations on its decision-making autonomy and soft budgetary constraints (Bałtowski and Kwiatkowski 2018, Chapter 1.4.3).

The multiplicity of goals is also compounded by the agency problem in all companies where ownership and management functions have been separated, but in the case of state corporate control it may be exacerbated by the fact that the notion of the principal (is it, e.g., the government? the society?) is blurred and motivations to control the agent's behavior weaken, usually due to the lack of personal financial benefit for the principal (Musacchio and Lazzarini 2014, pp. 70–73). It would therefore seem reasonable to limit the objectives of a SOE to a certain minimum, but this may be difficult to achieve primarily because the multitude of objectives results from the inherent plurality of objectives of the state owner and other stakeholders of state-owned enterprises.

The multiplicity and diversity of objectives (and their mutual contradiction) is one of the fundamental barriers to the functioning of SOEs and a huge challenge to state-controlled corporate governance. It is not only a matter of putting these objectives in order with the least harm to their achievement and working out ways of their pursuing, but also of establishing and monitoring the effectiveness criteria for these enterprises.

From the perspective of the reasons of SOEs' existence, the analysis of their economic and financial effectiveness, which is widely used as the main means of evaluation of their functioning, in most cases does not allow to obtain a full picture of the situation. Perhaps the main reason is that it is the easiest way of evaluation; additional verification of a similar kind is done by the financial market in the case of listed SOEs. Another argument in favor of such analysis is that even if profit is not the main objective of a state-owned enterprise, high microeconomic efficiency certainly helps the achievement of its other objectives (Matuszak and Szarzec 2019).

However, even in those, as practice shows, rather rare cases, where the main purpose of a SOE is to maximize its profit and/or value, the real picture may be distorted by the fact that such enterprises usually hold a dominant position on the market and achieve good results at the expense of their customers and other market players; they may also benefit from various types of preferences from the state, which also reduces pro-efficiency pressures. In all other cases, financial performance, while important (as it is indeed one of the key factors for achieving non-financial objectives), cannot become the basis of the analysis. For the same reasons, I do not consider the numerous comparative analyses of financial performance of public and private enterprises to be relevant, either in the form of benchmarking (comparing similar enterprises from both sectors) or through a sequential analysis of enterprises before and after privatization (even without taking into account problems of statistical comparability of data). These results may serve to justify privatization (which has its own goals and leads to changes in enterprises' objectives), but they usually do not show how effectively SOEs meet the whole set of objectives that have been set for them.

Therefore, it seems reasonable to assess of the broadly understood efficiency of a SOE by achieving its objectives (Florio 2014; PwC 2015, pp. 22–29). Bałtowski and Kwiatkowski (2018, Chapter 8.1.3) also suggest to include in the analysis a broader perspective of the SOEs' impact on the functioning of the entire economic system and on interest groups which function in the economy. Methodologically, this is a very complicated task, as it requires the precise identification of SOEs objectives and their hierarchy, finding the ways of formalizing them and measuring their implementation. A comprehensive list of SOEs' successes and failures must be created and, as far as the effects at the macro-level are concerned, the impact of state-owned enterprises must be separated from the whole bunch of other factors. It seems impossible to use only quantitative analysis here, and qualitative conclusions are subject to a high risk of error.

Besides, it seems particularly difficult to identify and prioritize real SOEs' objectives because, firstly, very often they are not formulated in a sufficiently transparent comprehensive way. Secondly, a significant proportion of important objectives may, in principle, be of a hidden, officially undisclosed nature (e.g., distribution of rents) or officially announced objectives may conceal the real ones (e.g., behind the economic patriotism slogans may hide the real objective to limit competition for the SOEs). But it makes sense at least to attempt to take into account the nexus of SOEs objectives.

Of course, the scope of such analysis also depends on its purpose. It will be another for the enterprise's boards, different for decision-makers in the government (broader, taking into account the context of their responsibility), another for the researchers (perhaps the widest but less focused on issues affecting individual enterprises).

3.3.5 *Legal Challenges*

The problems of the legal basis for SOEs' functioning are mainly related to two interrelated issues: the legal form of a state-owned enterprise and the dilemma of whether SOEs need special legal regulations or are to operate under general corporate law.

In the communist times, SOEs constituted a specific legal entity reflecting its functions in the communist system (as shown in Sect. 3.1 of this chapter). They were not usually independent entities, and the SOEs' management system was a part of the administrative system which steered the economy. The activity of state-owned enterprises was regulated by a system of legal acts tailored to the specific position and tasks of these enterprises in the command economy. In many of the countries of the Eastern bloc, there was not even a law on state-owned enterprises or it was adopted only when attempts were made to reform the command economy through partial autonomy of enterprises.

The transition towards market economy led to the diversification of the ways in which the state started to exercise control over SOEs (not only in administrative way but also through ownership tools). It resulted in the need for adjustment of the legal situation of SOEs and, more broadly, the need to define the legal mechanisms for the state to perform its ownership functions.

In developed market economies which may be treated as a benchmark, there was (and still is) a great diversity of solutions in this area which can be reduced to two models. It's either a special law regulating the functioning of state-owned enterprises or making them a subject of general corporate law, and both have their pros and cons. There are arguments in favor of the second solution, as it allows to improve SOEs' performance through their more efficient exposure to market relations, strengthening the commercial character of their functioning, their autonomy. However, the unification may have serious drawbacks (World Bank 2014, p. 32) such as politicization of appointments on enterprises' boards, making SOEs finance their social tasks at the expense of their profits, and inability to exert efficient corporate control. On the other hand, the World Bank's (2014, pp. 31–32) list of possible drawbacks of special regulations for state-owned enterprises is much longer and this form of regulation does not necessarily resolve the main drawbacks of using the general laws, such as the threat of inefficient corporate control and overburdening SOEs with non-commercial tasks. Additionally, special regulations may limit SOEs' autonomy and responsibility, hinder decision-making processes and encourage decisions that are harmful to their economic and financial standing.

In practice legislative changes in many developed economies are heading towards unification of legal environment of SOEs with the rest of the enterprise sector. But still the diversity of solutions is high; in many countries the state's ownership functions are still performed through special legal provisions which regulate the functioning of all the SOEs, or SOEs functioning in selected sectors of the economy in which the state maintained monopoly on business activity. There was and still is a widespread practice of introducing legal regulations for specific, most important SOEs or their groups, depending on the specificity of their objectives.

Accordingly, the legal forms of state-controlled enterprises may be different: they may be either non-corporatized (managed directly by a government's body) or corporatized (when the state's ownership functions are carried out under general corporate governance rules). In line with the unification of the legal environment in developed economies, nowadays the dominant form of a SOE is incorporated company subject to general corporate law sometimes with some additional regulations which allow SOEs to realize their special tasks.

It should be also noted that if a government wants to attract private capital to its enterprises, even from just technical point of view they have to be corporatized and function under the general corporate governance legal regime. Although in this case, even in developed market economies special solutions exist, when in mixed-ownership companies the state may have more corporate powers than other owners, as, e.g., in France (whereas in many other countries equal rights of state and non-state owners are regarded as the key for success). This means that such a company operates under general corporate law, while the state as a shareholder has additional rights, such as a "golden share," voting cap for non-state shareholders, special rights for the government in appointing boards' members, etc. A catchy term of "reluctant privatization" has been coined by Bortolotti and Faccio (2004) for the way the state resolves the "to eat a cake and to have a cake" dilemma transferring property rights to a private investor without appropriate transferring control rights.

The experience of many developed market economies has shown that there is another challenge: it turned out that creating an appropriate legal and organizational regime (the latter discussed in more details later) is not fully sufficient for making corporate control of the state rational and efficient (Aguilera and Cuervo-Cazurra 2011; Monks and Minow 2011, p. 268). Existing legal and organizational solutions inevitably create, first and foremost, a certain framework for the exercise of the state ownership functions, leaving more or less discretionary powers to make specific decisions. Since the beginning of the twenty-first century, there has been a growing awareness among researchers and decision-makers that the effective implementation of the multiple objectives of SOEs requires additional, extra-legal solutions. The new solutions were mostly of a "soft" nature, i.e., suggesting certain behavior rather than forcing it. These were various recommendations and best practices codes which dealt both with the level of the state corporate control and the state-owned enterprises. The general idea was taken from the private sector, where since the late 1980s, at the initiative of entrepreneurs, stock exchanges, and third party organizations best practice codes started to appear.

First recommendations on the policy of the state corporate control appeared at the international level, such as publications by OECD (2005b) and later by the World Bank (2014) which have already been extensively referred to in this book. These tools were created mainly with developed market economies in mind. However, they could be particularly important in the post-communist countries, which had to create a new system of the state corporate control, and thus apart from the legal framework, some kind of instructions on how to effectively introduce these new mechanisms was necessary. The problem is that in world practice such tools appeared too late, when the post-communist transition already lasted for more than a decade. In the countries of the Eastern Bloc, including Poland, an institutional and legal system of control of state assets has already been formed—to a large extent dysfunctional, as I will show in the next chapters of the book.

3.3.6 Organizational Challenges

A review of the organizational and technical solutions used worldwide for the state corporate control shows their great diversity. According to OECD (2005a, p. 42), at the beginning of the twenty-first century, three basic models could be distinguished, although of course numerous mixed solutions existed:

- decentralized, or sector ministry model, in which line ministries or special state agencies were responsible for the functioning of SOEs;

- dual, where responsibility was shared between a certain "central" ministry which coordinates the state's corporate policy, and the relevant sector ministries;
- centralized, where one department in the system of state administration was responsible for the whole state ownership policy.

About a decade later, the World Bank's researchers (World Bank 2014, p. 70) also distinguished a fourth model, the advisory model, which combined certain features of the decentralized and the dual model: ministries which perform state ownership supervision were assisted by a central body with advisory and coordination functions. The second OECD (2018) study confirms the existence of this model calling it "coordinating agency." It also distinguishes one more model, in fact a variant of the centralized one, where there are two government bodies which separately supervise two different groups of SOEs. But still we can talk about three basic models of organizational solutions: decentralized, partly centralized and centralized.

In the past, the decentralized model has been most widespread: both in communist countries (which is obvious) and in many capitalist countries because of the treatment of state-owned enterprises as one of the state's essential tools in the implementation of its development policy. The perceived advantages of this model included the possibility for the state to pursue an active industrial policy, the use of "sector expertize" accumulated in the ministries (Vagliasindi 2008). Over time, however, its drawbacks have become increasingly obvious, including the lack of a clear division between the ownership function and other functions of the state, and difficulties in determining who actually manages state-owned enterprises: the ministry or the management of the SOE (OECD 2005a, p. 45). To these drawbacks I would add another one, probably the most important one from the perspective of the tasks of post-communist transition. The ministerial nature of the state corporate control is generally poorly coordinated and easily subject to the influence of sectoral interest groups (which were particularly strong in late communist era), which fundamentally hinders the creation of coherent and comprehensive state ownership policy. In any case, in developed market economies, as the belief in the long-term pro-development potential of state-owned enterprises was waning and the disadvantages of the decentralized solution became increasingly apparent, a process of moving away from this model has been observed.

A dual model is still widespread, which is supposed to combine the advantages of centralized solutions (better coordination, etc.) with the knowledge and experience of line ministries, which have a better insight into the situation in "their" industries and enterprises they supervise. In fact, according to OECD (2005a, p. 47) this model was usually not deliberately created, but with a few exceptions, it was shaped spontaneously, as certain governmental agencies (e.g., the office of the Prime Minister or the Ministry of Finance) had more influence in the government than others and therefore took on more functions, including coordination of the state corporate control policy. With the generally acceptable effectiveness of this model, its main problem is often the insufficiently precise division of competences between the "central" body and the line ministries. This model is also increasingly being abandoned.

Presently, the most popular model (and a model towards which the state corporate control policy of the governments which previously have adopted other models is eventually moving to) is the centralized model, which is characterized by a very strong concentration of different elements of the state's ownership function in the hands of one body: a ministry (of industry, finance, etc.) or a special agency. This model is widespread not only in developed market economies, but also in post-socialist countries, where the additional motivation for its introduction was to strive to overcome as quickly as possible the negative effects of the sectoral nature of governance of the economy under the previous system.

Studies on the effectiveness of state corporate governance show that the centralized model is currently the most effective and is recommended as optimal not only by the OECD, but also by other researchers (Vuoria 2004). The main advantages are the possibility of conducting a coherent ownership policy, less politicized supervision and reduced rent-seeking (through limiting the influence of sectoral interest groups on the policy of state corporate control). However, it is certainly not devoid of flaws, the main one being related to the limited access to knowledge on the specificity of individual sectors by the centralized governmental body. It may be of particular importance, e.g., in infrastructure industries (Vagliasindi 2008; Bałtowski and Kwiatkowski 2018, Chapter 2.4). Another one, in the economies with extensive state sector but flawed institutional setup, is attractiveness of such a centralized agency with a very high value of controlled assets for various types of private interest groups which may severely distort the corporate governance of the state. As, among others, the Polish experience shows (Kozarzewski and Bałtowski 2017), this threat has proved to be far from purely theoretical.

Legal and organizational dilemmas were not limited to the choice of the right model, it was also crucial to create specific mechanisms, to choose specific tools in order to achieve the goals of the state corporate control, including safeguards against possible dysfunctions. One of the most important sources of such is contradictions between the state's role as the owner and regulator. Regardless of how centralized the adopted model of corporate control is, developed capitalist countries had to introduce a wide range of safeguards against this particular threat. Here, the experience of countries with high share of state ownership in the economy may be of special interest for transition countries. For example, Norway, which in the 1990s was moving towards the centralized model of the state corporate control, retained a special kind of decentralization for several largest SOEs when one state body was in charge of managing their assets, and another played the role of the regulator (OECD 2003). This allowed to separate the ownership and regulatory functions of the state. In Columbia ministers and state bureaucrats cannot sit on the state-controlled companies' boards. Singapore has introduced an intermediate body between the SOEs and the government in the form of a holding company; additionally, nominations to the boards of the holding and subsidiary companies have to be done according to professional and non-political criteria; there were no representatives of the government even on the holding's board (Milhaupt and Pargendler 2017).

However, the post-communist transition created one more challenge of an administrative kind, non-existent in market economies, so no knowledge transfer from developed economies was possible. It reflects the fact that corporate control policy was one of the key elements of a wider policy—an ownership policy of the state, the second pillar being ownership transformation. Here, the main organizational dilemma (and the transition experience of many post-communist countries has shown that this was a real problem indeed) was whether the state's corporate control functions and ownership transformation functions should be merged or separated.

These functions may be merged not only at the central level, but also, in the case of decentralized models, at the ministry level. The advantage of such a solution would be a better coordination of the overall ownership policy. However, it creates a conflict between the owner and the seller functions of such a body and in the case of the centralized model it would mean the creation within the government of a super-ministry, a center of power, which could cause its institutional petrification, a tendency to postpone its future modification or even liquidation (e.g., when after privatization is over, the seller function of the body becomes redundant and the state assets are too small to justify the existence of a separate supervisory agency).

Separation of privatization and corporate control functions into different bodies would avoid this conflict of functions and reduce the political weight and institutional inertia of these offices. But the coherence of the state ownership policy could be jeopardized by, firstly, problems with the precise division of responsibilities (e.g., whether supervision over enterprises which are in the process of privatization belongs to the privatization or state corporate control body—there are various solutions in the world in this respect). Secondly, one can expect the inherent conflict between these agencies, as they have opposing vested interests (to privatize as much as possible vs. to have as much assets as possible under the state control), which may be used in political games. However, this seems to be a lesser evil than the internal conflict of functions performed and the excessive political weight of the agency combining these functions under one roof and responsible for the state ownership policy in the entire economy.

In other words, it seems that there is no ideal organizational solution even in theory, let alone in practice, the latter being discussed in the chapters that follow.

References

Aguilera, Rith V., and Alvaro Cuervo-Cazurra. 2011. "Codes of Good Governance." *Corporate Governance: An International Review* 17 (3): 376–387.

Aharoni, Yairo. 1986. *The Evolution and Management of State-Owned Enterprises*. Cambridge MA: Ballinger.

Bałtowski, Maciej. 2009. *Gospodarka socjalistyczna w Polsce. Geneza, rozwój, upadek*. Warsaw: PWN.

Bałtowski, Maciej, and Grzegorz Kwiatkowski. 2018. *Przedsiębiorstwa państwowe we współczesnej gospodarce*. Warsaw: PWN.

Bałtowski, Maciej, and Piotr Kozarzewski. 2014. *Zmiana własnościowa polskiej gospodarki 1989–2013*. Warsaw: PWE.

Bałtowski, Maciej, and Piotr Kozarzewski. 2016. Formal and Real Ownership Structure of the Polish Economy: State-Owned versus State-Controlled Enterprises. *Post-Communist Economies* 28 (3): 405–419.

Bar, Ludwik. 1995. "Prawna reprezentacja pracowników najemnych w gospodarce rynkowej." In *Partycypacja i akcjonariat pracowniczy w Polsce*, edited by Leszek Gilejko, 35–48. Warsaw: ISP PAN and SGH.

Bator, Francis M. 1958. The Anatomy of Market Failure. *Quarterly Journal of Economics* 72 (3): 351–379.

Błaszczyk, Barbara. 1995. "Doświadczenia międzynarodowe za i przeciw wprowadzaniu akcjonariatu pracowniczego w Polsce." In *Partycypacja i akcjonariat pracowniczy w Polsce*, edited by Leszek Gilejko, 113–119. Warsaw: ISP PAN and SGH.

Borisov, Evgeniy. 2005. *Ekonomicheskaya teoriya*. Moscow: Urait.

Bortolotti, Bernardo, and Mara Faccio. 2004. "Reluctant Privatization." Nota di Lavoro 130, Fondazione Eni Enrico Mattei (FEEM), Milano. https://www.econstor.eu/bitstream/10419/118014/1/NDL2004-130.pdf. Accessed July 30, 2020.

Böwer, Uwe. 2017. "State-Owned Enterprises in Emerging Europe: The Good, the Bad, and the Ugly." Working Paper 17/221, International Monetary Fund, Washington, DC. https://www.imf.org/~/media/Files/Publications/WP/2017/wp17221.ashx. Accessed July 27, 2020.

Bremmer, Ian. 2010. *The End of the Free Market: Who Wins the War between States and Corporations?* New York: Penguin.

Chadeau, Emmanuel. 2000. "The Rise and Decline of State-Owned Industry in Twentieth-Century France." In *The Rise and Fall of State-Owned Enterprise in the Western World*, edited by Pier A. Toninelli, 185–207. Cambridge: Cambridge University Press.

Christiansen, Hans. 2011. "The Size and Composition of the SOE Sector in OECD Countries." OECD Corporate Governance Working Papers 5, OECD, Paris. https://www.oecd-ilibrary.org/the-size-and-composition-of-the-soe-sector-in-oecd-countries_5kg54cwps0s3.pdf. Accessed August 5, 2020.

Christiansen, Hans. 2013. "Balancing Commercial and Non-Commercial Priorities of State-Owned Enterprises." OECD Corporate Governance Working Papers 6, OECD, Paris. https://www.oecd.org/corporate/OECDCorporateGovernanceWorkingPaper6.pdf. Accessed July 28, 2020.

Coase, Ronald. 1964. "The Regulated Industries: Discussion." *American Economic Review* 54 (2): 192–197.

Demandt, Alexander. 2011. *Ungeschehene Geschichte. Ein Traktat über die Frage: Was wäre geschehen, wenn...?* Göttingen: Vandenhoeck & Ruprecht.

Engels, Frederick. 1951. "Socialism: Utopian and Scientific." In *Selected Works in Two Volumes*, edited by Karl Marx and Friedrich Engels, Vol. II, 86–142. Moscow: Foreign Languages Publishing House.

Engels, Frederick. 2010. "Anti-Dühring." In *Collected Works*, edited by Karl Marx and Friedrich Engels, Vol. 25, 1–309. London: Lawrence and Wishart.

Evans, Peter. 1995. *Embedded Autonomy: States and Industrial Transformation*. Princeton: Princeton University Press.

Fischer, Stanley, and Alan Gelb. 1991. "The Process of Socialist Economic Transformation." *Journal of Economic Perspectives* 5 (4): 91–105.

Florio, Massimo. 2014. "Contemporary Public Enterprises: Innovation, Accountability, Governance." *Journal of Economic Policy Reform* 17 (3): 201–208.

Friedman, David D. 1990. *Price Theory: An Intermediate Text*. Mason: South-Western Publishing Co.

Gaidar, Yegor. 1997. *Anomalii Ekonomicheskogo Rosta* [Anomalies of Economic Growth]. Moscow: Evraziya.

Gilbert, Ronald. 1995. "Efektywność ekonomiczna przedsiębiorstw ESOP w Stanach Zjednoczonych A. P." In *Partycypacja i akcjonariat pracowniczy w Polsce*, edited by Leszek Gilejko, 87–93. Warsaw: ISP PAN and SGH.

Goodman, John C. 2015. "Answer to Krugman on Market Failure: Government Failure is Worse." *Forbes*, January 24.

Gruszecki, Tomasz. 1990. *Prywatyzacja. Stan wyjściowy i analiza programu rządowego*. Warsaw: PAN.

Hall, Peter A., and David Soskice. 2001. *Varieties of Capitalism: The Institutional Foundations of Comparative Advantage*. Oxford: Oxford University Press.

Hausner, Jerzy, and Andrzej Wojtyna. 1993. "Evolution of Interest Representation in Poland." In *Institutional Change: Theory and Empirical Findings*, edited by Sven-Erik Sjöstrand, 339–350. New York: Routledge.

Kaliński, Janusz. 2015. "Kiedy zaczęło się odradzanie gospodarki rynkowej w Polsce?" *Optimum. Studia Ekonomiczne* 1 (73): 3–13.

Kankaanpää, Jari, Lasse Oulasvirta, and Jani Wacker. 2014. "Steering and Monitoring Model of State-owned Enterprises." *International Journal of Public Administration* 37 (7): 409–423.

Kołodko, Grzegorz W., and Walter W. McMahon. 1987. "Stagflation and Shortageflation: A Comparative Approach." *Kyklos* 40 (2): 176–197.

Kornai, Janos. 1992. *The Socialist System: The Political Economy of Communism*. Princeton, NJ: Princeton University Press.

Kowalik, Tadeusz. 1995. "Prywatyzacja, partycypacja i leasing." In *Partycypacja i akcjonariat pracowniczy w Polsce*, edited by Leszek Gilejko, 13–22. Warsaw: ISP PAN and SGH.

Kowalik, Tadeusz. 2005. *Systemy gospodarcze. Efekty i defekty zmian ustrojowych*. Warsaw: Fundacja Innowacja.

Kozarzewski, Piotr. 2006. *Prywatyzacja w krajach postkomunistycznych*. Warsaw: ISP PAN.

Kozarzewski, Piotr. 2019. *Polityka właścicielska państwa w okresie transformacji systemowej. Próba syntezy*. Lublin: Wydawnictwo Uniwersytetu Marii Curie-Skłodowskiej.

Kozarzewski, Piotr, and Maciej Bałtowski. 2017. "Change in the Ownership Policy Paradigm in Poland: State Control vs. Privatisation." *Acta Oeconomica* 67 (1): 1–20.

Lipowski, Adam. 1988. *Mechanizm rynkowy w gospodarce polskiej. Podstawy teoretyczne, perspektywy, dylematy.* Warsaw: PWN.

Mahboobi, Ladan. 2002. "Recent Privatisation Trends in OECD Countries." *Financial Market Trends* 82: 43–58.

Matuszak, Piotr, and Katarzyna Szarzec. 2019. "The Scale and Financial Performance of State-Owned Enterprises in the CEE Region." *Acta Oeconomica* 69 (4): 549–570.

Mazzucato, Mariana. 2013. *The Entrepreneurial State: Debunking Public vs. Private Sector Myths*. London: Anthem Press.

Milhaupt, Curtis J., and Mariana Pargendler. 2017. "Governance Challenges of Listed State-owned Enterprises Around the World: National Experiences and a Framework for Reform." *Cornell International Law Journal* 50 (3): 473–542. https://scholarship.law.cornell.edu/cilj/vol50/iss3/3. Accessed November 30, 2020.

Monks, Robert A.G., and Minow, Nell. 2011. *Corporate Governance*, 5th ed. Chichester: Wiley.

Moore, John. 1992. "British Privatization—Taking Capitalism to the People." *Harvard Business Review* 70 (1): 115–124.

Morawski, Witold. 2001. *Socjologia ekonomiczna. Problemy. Teoria. Empiria.* Warsaw: PWN.

Mühlenkamp, Hogler. 2015. "From State to Market Revisited: A Reassessment of the Empirical Evidence on the Efficiency of Public (and Privately-Owned) Enterprises." *Annals of Public and Cooperative Economics* 86 (4): 535–557.

Musacchio, Aldo, and Sergio G. Lazzarini. 2014. *Reinventing State Capitalism: Leviathan in Business, Brazil and Beyond*. Cambridge: Harvard University Press.

OECD. 2003. *Regulatory Reform in Norway: Marketisation of Government Services—State-Owned Enterprises*. Paris: OECD Publishing. https://www.oecd.org/regreform/32682052.pdf. Accessed August 3, 2020.

OECD. 2005a. *Corporate Governance of State-Owned Enterprises: A Survey of OECD Countries*. Paris: OECD Publishing.

OECD. 2005b. *Guidelines on Corporate Governance of State-Owned Enterprises*. Paris: OECD Publishing.

OECD. 2007. *Glossary of Statistical Terms*. Paris: OECD Publishing.

OECD. 2010. *Accountability and Transparency: A Guide for State Ownership*. Paris: OECD Publishing.

OECD. 2015. *OECD Guidelines on Corporate Governance of State-Owned Enterprises*, 2015th ed. Paris: OECD Publishing.

OECD. 2017. *The Size and Sectoral Distribution of State-Owned Enterprises*. Paris: OECD Publishing.

OECD. 2018. *Ownership and Governance of State-Owned Enterprises: A Compendium of National Practices*. Paris: OECD Publishing.

Prychitko, David L. 2002. *Markets, Planning, and Democracy: Essays after the Collapse of Communism*. Cheltenham: Edward Elgar Publishing.

Przeworski, Adam, Michael E. Alvarez, Jose A. Cheibub, and Fernando Limongi. 2000. *Democracy and Development: Political Institutions and Well-Being in the World, 1950–1990*. Cambridge: Cambridge University Press.

Putniņš, Tālis J. 2020. "Economics of State-Owned Enterprises." In *The Routledge Handbook of State-Owned Enterprises*, edited by Luc Bernier, Massimo Florio, and Philippe Bance, 215–238. New York: Routledge.

PwC. 2015. *State-Owned Enterprises: Catalysts for Public Value Creation?* Arlington: PwC.

Rychard, Andrzej. 1993. *Reforms, Adaptation, and Breakthrough: The Sources of and Limits to Institutional Changes in Poland*. Warsaw: IFiS Publishers.

Sadowski, Zbigniew. 1991 "Niezależne spojrzenie na prywatyzację w Polsce." *Gospodarka Narodowa* 3.

Shleifer, Andrei, and Robert W. Vishny. 1994. "Politicians and Firms." *Quarterly Journal of Economics* 109 (4): 995–1025.

Stypułkowski, Cezary. 1986. *Samodzielne i samorządne przedsiębiorstwo*. Warsaw: PWE.

Vagliasindi, Maria. 2008. "Governance Arrangements for State Owned Enterprises." Policy Research Working Paper 4542, The World Bank, Washington.

Venediktov, Anatoly. 1948. *Gosudarsvennaya Sotsialisticheskaya Sobstvennost' [State Socialist Property]*. Moscow: Izdatel'stvo AN SSSR.

Vuoria, Matti. 2004. "Evaluator Report of the State's Ownership Policy." Studies and Reports 3, Ministry of Trade and Industry of Finland, Helsinki.

World Bank. 2014. *Corporate Governance of State-owned Enterprises: A Toolkit*. Washington: The World Bank.

Zespół "Okrągłego Stołu" ds. Gospodarki i Polityki Społecznej. 1989. *Stanowisko w sprawie polityki społecznej i gospodarczej oraz reform systemowych*. Warsaw.

CHAPTER 4

Evolution of the State Corporate Control in Poland During the Transition

4.1 Introductory Remarks

After the transition started, the policy of the state corporate control began undergoing an evolution, a slow, gradual and often inconsistent, which creates problems with its description and analysis, especially in attempts of its periodization. However, several stages of this evolution can be seen, albeit usually with very fuzzy borders. The periodization of the corporate control policy of the Polish state presented in this chapter is based on observation of real changes in this policy and also takes into account political factors, assuming that these were one of the main driving forces of the observed changes. All the stages identified were characterized by the evolution of the state corporate control policy mostly in the following areas:

- place of state corporate control in the overall state ownership policy;
- objectives of state corporate control (formulated or deduced from the observation of successive governments' actions), primarily in terms of the role attributed to the state sector in the economy;
- tools od state corporate control.

Two phases have been identified, the first one, very long (it lasted for about 25 years), consisting of four stages. The second phase so far consists

P. Kozarzewski, *State Corporate Control in Transition*,
https://doi.org/10.1007/978-3-030-78562-8_4

of only one stage. The phases and stages were given names which reflect their essence in a concise form:

Phase One: From invigilance to statism (1989–2015).

1.1. The initial stage: Fighting the crisis and starting the transition (1990–1993).
1.2. Politicization of the state corporate control: The bounty for winners (1993–2001).
1.3. Attempts to consolidate the state corporate control (2001–2011).
1.4. Expansion of statism (2011–2015).

Phase Two: Towards State Capitalism (since 2016).

The periodization presented here is (like any attempt of this kind) quite conventional due to the problems with determining the caesura separating the individual stages. This was particularly evident in the case of the border between the third and fourth stage of the first phase, where the elements of continuation were particularly strong (especially one, concerning the achievement of the fiscal objectives of state's corporate control).

The last stage (which at the same time denoted entering the state corporate control into a new phase) is discussed in this book in greater detail than the previous ones due to two reasons. Firstly, it is still understudied. Secondly, what is more important, this stage seems to be of crucial importance for the development of the current system of corporate control of the state, which is part of the revised paradigm of the role of the state in the economy. The changes occurring at this stage reflect the long-term (started much earlier), fairly stable political and social trend, which will be crucial for the development of state corporate control and the state's ownership policy as a whole in the coming years.

4.2 Phase One: From Invigilance to Statism—Stages of the Evolution in 1989–2015

This phase covers a long period of a quarter of a century when the corporate control of the state was shaping up. The process was inconsistent, with numerous dysfunctions, perhaps the most important of which was growing politicization of ownership control over SOEs ad failure to create a clear strategic vision of the role of this sector in the economy. It resulted in evolution of the policy towards this sector from fairly liberal attitudes towards more and more pronounced state interventionism. Despite this, the general paradigm of the role of the state in the economy retained its liberal features, which has been changed only in the next phase, when the populist-conservative coalition came to power at the end of 2015.

4.2.1 The Initial Stage: Fighting the Crisis and Starting the Transition (1989–1993)

The first stage covers the period from the start of the post-communist reforms marked by the adoption of the reform plan in autumn 1989 (the so-called Balcerowicz Plan) up to parliamentary elections of 1993, when the liberal coalition lost power and was replaced by a left-wing coalition. During this stage, the problem of the state's corporate control was treated marginally; the policy towards state-owned enterprises was regarded mainly in the context of the privatization of the economy. Nevertheless, a largely centralized model of the state corporate control slowly began to take shape, and attempts were also made to improve the quality of state supervision. However, these measures were predominantly partial, inconsistent and often introduced in an ad hoc way.

The new government apparently expected that the problem of managing the state's assets would be solved mainly through changing the economic environment of state-owned enterprises and by liquidating the largest part of this sector as a result of privatization. Although it was never openly decaled due to political considerations, the government expected that those remaining SOEs that could not adapt to the market would simply be eliminated from the market, and the labor force freed up in this way would feed the thriving private sector. From this perspective, there was no need in a radical reform of the state corporate control.

As for the non-ownership tools of state influence on enterprises, for the government it seemed sufficient to remove both the existing restrictions on the activities of SOEs (especially in contracting supplies) and their privileges (e.g., soft budget constraints). The package of laws implementing the Balcerowicz Plan, apart from the introduction of market mechanisms also introduced in practice the equality of all forms of ownership through the elimination of privileges for SOEs in the area of finances, foreign trade, taxation, etc. What is more, in 1991, a very restrictive tax on excessive salary increase, introduced in the mid-1980s, ceased to apply to private companies. Thus, SOE became even discriminated in this area because the government believed that SOEs still were insufficiently subject to market discipline; the tax was finally abolished only in 1994. In 1992, corporatized SOEs were exempt from this regulation, which had to motivate them to undergo commercialization and become a subject not of the 1981 law on SOEs, but of the general corporate law.

The fact that almost all SOEs at that time were not a subject of the general corporate regulations meant that they still operated in the legal environment which did not provide them with efficient state corporate supervision scattered among line ministries with limited control rights. Through the whole stage, the government did almost nothing about it, apart from delicate attempts to make commercialization an attractive perspective for the SOEs and liquidation one of the biggest pathologies, "nomenklatura privatization," through prohibiting uncorporatized state-owned enterprises from establishing ventures with private firms.

Virtually all efforts of the government in streamlining the state corporate control were focused on a small, albeit growing number of corporatized SOEs (called sole shareholder companies of the Treasury, Polish acronym: JSSP). No special regulations were introduced, but the government took some practical steps towards this group of enterprises, whose commercialization was regarded as the first step towards their privatization. Ministry of Ownership Transformations (Polish acronym MPW—Ministerstwo Przekształceń Własnościowych) was created which apart from selling state property also started to perform some functions of the Treasury towards JSSPs. Here, a system of selection and nomination of supervisory board members[1] was created: the commission in charge of these activities was established, and a system of courses and exams for candidates for board members was introduced. Together with a private foundation Centrum Prywatyzacji (Privatization Center) the Ministry prepared recommendations for supervisory boards and management boards of JSSPs, thus a bit informally filling the regulatory void in this respect. In 1991–1992 this system operated relatively efficiently, in a fairly transparent way and without excessive interference of the Ministry in the functioning of JSSPs (Bałtowski and Kozarzewski 2014, pp. 321–322). But state corporate control based more on the enthusiasm and sense of mission among the Ministry's employees, than on coherent rules and regulations failed to ensure its sustainability in the coming years.

The lack of coherent systemic solutions in the sphere of state corporate control affected the state ownership policy as a whole. From the very beginning of the reforms, the activity of MPW was opposed by two strong forces which did not want to lose control over SOEs either through privatization, commercialization or creation of the state corporate control agency. The first was line ministries which successfully lobbied for creation of the list of so-called enterprises of particular economic and political importance (coal and lignite mines, power plants, the arms industry, etc.) exempt from privatization and which largely remained under the control of the line ministries. This not only slowed down the privatization processes, but also helped to preserve the influence of branch interest groups in the enterprise sector which were lobbying for a policy of support for large state-owned enterprises, primarily just because they were state-owned, under the slogan "the owner must take care of his assets." The second group of opponents was employee councils which controlled most of the SOEs, as they would be liquidated in the course of commercialization and privatization or lose most of the autonomy in the case of creation of the corporate control agency.

The lack of proper state corporate control over the vast majority of SOEs had also practical negative consequences and hardly ended in mass bankruptcies and a banking crisis. Most SOEs experienced problems in adapting to changing environment, to the development of market institutions. Their management was usually not qualified enough to carry out strategic changes, so their actions were limited to ad hoc and shallow defensive ones. At the same time, state-owned commercial banks, just a few years before separated from the National Bank of Poland, had no necessary skills in risk assessment in their loan policy towards SOEs. In the 1991–1992, in a fairly large group of SOEs (which accounted for about 10% of the value of the sector's sales) started rapidly accumulating outstanding debts towards banks which was also dangerous not for the banking sector (Gomułka 1993). Contrary to the standard recommendations of the World Bank (creation of an agency that would take over the debts of enterprises from banks), the Polish government decided to undertake measures which would not only eliminate "bad debts," but also would prevent their mass re-appearance in the future. In 1993 the settlement procedure was introduced where SOEs and state-owned commercial banks had to reach an agreement on the conditions for restructuring and repayment of the SOEs' debts, without the government's interference. This approach proved to be mostly successful (Gray and Holle 1996; Kochanowicz et al. 2005, pp. 67–69). It prevented a crisis of the banking system, mass bankruptcy of state-owned enterprises, and was an effective lesson of the market economy both for SOEs and commercial banks.

Unfortunately, it remained a rare example of the really effective behavior of the government towards its assets: SOEs and banks. No conclusions have been drawn to improve the mechanisms of state corporate control either.

4.2.2 *The Second Stage: Politicization of the State Corporate Control: The Bounty for Winners (1993–2001)*

This stage covers quite a long period from late autumn 1993 to late autumn 2001. It begins with the establishment of the left-wing coalition of several parties with the leading role of the Democratic Left Alliance party (Polish acronym SLD—Sojusz Lewicy Demokratycznej), an "heir" to the Polish United Workers' Party, the communist party which ruled Poland in the command economy times and which was dissoluted in 1990. The new party was following the social democratic ideology rather the communist one, though. The stage in question ends with the end of the term of the conservative AWS coalition (Akcja Wyborcza Solidarność—Solidarity Election Action) grouped around the "Solidarity" trade unions. The stage was characterized by a gradual erosion of the already ineffective state corporate control: its politicization and its increasing subordination to private interests groups. It is worth noting that this stage included two terms of the Sejm and four governments when different configurations of political forces were in power, both on the "right" and the left" side of the political spectrum. (Although in Poland the common use of the terms "left" and "right" is often misleading, as representatives of the both camps, e.g., usually support high level of state interventionism and generous social policy.) It was during this period that the attitude towards SOEs as a political bounty for parliamentary election winners was formed. The attitude which survived till today and have especially flourished under the rule of the populist-conservative coalition led by PiS (Prawo i Sprawiedliwość—Law and Justice) which took power in autumn 2015.

In general, the system of corporate control of the state during this stage was characterized by two fundamental flaws. Firstly, it was still the lack of uniform and formalized corporate governance rules. The opportunity offered by the new Privatization Act adopted in 1996, under which the Ministry of the Treasury (Polish acronym MSP—Ministerstwo Skarbu Państwa) was established, was not used. The establishment of the Treasury institution turned out to be a mainly formal act, not leading neither to a more precise definition of ownership rights of the state (new regulations, very general, still concerned only commercialized SOEs), nor to development of comprehensive tasks of the state ownership policy and ways of their implementation. The really executed principles (more often than not being unwritten) of the state corporate policy resulted mostly from the will, knowledge and convictions of the head of the Ministry and the political environment. What is more, the new legal regulations introduced additional chaos, treating in a different way JSSPs created as a result of commercialization of SOEs and similar companies established in a different way. Also nothing was done to unify the regime of corporate control over still quite a large number of non-corporatized SOEs and corporatized ones.

Systemic weaknesses of state corporate control were augmented by dysfunctional actions of successive governments. Although the first signs of these negative processes could be observed earlier, they accelerated in the autumn of 1993 after the SLD-led coalition took power. The system of selecting members for the supervisory boards of commercialized SOEs began to be dismantled. Examinations for candidates for supervisory boards became a formality. Under the "right-wing" governments of the AWS coalition which took power in 1997, the situation deteriorated even further. The list of candidates for supervisory boards was discontinued, and filling positions on the boards has since become the primary task of heads of political cabinets of successive Treasury ministers, which has further strengthened the discretionary, politically motivated nature of this procedure.

It created the situation, when group interests, regardless of their political provenance, increasingly took precedence over general interest. With the consent of all major political parties, a pathological system of political rotation in positions in the management of companies controlled by the State Treasury has been created which made JSSPs a bounty of the winning coalition which decided about nominations on the enterprises' boards purging them from the representatives of the previous ruling coalition. Therefore, major political parties were not interested in repairing the system, introducing clear, apolitical rules of ownership control, and just waited for their turn to put "their people" on the boards (Bałtowski and Kozarzewski 2014, p. 323). Concentration of power over JSSPs in the hands of politicians led to marginalization of supervisory boards in favor of general meetings of shareholders, i.e., in practice to MSP bureaucrats. (Bałtowski and Miszewski 2007, pp. 286–287).

Another negative trend in the state corporate control was re-concentration (mainly at the initiative of the government) of state-controlled assets—e.g., in the sugar industry, banking, fuel and shipbuilding industries. The official reason was the need for pre-privatization strengthening of enterprises in selected industries, obtaining economies of scale and synergies through concentration. Most often than not, however, concentration was not followed by privatization, and its beneficiaries turned out to be mainly industry lobbyists and interest groups among the political elite. As a rule, the concentration was accompanied by "soft" financing of SOEs by the state-controlled banking sector, and lucrative positions on supervisory boards were created.

At the end of the stage, the government started increasing its influence in the privatized SOEs, where for some reason the state retained a minority block of shares. Before, the unwritten rule was followed, that after privatization, even when a significant block of shares remained in the hands of the state, the government supported the new owner (in voting at the general meeting of shareholders) or at least remained neutral. This approach was replaced by a more active policy on the boards of such enterprises and was aimed at restoring control over them by the MSP which became more pronounced on the next stages.

The government failed to effectively address the growing dysfunctions in the state corporate control. Neither a coherent vision of the objectives of the state corporate control was created nor any serious attempts to stop growing entangled of SOEs in the maze of party and private interests were made. The government undertook only a few superficial steps mainly to improve the public perception of the economic policy of the government rather than to eliminate the growing dysfunctions (e.g., limiting remuneration introducing some disclosure requirements for JSSPs' boards members).

Paradoxically, the growing dysfunctions in the state corporate control was accompanied by the acceleration and streamlining of the processes of creation of the private enterprises' sector in Poland. Privatization, especially towards the end of the 1990s, started including new enterprises, also in the sectors that had previously been de facto excluded from ownership transformation. At the same time, conditions were created for effective functioning and development of the private sector in the Polish economy.

4.2.3 The Third Stage: Attempts to Consolidate the State Corporate Control (2001–2011)

The third stage covers the longest period of ten years and as many as three terms of the Polish parliament. It begins with the term of the left-wing coalition (led by SLD again) starting November 2001 and ends with the end of the first term of the PO-PSL (Polish acronyms which stand for Platforma Obywatelstka—Civic Platform and Polskie Stronnictwo Ludowe—Polish People's Party) centrist coalition rule in October 2011. This stage is characterized by attempts to improve the state corporate control, not only in organizational but also, to some extent, conceptual dimension. However, this did not lead to de-politicization of corporate control of the state. The boundaries of this stage are quite arbitrary, as the first attempts at improvement can be witnessed in the previous stage; the end of the stage also includes a number of important "cross-border" processes with the next stage.

The leftist SLD-led coalition wanted to confront itself to its predecessors, which identified itself as a right-wing one. In May 2002, the new team of the Ministry of the Treasury published the so-called "Opening Report" (Ministry of the Treasury 2002), which contained an analysis of the situation in enterprises controlled by the government and suggested directions for improvement of the state corporate control. The criticism towards the policy of the previous government was overwhelming: the report provided numerous examples of dysfunctions and even pathologies and concluded that the irregularities and abuses were of unprecedented scale and character. However, despite all the real dysfunctions of the state corporate control, the report could deliberately use too dark colors and to certain extend could serve the political goal of discrediting the previous coalition. In any case, the Supreme Audit Office (Polish acronym NIK—Najwyższa Izba Kontroli) analyzed the cases of mismanagement mentioned in the report and did not confirm most of them (Supreme Audit Office 2003). At the same time, according to the NIK report, the previous MSP's activity was not efficient enough.

The "Opening Report" also contained the promises of improvements. Among others, the Ministry of the Treasury had to develop unified standards and mechanisms of corporate control to be applied by all public authorities which performed the ownership functions.

Regardless of how politicized the objectives of the Report were and how reliable it was, it played an essentially positive role, providing evidence of the low quality of systemic, institutional and legal solutions in the area of state corporate control, or rather the lack thereof. It also initiated a new stage in the debate on improving the role of the state as the owner which so far had been a neglected problem of economic transition in Poland.

At the beginning of the analyzed stage, it seemed that things started to go in the right direction. The Ministry of the Treasury started working on increasing efficiency of the state corporate control. undertook work on improving the state corporate control. At the end of 2002 the Sejm passed an amendment to the Law on Commercialization and Privatization of State-owned Enterprises. It introduced, among others, the requirement to conduct mandatory qualification proceedings when appointing board members in companies where more than half of shares belong to the state. In March 2003 the Council of Ministers issued an executive act on conducting qualification proceedings for the members of managing boards in Treasury companies which regulated in detail the principles and procedure of such proceedings, as well as the requirements towards candidates for the boards. Both acts were to put an end, at least formally, to the politically motivated practice of appointment members of the boards in state-controlled enterprises.

Another important step in the same direction was the preparation in 2004 by the Ministry of the Treasury (2004) of the document which contained basic principles of the state corporate control in Treasury companies—which was a pioneering initiative, as it took place a year before the famous OECD (2005a) guidelines for SOEs were published. A year later the second edition of the Ministry's guidelines was prepared (Ministry of the Treasury 2005), which took into account the abovementioned OECD publication and even included its Polish translation as an annex. The guidelines described in detail the competences of SOEs boards, the principles of appointing their members, monitoring of SOEs, principles of cooperation between the Ministry and company boards. The document differentiated corporate control principles depending on the size of the block of shares in the hands of the state.

The real importance of those activities was limited. It was undoubtedly a step forward in comparison with the previous stage, when the government tried to address only the grossest dysfunctions. The new approach was more systemic, albeit still fragmented. Firstly, despite the declarations, the government failed to create corporate control rules valid for the whole set of SOEs. The documents of the MSP were not binding for other ministries which also exercised corporate control, such as the Ministry of Economy and others. Secondly, what seems to be more important, the criteria for the *raison d'être* of the state enterprise sector, fundamental goals of its functioning and ways of assessing how much these rationale were respected and the objectives were achieved were not defined. All the documents adopted during the stage in question seem to have tacitly assumed that these fundamental issues had already been resolved and the main task now was to ensure their implementation. Therefore, the official wording on corporate control goals and objectives was more technical than conceptual.

Both editions of the ministerial guidelines claimed in a very similar and general way that the purpose of the state's corporate control is to increase the profitability and value of companies, to increase effectiveness of execution of the state's ownership rights, to increase transparency, etc. As the only strategic goal, preparation of SOEs for privatization was mentioned. Meanwhile, the Polish government never had a goal of privatizing all the SOEs; it was obvious that a certain state-owned sector would always exist. A lot of SOEs had been formally or just in practice exempted from privatization programs; what is more, the beginning of the 2000s was marked by a radical privatization slowdown which was caused not only by the world economy recession, but also by changes in the economic policy introduced by the leftist government which opposed "selling out" of public assets. Thus, the key issue of corporate control over SOEs which had to remain controlled by the state for indefinite perspective was completely neglected.

In 2005, there was another change in the ruling coalition followed by the change of the government. Power was regained by parties which called themselves "right-wing," with PiS as a leader, but in fact they could be described rather as populist-conservative. Despite declarations, the new staff of the Ministry of the Treasury undertook no real steps in streamlining the state corporate control. Nothing fundamentally new has been achieved either after the next change of the ruling coalition, which took place in 2007 and when the PO-PSL coalition, which in those years could be described as centrally liberal with some reservations, took power (and kept it through two four years terms, up to autumn 2015). Aleksander Grad, the new Minister of the Treasury, was a zealous supporter of liberal economy, so he focused his attention on privatization rather than on state corporate control, apparently considering this area of the ownership policy as something naturally vanishing and thus much less important. However, his ministry promptly introduced open and partially public qualification procedures for supervisory boards in Treasury companies. For the first time in the history of Polish transition, the procedure of appointment of state representatives to supervisory boards was formalized, albeit only partially, as the minister was left with quite a large field for discretionary decisions.

In the following years, the only attempt at a more systemic approach to the role of the state in the enterprise sector, albeit still partial and ultimately unsuccessful, was the draft National Program of Ownership Supervision prepared in 2010 by the Economic Council to the Prime Minister (Economic Council 2010). It assumed that the state as the owner was to focus its attention on a dozen or so largest and most important companies of European potential and strategic importance. Ironically, the main idea of the program on the strategic role of the state in the business sector eventually resurrected after the PO-PSL coalition lost power in 2015, as one of the pillars of the Responsible Development Strategy prepared by their ideological opponents from the PiS (see Sect. 4.3.1 of this chapter).

An important feature of the stage in question was that conceptual and regulatory attempts to repair the state corporate control failed to improve its practical implementation. Still, nominations on supervisory boards of SOEs, especially the larger and more important ones, were often politically motivated. Thus, after each change of the ruling coalition, deep changes in their composition took place. What is more, those who had the opportunity to observe those processes at close range, point at increasing consolidation of the mechanisms of politically motivated nominations taking place since the beginning of the twenty-first century. While earlier, opinions and proposals of a wide range of stakeholders (local authorities, trade unions, expert and academic community) were taken into account in the selection of candidates for positions on supervisory boards, later the real group of candidates for these positions had become narrowed down and decisions on nominations were concentrated in the hands of the Ministry of the Treasury.

All political parties officially condemned the practices of political nominations on the SOEs boards, as well as other manifestations of state capture but did nothing to really stop them. Probably one of the most striking examples of the discrepancy between political promises and practice in this respect was the behavior of the PO-PSL coalition, the last one to take power in the analyzed period. In his exposé before the Parliament, the PO party leader and the new Prime Minister Donald Tusk (2007) declared, that his government would end "the several-year-long political procedure of appropriation of these companies [SOEs] by the bureaucratic and party apparatus." In 2012, after the end of the PO-PSL first term, the journalistic investigation entitled "Civic Platform's List of Shame" (Tokarz 2012) was published enumerating 428 politicians of this party who had been appointed to the SOEs boards.

As we can see, in 2001–2011, despite the quite high political diversification of the successive governments and the cyclical "purges" of the SOEs' boards, and despite some statist trends which will be discussed later, the policy of state corporate control was characterized by a peculiar kind of stability—the stability of principles, according to which it was conducted in practice, and stability of the tools used. A peculiar manifestation of stability was also a continuing lack of a real long-term strategy of the state for its assets.

However, in one respect a certain kind of a strategy could be seen: it was protection of the largest and economically and politically strongest SOEs with dominant market position against the threats of deregulation and market competition. Demonopolization (both of the structures that were formed historically and those created by the re-consolidation policy of the 1990s) met great resistance and in many areas took place mainly due to the need to meet the EU requirements. One of the most persistent state-owned monopolists was Poczta Polska S.A., still the largest mail-handling company in the country. Its monopoly for basic letter mail service was formally abolished only at the end of 2012; in practice, Poczta Polska S.A. maintained its privileged market position thanks to amended provisions of the Postal Law regarding the so-called designated operator. Another example was railways. Changes in this sector, including restructuring of the PKP (a state-owned giant which included virtually all the railway infrastructure and services) and allowing competition on the railway market, were conducted with great difficulty and extremely slowly.

In a number of sectors, the SOEs even obtained additional privileges (although the first cases of such practices could be witnessed at the previous stage). Among others, these were collective agreements in the state-controlled power and mining sectors which provided employees with numerous wage and employment privileges. More or less hidden forms of state aid to SOEs were also maintained. At the end of the discussed period, 37.5% of official state aid for the entire enterprise sector was directed to SOEs (Kozarzewski 2014, p. 382), despite the much lower share of the state sector in the national economy.

However, the stability of the general principles and tools of state corporate control was accompanied by certain changes, usually very mild. They clearly did not correspond to the changes of ruling coalitions, looking like more or less linear processes. It is also worth noting that they represented some convergence with the ownership transformation pillar of the ownership policy of the state. It meant the reverse of the trend of the late 1990s, when growing efficiency of the privatization policy was accompanied by growing dysfunction and losing focus in the corporate control policy.

These changes occurred primarily in two areas. The first area was the gradual increase of state interference in the functioning of the business sector which could be seen in both pillars of the ownership policy. In the area of ownership transformation the cases of "reluctant privatization" became increasingly numerous, when the state sold its shares regaining corporate control over formally privatized enterprises. There were also cases of even restoring state ownership control over several companies. In the area of corporate control, the state made steps which violated the principle of equality of ownership forms. One of the first (unsuccessful, as contested by the European Commission) attempts was made by the PiS coalition in 2005, when a law was passed which essentially introduced the "golden share" right for the government in "strategically important" companies with minority state ownership. The next quite similar attempt, also unsuccessful because of the European Commission resistance, was made in 2010 by the PiS' political adversary, the PO-PSL coalition. Only the third attempt, undertaken a few years later on the next stage, was successful.

The second area, and this is where the greatest changes took place, was the fiscalization of the objectives of state-owned enterprises, which had a direct equivalent in the ownership transformation policy in the form of fiscalization of privatization objectives. While the importance of privatization revenues for the state budget began to be recognized as early as in the late 1990s, the possibilities of increasing the budget revenues from the state's corporate rights started to be appreciated from 2005, probably due to, inter alia, a sharp decline in privatization revenues (Kozarzewski 2017). In the case of commercialized SOEs, these were dividends, and in the case of uncorporatized ones there were para-dividend payments for using of state assets by SOEs. These two sources of the state budget revenues existed before, but they were small, not exceeding several million zlotys annually. In 2005 these payments increased almost 5 times comparing to the previous year. Since then, until 2016, when the role of the state sector in the economy was radically revised, the dividends were been treated as a permanent and significant source of budgetary revenue. Starting with the 2006 budget law, the amount of the dividend was officially planned. In 2006–2009, the dividend revenues were higher that the revenues from selling the state property, in 2006 they were higher even fivefold (Table 4.1). They were higher even in 2008–2009, the first two years of the PO-PSL coalition which re-accelerated privatization.

This source of income proved to be much more stable than privatization revenues, as it did not depend on fluctuations on the global markets and political situation in the country which affected the demand and supply of assets to be privatized. That's why since 2006, when dividend income started being planned, the plans for its acquisition were usually exceeded, in contrast to the plans for privatization revenues, which usually fell short of the target figures. On the other hand, the policy of stripping of SOEs from profits posed a threat to development prospects of these enterprises, as it depleted the funds which could be allocated for investments. Unfortunately, there are no studies that would attempt to estimate the real losses generated by such a policy.

It is worth noting that not only the dividend policy of the state was resistant to external factors, but also the whole corporate control policy as well. It was not significantly affected by the global financial crisis of 2008–2009, which (with the support of many world-famous economists) contributed to a decline in the popularity of the neoliberal doctrine as a model of economic policy and to a redefinition of the role of the state in the economy in many developed market economies towards greater interventionism. Meanwhile, in Poland, the crisis management policy was based not on state interventionism, but primarily on the protection of market relations. This strategy proved to be highly successful as Poland was the only European country which had not experienced economic recession during this period. Important shifts in the state corporate control principles started much later, when Polish economy has mostly recovered from the crisis.

It should be also noted that the use of dividends as a source of budget revenue was the only fairly clear, albeit not directly formulated goal of the state enterprise sector on the discussed stage of evolution of the state control policy. Other objectives have never been clearly defined in any

Table 4.1 Central budget revenues from dividends[a] and privatization in 2001–2011

	2001	*2002*	*2003*	*2004*	*2005*	*2006*	*2007*	*2008*	*2009*	*2010*	*2011*
Privatization revenues planned, PLN bn	18.0	6.6	7.4	8.9	5.7	5.5	3.0	2.3	12.0	25.0	15.0
Dividend revenues planned, PLN bn	–	–	–	–	–	2.4	3.5	2.0	2.9	4.0	3.3
Privatization revenues achieved, PLN bn	6.8	2.9	4.1	10.3	3.9	0.6	1.9	2.4	6.6	22.0	13.1
Dividend revenues achieved, PLN bn	0.5	0.2	0.4	0.5	2.4	3.0	2.8	2.6	7.8	4.4	5.1
Privatization revenues plan realization, %	37.8	43.9	55.4	115.7	68.4	10.9	63.3	104.3	55.0	88.0	87.3
Dividend revenues plan realization, %	–	–	–	–	–	125.0	80.0	130.0	271.8	110.0	154.5

[a]Dividend payments from commercialized SOEs and Treasury companies and para-dividend payments for using of state assets by uncorporatized SOEs

Sources Ministry of the Treasury, Central Statistical Office, Ministry of Finance, own calculations

way. It could only be presumed that one of the goals was still using the SOE sector as a source of rents, because the treatment of SOEs as a bounty for election winners continued. What is worse, there were still no attempts to formulate the role of the state as the owner of enterprises in the long-term, strategic perspective.

4.2.4 *The Fourth Stage: Expansion of Statism (2011–2015)*

It was a relatively short stage, only four years long (November 2011–November 2015), covering the second term of the PO-PSL coalition. The beginning of the stage is set quite arbitrarily, as some features of this period could be observed earlier, such as attempts to increase control of the government over the most important (in its view) enterprises regardless their ownership structure. Behind this a certain change of the paradigm of the role of the state in the economy could be seen. The state was more and more reluctantly withdrawing from direct control over enterprises, and there was more and more evidence that it intended to remain a strong market player in the long-term. Gradually, state ownership was ceasing to be treated as a kind of necessary evil, an exception to the basic principles of the market economy being built.

It may be argued that the events of this short period created some ideological and institutional foundations for the radical statist turn which was made at the end of 2015 by the next government, of the PiS coalition. During this period, the concept of "domestication" of investments, institutionalization of the role of the state as an investor and extension of the range of tools for using SOEs as a source of resources to achieve social, economic and political goals were introduced into official and discourse, and (to a limited extent) into economic policy.

The fact that the same coalition won the parliamentary elections in autumn 2011, and the same person (Donald Tusk) took the position of prime minister, did not mean that its ownership policy remained unchanged. In the activities of the Ministry of the Treasury, there was a clear shift from privatization to management of state assets. The Ministry's actions were conducted in two main directions: attempts to improve state corporate control and strengthening the role of the state in the enterprise sector.

The new Minister of The Treasury declared focusing on improving the functioning of SOEs, among others, through de-politicization of the state corporate control. In early 2013 the Ministry presented new principles of corporate governance in Treasury companies (Ministry of the Treasury 2013) containing a comprehensive set of solutions for supervising companies with state shares, including (which previously had been neglected) subsidiaries in holding structures, appointment and dismissal of members of the boards of such companies, as well as principles of their remuneration. The Ministry also elaborated a set of principles to be followed by representatives of the state on supervisory boards, as well as plans towards de-politicization of nominations of the boards' members (Grochal 2013).

In the practical dimension, not much changed apart from unprecedented "intra-term" exchange of persons on the boards of Treasury companies; in the past, such changes originated only from changes of ruling coalitions. It is not clear what stood behind it. One of the versions (Grochal 2013) claimed that it was done in order to exchange political nominees with professionals in the framework of the de-politicization of the state corporate control. Another version (Kozarzewski 2019, p. 204) refers to the intra-party struggle within the PO and claims it to be just a sign of continuing politicization of the state corporate control.

Ironically, the minister under whose auspices all these changes had been prepared, in 2013 was revoked for allegedly undue control over one of the important companies of the Treasury. The next minister was a PO politician (i.e., without proper professional background) who effectively put on hold all the attempts to find systemic solutions to improve the state corporate control. However, he was very active in making personnel changes on the boards of Treasury companies. Again, the reasons for the "purges" were not entirely clear (as well as whether they were a continuation of his predecessor's policy): in most cases there was no official explanation of these decisions. Perhaps in some cases, particularly in energy companies, the reason was a difference of views on enterprises development between the state representatives on the boards and the Ministry.

A characteristic feature of those "purges" was resignation from adopted procedures and principles: quite often they were followed purely formally, if any, especially in the case of the largest companies. The nomination criteria were often "adjusted" to fit the desired persons—mainly those whom the minister personally trusted, often not having appropriate qualifications (Bałtowski and Kozarzewski 2014, pp. 334–335). The last two such nominations were made by the minister just a few hours before his resignation (Kublik 2015). This minister had to resign just five months before the PO-PSL coalition lost power in autumn 2015. No official reason was made public; one of the most plausible versions was his too nepotistic policy of nominations on the companies' boards (Arłukowicz 2015). The next and the last Minister of the Treasury nominated by the PO-PS coalition had no time to start elaborating an implementing any new strategy. He just put aside the personnel policy and attempts to reform the state corporate control, focusing on the second main direction of the Ministry's activity, i.e., on the consolidation of the role of the state in the enterprise sector (which nevertheless included drastic personnel decisions).

Within this direction, on the stage in question, important changes started shaping up. During the second term of the PO-PSL coalition, it became clear that the statist drift which could be seen earlier was developing into a new quality of state corporate control policy. What is important, as it was mentioned before, a quite spectacular growth of statism in Poland took place only after the global financial crisis had ended. At that time in many other countries a return to less statist policy could be already observed. There were two areas where the government tried to increase its impact.

The first area was re-nationalization of selected sectors of the economy, at those times being rather a loose concept than an action plan. On the surface, the concept had nothing to do with nationalization, but later it became a good tool for currying it out, when these ideas were further developed and started being implemented in practice by the next coalition (PiS-led) which took power at the end of 2015. This was a concept of "domestication" or "re-polonization" initially of only one sector—financial. It seemed quite paradoxical, because Polish financial sector was the only one of all the post-countries countries not to have experienced a crisis during the entire period of the transition; it also proved resilient to the impact of the global financial crisis of 2008–2009. Nevertheless, one of the authors of this concept, Stefan Kawalec (2015), who nota bene previously was a liberal-minded co-creator of Polish reforms and co-author of the program that prevented the outbreak of the financial crisis in Poland in 1992 (discussed in Sect. 4.2.1 of this chapter), claimed that the domination of foreign capital in the banking sector (which controlled more nan 70% of the assets) posed a risk of decisions violating the interests of the Polish economy in favor of some political interests of foreign entities. This would result in restrictions in access to credit capital and threaten the development prospects of the Polish economy. The remedy was to ensure a predominance of domestic capital in the banking sector, although no specific recipes were formulated on how to achieve this. This idea met with both approval (also among the political opposition) and criticism. Skeptics (also, like Kawalec, with extensive reform experience, such as Leszek Balcerowicz and Stanisław Gomułka) claimed that the domination of domestic capital may lead to the politicization of decisions in banking, as such banks may more easily succumb to pressure from the government encouraging imprudent lending and investment policies (Kwaśniak 2010).

The second area of growing state interventionism was increase in the role of the state as an investor. In October 2012, the government announced the "Polish Investments" program which assumed, among other things, investing state funds, including those obtained from privatization, in public–private investment projects in areas that were not attractive for independent investment by private capital. As a part of its implementation, in 2013 Polish Developmental Investments (Polskie Inwestycje Rozwojowe, PIR) was established, a new governmental agency with the aim of providing financing, together with the state-owned bank BGK (Bank Gospodarki Krajowej), for long-term infrastructure investments.

From the point of view of corporate control, this meant recognizing the superiority of state ownership over private ownership: it was expected that a government agency (without any experience) together with a state-controlled commercial bank (with little experience in financing big innovation projects) would be far more effective than private investors. They were supposed to undertake commercially viable investments in areas which the private sector considered insufficiently attractive due to the expected revenues or the degree of risk.

By the end of 2015, the program planned to invest about PLN 40 billion (USD 10.5 billion). According to the Supreme Audit Office (2015a) report, during this period, agreements were signed for three quarters of this amount, PLN 30.5 billion (USD 8 billion). About 80% of these funds were directed to the public sector; public–private investments were only 20% of the contracted funds. The Supreme Audit Office criticized the program not only for the underspending of the funds, but also for the flawed way in which the program was developed, its limited transparency and accountability. Moreover, contrary to the original assumptions, the program contributed to the increase of public debt (by PLN 3 billion—USD 790 million).

It should be added that the "Polish Investments" was never criticized by the PiS politicians who were in opposition at that time; they also did not criticize the program after PiS took power at the end of 2015. What is more, the PiS-led coalition further developed and expanded it. It was a quite unusual behavior because PiS politicians used to heavily criticize almost all actions of the PO-PSL government claiming that they ruined Poland. Especially fiercely PiS criticized privatization policy of its predecessors who, despite by the end of 2015 privatization was virtually halted, allegedly "have sold out everything that could be sold" (Rzeczpospolita 2016). The statist ideology which stood behind the "Polish Investments" program was in many respects shared by PiS, so unlike privatization, it was not to be (using their wording) "extinguished," but continued and developed. The same as PiS approved the concept of "domestication" of the banking sector and started to implement it after getting power in 2015.

Another practice that developed at this stage was the use of SOEs as a source of financing for economic and non-economic purposes.

First of all, this manifested itself in a shift from a policy of restructuring unprofitable, albeit socially and politically important industries towards attaching them to profitable ones. The most clear example was the policy change towards coal mining. The restructuring plan for this sector approved by the parliament in January 2015 assumed the completion of restructuring measures launched at the beginning of the century which meant a radical solution to the problem of chronic unprofitability of many state-owned coal mining companies, at the same time avoiding their privatization. This was an ambitious and politically bold plan, combining deep state interference (also in the form of financial support) with intentions of actual restructuring the state-owned coal mines and closing down those unviable. However, its implementation was not successful. On the one hand, the European Commission promptly questioned the state financial aid to the mining sector. On the other hand, the PiS coalition which came to power in a few months, for political reasons was against closing any mines, even unprofitable ones.

However, the PO-PSL government had another tool to save the mines: energy holdings. They started to emerge on the basis of energy groups created in the 2000s, combining mining companies and power plants in one capital structure. In addition to the expected effects of vertical integration, such structures also began to serve as support for low profitable or unprofitable mining plants by high-profitable power companies.

The creation of such holdings has not always been done in a conflict-free manner: in the summer of 2015, the management of state-owned Tauron power generating company questioned the economic sense of the acquisition of the collapsing Brzeszcze mine (previously destined for liquidation) imposed by the Ministry of the Treasury. The dispute was resolved by the Ministry which promptly revoked those members of the managing board, who opposed the transaction, and replaced them with more compliant persons. The refurbished board immediately finalized the acquisition. Interestingly, already in December 2015, the new Minister of the Treasury freshly nominated by the new PiS government made further changes to Tauron's managing board, leaving only the "compliant" members appointed by the predecessor several months before.

Secondly, during the discussed stage, companies controlled by the state continued to perform functions of a source of revenue for the state budget through an aggressive dividend policy. Since 2013, this has become the main source of income generated by the ownership function of the state, as privatization revenues were declining and eventually virtually disappeared in 2015. The SOEs funds have also increasingly been used for sponsorship purposes, especially in the areas of cultural and sport events. There are grounds to believe that these activities went beyond the implementation of the enterprises' marketing strategies, as the scale of such sponsoring definitely exceeded the scope of similar activities undertaken by private companies (Deloitte 2012; Senderski 2015) and may mean, e.g., that in fact SOEs partly financed the social policy of the state in supporting cultural and sport life in the country.

During the analyzed stage, the state kept increasing its control over the enterprise sector using both ownership and non-ownership means, expanding practices that had emerged on the previous stages. The third attempt (after the aforementioned two blocked by the European Commission at the previous stage) of the government to get special rights towards the companies it regarded as strategic was successful. In 2015, just before the PO-PSL coalition lost power, it managed to pass the Act on Control of Certain Investments which raised no objections from the EC and which provided the Minister of the Treasury with the right to block acquisition transactions of companies operating in strategic sectors of the economy (put on the special list), even if they were fully private. However, it was only the next government formed by their political adversaries that took advantage of this regulation for the first time.

Another non-ownership mechanism, which ultimately took shape during the period in question, was the practice of granting privileges to the state owner vis-à-vis other shareholders. One of the most popular instrument was used in all the largest companies in which partial privatization was carried out and the state retained a minority block of shares. The government resolved the "cake dilemma" through introducing special provisions in companies' charters which were introduced basing on the general corporate law, without the need of special regulations. One of the popular provisions of this kind was introduction of the voting cap (usually 10–20%) for new shareholders; the old one, i.e., the state, had no such restrictions. In some companies with minority state ownership (e.g., PKN Orlen SA, the largest oil refiner and petrol retailer in Central Europe), as well as majority (e.g., PGE SA, the largest power producing company in the country), another instrument was used which increased the rights of the state shareholder through statutory provisions: the right to directly appoint one member of the supervisory board by the Minister of Treasury (Bałtowski and Kozarzewski 2016). Also the provisions of the corporate law were used to give the state owner supervoting privileges.

The government also used ownership instruments to expand its role in the enterprise sector though acquisition of companies controlled by private owners. This was usually a re-nationalization of previously privatized state-owned enterprises. The Bogdanka mine, privatized in 2009, was bought out by the state-controlled energy company Enea in 2015, in the last weeks of the PO-PSL government. It was done in a rather ruthless way: Enea resigned from purchasing coal from Bogdanka and when the price of the mine's shares fell sharply because of this, took it over. In the financial sector, the main perpetrator of the expansion of the role of the state as entrepreneur was PZU SA, the largest insurance company, over which the state had regained control several years earlier. PZU SA took up the creation of a holding financial empire which included banking services. In 2015, it bought out shares of Alior Bank (a listed company established by private domestic investors), which in turn a year later bought out a part of the former Bank BPH which had been acquired by a foreign investor during privatization of the banking sector. The next objective was to buy almost 33% of the shares of the largest bank Pekao SA (also a privatized state-owned bank) from an Italian investor Uni Credit, who was experiencing financial difficulties. This was achieved by the next government formed by the PiS-led coalition.

4.3 Phase Two: Towards State Capitalism—Since 2016

So far the last stage in the evolution of the state corporate control in Poland began at the end of 2015, with the formation of the PiS coalition government. It was different from all the previous stages marking a new phase not only in the corporate control policy and ownership policy of the state in general, but also in the whole paradigm of the role of the state in the economy. Already at the outset, in line with its electoral program, the new government had declared that during all the previous 25 years the transition was conducted in a wrong, dysfunctional way, and one of the greatest disasters was the ownership policy of the state which failed to create strong national productive forces and direct the Polish economy on the modern development path. According to the official narration, from now on the state would play a decisive role in creating the developments prospects for the economy and the society, including being an active owner and investor.

In the area of state corporate control (and the whole ownership policy of the state), we indeed can speak of a paradigm shift. The previous paradigm which was followed basically by all political forces which ruled since 1990 assumed, in principle, a limited role of the state as an owner, and in the ownership policy, the emphasis was placed on privatization. Whereas the new paradigm assumed, on the one hand, the effective liquidation of privatization policy, and even certain nationalization measures. On the other hand, it assumed a radical expansion of the ownership functions and the role of the policy of the state corporate control. In this sense, this new paradigm can be treated as a conscious or unconscious reference to the concept of state capitalism, hence the name of this phase and its so far only stage.

At the same time the radical statist turn in the policy of state corporate control (and in the policy of ownership transformation as well) at some extent was a continuation of the statist trends established by the predecessors, especially during the second term of the PO-PSL coalition. Although the new coalition cut off ideologically from the previous one, claiming to be virtually a total denial of it, it was very active in taking advantage of the statist conceptual and institutional achievements of its adversaries. However, the main novelty was the scale of statism and the almost system-changing nature of these trends. As Wojtyna put it, the new coalition broke the consensus that had existed within the political class for a quarter of a century on the relative independence of the economy from politics and started to dismantle the economic system that worked well enough (Ekonomiści o zagrożeniach dla polskiej gospodarki 2018, p. 6).

4.3.1 The Paradigm Change

4.3.1.1 The New Development Paradigm: The State Will Make Poland Great Again

The new development paradigm was based on almost total criticism of the economic policy in the entire period after 1989, primarily the development policy based on foreign direct investments, which allegedly led to the creation of a colonial-type dependent economy in Poland. It was also stated that the economic policy to date was of an ad hoc nature, without any strategic planning. All this left "Poland in ruins," which was one of the slogans of PiS in the parliamentary election campaign of 2015. The new concept of development was based on using mainly internal resources and on selective support through state investments of sectors of the economy or even individual enterprises ("national champions") with the largest export potential and ability to face competition on world markets. The increasing role of domestic capital was to be accompanied by limiting the role of foreign capital, which was to be encouraged to invest only in selected sectors of the economy. From the perspective of the Block's (1994) typology, this meant a departure from the moderately interventionist concept of a macroeconomic stabilization state and the announcement of the construction of the so-called developmental state, the most interventionist state after the socialist state. The new concept was inspired, among others, by the idea of an "entrepreneurial state" by Mazzucato (2013) and the slogan of "economic patriotism." Theories and concepts from the past were also referred to, such as the dependency theory, which had been popular in the "third world" countries which saw increasing economy autarky as a recipe for development problems (Ferraro 2008), and the world-systems theory by Wallerstein (1974), which assumed similar recipes.

Another aspect of the paradigm change was declaration of resignation from the FDI-led development path and replacing it with the concept of development based on domestic resources. The then Minister of Development (and later Prime Minister) Mateusz Morawiecki, the main ideologist of the paradigm change, had coined a maxim "There is not enough Polish economy in the Polish Economy." He claimed that the high share of the

FDIs in the Polish economy had disastrous consequences—referring to Thomas Piketti, his favorite economist, who allegedly stated that Poland from an economy that was an internal economy of the USSR became an economy colonized by the West (Do Rzeczy 2017).

The new economic policy paradigm began to be widely promoted by the PiS-led government, especially the very eloquent Morawiecki, as well as by the pro-government part of the media. The public discourse was dominated by the concept of superiority of national capital and state ownership over private and foreign capital, usually with domestic capital being identified with state (public) capital. Politicians of the ruling coalition and the publicists who supported them proclaimed that all the most important areas of the economy should be supervised by the state and financed by national, preferably public capital. Foreign capital can participate only in those areas that could not pose a threat to the vital Polish interests (in a very broad sense). What is more, private domestic capital may be far inferior to the public one as also potentially harmful to national interests because, according to the Minister of State Assets Jacek Sasin, it "often has its roots in criminal activities or in the communist period" (PAP 2020).

The new development paradigm in its most full form was formulated in an extensive "Strategy for Responsible Development" adopted by the Council of Ministers in February 2017. Due to the person of its main promoter, it was commonly called the "Morawiecki Plan." According to this document, one of the main areas of concentration of the government's efforts aimed at ensuring sustainable economic growth was to be "re-industrialization based on Polish resources" understood as state-controlled development of modern, innovative industry. At the same time, there was to be a "qualitative change in the competitive model of industry, so far based on low labor costs, towards the use of modern mechanisms of generating knowledge and technology" (Council of Ministers 2017, pp. 51, 73). The "Strategy" listed 10 strategic sectors which could become "future engines of the Polish economy" (vehicles production, professional electronics, information and communication technologies, aerospace sector, medical devices and services, mining systems, raw material recovery, eco-construction, food processing and military systems). Five "directions of intervention" were enumerated: development of modern industry, development of technical infrastructure and qualifications, support for the quality management system in industry, access of industry to raw materials and support for professional education. Within each of these directions, the so-called strategic projects were proposed (devoted to development policies in a given field), and the first direction also included 9 programs which contained 12 flagship projects (supporting specific directions of production activities).

Already at the stage of public consultations, the "Strategy for Responsible Development" became the subject of a wide criticism by economists. Wojtyna (2016) called this document a strategy for reversing the achievements of the Polish transition, a strategy of counter-transition because the "Strategy" was going to introduce "manual control" of development processes. In his view, it was a plan for a technocratic modernization inspired and to a large extent financed by the state or state-owned enterprises, resembling the failed economic strategy of modernization of the Polish economy in the 1970s. Nota bene, the somewhat outdated approach towards modernization of the economy was visualized by the Ministry of Development which decorated the draft version of the re-industrialization part of the new concept on their site (now defunct) with a picture of a factory with smoking chimneys.

Critics of the "Strategy" (Bukowski 2016; Łaszek et al. 2016) also pointed at the strategy's structural and conceptual chaos, an attempt to use an autarchic approach to boosting innovations and achieving competitive advantages on the world markets, lack of definition of measurable effects and the amount of necessary resources, omission of labor productivity issues and the lack of deeper reflection on the place and role of the service sector in the Polish economy (which in the "Strategy" was of secondary importance vis-à-vis industry). They also warned about adverse political effects of giving more power in the hands of officials and politicians such as politicization of economic decisions and a strengthening of sector lobbying.

Despite the "Strategy" was claimed to be "a key document of the Polish state in the area of medium and long-term economic policy" (Council of Ministers 2017, p. 1), the real economic policy was significantly different from the one declared in this document and contradictory. The fundamental contradiction was systemic. On the one hand, both the "Strategy" and a number of investment activities undertaken by the state significantly indicated the implementation of the "entrepreneurial state" concept. On the other hand, in the rhetoric and specific actions of the government (including the flagship "Family 500 Plus" program of financial support for all the families with more than one underage child) one could see rather the implementation of the "welfare state" concept, and these two concepts are difficult, or practically impossible to reconcile. The former assumes increased investment, e.g., based on savings, while the latter promotes consumption; there may be also problems for the state budget to generously finance both investment and social programs. From the very beginning, this dilemma was disregarded by the government (the famous statement "it is enough not to steal" by the then prime minister Beata Szydło), which focused on increasing state budget revenues, mainly through the so-called sealing of the tax system, especially closing the VAT gap. Morawiecki, who took up the post of prime minister in autumn 2017, publicly recognized this dilemma as non-existent stating that "development and social issues are one and the same. A flourishing economy is a condition for conducting a generous social policy" (Do Rzeczy 2017).

Even the rhetoric of the authorities and the actions implemented within the framework of the new statist paradigm were incoherent. One of the best examples was the attitude of the government towards foreign direct investments and main factors of development. Minister Morawiecki, who in his public speeches postulated the re-polonization of the economy and the need to switch to innovation-based development path which included resignation from competing with labor costs, at the same time, as one of the greatest achievements of the PiS government, used to mention attracting the investments of the German concern Daimler AG, which decided to build an engine factory in Lower Silesia. This achievement looked somewhat incompatible with the new paradigm.

These contradictions and inconsistencies may mean that the "Strategy for Responsible Development" failed to become a document playing the key role in the economic policy of the PiS government, although for sure it marked a general paradigm shift in the role of the state in the enterprise sector. It started gradually disappearing from the official discourse; many of the actions provided for in the "Strategy" were not implemented or were implemented only for show, such as the ceremonial commencement of the construction of a ferry in the "Gryfia" ship repair yard without a project and cost estimate. Analyzing the list of projects in the Strategy, Wojtyna (2018) comes to a conclusion that the government in fact is not interested in their realization because it would be an increasing unnecessary burden for it.

The only project from the "Strategy" which seems to be still on the government's agenda is the development of the "national electric car," although its realization deviates more and more from initial assumptions and looks more like an element of political show on, paraphrasing Donald Trump, "making Poland great again." The project started in 2016 with creation of the ElectroMobility Poland company owned by four major state-controlled energy companies and a national competition for the best picture of the future car held in 2017 (without previously deciding on its general concept and basic parameters). In August 2019 the task of preparing its production was contracted to a German integrator EDAG Engineering. The initial ambitious plans of building 1 million "national electric cars" by 2025 were lately downsized to 600 thousand by 2030. In July 2020, a body prototype developed by Italian designers was presented to the public (having nothing in common with pictures that won the 2017 competition). The current (as of the late summer of 2021) plan is to produce this car in a state-owned factory (yet to be built) on a platform yet to be licensed from one of the Western carmaker giants and using components provided by global suppliers yet to be found. To make this plan more feasible, in July 2021 the government has decided to make a previously unforeseen direct investment of PLN 250 million (USD 65 million) into the ElectroMobility Poland.

At the same time the government started launching big developmental projects not included in the Strategy, such as reactivation of old plans to build a canal across the Polish section of the Vistula Spit that would allow to get to the Vistula Lagoon from the Gdańsk Bay without crossing the Russian territory. This project, fully financed by the government, was widely criticized (Dobrzycka-Krahel and Kozakiewicz 2011; Woźniak 2019; Figura 2020) for its adverse environmental impact and lack of practical sense. In 2017, the PiS government has also launched a much bigger, ambitious and controversial megaproject of building the Central Communication Port, a hub which would include a gigantic airport with a system of connections to the rail and road network, with an expected cost of about PLN 30 billion (nearly USD 8 billion). This project was merely mentioned in the Strategy as one of the possible alternatives to be studied within the Strategy's timeframe; alternative solution was the use of the already existing network of airports. This project was also widely criticized (Sadurski 2017; Ćwiklak 2018) first of all for lack of economic sense, as there would no demand among carriers for such a hub. Critical opinions on these two projects which are treated by the government as priority ones induce sharp reactions of the ruling political class. The critics are accused of ignoring the Polish *raison d'état* and even of being agents of influence of other countries, such as Germany or Russia (Polskie Radio 24 2020).

The COVID-19 pandemic created a fertile ground for state interventionism. In March 2021 the ruling PiS-led coalition announced the outline of the Polski Ład (Polish Order) strategy which aimed at overcoming the impact of the pandemic on the Polish society and economy. It includes a wide-scale investment program financed through the EU and domestic public funds, where the state assumes the role of the main vehicle not only in the crisis management, but also in future development of the Polish economy—thus re-confirming the new state-led development paradigm pursued by the government since the end of 2015. Within the strategy, a Program for Strategic Investments has been announced by the government. The ultimate goal of the Polski Ład is in about ten years to make a civilizational leap towards the most developed European countries (Polski Ład 2021).

4.3.1.2 Return of SOEs: The New Objectives of the State Corporate Control

Notwithstanding the high degree of chaos in the government's economic policy and its contradictory corporate policy, since 2016 the change in the state corporate control goals can be clearly seen, although they have still not been officially formulated in full detail. Observations show that there are two types of changes: those resulting from the paradigm shift in the role of the state in the economy and those resulting from other reasons.

The paradigm shift which manifested itself in combining the concepts of the "entrepreneurial state" and "economic patriotism" led to an increased role of the state as an entrepreneur and an investor for two main reasons. Firstly, because SOEs were to be used as locomotives for economic modernization and growth. Secondly, because the "re-polonization" of the economy in practice meant nationalization: foreign capital (especially in the financial and energy sectors) was indeed replaced by national capital, but this was state capital only and not private capital.

The use of the state sector as the main development factor also had to change the attitude to the objectives of SOEs, redefining what resources of these enterprises were particularly important for the implementation of the government's policy. Previously, the policy towards SOEs, which had not been officially formulated, but was openly conducted, was based primarily on the ability of SOEs to generate funds for meeting the fiscal needs of the state (although there were more and more actions aimed at saving selected industries or individual enterprises, e.g., in mining). Such a policy might have made sense when the state sector as a whole was not considered an important long-term resource for the economy from the point of view of its pro-development potential, because exactly this potential was jeopardized by the aggressive policy towards the SOEs profits. In this respect, the policy of the PiS government, which since 2017 has radically eased the dividend burden on SOEs, seems quite logical. In 2016 the Ministry of the Treasury developed a new, exceptionally lenient dividend policy for 2017–2019 (Kacprzak 2017). Table 4.2 shows a decrease in the collected dividend since 2016 and planned dividend since 2017 as compared to the previous stage of the evolution of the state corporate control. Apparently due to the growing fiscal needs of the government in 2018–2019 dividend payments were substantially higher than planned, though. At the beginning of 2020, the Minister of State Assets government declared to lower the dividend burden on SOEs once again in order not limit the development possibilities of SOEs (Money.pl. 2020). Plans for 2020 were reduced almost twofold comparing to the previous years—and later again reduced three times because of the COVID-19 crisis which negatively affected the profit prospects of Treasury companies. In practice, however, the government, apparently due to the need to cover the dramatically high expenditures caused by anti-COVID measures, did not release its grip over SOEs. In 2020, the plan for collecting dividends was exceeded almost five times.

The profits remaining in the SOEs were to be used for investments, restructuring and employment reduction. SOEs were also encouraged to use these funds to take control of other companies, not only for business, but also for "patriotic" reasons—to limit the impact of foreign and "bad" private domestic capital. The problem of ensuring budget revenues,

Table 4.2 Central budget revenues from dividends in 2012–2020

	2012	*2013*	*2014*	*2015*	*2016*	*2017*	*2018*	*2019*	*2020*
Planned, PLN bn	8.0	5.0	4.6	4.5	4.5	2.4	2.2	2.8	0.5[a]
Collected, PLN bn	7.8	6.4	3.8	4.6	2.8	2.4	2.8	3.5	2.4
Plan realization, %	97.5	128.0	82.6	101.1	62.6	99.4	124.2	126.2	488.0

[a]Reduced from the initial planned amount of PLN 1.5 bn due to COVID-19 pandemic
Sources Ministry of the Treasury, Central Statistical Office of Poland, Ministry of Finance, own calculations

which became more urgent because of high expenditures on social and investment programs, was resolved in other ways, primarily by increasing tax pressure and making adjustments to use other sources of revenue, including the exotic idea of forcing Germany to pay out multi-billion war reparations. Till the end of 2019, in the situation of a good economic climate throughout the world, the country's fiscal situation was good and in a short time perspective the government could afford high spendings while resigning from a large part of dividend revenues. However, from the longer perspective, probably the "fat years" could have been better used, as many other countries did, to accumulate resources for the "lean years" and take care of the reduction of public debt. Which PiS government didn't do. The end of the "fat years" came unexpectedly fast due to the coronavirus pandemic crisis which created a very tough challenge for the government which had created a lot of rigid expenditure positions in the central budget and a lot of expectations from various social groups.

As it was discussed in Sect. 3.3.4, SOEs have a broader set of objectives than private enterprises, not necessarily within an economic and financial dimension only. Comparing to the previous stages, the PiS government have extended these primarily non-commercial objectives of SOEs. The large-scale sports and cultural sponsorship were supplemented with quasi-political activities aimed, among other things, at consolidating the position of the current ruling coalition.

One of the tools was the support for the mass-media favorable to government and the parliament majority in the form of mass publication by SOEs of advertisements and announcements in such newspapers, magazines and TV channels. At the same time SOEs withdrew advertising expenses from the media opposing the current ruling coalition. For example, as early as in 2016 the net profit growth of Niezależne Wydawnictwo Polskie, publisher of "Gazeta Polska" weekly, very supportive to the government, accounted for 692% comparing to the previous year, while that of Forum SA, publisher of "Gazeta Polska Codziennie" daily, also very supportive towards the government, was 731%. And this despite shrinking the overall Polish press advertising market in 2016 by 15–20% (Mejer 2017).

Another tool of such consolidation is installing state control over the media market—the need for it was numerously proclaimed by PiS politicians as in Poland media had been allegedly captured by hostile domestic and especially foreign interest groups. Thus, the "re-polonization" was needed in order to defend national Polish interests. This narration became especially strong during the presidential campaign in Summer 2020, when other countries, especially Germany, were openly accused in intervention in the domestic affairs of Poland—including by President Andrzej Duda who called critical attitude of the press towards him an "an another installment of the German attack," "a dirty campaign of the worst kind" and "an attempt of Germans to elect our president" (Rzeczpospolita 2020).

SOEs were expected to take part in counteracting these hostile activities through nationalization of the media. As vice premier Piotr Gliński put it, "there is a huge advantage of media that are not in the hands of capital connected with the Polish government" and state-owned companies, when they can, must buy out these media from foreign owners (Kośmiński 2020). In the second half of 2020, Orlen, the state-controlled oil industry giant, took a 65% stake in Ruch (from a domestic private owner), one of three largest press distributors in Poland. At the beginning of 2021, it also bought Polska Press from a German owner, a publishing group which edited 20 regional newspapers and possessed a dozen of Internet services—thus concentrating in its hands a substantial market share both in media publishing and distribution. While the management of Orlen stressed the purely business character of these transactions, the latter one was conducted in line with the patriotic, country-saving narration of the authorities. And the former transaction may be also regarded as helping the government to install control over the media market. Given the fact that before the takeover Ruch was at the verge of bankruptcy, it was hardly an attractive asset to buy by an oil company from the perspective of its business.

Another example of using state corporate control for political purposes is the establishment in 2016, on the initiative of then Prime Minister Beata Szydło, of the Polish National Foundation (the Polish acronym PFN—Polska Fundacja Narodowa) with a target amount of funds of PLN 633 million (about USD 170 m). Its founders were 17 large SOEs (10 of which were included in WIG20 Warsaw Stock Exchange flagship index). The foundation's mission was to improve Poland's image abroad, to build its brand and to promote the Polish economy (Sudak 2016). The initial version of the foundation's statute also contained the objectives of direct support for the Polish economy, e.g., for SOEs and private entrepreneurship, promotion of good market practices, support for market development and innovation. In practice, the PFN has been involved in the organization and financing of propaganda support for government activities and the promotion of patriotic attitudes. The first project implemented by the PFN was a nationwide billboard campaign supporting the controversial court reform; the foundation also ran several programs devoted to de-communization and celebration of the centenary of Polish independence. In mid-2017, the PFN removed all references to economic objectives from its statute, introducing provisions on promoting patriotic attitudes, protecting Poland's image and fighting defamation of the nation. The functioning of the foundation is not transparent, which is explained by its representatives as the need to keep trade secrets. Controversy is aroused both by the content of the implemented projects and by the unclear manner of their selection and cost estimation. According to independent investigations, the selection of contractors and the personnel policy of the PFN have clear features of nepotism (Kondzińska and Szpala 2018; Newsweek Polska 2018).

Using SOEs for the agenda not directly related with their goals and mission is facilitated by the fuzzy boundary between what may be regarded as state-owned and non-state-owned discussed in Sect. 3.2.4. The practical consequence of this fuzziness is the possibilities to avoid disclosure of some actions of state-controlled companies which gives the politicians and bureaucrats much more room for discretionary use of the SOEs resources than it would be possible under the strict public control. Both Orlen and the PFN consistently refuse to disclosure information on their controversial financial operations under the pretext that they do not use public funds. The latter denied access to financial data even for its founders and the Supreme Audit Office.

The PFN has a good reason to do this. The growing non-commercial activity of SOEs was criticized not only by watchdogs, but also by the Supreme Audit Office (2018a). It negatively assessed the practice of sponsoring in conditions of a negative financial result of a SOE, as well as lack of control over the activities of the PFN on behalf of the founders. In addition, many companies were accused of not complying with internal sponsoring rules and commissioning consulting or media services, which often led to mismanagement.

In order to streamline the state corporate control and counteract the dysfunctions in SOEs' functioning, in autumn 2017 the Chancellery of the Prime Minister issued a document entitled "Principles of Corporate Governance in Companies with Treasury Shareholding." Despite its rather general character, it clearly reflected the growth of statism in the state's economic policy. The principles assumed (Chancellery of the Prime Minister 2017, p. 3):

- long-term increase in the value of national assets through an increase in the value of SOEs;
- strengthening state corporate control through introduction of high corporate governance standards which include selection criteria and procedures of nominations on the SOEs boards and requirements towards state representatives in SOEs;
- increased protection of key economic interests of the state through keeping or increasing the share of the Polish capital in companies of significant importance for the national economy (here, the document de facto equates domestic capital with state capital);
- ensuring coherence of strategies implemented by SOEs of significant importance for the national economy and by SOEs which perform public mission with the governmental programs.

4.3.2 Organization of State Corporate Control Under the New Paradigm

4.3.2.1 The Quest for New Organizational Solutions

The changes in the paradigm of the role of the state in the economy towards more interventionism and changes in the goals of the state corporate control required organizational changes. This was reflected, firstly, in the creation of new central agencies. Within the entrepreneurial state paradigm, already at the end of 2015, the Ministry of Development with a very broad range of tasks was established; later, in 2018, two ministries were established in its place: the Ministry of Investment and Development and the Ministry of Entrepreneurship and Technology.

Secondly, major changes have taken place in the organization of the state corporate control. On January 1, 2017, the Act of 16 December 2016 on the principles of state property management came into force and became the first legal act in the history of the post-communist Poland which regulated execution by the state of its corporate rights. Unfortunately it contained a number of gaps and unclear wording, allowing for great freedom of interpretation of its provisions. In particular, the objectives and methods of the state corporate control were formulated too vaguely, as well as the methods of assessing the activities of companies controlled by the State.

The content of this Act clearly indicated the government's intentions to strengthen its ownership functions at the same time practically completely resigning from privatization. The official language even got rid of the word "privatization," from now on selling state assets is enigmatically called "disposal of shares." The notion of companies of significant importance for the national economy was introduced. The Prime Minister could include companies operating in as many as 23 sectors into this category. Apart from areas traditionally considered strategic, such as the financial, energy and arms industry, the Act also listed such industries as the chemical industry, fertilizer production, hard coal mining, real estate trade, land, sea and air transport and the food industry. Already on January 13, 2017, the Prime Minister announced the list of 30 such companies. However, the Act did not present in a comprehensive manner the specificity of corporate control over this type of companies. Specific provisions were scattered throughout the document and stated, among others, that the shares of these companies could not be transferred as a donation to a local government, that a representative of the state at the general meeting of such a company was to act on the basis of a written voting instruction drawn up by the state agency in charge of state corporate control, and that such a representative should have appropriate knowledge or professional experience.

As promised during the election campaign of 2015, at the end of 2016 the Ministry of the Treasury was liquidated. This was caused not only by the official completion of privatization, but also by a significant change in the organizational principles of the state corporate control. The majority of the control functions were moved to the Prime Minister, including exercise of all rights from shares. In fact, that meant decentralization of management of state assets because the Prime Minister got mostly coordinating functions: the Act on the principles of state property management provided for the possibility to delegate Premiers' rights to particular ministers or other state agencies. And this right was immediately used: already on January 3, 2016, the corporate control over 432 Treasury companies was divided among 10 ministries and the principle of centralized ownership supervision over state property, which has been in force (with some exceptions) for over 20 years, was effectively abolished. The authors of the act foresaw this course of events which in their view was advantageous for the state corporate control. In the supporting document for the act draft (Chancellery of the Prime Minister 2016), they argued that SOEs would be provided with better supervision by professionals in the relevant industry and better engage in meeting the economic policy objectives. In practice, assignment of SOEs to ministries did not always seem logical and sometimes rather reflected the strength of a given ministry. The largest beneficiary of the decentralization was Mateusz Morawiecki, who at that time was the Minister of Development and Finance. He took over the supervision of 245 companies, i.e., more than a half of their total number.

Decentralization of the state corporate control immediately resulted in a deepening of the dysfunction of supervisory functions of the state, fully in line with the results of empirical studies conducted by the OECD (2005b), which clearly indicated that the dispersed model was the worst as inevitably leading to various pathologies. In Poland after the state corporate control decentralization, the dysfunctions manifested themselves, firstly, in the struggle between ministries for control over companies. The original distribution of SOEs was subject to several partial changes, which included the transfer of subsequent companies from the Prime Minister's authority to the ministries. After the "government reconstruction" at the beginning of 2018, 48 companies from 396 remained under the Prime Minister's control, with 12 ministries being responsible for the rest, and the largest "owner" was the Minister of Entrepreneurship and Technology controlling blocks of shares in 179 companies. Secondly, it was deteriorating quality of the state control over the enterprises, i.e., lack of coordination of the state ownership policy, further politicization of appointments on the SOEs boards which, as will be shown further in the chapter, led to accelerated rotation of members of these boards, growing problems with appointing board members with proper qualifications, and more and more widespread use of state assets to satisfy groups of private interest.

In November 2018 the Supreme Audit Office (2018b) published a report devoted to the effects of introduction of this model of the state corporate control. Despite a generally positive overall assessment and the absence of significant formal irregularities, the report presents a very unfavorable picture of both the new model and the manner of its implementation. The biggest drawbacks included the lack of a uniform control system: about 60 companies owned by the state were still subject to special regulations. Meanwhile, even in companies subject to general regulations, no new principles of supervision were introduced and no restructuring or consolidation activities were undertaken, which would have been especially critical in the case of numerous (about 1/5 of the total number of SOEs) companies in a very bad financial condition. The method of transfer of control by the liquidated Ministry of the Treasury was chaotic and often resulted in incomplete disclosure of information to new bodies performing ownership functions. Moreover, from March 2017, access to the archives of the Ministry of the Treasury was definitely closed. The main recommendation of the Supreme Audit Office was a real unification of corporate control of the state coordinated by the single decision-making center, i.e., the Prime Minister. Following these recommendations would de facto mean a return to, this time a more coherent, centralized model valid for over 20 years.

The government was growingly aware that the new, de facto decentralized state corporate control instead of getting improved, became even less effective which posed a serious threat to the implementation of the new development paradigm based on the role of the state as an owner and investor. Just a year later, during the so-called government reconstruction (December 2017–January 2018), Morawiecki, who became Prime Minister, significantly consolidated economic power in his hands, including the state corporate control. Control over many large and most important companies was transferred from the ministries to the Prime Minister's office, including the Industrial Development Agency, the Polish Development Fund, the Warsaw Stock Exchange, the largest state-controlled bank PKO BP and the largest insurance company PZU, PKP (railways), the Polish Post Office, as well as the biggest Polish refiners and petrol retailers PKN Orlen and Lotos.

In Autumn 2019 the centralized state corporate control model was formally re-installed through to a great extent "resurrecting" the Ministry of the Treasury (stripped of its privatization functions) under the new name of the Ministry of State Assets. Additionally, the Ministry became responsible for mineral deposit management. Jacek Sasin, a loyal PiS party official, became the Minister of State Assets. However, as in the times of the Ministry of the Treasury, the centralization of the state corporate control was not complete. The new ministry got control over only 200 treasury companies out of the total number of 367 companies at that time with blocks of shares of the rest of the enterprises in the hand of various governmental agencies. In mid-2020, out of the total number of 349 enterprises with the state participation, the Ministry of State Assets possessed 206 blocks of shares of (59% of the total number of companies), 93 blocks of shares were held by the Industrial Development Agency, 22 by the Ministry of Culture and National Heritage, 20 by the Ministry of Marine Economy and Inland Navigation, one each by the Ministry of Interior and Administration, and the Ministry of Health, and four were controlled by the Prime Minister office (Chancellery of the Prime Minister 2020).

Apart from only partial re-centralization of the state corporate control there are controversies about the obscure criteria of directing state block of shares to given ministries. It seems logical that the state corporate control over 16 regional state-owned RTV broadcasters was put in the hands of the Ministry of Culture and National Heritage and not the Ministry of State Assets. However, a number of other decisions were not so obvious, such as keeping under auspices of the Industrial Development Agency, whose main task is taking care of insolvent and in other ways problematic enterprises, also a few firms which functioned normally. This and other hard to understand cases of non-transfer of state assets under the control of the new ministry may be explained by some political considerations, such us political weight of the relevant ministers (Szymański 2020). On the other hand, depriving the Ministry of Defense of corporate control over the defense industry may also be regarded as a controversial, politically motivated move reflecting rather the political weight of the Minister of State Assets rather than practical considerations (Świerczyński 2019).

4.3.2.2 *Evolution of the Personnel Policy*

The government formed by the PiS-led coalition at the end of 2015, made a traditional move, which previously had been made by all its political predecessors, i.e., started "purging" SOEs' boards from the representatives of the political adversaries. Even before the decentralization of the state corporate control, this personnel change differed much from such previous campaigns in its pace and scope: it was carried out faster and took up more positions, including much more active changes in the composition of the managing boards. During the first few months of the PiS-led term of office, practically all SOEs were covered by these "purges." After a year of the PiS rule, the "Puls Biznesu" daily identified about a thousand political nominees on the SOEs boards and put them on the "List of Shame" of the new government (Tokarz 2017), which was more than twice as many than the population of the already mentioned "List of Shame" devoted to the PO-PSL government (Tokarz 2012) created after five years of PO-PSL rule. The decentralization of the state corporate control which had led to the strengthening of the individual ministries and created a kind of patrimonies governed by them contributed to the further acceleration of the personnel carousel in Treasury companies: change of the administrative body which exercised state corporate control was accompanied by the desire of the new body to put "their own people" on the companies' boards. The gradual re-centralization also contributed to personnel changes when SOEs started changing their governmental patrons again.

The accelerated personnel change on the SOEs boards created a new problem: lack of a sufficient reserve of qualified members of supervisory and managing boards which would at the same time meet the political goal of purging the SOEs from the political enemies and supplying their boards with political allies. Despite all the politicization of the nominations on the SOEs boards under the PO-PSL governments, the state nominees, with some exceptions, were competent enough to perform their tasks as supervisory and managing boards members, being both professional and loyal enough to the government. The new government of mostly populist origin had obvious problems in attracting such people; besides, it seems that in its corporate control personnel policy the "bounty factor" became much stronger than on the previous stages, where the governments tried to find (with various degree of success) an equilibrium between treating the state assets as a political loot and keeping the state corporate control efficient. Thus many managers who would be suitable for positions in SOEs may have been deterred by the progressive politicization of state corporate control.

All this led to rapid deterioration of the quality of the personnel nominated to the SOEs boards by the state owner. More and more often positions in supervisory boards of Treasury companies started to be held by people without sufficient qualifications including bizarre cases when, for example, already in December 2015, the position on the supervisory board of Warszawskie Zakłady Mechaniczne SA (automotive parts producer) was taken over by Kaja Godek, a young pro-life activist with a philological education, or when in July 2016 Łukasz Dudkowski, previously the director of the municipal cultural center, became the new CEO of the state-owned bus and truck producer Jelcz. It should be noted that in order to appoint these people, the government had to break the rules and procedures of nominations in Treasury companies especially those which had to ensure proper qualifications of nominees. Sometimes the regulations were only "bypassed," when the political nominees on the boards formally represented not the state owner, but employees (where qualifications requirements practically did not exist). But the regulations were broken in outright way too. For example, the legal regulations requiring that supervisory board members on behalf of the state must have higher education and pass a state examination for supervisory board members were simply ignored in the case of 22 out of 25 companies belonging to the state-owned Polish Armaments Group (Polska Grupa Zbrojeniowa) by deleting (illegally, but never challenged) the relevant requirements from their statutes (Radecki-Mikulicz 2016).

In fact, the politicization of personnel policy has taken over not only positions in companies' boards, but also those responsible for the state corporate control in the state administration. Just after the PiS coalition won the 2015 elections, it amended the Civil Service Act replacing contests for higher positions in the civil service with appointments. From now on, all senior positions up to the deputy director of the department were filled in a discretionary manner directly by ministers and heads of other central offices. The requirement for the persons occupying top positions in the civil service to have managerial experience in government administration or public finance, as well as the requirement to be apolitical (not to be a party member in the previous five years), was removed.

The lack of control over the quality of the personnel policy quickly led to numerous abuses, when government-nominated members of the boards started pursuing their private interests, including asset stripping and tunneling, e.g., by ordering overpriced services from "friendly" outsider companies. The scale of the abuse of such kind forced the government and law enforcement agencies to take appropriate steps. As early as in September 2016, Dawid Jackiewicz, the first Minister of the Treasury in the PiS government, was accused of cronyism when filling positions in Treasury companies (an also for continuing the aggressive dividend policy of the previous coalition's government) and dismissed. The Central Anticorruption Bureau became interested in several cases, arresting, among others, the Chairman of the Supervisory Board of the state-controlled Grupa Azoty SA, the leading chemical industry company in the country. The government managed to eliminate a number of the most drastic and popular in the media cases of nepotism, such as the illegal appointment of Bartłomiej Misiewicz, a Law and Justice activist previously working an assistant in a chemists shop, without higher education, as a member of the supervisory boards of Energa Ciepło Ostrołęka power plant and Polish Armaments Group. However, these actions have not significantly reduced the pathologies of the state corporate control.

A kind of a systemic attempt within the PiS party structures to limit access of politicians to seats on SOEs boards was made in 2018, on the occasion of the local government elections. The PiS leadership had introduced restrictions on running for local government for those holding such positions. The official explanation voiced by the PiS Chairman Jarosław Kaczyński was that "one does not go to politics for money" (Rzeczpospolita 2018), which could mean a desire to please the electorate. One can also suppose that it was also about preventing excessive concentration of positions in authorities and companies so as not to deplete too much these resources that could be distributed among the larger number of cronies. Paradoxically at the first sight, one of the beneficiaries of this approach could be politicians from the opposition, as quite a lot of them were approached before the local elections with propositions to resign from taking part in them in exchange for positions in SOEs boards. Several opposition politicians, who had won the 2018 local elections, also got similar propositions (Rogojsz 2018; Wroński 2018). The higher priority of getting control over representative bodies over nepotistic policy towards SOEs boards seems quite logical, though, as political power is a pre-requisite for the latter.

No wonder that the almost complete exchange of persons on the positions on the SOEs boards at the beginning of the PiS coalition rule did not mean the end of the personnel carousel. After just a few months, especially after the resignation of minister Jackiewicz, there was another wave of the changes. The persons appointed to the positions by the PiS government were in many cases dismissed and replaced by other persons, who, in turn, sometimes did not hold on to them any longer and were replaced by others. The record in this respect belongs to the Energa energy company where in December 2019 the ninth president was appointed since the PiS coalition took power at the end of 2015 (which makes the rotation at the average speed of 2.25 presidents per year). In the same period, the presidents of the state-controlled PZU insurance company, Bank Ochrony Środowiska (Environment Protection Bank) and Polska Wytwórnia Papierów Wartościowych (Polish Security Printing Works), were changed five times each, and four times the presidents of Lotos Group and KGHM copper and silver producer. According to calculations by "Dziennik Gazeta Prawna" daily (Miłosz 2018), during the first three years of the PiS coalition rule, in the group of 30 Treasury companies which the government regards as having "significant importance for the economy" there were 100 persons holding the positions of chairmen of supervisory boards, i.e., on average one person held this position for less than a year. The personnel carousels and their mechanisms were described in detail by Kopińska (2018) and Roguski (2018).

All in all, according to data provided by the Chancellery of the Prime Minister, from the beginning of the PiS coalition government until the end of January 2018, decisions were made to fill positions in Treasury companies with 2534 people (about 7.25% per company), which also included situations of reappointment to supervisory boards and boards of directors. In practice, there were even more of such decisions because there is no information about personnel changes in several hundred subsidiaries of state-owned companies (Kacprzak 2018). The studies by Błaszczak (2018, 2019) and Szarzec et al. (2020) show that, comparing to the previous stages of the evolution of the state corporate control the PiS government was unprecedentedly active both in "initial" personnel changes on the SOEs boards and in further rotation. Perhaps the attention towards control over SOEs is a characteristic feature of PiS, because the second most intensive rotation on the board was registered by both studies in 2006–2007, during the previous two-year rule of this party. Although another regularity has been preserved: rotation on the management boards were still much less intense than on supervisory boards (Szarzec et al. 2020) which may be explained by the fact that qualifications of persons on managerial positions were much more important for the companies' performance than that of supervisory board members who have more possibilities for relatively harmless free riding. Thus, positions on the supervisory boards became more prone to political nominations and overriding of qualifications requirements.

High pace of personnel changes created additional problems. By 2019, one of the biggest problems of the state owner was to find candidates who would replace the dismissed board members and it probably contributed to slowing down the personnel carousel (Błaszczak 2019). Perhaps one of the side effects of this personnel deficit was a rotation of the same persons affiliated with the PiS coalition hopping from one board to another. For example, Daniel Obajtek, an agricultural technician and former mayor of small Pcim municipality (about 4900 inhabitants), at the end of 2015, became president of the Agency for Restructuring and Modernization of Agriculture; in March 2017 he moved to the position of president of Energa energy group and in February 2018 became president of PKN Orlen.

The government made several rather unsuccessful attempts to improve its personnel policy towards the SOEs boards through its depoliticizing and ensuring the quality of candidates for positions in companies. In 2017, a Council for Treasury Companies and State Legal Entities was established with members appointed by the Prime Minister, the Minister of Development and the Minister of Energy, which was to be responsible for providing opinions on candidates for the boards of companies controlled (directly or indirectly) by the state and on a number of other decisions concerning state corporate control. However, the real effectiveness of this body was very limited. Firstly, the opinions of the members of the Council, who were middle-level officials from the ministries, had no real weight. Secondly, because the criteria for evaluating candidates for the boards were formulated in a too broadway which gave grounds for controversial positive opinions, e.g., on nominating persons who only had political career behind them. Thus, in practice, the Council did not contribute to depoliticizing the state corporate control. Thirdly, the requirement for the Council to give an opinion on a candidate could in many cases be relatively easily omitted: a candidate for a supervisory board member could be proposed not by the state administration, but by another entity controlled by the state. For example, this made possible to nominate two persons to the supervisory board of the Warsaw Stock Exchange with no experience in the capital market, because it was proposed by the state-controlled PKO BP bank.

Another attempt was made in 2018 through the amendment to the Act on the principles of state property management which increased the qualifications requirements for the candidates to the SOEs boards (holding MBA degree, CFA, CIIA, ACCA, CFF certificates, being a professional auditor, legal advisor, advocate, etc.). Provisions were also introduced to limit the conflict of interest and the possibility of the same person sitting on more than one supervisory board.

Another direction of streamlining the state corporate control was motivating the board members to work more efficiently and limiting the possibilities of rent-seeking. In 2016, the special act was adopted which introduced the new a new system of hiring and remunerating board members of companies with the participation (even minority) of the state or municipalities. Among other things, employment contracts with members of management boards were abolished, and their remuneration started to depend on the size of the company and the degree of achievement of its goals. The possibility of receiving additional remuneration from subsidiaries was also eliminated. The public owner of the shares was to conduct such a personnel policy regardless of the number of votes possessed. In fact, even if it was a minority owner, a private majority owner was rather interested in proper cooperation with it as could create better conditions for the company's functioning (PwC 2017).

The financial effectiveness of the act was limited: the new system, although it significantly reduced the earnings of managers and members of supervisory supervisors in the largest companies, sometimes allowed for their significant growth (Krześnicki 2017). Moreover, taking into account the rapid rotation on the management positions in Treasury companies, lower earnings could be compensated by high severance pay (Jóźwik 2017a). Besides, reducing the earnings of senior managers might make these positions less attractive to highly qualified persons who would choose working in the private sector instead. It could only aggravate the general problem of the government with finding qualified candidates for board members and create additional possibilities for filling managerial positions with people of lower value on the labor market, i.e., less qualified. So far there is no robust evidence that this effect actually exists, the relevant studies are yet to be done (Szarzec et al. 2020).

In 2017 an attempt was made to reduce the corruption-generating conflict of interests of persons performing public functions which could also limit the rent-seeking potential of the SOEs boards. A draft law on openness of public life was submitted to the parliament by the government, which, among other things, extended the notion of a person performing public functions to include members of supervisory boards and management boards, as well as proxies in the companies where the state holds at least 20% of shares. Such a person had extensive obligations to disclose his or her income and assets, and at the same time was prohibited from conducting private business activities, holding positions on commercial companies' boards or holding over 10% of their shares. These restrictions in the draft law were criticized by experts as insufficient or too easy to overcome (RPO 2018; Ojczyk 2018). At some moment, the government lost interest in this law, allegedly because it would reveal too much information about the wealth of the members of the political elite (Newsweek Polska 2019), so the law was never passed.

4.3.3 *Ownership Policy*

According to the new logic and tasks of state corporate control, the government has taken numerous practical steps to ensure the survival and expansion of the state-controlled enterprise sector. Three main sets of instruments were used: increasing ownership control of the state in the enterprise sector, creation of privileged position for SOEs on the market and limiting private property rights.

4.3.3.1 *Crawling Re-Nationalization*

In line with the new paradigm, privatization was finally put on hold (along with accusing of the previous governments of selling out the whole economy). The PiS government started gradual re-nationalization of selected state assets both in an open way, proclaiming the advantage of the state as an investor over private capital and the need of support for Treasury companies in their expansion, including acquisition of other firms, and in a somewhat veiled way, through so-called re-polonization and formally apolitical business decisions of Treasury companies.

As it was mentioned before, the notion of advantages of state ownership often went together with arguments against FDIs. The PiS coalition made use of the re-polonization concept elaborated in early 2010s by its political adversaries which were close to the PO-PSL government, substantially developing it. Now it had to be applied not only to the banking sector (although in this sector it was most advanced), but to the whole economy and was claimed to be a radical change of the country's development path. In practice, however, re-polonization led to the replacement of foreign capital by state capital rather than private domestic capital (it should be mentioned that the authors of the original concept of re-polonization of banks decisively rejected the ideas of their nationalization). There is much to suggest that this was largely not the result of a lack of willing national capital, but the effect of a deliberate nationalization policy resulting from a new perception of the state's role in the economy—which recently the members of the political elite started admitting.

The main tool of nationalization was, as before, the acquisition of control over private enterprises by Treasury companies which were even encouraged to do it through reduced dividend payments to the state budget. The novelty introduced by the PiS government compared to previous governments was that while previously such acquisitions were explained solely by business decisions of companies owned by the state, now an important state interest was stressed. It was, among others, the need to fight against enemies of Poland, what was discussed in Sect. 4.3.1 of this chapter, or contribute to economic security of the country. For example, with regard to energy companies, the Minister of Energy, Krzysztof Tchórzewski, publicly stated that "there should be no place for profit-oriented entities in the Polish energy sector, but long-term activities increasing the country's energy security are important" (Graniszewska 2016).

Another important source of financing for public investments of nationalization character was public funds. Polish Developmental Investments agency established by the predecessors changed its legal form and was transformed into the Polish Development Fund (Polski Fundusz Rozwojowy, PFR). The fund took part in the buyouts of shares in companies that were to be taken under state control. In 2017 state insurance company PZU took over PKO S.A. bank. Not having the necessary funds (10.6 billion zlotys, about USD 2.8 billion), it benefited from the assistance of the PFR, which added 4.1 billion zlotys (USD 1.1 billion) of public money to the transaction. In 2018 the PFR took over 70% of the shares in Pesa (rail vehicles production) and took part in the re-nationalization of previously privatized segments of Poliskie Koleje Linowe, a mountain cableway operator.

The state domain in the enterprise sector could be also extended by allowing the state agencies to freely purchase shares of companies traded on the stock exchange. Funds for this purpose were among other things, delivered through the creation in 2019 of a Capital Investment Fund (Fundusz Inwestycji Kapitałowych) with an annual budget of 2 billion zlotys (about USD 530 million), supervised by the Prime Minister and fed by part of the dividends collected by the state.

Another helpful tool was the Act on Control of Certain Investments passed by the previous coalition and which allowed blocking acquisition transactions in companies put on the special list of "protected entities." In 2017 the state, against the will of the French concern EDF, blocked the sale of EUR 1 billion worth of shares in the EDF Polska group (consisting of, among others, eight heat and power plants and one large power plant) to another private investor and forced their sale to the state-controlled Polish Energy Group (Polska Grupa Energetyczna, PGE) (Kaczmarczyk 2017). The same happened to Połaniec power plant acquired in the same year from the French company Engie, which also had intended sell its shares to another private investor. The government had entered conflict with the Russian Acron which possessed 20% of shares of Grupa Azoty chemical factories. The government used the Act to block Acron's plans to acquire the controlling stake and tried to buy out the shares it possessed. Despite substantial reduction of the market value of shares held by Acron, it resigned from the suggested transaction, but in return started to block investment plans of Grupa Azoty, apparently not being satisfied with the dividend policy of the state as the majority investor (Jóźwik 2017b; Frączyk 2019).

Many nationalizations expanded the state domain in areas relevant to the new economic policy. Sometimes they performed dual function, being at the same time rescue investments. In the area of re-industrialization, which included support for domestic industrial producers, these were the above-mentioned buyout of Pesa, one of Poland's largest manufacturers of rail vehicles with a pan-European reputation, which was on the verge of bankruptcy, and the repurchase in 2016 by two companies belonging to the Polish Armaments Group of the assets of the bankrupt Autosan truck and bus manufacturer. The Industrial Restructuring Agency renationalized two companies in the shipbuilding industry by purchasing shares in the Gdańsk Shipyard and GSG Towers from a Ukrainian private investor. As a part of realization of the gigantic plan of creating a transportation hub, the collapsing local airport in Radom (100 km from Warsaw) was taken over from the local government by the state-owned company Polskie Porty Lotnicze.

Compared to the second term of the PO-PSL governments, an important novelty in the field of expansion of state ownership control was the announcement of a revision of some privatization transactions that allegedly led to the sale of assets at too low a price or violated the Polish national interest. To support the first argument, the Supreme Audit Office (2015b) report published at the end of 2015 was referred to which highly critically assessed 4 out of 15 major privatization transactions that had been conducted by the PO-PSL governments of both terms. The main allegation was too low transaction prices which allegedly did not reflect the actual value of the enterprises. However, several experts were of a different opinion, stressing that the NIK valuations were overestimated because they did not take into account the companies' debts, necessary investments and lack of interest from potential buyers (Bartuś 2015).

The second criterion (violation of the national interest) was never precisely formulated and could not be credibly deducted from the practice. Some cases were understandable from the point of view of the new development paradigm, such as questioning the privatization of PKP Energetyka electricity Polish railway network' distributor as an important infrastructure entity. However, cases with unclear agenda existed—like the (eventually successful) attempts to re-nationalize Polskie Koleje Linowe, a cableway operator in Tatra mountains region which had been privatized to a foreign investor. Officially the state wanted to return from the foreign hands a piece of infrastructure having exceptional historical and landscape values. Anyway, this was not the only notion of non-economic value of objects which had to be re-privatized (or saved from privatization). For example, in 2017 the government unsuccessfully tried to re-nationalize (under the slogan of re-polonization) Polskie Nagrania record label which had bankrupted in 2010 and had been sold to Warner Music Poland in 2015. The main justification was returning to Polish hands the large musical archive operated by the company, although nor Polskie Nagrania, neither Warner Music Poland had copyright for them, so it could not be used the company's owner discretion. The fact that Warner Music Poland, in compliance with the contract, has digitalized the archive and passed it free of charge to the state-owned National Digital Archives, was also ignored. The government was ready to pay much higher price that it had sold the label for; however, the buyout transaction was never completed.

This example shows that one of the biggest obstacles to revising the results of privatization was the lack of efficient ways of doing it. The possibility of annulling privatization contracts was discussed but never used—perhaps due to the lack of efficient procedures (the only such attempt stuck for good in the court). Besides, there could be fears of unfavorable reactions of the financial markets. In this situation, the government started to try buying out enterprises—but this method proved to be only partially efficient. Quite often the new owners were not interested in the transaction, such as CVC Capital Partners fund which had bought PKP Energetyka and in 2018 declined the buyout offer by the Ministry of Infrastructure. In some cases, the government was very persistent: in the fall of 2018, after a laborious process of discouraging the existing investor (partial expropriation to the State Treasury, resumption of the prosecutor's investigation, obstruction by local authorities), the Polish Development Fund managed to buy out Polskie Koleje Linowe.

So far, transactions expanding the state domain in the economy were of a sporadic character, but usually included assets of high value. While it was still too early to speak of a noticeable growth of the state sector in the Polish economy as a whole, in some sectors it was already becoming important, first of all in the banking sector. Re-consolidation of the banking sector in the hands of the state (in the framework of its "re-polonization") started already under the PO-PSL government; this process accelerated under the PiS government. Compared to 2008, in 2017 the share of domestic capital in the banking sector more than doubled and reached 54.5% (Polish Financial Supervision Authority 2018, p. 7). Then the process of "re-polonization" stopped, although semi-officially, the government announced the goal of achieving 90% of the domestic capital in banking (wPolityce.pl 2017). Observing the history of the acquisitions, it can be concluded that this growth has been achieved only through the involvement of state-controlled capital and currently almost all the largest domestically owned banks are in fact state-owned. Officially, the state possesses only about 46% of the domestic banking capital (Polish Financial Supervision Authority 2020, p. 5), but in reality this share is highly underestimated as not taking into account assets controlled indirectly, through other state-own entities.

In the energy sector, the state already controlled a substantial part of it: in 2016, it was 6 out of 16 energy companies on the list of 500 largest enterprises by the Rzeczpospolita (2019) daily employing a total of 88.6% of the employees; the above-mentioned acquisition of power plants from French owners increased this ratio to 90.7%. According to unofficial sources, the PiS government was aiming for practically 100% state dominance in the energy sector.

4.3.3.2 Consolidation of the State Sector

According to the new logic and tasks of state corporate control, the government has taken numerous practical steps to ensure the survival and expansion of the state-controlled enterprise sector which Barbara Błaszczyk (2017, p. 213) described as "consolidation of the state sector at the expense of the market"—and sometimes this was done even against the interests of individual SOEs. Actions that were increasing the state's influence in the enterprise sector correlated with the direct expansion of the state ownership through the acquisition of private companies or the expansion of power in companies in which the state held shares. All these activities have directly or indirectly affected market relations and the situation of the private sector, limiting the functioning of market mechanisms and fair competition.

A special example of consolidation of the state sector was the hard coal mining industry. The government tried to reduce as much as possible the number of mines threatened with liquidation as part of the restructuring of the mining industry. However, due to EU regulations, public aid could be directed only to the restructuring of the mines and not to keeping them alive. To bypass this restriction, the government expanded the practice developed by the predecessors: forming capital groups, where weak companies were kept by strong ones. This was done both in a capital way and through an obligation for power plants to purchase coal from the supported mines. In 2016, the Polish Mining Group (Polish acronym PGG—Polska Grupa Górnicza) was established, which took over the assets and liabilities of the state coal mining giant Kompania Węglowa (mentioned in Sect. 4.2.4 of this chapter) and later all mines of the bankrupt Katowice Coal Holding. The new group's shareholders were the largest energy companies which recapitalized it, and five banks, including two state-controlled ones, which bought out PGG bonds to cover the debt of the Kompania Węglowa. At the same time, Spółka Restrukturyzacji Kopalń (also mentioned in Sect. 4.2.4 of this chapter) which initially had to be in charge of closing down unprofitable mines took over non-productive assets of both Kompania Węglowa and the Katowice Coal Holding. As a result of these activities, only the non-productive assets of the mining industry had to be liquidated, while every effort had to be made to preserve the mines, as well as miners' privileges as yearly bonuses called 13th and 14th wages and bonuses in-kind.

Under the threat of declining demand for coal in the medium and long-term, rescuing the mining industry had to involve its artificial maintenance. First of all, through long-term contracts: state-controlled energy companies Energa and Enea decided to build a new block in Ostrołęka thermal power plant and signed a letter of intent with PGG to supply coal for 30–40 years (Energa 2016). Secondly, by hindering the transition to alternative energy sources, including renewables (RES). The issue of nuclear power plant construction was still in the initial phase, while the development of RES was de facto halted in 2016 by the enactment of the Wind Power Plant Investment Act, commonly known as the Distance Act. It made the development of wind energy practically impossible, radically tightening the requirements for the distance between wind turbines and buildings and increasing the tax burden on wind power plants several times. The act was aimed at limit competition on the electricity production market, preferring coal-based power generation and state entities.

The described actions had an ambivalent effect on companies controlled by the State Treasury. On the one hand, it allowed these entities to achieve a dominant position on the market and to certain extent increased their profitability (or at least limited losses). On the other hand, such attention at coal energy depleted the capabilities and financial results of better functioning energy generation companies and from time to time caused protests both in these companies and among non-state minority shareholders of listed companies. Directing a significant portion of investments not at development (or dividend), but at rescuing unprofitable members of the holding structures (as well as ensuring the sale of their production through its forced purchase by the group's profitable companies) violated the interests of minority private shareholders. As a side effect, there was a significant drop in the value of shares of these energy companies listed on the WSE.

Another adverse effect was triggering negative reactions from investors, primarily foreign ones, involved in RES, who announced that they would file suits for international arbitration (Business Insider Polska 2018). The lawsuits for billions of zlotys also were filed against state-controlled energy companies (Enea and Tauron), which began to withdraw from the agreements signed with foreign companies concerning the construction of wind power plants and the purchase of so-called green certificates, i.e., certificates of origin for electricity generated from renewable energy sources (Sudak 2017a, b).

All in all, the government's strategy of rescuing coal mines did not work well: the Polish coal was less and less attractive because of its high price (which in mid-2020 was two times higher than world market prices) caused by worsening conditions of extraction and high labor costs, as well as often its inferior quality. Even state-owned power plants did everything to avoid buying Polish coal, which boosted import (in 2015–2018 it increased more than twofold). Additional negative factor was decreasing demand on coal for electrical energy production because of exceptionally mild winters in the recent years. However, the coal mines did not reduce production and accumulated huge amounts of unsold coal. The government tried to resolve the crisis through unsuccessful attempts to restrict import of coal and ordering the state Material Reserves Agency to increase its strategic stock of coal, but the amount bought by the agency was too small to stop skidding the PGG into more and more severe losses which by the end of 2019 amounted to more than PLN 2 billion (over USD 500 million) (Grabowski 2020). At the same time Poland had to bear high costs under the EU Emissions Trading System, because about 75% of total electrical energy production in this country is still coal-based.

In these circumstances, the government had to resign from the plans to expand coal-based electrical energy production and in 2020 to revert to the plans of phasing out this sector—going beyond the previous plans of reducing labor costs and closing down the most unprofitable mines. The government decided to gradually phase out this sector. The first decision was to abandon the plans of building a new block fueled by coal in Ostrołęka power plant and to erect gas-fueled one instead—the costs of the demolition of the already built structures and building of a brand new power bloc are to be covered by state-controlled Energa and Enea, which had signed the initial contract. Besides, the government set the deadline for completion of hard coal production had been set at the end of 2049. Resignation from support for coal-based energy production met with the fierce resistance of the trade unions which claimed that the government was fully responsible for the crisis in coal mining, so it had to bear all the costs of keeping it alive (although in practice it would mean that these costs would be borne by the rest of the society). At the time the book was finished (March 2021), the government has not reached agreement with trade unions on the conditions and schedule of closing down the industry.

The consolidation of the state sector also included other branches: armaments (within the Polish Armaments Group) and fuel. In the case of the armaments sector, the tendency to push private entities out of the market and rescue bankrupt companies was particularly evident. A striking example was the policy towards the bankrupt bus manufacturer Autosan, which first was bought out by the armaments industry companies to save it. However, Autosan got into trouble again because it did not manage to send an offer for a tender for equipment for the army on time. The tender was canceled, and the next tender for the same order was won by Autosan which this time was not late (Mikołajewska 2017). In military procurement, state contractors began to be preferred, regardless of the fact that private contractors were able to provide better conditions for the execution of contracts (Dziennik Gazeta Prawna 2017). In the liquid fuels market, two largest companies (both controlled by the state) Orlen and Lotos merged in 2020.

Restricting competition in favor of companies directly or indirectly controlled by the state gradually included another strategic sector, the financial one. The "domestication" and, in fact, the nationalization of the banks still left a large margin for competition, but created a group of privileged banks, participating in financing government programs. Radical changes took place in the insurance market segment. The government firmly urged public entities, not only enterprises, but also local governments, to insure themselves in the Towarzystwo Ubezpieczeń Wzajemnych Polskiego Zakładu Ubezpieczeń Wzajemnych (Polish Mutual Insurance Company, Polish acronym TUW PZUW) established in 2015 by the state-controlled PZU insurance company. Joining the PZUW TUW was possible without a tender procedure. The official justification for the advantages of this solution was the reduction of insurance costs and better risk management (TUW PZUW 2020).

In 2020, the government announced and started realization of a large consolidation project in the agri-food sector based on the creation of the state-controlled Polish Food Holding which would include the whole chain from agricultural procurement to retail trade. The official objective is to serve both consumers and farmers: the former would enjoy attractive retail prices, the latter would receive generous payment for their products (WitualneMedia.pl 2020). The government plans to create state-controlled store chain through buying out the existing private retail chains which additionally would, as a government official put it, end the domination of foreign networks on the Polish market (Święcki 2020).

More and more often, according to the new paradigm, the state sector was used to implement the government's huge investment projects. One of such flagship projects was the aforementioned electromobility development program. In October 2016, ElectroMobility Poland was established, whose shareholders were four state-controlled energy companies: PGE, Energa, Enea and Tauron. It was supposed to implement the assumptions of the Strategy for Responsible Development, which aimed to produce one million electric cars by 2025.

Somewhat parallel to the governmental electromobility project, Lotos (which is a vertically integrated group of fuel companies previously having nothing in common with the electromobility or automotive branch) undertook to develop the so-called functional prototype of an electric car and concluded a cooperation agreement with Polish Post and the state television company. The latter two organizations were to purchase from Lotos electromobile products and services. Besides, Lotos developed a program of building fast charging stations. In turn, two other Treasury companies, Enea (energy) and Kolejowe Zakłady Łączności (railway telecommunications infrastructure) signed letters of intent concerning the production and distribution of chargers for electric cars. It is important to note that all these decisions were officially explained by business rationale, but they were outside most of these companies' specialization and were taken in the situation of rather moderate interest in such investments expressed by private investors, including foreign ones. Therefore, one can suspect that behind these projects some government's plans to increase the state participation in the electromobility branch could be hidden.

Even if the projects did not exclude the participation of the private sector, state-controlled companies were usually expected to play a leading role in them (e.g., being the core investor or the ordering party). For example, this pattern was used by the state-owned railroad carrier PKP Intercity, which, as part of the "Luxtorpeda 2.0" speed train project included in the "Strategy for Responsible Development," announced a program of the so-called innovation partnership (when the ordering party finances the development of a new product and guarantees the purchase of large batches of it if it meets the assumed requirements). The program was to support Polish railway stock producers; it is worth noting, that in this branch the state also expanded its corporate control through acquiring in 2018 one of the largest companies (Pesa).

4.3.3.3 Limiting Private Property Rights

Compared to the previous stages, the property-rights-restricting government intervention, mainly through regulatory pressure of the state on the private sector, has also been intensified.

As it was mentioned above, the PiS government took advantage of the Law on Control of Certain Investments passed by the previous coalition (see Sect. 4.2.4 in this chapter), blocking the change of owners in private energy companies, which led to their nationalization; the law also made possible to block selling the stake in Azoty Group. In 2020, new restrictions against acquisitions were introduced within the coronavirus pandemic crisis management package. They apply to all the smaller listed companies, i.e., whose sales in Poland has not exceeded the equivalent of EUR 10 million in any of the two previous financial years. The government openly admits that this measure has to block hostile takeovers by foreign capital. As Deputy Prime Minister Jadwiga Emilewicz put it, "Polish economy is not for sale" (Maciejasz 2020).

In 2016 the Ministry of Defense has prepared a draft law which would impose strict control on a wide range of companies "of particular economic and defensive importance" functioning in 15 widely defined areas (including transport and distribution companies, telecommunications services, mining, production and repair of motor vehicles, etc.) in imprecisely defined "conditions of external threat to the state and during the war." However, the parliament failed to process this draft law in time and the new parliament which has formed in autumn 2019 did not resume the works.

Restrictions on ownership rights of private entities did not necessarily mean direct state interventions or direct and indirect preferences for the state or enterprises controlled by it. It could also take the form of actions limiting competition in selected industries, blocking access of new entrants to the market. In April 2016, under the slogan of fighting against land concentration and protection and development of family farms, the trade of agricultural land was drastically restricted. It radically limited the categories of private buyers (to members of family, farmers and the church) and practically withheld selling agricultural land from state resources. However, the rules introduced had not very precise exceptions, which favored the discretionary decisions made by the authorities responsible for controlling the land trade.

In the summer of 2017, the Pharmaceutical Law was amended by introducing restrictions on the number of pharmacies (according to the criterion of their spatial density and population density) and the entities that may establish them (only pharmacists or businesses established by them). As of January 1, 2019, an amendment to the Act on the State Medical Rescue came into force which de facto liquidated the market for medical emergency services by prohibiting local governments from signing contracts with private entities. One should also mention the so-called Distance Law passed in May 2016 (discussed before), which limited competition on the energy market and de facto favored state-owned energy producers.

Other legal regulations restricting market access combined with a clear preference for state entities were also developed. These are the plans to restore the monopoly of the Polish Post for handling official correspondence (where this company already de facto restored its monopoly position) and to grant the status of National Printing House to the State

Security Printing House (this would give it a monopoly for official and security printing).

A potential threat of limiting private property rights was brought by the Supreme Court Act passed in December 2017. It introduced the so-called extraordinary complaint against valid court decisions that could be filed by selected public bodies (Prosecutor General, Ombudsman, General Prosecutor's Office, the Polish Financial Supervision Authority, antimonopoly and consumer protection agency, etc.). During the three-year transition period, i.e., till the end of 2021, decisions that became final after October 17, 1997, i.e., up to 20 years back, could be challenged. This raised concerns about the creation of a legal basis for challenging any judgment concerning economic transactions, including ownership ones.

Note

1. According to the Commercial Code, in Poland companies have the two-tier system of the boards: supervisory board and management board.

References

Arłukowicz, Bartosz. 2015. "Co mają na sumieniu odwołani ministrowie?" *Polityka*, June 11.

Bałtowski, Maciej, and Maciej Miszewski. 2007. *Transformacja gospodarcza w Polsce*. Warsaw: PWN.

Bałtowski, Maciej, and Piotr Kozarzewski. 2014. *Zmiana własnościowa polskiej gospodarki 1989–2013*. Warsaw: PWE.

Bałtowski, Maciej, and Piotr Kozarzewski. 2016. "Formal and Real Ownership Structure of the Polish Economy. State-owned Versus State-controlled Enterprises." *Post-Communist Economies* 28 (3): 405–419.

Bartuś, Zbigniew. 2015. Sprzedaż ZGH Bolesław. „Cena zaniżona, bo... to był jedyny dobry kupiec." *Dziennik Polski*, December 22.

Błaszczak, Anita. 2018. "Miotła hula na państwowym." *Rzeczpospolita*, November 13.

Błaszczak, Anita. 2019. "Prezesi państwowych spółek mogą odetchnąć. Karuzela wyhamowała." *Rzeczpospolita*, July 22. https://www.rp.pl/Biznes/307219938-Prezesi-panstwowych-spolek-moga-odetchnac-Karuzela-wyhamowala.html. Accessed September 1, 2020.

Błaszczyk, Barbara. 2017. "Zmiany w systemie instytucjonalnym polskiej gospodarki. Wypieranie własności prywatnej, rynku i konkurencji przez państwo w ramach dobrej zmiany." In *Perspektywy dla Polski. Polska gospodarka w latach*

2015–2017 na tle lat wcześniejszych i prognozy na przyszłość, 203–248. Warsaw: FOR.

Block, Fred. 1994. "The Roles of the State in the Economy." In *The Handbook in Economic Sociology*, edited by Neil J. Smelser and Richard Swedberg, 691–710. Princeton: Princeton University Press.

Bukowski, Maciej. 2016. *Blaski i cienie Strategii Odpowiedzialnego Rozwoju*, Warsaw: Instytut Obywatelski.

Business Insider Polska. 2018. "Wiatraki przestają się kręcić." *Business Insider Polska*, January 4. https://businessinsider.com.pl/wiadomosci/firmy-wiatrowe-beda-walczyc-o-odszkodowania/8x9dtcl. Accessed September 3, 2020.

Chancellery of the Prime Minister. 2016. *Rzadowy projekt ustawy o zasadach zarządzania mieniem państwowym*. Warsaw: Kancelaria Prezesa Rady Ministrów.

Chancellery of the Prime Minister. 2017. *Zasady nadzoru właścicielskiego nad spółkami z udziałem Skarbu Państwa*. Warsaw: Kancelaria Prezesa Rady Ministrów.

Chancellery of the Prime Minister. 2020. *Spółki z udziałem Skarbu Państwa*. https://www.gov.pl/web/nadzor-kprm/wykaz-spolek. Accessed August 31, 2020.

Council of Ministers. 2017. "Strategią na rzecz odpowiedzialnego rozwoju do roku 2020 (z perspektywą do 2030 r.)." *Monitor Polski* 260.

Ćwiklak, Dariusz. 2018. "Centralny Port Komunikacyjny im. Stanisława Barei." *Newsweek Polska*, June 8.

Deloitte. 2012. *Sponsoring – podstawowy instrument marketingu sportowego. Analiza rynku sponsoringu sportowego w Polsce z uwzględnieniem działalności spółek z udziałem Skarbu Państwa*. Warsaw: Deloitte.

Dobrzycka-Krahel, Aldona, and Jadwiga Kozakiewicz. 2011. "Przekop przez Mierzeję Wiślaną czy ingerencja w bioróżnorodność Zalewu Wiślanego?" *Journal of Ecology and Health* 15 (5): 211–218.

Do Rzeczy. 2017. "Morawiecki: Wolność rośnie siłą przedsiębiorczości, a przedsiębiorczość siłą wolności." *Do Rzeczy*, November 16.

Dziennik Gazeta Prawna. 2017. "Dwa lata dobrej zmiany: centralizm państwowy w praktyce." *Dziennik Gazeta Prawna*, October 31.

Economic Council. 2010. *Narodowy Program Nadzoru Właścicielskiego – nowy ład korporacyjny w spółkach Skarbu Państwa*. Warsaw: Rada Gospodarcza przy Prezesie Rady Ministrów.

Ekonomiści o zagrożeniach dla polskiej gospodarki. 2018. Conference transcript. Polish Economic Society, Warsaw, April 24. http://www.pte.pl/pliki/2/1/autoryzowany_stenogram_24_kwietnia_2018.pdf. Accessed August 14, 2020.

Energa. 2016. *Energa zawarła z Eneą i PGG porozumienia przybliżające realizację Ostrołęki C*. https://media.energa.pl/pr/326908/energa-zaw

arla-z-enea-i-pgg-porozumienia-przyblizajace-realizacje-ostroleki-c. Accessed September 3, 2020.

Ferraro, Vincent. 2008. "Dependency Theory: An Introduction." In *The Development Economics Reader*, edited by Giorgio Secondi, 58–64. London: Routledge.

Figura, Magdalena. 2020. "Przekop Mierzei Wiślanej zniszczy jedyny w swoim rodzaju fragment Polski." https://www.onet.pl/biznes/biznesalert/przekop-mierzei-wislanej-zniszczy-jedyny-w-swoim-rodzaju-fragment-polski/4rmh9wr,30bc1058. Accessed August 18, 2020.

Frączyk, Jacek. 2019. "Rosjanie mogą zablokować inwestycję Azotów na półtora roku." *Money.pl*, November 15. https://www.money.pl/gielda/rosjanie-moga-zablokowac-inwestycje-azotow-na-poltora-roku-ogromny-cios-w-kluczowy-projekt-6446394761172609a.html. Accessed September 4, 2020.

Gomulka, Stanisław. 1993. The Financial Situation of Polish Enterprises 1992–1993 and Its Impact on Monetary and Fiscal Policies. Studies and Analyses 6, CASE—Center for Social and Economic Research, Warsaw.

Grabowski, Paweł. 2020. "Restrukturyzacja Polskiej Grupy Górniczej to jedyny ratunek dla górnictwa." https://bezprawnik.pl/restrukturyzacja-polskiej-grupy-gorniczej/. Accessed September 3, 2020.

Graniszewska, Magdalena. 2016. "Państwo wchodzi do gry o EDF." *Puls Biznesu*, September 15.

Gray, Cheryl W., and Arnold Holle. 1996. Bank-led Restructuring in Poland: An Empirical Look at the Bank Conciliation Process. Policy Research Working Paper 1650, The World Bank, Washington.

Grochal, Renata. 2013. "Minister skarbu czyści spółki z partyjnych kolegów." *Gazeta Wyborcza*, March 3.

Jóźwik, Tomasz. 2017a. "Tańsze bilety na kadrową karuzelę." *Dziennik Gazeta Prawna*, June 21.

Jóźwik, Tomasz. 2017b. "Rosjanie wywieszają białą flagę w sprawie Azotów." *Dziennik.pl*, April 5. https://gospodarka.dziennik.pl/news/artykuly/546742,acron-azoty-akcje-rosja-rosjanie-polska-firma-chemiczna-gospodarka-wiaczeslaw-kantor.html. Accessed September 4, 2010.

Kacprzak, Izabela. 2017. "Państwo już nie dusi dywidendami." *Rzeczpospolita*, October 10.

Kacprzak, Izabela. 2018. "Powyborcze tsunami kadrowe." *Rzeczpospolita*, April 6.

Kaczmarczyk, Marcin. 2017. "Transakcja za miliard euro? Polska Grupa Energetyczna kupuje elektrociepłownie od Francuzów." *Gazeta.pl Next*, May 11. https://next.gazeta.pl/next/7,151003,21798406,transakcja-za-miliard-euro-polska-grupa-energetyczna-kupuje.html. Accessed September 4, 2020.

Kawalec, Stefan. 2015. „Udomowienie banków uniezależni je od zagranicznych central." *Gazeta Prawna*, March 1.

Kochanowicz, Jacek, Piotr Kozarzewski, and Richard Woodward. 2005. Understanding Reform: The Case of Poland. CASE Reports 59, CASE—Center for Social and Economic Research, Warsaw.
Kondzińska, Agata, and Iwona Szpala. 2018. "Polska fundacja swoich." *Gazeta Wyborcza*, April 9.
Kopińska, Grażyna. 2018. *Stanowiska publiczne jako łup polityczny. Polityka personalna w okresie od 16 listopada 2015 do 31 października 2017 roku*, Warsaw: Fundacja im. Stefana Batorego.
Kośmiński, Paweł. 2020. "Gliński: Tam, gdzie to możliwe, państwowe spółki powinny kupować media." *Gazeta Wyborcza*, October 13.
Kozarzewski, Piotr. 2017. "Fiscalization of Ownership Policy of the Polish State During the Post-Communist Transition." *Annales Universitatis Mariae Curie-Skłodowska, Sectio H—Oeconomia* LI (4): 173–181.
Kozarzewski, Piotr. 2019. *Polityka właścicielska państwa w okresie transformacji systemowej. Próba syntezy*. Lublin: Wydawnictwo Uniwersytetu Marii Curie-Skłodowskiej.
Krześnicki, Jakub. 2017. "Nowa ustawa kominowa w akcji. Na co mogą liczyć zarządy spółek Skarbu Państwa?" *Bankier.pl*, August 8. https://www.bankier.pl/wiadomosc/Nowa-ustawa-kominowa-w-akcji-Na-co-moga-liczyc-zarzady-spolek-Skarbu-Panstwa-7536626.html. Accessed September 1, 2020.
Kublik, Andrzej. 2015. "Minister skarbu rozdaje awanse last minute." *Gazeta Wyborcza*, June 18.
Kwaśniak, Wojciech. 2010. "Państwo w bankach – sądy wzajemnie sprzeczne." *Obserwator Finansowy*, October 6.
Łaszek, Aleksander, Rafał Trzeciakowski, and Karolina Wąsowska. 2016. *Władza w ręce urzędników, czyli rozwój według planu M. Morawieckiego*, Warsaw: Forum Obywatelskiego Rozwoju.
Maciejasz, Dominika. 2020. "Emilewicz o wrogich przejęciach: Polska gospodarka nie jest na sprzedaż." *Gazeta Wyborcza*, June 8.
Mazzucato, Mariana. 2013. *The Entrepreneurial State: Debunking Public vs. Private Sector Myths*. London: Anthem Press.
Mejer, Jakub. 2017. „731 proc. wzrostu zysku ma wydawca Gazety Polskiej Codziennie." https://www.press.pl/tresc/50016,731-proc_-wzrostu-zysku-ma-wydawca-_gazety-polskiej-codziennie_. Accessed August 19, 2020.
Mikołajewska, Katarzyna. 2017. "Autosan wygrał przetarg na dostawę 28 autobusów dla Sił Zbrojnych RP." *Money.pl*, November 16. https://www.money.pl/gospodarka/wiadomosci/artykul/autosan-sily-zbrojne-rp-kontrakt-na-autobusy,237,0,2389997.html. Accessed September 3, 2020.
Miłosz, Maciej. 2018. "Stu szefów na stulecie niepodległości." *Dziennik Gazeta Prawna*, October 30.

Ministry of the Treasury. 2002. *Informacja o sytuacji w wybranych spółkach Skarbu państwa i przedsiębiorstwach państwowych—Raport otwarcia*. Warszaw: Ministerstwo Skarbu Państwa.

Ministry of the Treasury. 2004. *Zasady nadzoru właścicielskiego nad spółkami z udziałem Skarbu Państwa oraz innymi państwowymi osobami prawnymi*. Warsaw: Ministerstwo Skarbu Państwa.

Ministry of the Treasury. 2005. *Zasady nadzoru właścicielskiego nad spółkami z udziałem Skarbu Państwa oraz innymi państwowymi osobami prawnymi*. Warsaw: Ministerstwo Skarbu Państwa.

Ministry of the Treasury. 2013. *Zasady nadzoru właścicielskiego nad spółkami z udziałem Skarbu Państwa*. Warsaw: Ministerstw https://www.gov.pl/web/aktywa-panstwowe/spolki-objete-nadzorem-wlascicielskim-ministra-aktywow-panstwowycho Skarbu Państwa.

Miszewski, Maciej. 2012. *Polska transformacja gospodarcza i jej uwarunkowania*. Katowice: UE w Katowicach.

Money.pl. 2020. "Sasin: Dywidendy spółek Skarbu Państwa nie powinny ograniczać inwestycji." *Money.pl*, February 24. https://www.money.pl/gielda/sasin-dywidendy-spolek-skarbu-panstwa-nie-powinny-ograniczac-inwestycji-6482087876782209a.html. Accessed August 19, 2020.

Newsweek Polska. 2018. "Polska Fundacja Narodowa nie odpowiada na pytania." *Newsweek Polska*, April 9.

Newsweek Polska. 2019. "Ustawa o jawności życia publicznego mogła zaszkodzić interesom PiS?" *Newsweek Polska*, February 1. https://www.newsweek.pl/polska/polityka/ustawa-o-jawnosci-zycia-publicznego-mogla-zaszkodzic-interesom-pis-projekt-wstrzymano/437ysyn. Accessed September 1, 2020.

OECD. 2005a. *Guidelines on Corporate Governance of State-owned Enterprises*. Paris: OECD Publishing.

OECD. 2005b. *Corporate Governance of State-owned Enterprises: A Survey of OECD Countries*. Paris: OECD Publishing.

Ojczyk, Jolanta. 2018. "Projekt ustawy o jawności życia publicznego poszerza defi nicję osoby pełniącej funkcje publiczne." *Rzeczpospolita*, January 31.

PAP. 2020. Sasin: spółki Skarbu Państwa to duży polski kapitał, rząd będzie je wspierał i konsolidował, PAP Polish Press Agency, June 13. https://www.pap.pl/aktualnosci/news%2C661905%2Csasin-spolki-skarbu-panstwa-duzy-polski-kapital-rzad-bedzie-je-wspieral-i. Accessed March 12, 2021.

Polish Financial Supervision Authority. 2018. *Raport o sytuacji banków w 2017 r.* Warsaw: Urząd Komisji Nadzoru Finansowego.

Polish Financial Supervision Authority. 2020. *Informacja na temat sytuacji sektora bankowego*. Warsaw: Urząd Komisji Nadzoru Finansowego.

Polski Ład. 2021. http://polskilad.pis.org.pl/files/Polski_Lad.pdf. Accessed August 3, 2021.

Polskie Radio 24. 2020. "Ukłon w stronę Berlina." https://polskieradio24.pl/130/5925/Artykul/2523654,Uklon-w-strone-Berlina-Samuel-Pereira-o-sprzeciwie-Rafala-Trzaskowskiego-wobec-CPK. Accessed August 18, 2020.

PwC. 2017. *Zmiany w wynagradzaniu menedżerów wg nowej ustawy kominowej.* https://www.pwc.pl/pl/artykuly/2017/nowa-ustawa-kominowa-zmiany.html. Accessed September 1, 2010.

Radecki-Mikulicz, Konrad. 2016. "Ośmiornica Macierewicza. Setka nowych osób w spółkach Polskiej Grupy Zbrojeniowej." *OKO.press*, October 1. https://oko.press/osmiornica-macierewicza-setka-nowych-osob-zarzadach-spolkach-polskiej-grupy-zbrojeniowej/. Accessed August 31, 2020.

Rogojsz, Łukasz. 2018. "Walka o Mazowsze." *Gazeta Wyborcza*, November 16. http://wiadomosci.gazeta.pl/wiadomosci/7,114884,24174968,walka-o-mazowsze-kolega-radny-mial-klopoty-pis-przyszlo-z.html. Accessed August 31, 2020.

Roguski, Adam. 2018. "Chaos przy obsadzaniu władz firm z udziałem Skarbu Państwa." *Rzeczpospolita*, April 6.

RPO. 2018. Opinia RPO w sprawie projektu ustawy o jawności życia publicznego, Rzecznik Praw Obywatelskich, January 23. https://www.rpo.gov.pl/pl/content/opinia-rpo-w-sprawieprojektu-ustawy-o-jawnosci-zycia-publicznego. Accessed November 1, 2018.

Rzeczpospolita. 2016. "Jackiewicz: wygaszamy proces prywatyzacji." *Rzeczpospolita*, February 26.

Rzeczpospolita. 2018. "Kaczyński: Jest decyzja. Do polityki nie idzie się dla pieniędzy." *Rzeczpospolita* July 6.

Rzeczpospolita. 2019. „Lista 500 (Edycja 19)." *Rzeczpospolita*, April 26.

Rzeczpospolita. 2020. "Duda: Mamy kolejną odsłonę niemieckiego ataku w tych wyborach." *Rezczpospolita*, July 3.

Sadurski, Konrad. 2017. "CPK? Ludzie, trzeba się opamiętać. Podatnicy zapłacą dwa razy za Centralny Port Komunikacyjny." *Dziennik.pl*, December 21. https://wiadomosci.dziennik.pl/opinie/artykuly/565147,cpk-podatnicy-zaplaca-dwa-razy-za-centralny-port-komunikacyjny.html. Accessed August 18, 2020.

Senderski, Marcin. 2015. "Inhibited Privatization: A Hurdle Race over Vested Interests." *European Journal of Government and Economics* 4 (1): 46–66.

Sudak, Ireneusz. 2016. "Tworzy się Polska Fundacja Narodowa. 100 mln zł na promocję Polski" *Gazeta Wyborcza*, November 18.

Sudak, Ireneusz. 2017a. "Amerykańska firma składa pozew przeciwko Tauronowi, spółce skarbu państwa." *Gazeta Wyborcza*, July 3.

Sudak, Ireneusz. 2017b. "Energa nie czeka na sąd i przestaje płacić za zieloną energię." *Gazeta Wyborcza*, September 12.

Supreme Audit Office. 2003. *Informacja o wynikach kontroli w podmiotach gospodarczych opisanych w rządowym Raporcie otwarcia z 7 maja 2002 r*. Warsaw: Najwyższa Izba Kontroli.

Supreme Audit Office. 2015a. *Realizacja programu "Inwestycje Polskie". Informacja o wynikach kontroli*. Warsaw: Najwyższa Izba Kontroli.

Supreme Audit Office. 2015b. *Prywatyzacja wybranych spółek Skarbu Państwa. Informacja o wynikach kontroli*, Warsaw: Najwyższa Izba Kontroli.

Supreme Audit Office. 2018a. *Wydatki spółek z udziałem Skarbu Państwa na działalność sponsoringową, medialną i usługi doradcze. Lata 2015–2017 (I połowa)*. Warsaw: Najwyższa Izba Kontroli.

Supreme Audit Office. 2018b. *Nadzór nad spółkami z udziałem Skarbu Państwa. Informacja o wynikach kontroli*. Warsaw: Najwyższa Izba Kontroli.

Święcki, Radosław. 2020. "Utworzenie państwowej sieci sklepów. Rząd powinien zrobić ten krok?" *Biznes.info*, June 6. https://www.biznesinfo.pl/siec-sklepow-060620-pm-rzad. Accessed September 8, 2020.

Świerczyński, Marek. 2019. "PiS się poddaje, Sasin zabiera zbrojeniówkę z MON." *Polityka*, December 7.

Szarzec, Katarzyna, Bartosz Totleben, and Dawid Piątek. 2020. "How Do Politicians Capture a State? Evidence from State-owned Enterprises." *East European Politics and Societies*. https://journals.sagepub.com/doi/10.1177/0888325420953485. Accessed 22 September 2020.

Szymański, Damian. 2020. "Spółek Skarbu Państwa jest więcej, niż się wydaje." *Business Insider*, January 17. https://businessinsider.com.pl/firmy/spolki-skarbu-panstwa-w-polsce-ile-ich-jest-jak-wygladaja-ich-finanse-opinia-dot/7m9szef. Accessed August 31, 2020.

Tokarz, Dawid. 2012. "Lista wstydu Platformy Obywatelskiej." *Puls Biznesu*, November 5.

Tokarz, Dawid. 2017. "Teraz k... my. Na całego!" *Puls Biznesu*, January 16.

Tusk, Donald. 2007. "Tekst expose premiera Donalda Tuska." *Rzeczpospolita*, November 23.

TUW PZUW. 2020. "Kim jesteśmy?" https://www.tuwpzuw.pl/. Accessed 3 September 2020.

Wallerstein, Immanuel. 1974. *The Modern World-System I: Capitalist Agriculture and the Origins of the European World-Economy in the Sixteenth Century*. New York: Academic Press.

WitualneMedia.pl. 2020. "Rząd tworzy Rządowy Holding Spożywczy." *WitualneMedia.pl*, July 21. https://www.wirtualnemedia.pl/artykul/rzad-tworzy-polski-holding-spozywczy. Accessed September 8, 2020.

Wojtyna, Andrzej. 2016. "Czy gospodarka przetrwa plan Morawieckiego." *Rzeczpospolita*, December 5.

Wojtyna, Andrzej. 2018. "Czy premier wygasza plan Morawieckiego." *Rzeczpospolita*, February 11.

Woźniak, Adam. 2019. „Przekop Mierzei Wiślanej może okazać się transportowym fiaskiem." *Rrzeczpospolita*, February 18. https://www.rp.pl/Transport-morski/302189913-Przekop-Mierzei-Wislanej-moze-okazac-sie-transportowym-fiaskiem.html. Accessed August 18, 2020.

wPolityce.pl. 2017. "Minister Kowalczyk: Rząd PiS nie będzie prywatyzować firm państwowych." *wPolityce.pl*, February 4. https://wpolityce.pl/polityka/326195-minister-kowalczyk-rzad-pis-nie-bedzie-prywatyzowac-firm-panstwowych-zamiast-sprzedawac-zaklady-bedzie-odbudowywal-majatek. Accessed September 4, 2020.

Wroński, Paweł. 2018. "Anna Morawiecka przegrała, ale może rządzić. PiS urządza trzecią rundę wyborów?" *Gazeta Wyborcza*, November 16.

CHAPTER 5

State Corporate Control in Polish Transition: Main Outcomes

5.1 Introductory Remarks

Attempts to assess the effects of the state corporate control policy meet a lot of challenges. From the methodological perspective, apart from the obvious problems with studying ongoing processes, a problem of the criteria of the evaluation arises. The complex nature and multidimensionality of the issue under consideration, its impact on the basic spheres of functioning of the state and the society does not allow to choose one simple criterion, a universal indicator. This implies the need to use to some complicated ideal model describing what corporate control policy of the state (and the whole ownership policy) was supposed to achieve and a set of indicators describing its particular aspects. There are serious doubts as to whether such a universal model can exist because of both the varieties of capitalism being built, as well as the variety of tools that could be used. It may mean that researchers rather would built their point of references based on their personal views of what features an ideal target model should have and, accordingly, what the state policy should look like. Moreover, the corporate control policy of the state is a part of a high controversial subject of ownership policy of the state in transition and its impact on the country's development. The range of privatization impact assessments is particularly wide: from apologetics to blaming privatization for an alleged national disaster. But the range of conflicting views on the state corporate control also shows the whole possible spectrum from the

P. Kozarzewski, *State Corporate Control in Transition*,
https://doi.org/10.1007/978-3-030-78562-8_5

preaching of the state's fundamental inability to be an effective owner to the belief that only the state-owned enterprise sector can be a refuge of a stable, resilient economic system.

In order to at least partly eliminate the ideological bias in the assessment, the dual approach will be used in this chapter. On the one hand, the effectiveness of the state corporate control policy in transition will be assessed in the sense of the ability of the government to realize the goals it has set which is discussed in Sect. 5.2 of this chapter. On the other hand, the analysis would not be complete without assessing the outcomes in comparison with an idealized set of goals described in Sect. 3.3.1. However, one must be very cautious because the real economic policy, including the ownership policy, is limited by a multitude of economic, political, institutional, epistemic, etc. factors, so the question remains whether the quality of this policy and the ability of effective goal setting and their pursuing really were, realistically speaking, far from optimal in the given circumstances. This issue will be further discussed in Chapter 7 devoted to the experience of other selected transition countries which presented different approaches to the policy of state corporate control. Of course, the theoretically feasible range of ways of shaping and implementing the state corporate control policy in transition is not limited by those which really existed, but such an approach seems to be more secure, protecting against the tendency to build models that do not have sufficient support in reality.

Another obstacle is the necessity to separate the effects of the state corporate control policy from the whole range of factors shaping the social and economic reality such as other directions of the state policy, and multiple external factors that were beyond the government's control.

Last but not least, a serious practical obstacle exists which is deficiency of the data. There are large gaps even in quantitative data concerning the state's involvement in the enterprise sector, especially at the enterprise level (on finances, employment, and ownership) which will be discussed in detail in Sect. 5.3 of this chapter. The data characterizing the qualitative dimension of the state corporate control is even more difficult to access, and the methodological correctness of their creation often arouses great controversy. There is a lack of complete information about the state policy objectives and ways of their implementation (including their variability over time).

Despite all these obstacles, I believe that at least certain tentative conclusions can be made being one more step towards understanding the issues in question.

5.2 Achieving the Goals of State Corporate Control

It is not an easy task to juxtapose the goals of the corporate policy of the Polish state with the results achieved. One of the main difficulties lies in the necessity to reconstruct these goals and their evolution over the analyzed period. As already mentioned before, they have never been formulated in a comprehensive manner; what is more, for a significant part of the transition, they were not formulated by the authors of the economic policy at all. The goals of the state corporate control, albeit in a very general and fragmented way, started to be openly put forward only after the PiS coalition came to power in late 2015. Besides, unlike privatization (and later crawling nationalization) was the focus of interest of politicians, journalists and researchers through all these years, which provided additional information for further research, until recently the state corporate control was not a popular topic in these circles, except several sporadic boosts of public attention caused by scandals evoked by the controversial nominations on the SOEs' boards. So the possibilities to cover the information gaps were limited, especially before PiS came to power in 2015. After that, the increasing number of controversial decisions regarding SOEs (and general statization of the economic policy) helped to attract journalists' and researchers' attention towards the state corporate control and had a beneficial effect on gathering information in this area.

Besides, the real sets of goals and their mutual hierarchy, deductible from observations, were constantly modified, until the fundamental change of priorities, which started during the second term of the PO-PSL term (2011–2015) and obtained their final, so far, shape after the PiS coalition came to power. In the second decade of twenty-first century, some of the goals were not realized because they were simply abandoned. For this reason, it is impossible to adopt unambiguous criteria for the realization of state corporate control policy goals.

5.2.1 *Achieving the Goals of the System Area*

As it was mentioned in Sect. 3.3.1, this area covers goals of structural and regulatory kind: making the private sector dominant and moving away from the command economy principles in favor of the state being in charge of shaping the general conditions of economic activity. Both these sets of goals were indeed present in the ownership policy of the state, the first one being realized mainly through privatization and the second one being predominantly the subject of the policy of the state corporate control. These areas were interrelated, as regulatory changes could not be effectively implemented without the structural reform; on the other hand, structural de-statization of the economy was not possible without the willingness of the state to resign from "manual control" of the most part of the enterprise sector.

The assessment of the degree of achievement of the structural goals usually is based on the quantitative data which depicts the progress of privatization in the broad sense, i.e., including the creation of new private enterprises. In this respect, the progress in Poland has been very large: the economy with a predominance of state ownership has been transformed into an economy, where the vast majority of enterprises are controlled by private capital. By mid-2010s, in the sector of non-financial enterprises, the state share (even taking into account hidden and indirect forms of state corporate control) fell to 15–16% measure by employment or contribution to the country's GDP (Bałtowski and Kozarzewski 2016). At the beginning of the new century, the government (Ministry of the Treasury 2003, p. 7) sets an objective to achieve a 10–20% share of state ownership which would allegedly equal to the level of the state involvement in the "old" European Union countries (EU-15). So, formally, the structural goal set by the government was achieved. However, in practice, the situation did not look so unambiguous.

Even if we stick to purely quantitative criteria, the structural change does not seem to be complete. The Ministry of the Treasury overestimated the then state sector's share in highly developed economies: in the EU-15 countries, already at the turn of the century (at that time this indicator was counted for the last time for all EU countries) it amounted at 8.5% on average (CEEP 2000). Since then, numerous privatization transactions have been carried out in most of the EU-15 countries and, for example, in France, which is known for its relatively (comparing to most other developed economies) high degree of statism in economic policy, the discussed share (measured by value added) fell from about 25% in 1985 to about 5.5% in 2008 and stays roughly at the same level since then (INSEE 2019, p. 151). Also measured by the valuation of SOE sector relative to GDP, which is imperfect (Christiansen 2011), but for which data is available, the size of the state sector in Poland in the middle of the second decade of the twenty-first century was one of the highest in the region (15.7%), including most of the transition countries of Central and Eastern Europe. According to the European Bank for Reconstruction and Development (EBRD Database 2020), only small privatization has been fully completed in Poland, and the progress of large privatization was, together with Latvia, among the weakest. The state share in GDP was one of the highest, higher than in the Czech Republic, Slovakia, Hungary, and Estonia.

According to Bałtowski and Kwiatkowski (2018, p. 316), however, the formal scope of state ownership in Poland can be considered to be "within the upper limits of the standards of highly developed European countries." The problem, in their opinion, was that the scope of the hidden state control (when formally private companies are in fact largely controlled by the government) very significantly exceeded these norms creating multiple negative consequences which will be discussed later.

Quantity wise, the limiting of the state control over enterprises, was also quite heterogeneous in different sectors and enterprise groups according to their size, which will be discussed in detail in Sect. 5.3 of this chapter. The highest concentration of SOEs was observed in the group of the largest companies. At the end of 2019, exactly the half of the 20 largest (in terms of sales) non-financial enterprises formally or de facto was controlled by the state; these companies accounted for 63.2% of revenues and 57.8% of total employment in this group. In this respect Poland also stood out from other market economies. According to OECD estimates (Kowalski et al. 2013), in the countries belonging to this organization, among the companies listed in Forbes' list of 2000 largest companies in the world, a greater share of state-controlled companies than in Poland (12.5% of total sales) was observed only in Norway (25.0%). In the remaining OECD countries, it was a one-digit value, the highest in France: 7.9%.

The share of the state in the ownership differs very much across the sectors and branches of the economy, being low in trade, construction, accommodation, and catering, as well as in manufacturing. At the same time, the state, according to official data which is often underestimated (because they do not take into account indirect state control), controls about half or even more (measured by gross output or employment) of mining, energy supply and companies which provide water supply, sewerage and waste management. Measuring by the gross value of fixed assets, this differentiation in even much more pronounced, especially in water supply, sewerage and waste management, where in 2018, the state (mostly the local authorities) controlled as much as 92.6% of the assets (Central Statistical Office 2019). Although in developed economies in this branch, the share of public ownership is usually quite high as well, as it helps local governments to perform their duties towards the population, in Poland, it has become a source of dysfunctions caused by a conflict between their regulatory and entrepreneurial functions of the public authorities: these companies to a large extent have just captured the local market and enjoy protection from the private sector's competition (Office of Competition and Consumer Protection 2011).

What is more, as a result of the statist turn in the economic policy, the recent years show slight but measurable growing share of state ownership in industry as a whole and in all its main sectors but mining and quarrying (the latter may be explained not by withdrawal of the state, but just by steep decline in coal mining performance) and activities controlled by local governments. The highest growth rates in both in gross output and gross value of fixed assets can be seen in electricity and gas supply which reflects the policy of nationalization of thermal power plants.

The size of the state-owned sector and its dynamics are discussed in detail further in this chapter.

The analysis of the quantitative results of the change in the ownership structure of the economy does not give a full answer to the question to what degree the systemic goals of state corporate control reform have been achieved. The question is whether the scope of state corporate control became close to optimal—both in the government's perception of what should be the state's functions in the enterprise sector and from the researcher's point of view.

In Sect. 3.2.3, arguments were presented in favor of a minimalistic approach to the participation of the state sector in the economy. According to them, enterprises should remain in the hands of the state only in justified cases. However, the experience of developed market economies shows that no one common pattern exists in this respect: the extent of state ownership is very different both in the share of SOEs in the economy in general, and in specific sectors where SOEs play important role. Nevertheless, there are some common regularities: the government first of all usually controls large and very large enterprises of great importance for the economy (since it makes no sense to control a company of little economic importance), belonging to energy sources extraction and/or, to a greater or lesser extent, infrastructure sectors.

At first glance, the situation in Poland is similar. The more detailed look at the involvement of the Polish state in specific sectors shows, however, that in many cases, it is difficult to find analogies with developed market economies or any rational justification for the state to retain some enterprises or even control over whole branches. It is especially hard to do especially nowadays, after the radical paradigm shift on the role of the state in the economy performed by the PiS government. The idea of what kind of goods and resources the state sector is supposed to produce has expanded rapidly, unparalleled in developed countries. As a result, the state still keeps in its hands a number of enterprises (and even acquires new ones) due to reasons other than the need to overcome market failures, produce socially important goods or speed up economic growth.

The additional (compared to the minimalist approach) functions of the state domain in Poland can be divided into three not entirely separable categories because functions of a SOE may overlap. Firstly, this is saving companies from bankruptcy and closing down. There is an increasing number of rescue investments (in the form of buying out or just keeping enterprises alive through direct and indirect financial support) of the state in industries or even single enterprises, which from the social and economic point of view are not of key importance and in most developed countries are in the private domain and have no chances to enjoy state support. These are, for example, coal mines or companies producing buses and rail vehicles. The need to keep them alive raises controversy. From fiscal reasons, there seems to be no sound justification, for example, to keep state control over the Polish mining sector, a significant part of which devours more resources than it produces (and their product can be easily get elsewhere, often of better quality and/or for lower price), often being a burden for other SOEs which are ordered to help them to survive. Thus, the reasons for rescue investments are not always clear; in the case of the mining sector, it may be predominantly the social goal of keeping the workplaces. In the case of manufacturing enterprises and some other objects, such as highly unprofitable airport in Radom bought out from the local government, it's a part of the new development policy based on state assets and investments. At the same time, paradoxically, in Poland, unlike in many developed market economies, there were no short-term state rescue investments as a way to counteract the global economic crisis.

Secondly, the state did not fully resign from, inherited from the command economy, forcing SOEs to perform social functions such as providing employment for the population. What is more, there are signs that social functions of SOEs were in some respect even extended, the government delegating realization of some elements of social policy to SOEs which are forced to sponsor cultural, sports and other events.

Thirdly, since 2016, the SOEs perform political function of supporting the political class through, i.e., financing the "politically friendly" media and government's propaganda projects described in Sect. 4.3. This function is closely interleaved with the fourth function of the SOE sector which is being the source of rents for a number of private interest groups, which is discussed in detail in Sect. 6.1.

Last but not least, there is a peculiar function of preserving "national silver," i.e., enterprises whose *raison d'être* to stay in the public sector (or to return to it, such as the cable car to Kasprowy Wierzch) was mainly that it was a shame for them to belong to an "alien" (especially since 2016, when foreign capital started to be perceived as fundamentally unfavorable for the national interest of Poland, and there was no national capital that would want to take over these enterprises).

The microeconomic dimension of the regulatory goals included radical change of corporate governance objectives, principles, and tools in the state-controlled enterprise sector, including overcoming the situation of a very weak control of the government over its property "inherited" from the reforms of the last decade of the communist rule. Here, the successes were the most modest. Reforms of state corporate control never included all the SOEs, but only corporatized ones. Even at the time, this book was finished (spring 2021), about 50 uncorporatized SOEs still existed and were not the subject of the general corporate laws. But in corporatized SOEs, where the state formally got the necessary corporate governance tools, it failed using them in an effective way, first of all in the sense making SOEs perform their special functions in the economy and serve the interests of the whole society, and not private interest groups. The problem of inferior microeconomic efficiency of SOEs was also more often than not far from being resolved (which is discussed further in this chapter).

Under the new paradigm pursued by PiS, the problem of low state corporate control effectiveness became more important because of the expanded role of SOEs in the economy. But the PiS government failed to improve it and even caused its deterioration because of, among others, trying to make SOEs to perform often mutually contradictory functions and making the whole sector more prone to rent-seeking.

Looking at the meeting of the systemic goals from the government's perspective, the outcome is quite ambiguous. First of all, it results from changing plans and expectations of the government. As it was discussed in Sect. 4.2, before the mid-2010s paradigm turn, the state-owned sector was perceived in line with more or less minimalistic approach, although this attitude gradually deteriorated through the years. From this perspective, for the most part of the Phase One (1989–2015), the existing SOEs sector was perceived like being still too big; by the end of the PO-PSL coalition rule, when statist trends became more and more visible, privatization was effectively stopped in 2015, but in the official discourse, no declarations existed that some part of the economy was to be returned to the state hands. So right before the statist turn, the realization of the structural goal was, from the policymakers' perspective, apparently quite close to be achieved. According to the new narration introduced by PiS politicians (see Sect. 4.3), previous de-statization structural changes were an overkill and the growing engagement of the state as an owner and investor in the previous period was still inadequate to meet its extended tasks in the economy.

Quite similar picture can be seen in the regulatory dimension of the systemic set of goals. The governments before the mid-2010s statist turn, while gradually increasing the regulatory burden on the enterprise sector, never tried to restore deep interference in its functioning. The PiS government found the scope and tools of exerting the impact on the economy, which were "inherited" from the predecessors, to be highly insufficient and proclaimed the state the main vehicle of the Poland's economic development and expanded functions of SOEs. So far, the level meeting new goals and objectives presents a mixed picture. The state sector indeed started to expand and the overall level of state interventionism increased. But meeting specific objectives clearly lags behind. None of the great investment and innovation projects, especially those envisaged in the "Strategy for responsible development," are being realized according to initial plans and assumptions; many of them are not implemented at all. Many of the additional functions imposed on SOEs do not work well either. Rescue investments proved to be much less effective and, for example, in coal mining, the government reverted to the idea of further downsizing of this sector and eventually closing it down, thus resigning from saving the mines at all costs, including through keeping coal as the main source of energy production at the indefinite perspective. Thus, the social function of SOEs was undermined as well. Preservation of the "national silver," especially in terms of returning previously sold assets to the motherland, also has mixed results, not all the plans being realized. On the other hand, SOEs proved to be a reliable source of financial resources for supporting the social policy, the political elite and a number of interest groups (see more in Sect. 6.1).

Finally, the microeconomic dimension of the regulatory goals was perceived as rather unsuccessful not only by many researchers, including the author of this book, but also by decision-makers themselves. Through the whole analyzed period, the government failed in almost every attempt to create efficient state corporate control mechanisms. The policymakers and members of the government in charge of ownership functions of the state were increasingly aware of that, and kept trying to introduce regulations that would streamline the corporate governance of SOEs. Before the statist turn of mid-2010s, this problem was often regarded as of a rather minor importance, as the state sector was seen as generally vanishing. The situation has radically changed after the PiS coalition came to power in late 2015, and the new government started to treat the issue of effectiveness of the state corporate control more seriously, as inadequate performance of SOEs would undermine the new statist development strategy. So far, the increased efforts of regulatory, organizational, and law-enforcement kind ended with failure, of which the government seems to be aware, because it keeps trying to address the problem.

5.2.2 *Achieving the Economic Goals*

As it was discussed in Sect. 3.3.1, the economic goals consisted of two parts: micro and macro. At the micro level, the goal was to radically improve the effectiveness of enterprises and generally their ability to shape effective market strategies. It applied also to SOEs, even if the hierarchy of their goals and objectives did not put microeconomic effectiveness at the first place. At the macro level, the main goal was to contribute the corporate policy to fast, stable and sustainable economic development.

It is difficult to express a reasoned assessment of the achievement of the goals in this area due to various reasons. Firstly, these are methodological difficulties in determining the role of state corporate control policy in improving the functioning of enterprises and the whole economy against the impact of other factors, such as progress in economic liberalization and stabilization, the changes of economic situation in the country, and the selection bias introduced by the "constructivist" ownership policy of the state which used numerous criteria of directing an enterprise on the privatization path or keeping it under the state control. One of which quite often was its performance (and in practice it could affected the decisions both ways: promoting privatization or creating incentives to keep it sate-owned). Another obstacle is the problem of separating state and private ownership described in Sect. 3.2.4.

Secondly, the extended objectives of state-owned enterprises and the fact that their value and profitability could not be a top priority, meant a sophisticated impact of SOEs on the economy, going far beyond the simple mechanisms typical for private enterprises where value creation, paying taxes, hiring workforce, and introducing innovations in order to be competitive somewhat "automatically" contributed to economic development.

Thirdly, almost through the whole transition period in Poland the economic effects of state corporate control were practically outside the field of view of researchers. Only recently, because of increasing statism in the economic policy and more active playing by the state the role of owner and investor, these topics begin enjoying greater interest. Is must be admitted, however, that this was not the unique fault of those who studied Poland; the same can be said about studies on virtually all the post-communist countries.

So far, studies on the micro- and macroeconomic effects of state corporate control, both in Poland and in other post-communist countries, have focused mainly on forms of corporate control, largely ignoring their impact on the functioning of enterprises. A thorough review of these studies can be found in an article by Grosman et al. (2016). Microeconomic research conducted so far, on the other hand, has focused mainly on the effects of privatization and not on the state's corporate control, so the financial results of SOEs have only served as a benchmark for research on the progress of privatization. Therefore, it was assumed (most often tacitly) that financial indicators are the most important in the activity of a state-owned enterprise.

Such studies usually showed that while the improvement in the economic condition of privatized enterprises was of a long-term nature, there were strong fluctuations in the state sector, and periods of good financial results were largely caused by external factors (favorable changes in the economic situation, favorable state policy, etc.), or came from the dominant market position of SOEs which often allowed them to achieve higher profitability than private companies (Bałtowski and Kozarzewski 2014, pp. 378–379; Szarzec and Nowara 2017). The instability of the of SOEs was also manifested in the above-average volatility of their stock exchange listings, especially after 2015, both over time and between companies of different industries (Rudke 2018). One of the typical situations was falling capitalization of power companies involved in rescue investments in coal mines because they undermine the trust of the market. Such actions have caused understandable concern for private investors in power companies (a phenomenon that has already been noted during the second term of the PO-PSL government).

Research on the functioning of the SOE sector in the post-communist countries that joined the EU (Pula 2017), as well as studies analyzing these issues on a global scale (Tihanyi et al. 2019) prove that the situation in Poland was quite typical for many reasons. A significant part of the largest SOEs in CEE countries functioned relatively well and was able to face market competition. The majority of these prosperous SOEs remained in the hands of the state for strategic reasons, while in these countries, there was no oligarchization of the economies. However, SOEs often turn out to be in a privileged institutional environment comparing to private companies, which makes it easier for them to achieve good financial results (Estrin et al. 2019). At the same time, most of these companies have lower profitability, especially those which operate on markets with lower prices thus pursuing some social goals (Matuszak and Kabaciński 2019), and lower returns on capital and investments than in the private sector (Böwer 2017). The latter seems to reflect the fact many SOEs, having a kind of umbrella over them that shields them from many market rigors (either state support or simply a dominant position on the market), can invest relatively much without special care for the efficiency of these investments. The material result of such investments may be significant in the form of, e.g., construction of large facilities, but their costs are often unacceptable for the private sector. Besides, there are a lot of completely missed investments, such as made by the Polish SOEs abroad (Frączyk 2016).

A study of financial performance of SOEs must be complemented with an analysis of the implementation of a specific set of "extended" objectives which generally do not exist in private companies. This is a difficult task, and it is more feasible in the case of individual enterprises than when trying to assess the functioning of the whole SOE sector. In the latter case, it may even be impossible to do so on a wider scale due to the multiplicity and often vagueness of objectives, their variability and problems with selecting measurable criteria for evaluating their achievement. At most, certain hypotheses and assumptions can be formulated. It is also impossible to limit the analysis to effects at the micro level, because many goals of state-owned enterprises assume obtaining results at the macro level.

Even the PiS government, which conducted statist policy, had formulated the objectives of the SOE sector in too general and fragmented a way (as shown in Sect. 4.3). In order to systematize the observed and presumed objectives of SOEs imposed by the government's corporate control policy, one can refer to the "ideal models" of functions of state-owned enterprises described in Sect. 3.3.4 Mühlenkamp's (2015) "welfare approach," i.e., correction of market imperfections, can be found in the functioning of state-owned enterprises in Poland because, as official statistics show, public sector enterprises generally reach cost and productivity levels slightly better than private enterprises (Mühlenkamp rejects profitability indicators, as in his opinion, profit maximization cannot be a goal of a state-owned enterprise within this approach). However, it must be remembered that Mühlenkamp applied his principles of the analysis to developed market economies, where SOEs are subject to market rigors and state protectionism towards them, enterprises are generally kept in check. In Poland (and other post-communist countries), many state-owned enterprises, especially the largest ones, are in a privileged position compared to other market players.

Mühlenkamp's second perspective, the "public choice approach," is a very broad category that goes beyond the micro- and macroeconomic effects of state corporate control. Besides, Mühlenkamp did not use it in his empirical research. Generally speaking, this approach is about any use of state-owned enterprises for non-economic purposes. Here, we can use the classification of objectives of SOEs developed by PwC (2015) from the perspective of resources, a SOE is expected to deliver (discussed in Sect. 3.3.4). Most of them seem to be present in the corporate control policy of the Polish state. In all these areas, however, it is impossible to say whether the achievement of the objectives of SOEs was close to optimal. The goal of producing public goods and socially important private goods was pursued indeed. However, perhaps the state sector "appropriated" this function too much, as it might have been more efficient to delegate part of it to the private sector (e.g., in defense industry, some parts infrastructure, etc.). What is more, by the end of the 2010s, the dominance of the state sector in these areas increased. The goal of limiting the influence of private and foreign investors was more and more evident in Poland's economic policy, especially since mid-2010s; again, one can have doubts about its effects at the micro level (as to the efficiency of the state investor) and macro level (whether state investments, and not private and foreign ones, managed to become the main factor of development).

It is too early to assess the results of the goal of stimulating the development of the national economy with the help of SOEs and state investments; such a development model had both supporters and sceptics. The former counted above all on the state's great mobilization potential (like in the inter-war period in Poland or in contemporary China), among other things, eliminating the possible dangers of basing development solely on private capital, especially foreign one. Although such an approach is popular in public discourse, there are no significant publications based on the Polish realities; its supporters still refer to the world literature. The latter group, skeptics, has concerns about the abilities of SOEs to boost economic development because of inherent dysfunctionalities of its corporate governance. SOEs more often than other companies exhibit dysfunctions of politicization: earlier it was the omnipotence of managers and trade unions; later control over them was taken over by politicians of parties winning parliamentary elections (Senderski 2015; Kozarzewski 2016).

The most recent studies on corporate governance in Polish SOEs (Postuła 2013; Postuła and Wąsowska 2018) show an even wider range of dysfunctions in this area. Most of them seem to be of an immanent nature, as they are the result of the specific position of these companies vis-à-vis public administration and the specific set of objectives to be pursued by the state sector. The former has created sophisticated and contradictory mechanisms of corporate governance with a complex structure of stakeholders and agency relations, as well as collision of different forms of supervision and control over the company. This resulted, among other things, in the primacy of supervision of government officers over supervision by the company boards. Together with the lack of a clear legal basis, this led to both a lack of due consideration of the real needs of these companies and insufficient achievement by the companies of the objectives resulting from their state-owned status. The bureaucrats and members of the SOEs boards even had no precise idea of what these objectives could be. For example, realization of public interest was understood mainly from the fiscal perspective, i.e., to supply the state budget with company's profits—and accordingly, the company's main goal was perceived as profit generation. The second perceived goal was job creation, although, as the research shows, generally the implementation of socially important tasks was rarely considered a priority by all parties involved in SOEs' supervision. Similarly, the need to implement a government's policy towards SOEs was considered a relatively rare priority (Postuła 2013, pp. 110, 120–121).

Interestingly enough, a very similar set of dysfunctions was described as far back as in the 1980s and concerned SOEs in developed market economies (Aharoni 1986), despite much better institutional conditions than in post-communist countries. It can therefore be argued that in Poland, under unchanging or deteriorating institutional conditions, chances for SOEs to effectively fulfil their economic function are generally speaking rather slim. In such a case, the realization of the influence of the state's corporate control on the achievement of economic goals at the macro level is also questionable.

The experience of other post-communist countries seems to confirm these concerns. None of them managed to ensure sustainable economic development (or even simply economic growth) based on the state sector. Relatively, the greatest successes of statist stimulation of economic growth have been achieved by countries rich in a particular type of natural energy resources, such as oil and natural gas, by investing in their extraction and export. Nevertheless, this growth was neither stable nor sustainable. In terms of the level of social and economic development, these countries still lag behind the CEE countries, which based their development strategies primarily on the development of the private sector, including foreign-owned.

Research by the International Monetary Fund (Böwer 2017) shows that the extensive state sector in post-communist countries poses a threat at a sectoral and macroeconomic level. It jeopardizes the stability of public finances and the financial sector (through the creation of debt and sub-optimal activity of state banks). It also creates a threat to the productivity of the business sector and economic growth through the spillover effect as negative externalities of the state-owned enterprise sector functioning. The expansion of the state sector taking over key positions in new sectors of the economy are also detrimental to the development of the private sector, as it limits its field of activity (Radygin et al. 2015).

So far, the studies that would confirm of falsify these considerations using statistical methods are extremely rare and there are no studies devoted specifically to Poland. The study by Szarzec et al. (2020) on European economies provides ambiguous results showing that the impact of SOEs on the economic growth to a large extent depends on the institutional setup in a given country.

5.2.3 *Achieving the Fiscal Goals*

The fiscal goals of state corporate control were aimed at the improvement of public finances in both expenditure and income dimensions.

Within the **expenditure** dimension, it meant a reduction of the SOEs' burden on the state budget by shrinking this sector due to privatization and increasing the efficiency of the functioning of the remaining SOEs so it would mean few resources spent on keeping them alive. From the very beginning of the transition, measures have been taken in many directions, including introducing equal rights for all forms of ownership and eliminating subsidies (at least officially) for state-owned enterprises. It was a painful experience for SOEs and raised popular accusations against the government in the early 1990s that it had left its property to the mercy of fate. Despite this, during the first years of transition, there were no anticipated mass bankruptcies of SOEs, although many of them had to reduce their activity and get rid of excessive assets.

However, there is no confident answer to the question whether the SOEs really managed to adapt to the emerging market environment, or some form of public support was also helpful. It is not possible to accurately calculate the size and dynamics of state spending on supporting SOEs due to the variety of forms of support and their often not entirely transparent nature. According to the EBRD's estimates (EBRD Database 2020), in the first half of the 1990s, the value of public aid (direct and indirect) for the entire enterprise sector in Poland in relation to GDP fell twofold: from 5 to 2.5%, and then stabilized at about the same level. The data of the Office of Competition and Consumer Protection (2002–2019), which since 2001 has separated public aid for the public sector of enterprises (with a 100% or majority share of the central or local governments), shows that the value of its official forms was usually not high and in most years did not exceed 0.5% of GDP. After overcoming the effects of the global crisis, it stabilized at a level of about 0.35% of GDP.

Through all these years, the SOEs enjoyed relatively higher preferences than the private sector: their share in the public funds was higher than their share in the economy (however measured: share in GDP, value added, employment, etc.). According to the latest available data (for 2018), it amounted to 35.8% of the total amount of public aid (Office of Competition and Consumer Protection 2019), which is a typical value for the recent years (before 2015 it usually did not exceed 30%) and was at least twice as much as the share of the public enterprise sector in the economy. Moreover, the largest beneficiaries of the aid almost without exception in the entire period 2001–2018 were large state-owned companies, mainly from the infrastructure and mining sectors.

However, this level of public support for SOEs seems to be underestimated for two reasons. Firstly, because of the underestimation of size of the state-controlled enterprise sector (discussed in more detail in Sect. 5.3 of this chapter). According to Matuszak et al. (2020), who identified companies with indirect state control and added minority controlled enterprises to their study (as most of them are de facto still controlled by the government), the real share of state-controlled enterprises in the public aid in 2010–2015 was much higher, between 38.5 and 61.5%. In 2015, the companies with majority state ownership alone received as high as 58% of aid funds. The authors of the study conclude that state-controlled companies enjoy preferential treatment both as being more likely (52–68%) to receive state aid than private enterprises, and in the amount of resources received by a state-controlled company (on average 11–22% more than a private enterprise).

Secondly, apart from official public aid, there were also unofficial, hidden, and indirect forms. These included, among others, "rescue investments" which support SOEs by other SOEs and governmental agencies, as well as preferential treatment of selected SOEs in public procurement tenders. The value of such forms of hidden support has not yet been estimated.

There are arguments which justify the disproportionally big share of public aid received by the SOEs because of important social functions they perform. But as anecdotal evidence show, this was not always the case, and the SOEs may often just have stronger bargaining power than private firms or being granted with resources to achieve political goals. The scale of this "unjust" public support for SOEs is unknown, but nevertheless it may be argued that the goal of lifting from the state the unnecessary financial burden of supporting the state-owned enterprise sector has not been fully achieved.

Almost through the whole 1990s, the government did not treat its ownership policy as a source of fiscal **income**. Even in its privatization policy, where selling large amounts of state assets promised substantial budget revenues, it was of secondary importance, let alone SOEs where boosting any income from this sector (either through taxes or dividends) was not on the agenda at all. It was not until the end of the 1990s, that privatization revenues became one of the basic priorities of privatization policy. They began to be treated as an important source of financing for specific tasks of the government, including the social security reform, especially the pension reform, where privatization proceeds were to finance its pay-as-you-go pillar. This was one of the reasons why the government started privatizing companies with a very high market value, which resulted in a sharp increase in privatization revenues and a record of 2000 (PLN 27.2 billion, about USD 6.3 billion) could never be repeated, even in nominal terms.

The government started exploring the remaining SOEs as a source of budget revenues only later, in mid-2000s, when the global recession of early 2000s and anti-privatization policy of the ruling coalitions (both claiming themselves as left- and right-wing) led to dramatically falling proceeds from privatization up to pathetic PLN 600 million in 2006 (about USD 190 million) which was only 11% of the plan. As it was already mentioned in Sect. 4.2, since 2005, the government boosted dividend and para-dividend payments from SOEs, and since 2006 started to plan them. Gradually, it became the main source, and then practically the only one, that the state obtained on its property. The statist change in the paradigm of economic policy, apart from stopping privatization and renouncing its revenues, led to the policy of letting SOEs keep most of their profits to themselves, cutting dividend payments by a half since 2017 and planning the next almost six-fold cuts in 2020. However, this does not mean a proportional weakening of financial pressure on SOEs: they started being used more widely as a source of financing for government projects: formal and informal, including those of the ruling party, from taking part in megalomaniac projects through rescue investments to financing political propaganda projects of the PiS coalition. At the same time, the government rather did not treat taxes paid by SOEs as a valuable source of income (perhaps at least partly because in Poland CIT is generally a marginal source of budget revenues).

The exact value of this extra burden is still to be estimated which is not an easy task because many such schemes have a quite hidden nature, e.g., such as forcing SOEs to subscribe to "politically friendly" media or putting there their advertisements. But it may be guessed that still the total burden imposed by the government on the SOEs decreased.

The question arises to what extent this source of revenue has actually been successful in meeting budget needs. Only a partial answer can be given. Speaking about dividends and para-dividends, formally, the situation looked quite favorable: in 2006–2019, starting from the first year when these proceeds for the state owner started being planned, the target amount was not met only in five years, including two years where the amount of dividends collected was very close to the plan (97.5% in 2012 and 99.4% in 2017). The unweighted average of the plan fulfilment was 120.9%. On the other hand, the proceeds from dividends and para-dividends were not big and never exceeded 2.75% of the central budget revenues and 0.58% of GDP. Averagely, in 2006–2019, they amounted to 1.28% of budget revenues and 0.29% of GDP. In 2016–2019, under the new statist paradigm, the average share of dividends in central government revenues fell to 0.65% and to 0.14% of GDP.

From the perspective of the fiscal income goals of the whole ownership policy of the state, this level of revenues was highly inadequate; at most it could affect to some extent the level of the budget deficit. Besides, the government treated these proceeds (as well as privatization revenues) from a short time perspective, focusing on the current situation of public finances. Thus nothing was done to prevent one of the major failures, which was the inability to finance the pension reform (especially in the situation of falling privatization revenues) which eventually led to its erosion and effectively termination. This meant that not only the fiscal target, but also one of the main social goals of the state ownership policy was not achieved.

Turning to using SOEs for financing various projects, the outcome is quite mixed here as well. Rescue investments of different kind, from buying out insolvent enterprises to creation of capital groups where "rich" partners provide resources to "poor" ones, so far indeed more often than not saved falling, unprofitable companies from liquidation. At the same time, these transactions mostly failed to provide these firms with effective tools to improve their situation in a long run, create foundations for boosting their profitability and competitiveness. It is especially obvious in the case of the coal mining sector, among others because of unwillingness of the "poor" to be restructured and the reluctant attitude of the "rich" to play charity at the expense of their development prospects. So the coal mining sector's decaying was only being prolonged. The PiS government faced the necessity to eventually close this sector down because political gains of keeping it alive fade in the face of growing financial and international reputational costs.

Use of the state's resources for financing developmental and political projects, on the one hand, allowed the PiS government to raise substantial funds for propaganda projects and support for the "politically friendly" media. The latter, being on the periphery of the media market before, got an enormous financial support which allowed them to increase their budgets several times. It was much worse with financing development projects, among others because a substantial part of their resources was redirected to achieving political objectives, the evolution of the Polish National Foundation being one of the most striking examples (see Sect. 4.3). Another problem was forcing SOEs to finance unfeasible projects, such as the flagship investment project promoted by the PiS government—building the huge coal unit in Ostrołęka power plant. The terminated project generated about PLN 1.5 billion (about USD 400 million) of losses for the two SOEs involved (Frączyk 2020).

In this context, it should be also mentioned that extensive using resources of large profitable SOEs on meeting the fiscal needs of the state posed a threat for development prospects of these companies and their ability to realize objectives other than generating public funds. Many listed SOEs also faced decreasing value on the financial market which, among others, violated interests of private shareholders.

At the end of the analysis of the achieving of fiscal goals, it is worth noting that in the future, their role may increase again. Before the outbreak of the coronavirus lockdown, the government's finances continued to look rather favorable, the budget deficit and public debt remaining at a safe level despite implementation of the ambitious and very costly programs within the PiS coalition's social and economic policy. It was possible because of the favorable situation in the global economy and good condition of the Polish economy, with quite efficient regulations, "inherited" by the PiS coalition. Sooner or later both these positive factors would start depleting, which could be accelerated by the coronavirus crisis, i.e., both the effects of slowing the economy by the lockdown and crisis management measures which are extremely costly for the public finances. In the situation of growing problems with maintaining the fiscal balance, it may be expected that even such a statist-oriented government would be forced to use the old recipe of using SOEs as an "emergency" source of budget revenues—by increasing drainage of their profits or even re-launching their privatization.

5.2.4 *Achieving the Social Goals*

Within the overall ownership policy of the state, the realization of social goals took place mainly through the policy of corporate control over SOEs; within the privatization policy, their role was basically only to support ownership change and the achievement of other goals of the post-communist transition. The policy of state corporate control was much more "predestined" to pursuing social goals because, as it was mentioned in Sect. 3.3.4, most of the objectives of state-owned enterprises carry a certain social element. Besides, the government had much more tools to steer SOEs in order to achieve social effects, than within its privatization policy and policy towards private enterprises.

In Poland, the social dimension of the state corporate policy mostly covered the protection of selected groups of employees from the negative effects of market mechanisms. This was particularly true for the most vulnerable industries, such as mining and shipbuilding, when successive governments tried to keep alive enterprises that would have been liquidated without the public support. At the beginning of the transition, such support mainly took the form of various kinds of soft budget constraints, abstention from privatization of these enterprises or entire industries, as well as abandoning the demonopolization of certain sectors. In the twenty-first century, new forms of support emerged and began to spread, such as recapitalizing "too important to fail" companies and providing them with markets. This was primarily due to the creation of mining and energy concerns in which profitable energy companies supported unprofitable mines with capital and through purchasing their production, as well as the change of the government's energy policy after 2015, which, contrary to global trends and Poland's climate commitments, limited the use of RES in favor of coal-based energy.

To what extent have such social goals, implemented within the framework of the state corporate policy, been achieved? In the short term they have as the government manages stopping the bankruptcy of enterprises or preventing a very large reduction of their activity. However, the implementation of "protective" social measures led to numerous negative side-effects, both economic and non-economic (slowing down of restructuring, burdening both enterprises and society as a whole with costs, promoting egoistic behavior among social groups which enjoy support, etc.). And, as it was discussed before, the protective effects of such measures quite often do not go beyond the short- to medium-term perspective, as they failed to improve long-term viability of these enterprises and even the whole industries, such as mining.

Social goals the state corporate control were closely linked to other objectives, both of corporate control and economic policy as a whole, often being not so much objectives in themselves, but rather as a tool for achieving other objectives or being their by-product. For example, they helped to achieve political objectives of obtaining the favor of certain social groups (not only employees of the enterprises in question, but also other interest groups, primarily industry-related) pursued by successive governments both on their own initiative and under pressure from these groups (which is discussed in detail in Sect. 6.1). After the PiS coalition took power in 2015, the meeting of social goals of the state corporate control became a part of the new policy of increased state interventionism.

5.2.5 *Achieving the Political Goals*

As it was mentioned in Sect. 3.3.1, these goals could be basically of two kinds: de-politicization of the economy and creating a social and political base of the new system.

At the macro level, the main vehicle of the de-politicization of the economy were changes of ownership structure of the economy towards making the private sector dominant and leaving the state ownership only in the areas where it was necessary to realize public interests. In other words, here the level of meeting the de-politicization goal was to a large extent provided by achieving the structural systemic goal. From this perspective, the "structural" de-politicization of the corporate sector in Poland is far from complete, and in the recent years, we witness even signs of its re-politicization through the expansion of the state control over enterprises.

The situation is aggravated by the fact that there was no comprehensive reform of the state corporate control which would create effective mechanisms of making SOEs serve public interests. After the initial successes in counteracting the legacy of the late years of the command economy in Poland, especially limiting the role of the ministries which exercised the function of the "founding bodies" towards SOEs (see Sect. 3.1.2), the role of various special interest groups which exerted pressure on the public authorities (including the parliament and the government) to achieve their private goals quickly began to grow. These were, for example, industry interest groups that opposed the deep restructuring and privatization of "their" enterprises and the introduction of general rules of the game for the entire economy, including the SOEs sector, which would threaten their historically privileged position. Already in the mid-1990s, SOEs began to be treated as a political asset by political parties which won the elections (and were interested in the seats on SOEs boards) and by the government agencies in charge of the state corporate control (which distributed these seats and thus increased their political weight in the eyes of the ruling coalition and among the rest of the state bodies). From the beginning of the 2000s, the politicization of the functions of state-owned enterprises made a step further, as they began to be increasingly treated as a political tool by the government and politicians for centralization of power of the state over the enterprise sector and consolidating the power of the currently ruling parties over SOEs, which led, among other things, to the politicization of the civil service (Mazur et al. 2018). It can be argued that the state sector has become one of the main sources of rents for various interest groups, contributing to the creation of a broad peculiar anti-reform coalition..

In its turn, this means that the erroneous corporate control policy of the state which was to a large extent captured by interest groups contributed to very ambiguous outcome in attempts to create a broad pro-reform coalition which would exert strong pressure on the government helping it to continue reforms and restrain the anti-reform activity through limiting the political influence of interest groups associated with the previous regime and its institutions. The discussion on the extent of successes and failures in creation of the social and political base of the transition, as well as their sources, lies beyond the thematic scope of this book. It should be only briefly noted that, on the one hand, a class of private owners has been indeed created which became a political force in the sense that it generally proved to be able to ensure the functioning of their businesses independently of the political turmoil that has been going on for three decades in Poland. The success or failure of private economic activity depended mainly on the adopted market strategies and market situation, and not on the connections with the government and/or political parties. It is worth noting that due to the creation of quite sound political institutions, including political competition, no class of oligarchs, i.e., large entrepreneurs influencing the economic policy of the state, has ever emerged in this country.

On the other hand, the class of private owners proved to be not strong enough to become the main driving force behind the continuation of reforms and to prevent first crawling and after 2015—open statization of the economic policy. The reasons behind this (Kozarzewski 2019, pp. 276–278) may lay, firstly, in the fact that a majority of large businesses were in the foreign hands and their ability to influence the policy of the Polish state through democratic mechanisms were limited. Secondly, as the research conducted at the beginning of the 2010s shows (Gardawski 2013), local businessmen preferred a market-based but nevertheless paternalistic socio-economic model with the state being the owner of strategic assets and the main vehicle of economic modernization. I.e., something which later was proposed by the PiS coalition; although, ironically, despite all the patriotic rhetoric, the coalition does not treat Polish entrepreneurs as its major political base, counting on the support of interest groups gathered around SOEs instead as well as the population which does not conduct economic activity.

5.3 The Place of the SOE Sector in the Polish Economy

The SOE sector can be portrayed using different approaches, from purely quantitative to those which use more qualitative criteria. In the analysis presented below, three dimensions are used:

- the scale of the SOE sector in absolute (which depict its size) and relative values (which show the share of SOEs in the whole Polish enterprise sector);
- the extent of the SOE sector, i.e., how far the state (still) controls sectors and branches of the economy, because average values for the whole economy do not take into account uneven distribution of

the state control across sectors and branches of the economy; areas where the state ownership is extremely extensive or very limited may exist;

- the importance of the SOE sector is a more qualitative category than the previous ones, which is still based on quantitative data; it shows the share of SOEs among the most important companies in the country.

Estimation of the real scale, extent, and importance of the state-controlled enterprise sector in the Polish economy is the task which is both very important and hard to complete. The importance derives from the need to assess the real role of the state ownership in this country, especially against the claims that during the post-communist transition, it was reduced to the optimal level or even the process of de-statization of the enterprise sector went too far.

Studies on the SOE sector using these dimensions are difficult because of a number of methodological and practical problems. The former is related to setting a formal border between enterprises which are controlled and not controlled by the government. The existing approaches to solving this problem which go beyond the formal majority and/or just using ownership categories presented in official statistics, usually try to identify two additional groups of cases. Firstly, these are enterprises where minority stake in the hands of the government still gives it full control rights. For this purpose, some formal threshold is set by the researchers, such as just 25% of shares (Bałtowski and Kozarzewski 2016) or 25% of shares provided that the rest of shareholders are small and dispersed (Matuszak and Szarzec 2019). Also situations when the government, regardless its minority stake (sometimes really small) secured preserving control over an enterprise trough provisions it its statute, should be taken into account. However, the issue of "border" cases remains unresolved, when the state control is contextual and depends, e.g., on the character of decisions taken by general assembly or the boards.

Secondly, these are cases when the government controls an enterprise indirectly, through other state-controlled enterprises, or through state funds or other state-controlled agencies. The Polish government in its official documents usually does not treat such enterprises as state-owned which makes no sense from the state corporate control perspective, because all directly and indirectly government-controlled companies are a subject of the Act of December 16, 2016, on the Principles of State Property Management. How far misleading the government's documents may be, can be shown on the example of Polish Mining Group (PGG—Polska Grupa Górnicza) in which according to the Prime Minister Office, the government possesses only one share out of 39,167,182 (0.000003%). In reality, the state fully controls the PGG because it has the majority of votes in all the shareholders of the PGG. What is more, the whole ownership control over them is concentrated in the hands of one governmental agency: the Ministry of State Assets (Table 5.1).

The Central Statistical Office (2019, p. 30) has a more sensible definition of public sector which covers enterprises directly and indirectly controlled by the central government and local governments with the threshold of 50% of shares. It allows including many enterprises disregarded in the government's sources, although still does not take into account situations where the government has minority, but still

Table 5.1 Capital structure of the Polish Mining Group (PGG—Polska Grupa Górnicza) in 2020

Shareholder	*% of shares*	*Level of control over the shareholder by the government*
PGNiG Termika S.A	20.43	Member of the PGNiG group where the government (Ministry of State Assets) has 71.88% of shares
Węglokoks S.A	18.30	100% of shares (Ministry of State Assets)
PGE GiEK S.A	15.32	Member of the PGE group, where the government (Ministry of State Assets) has 57.39% of shares
Energa Kogeneracja Sp. z o.o	15.32	Fully controlled by PKN Orlen where the government (Ministry of State Assets) has 27.57% of shares, but de facto has the majority of votes
TF Silesia Sp. z o.o	15.32	100% of shares (Ministry of State Assets)
Polish Development Fund (Polski Fundusz Rozwoju)	7.66	99.39% of shares (Ministry of State Assets)
Enea S.A	7.66	51.5% of shares (Ministry of State Assets)
Ministry of State Assets	0.000003	–

Source Chancellery of the Prime Minister (2020), companies' websites, own calculations controlling block of shares. Besides, no Polish agency takes into account ownership control exerted by foreign state-owned entities. All such cases are presented as just foreign ownership and it is tacitly assumed that there is no difference between private and public FDIs. The latter does not pose an important problem in Poland though, as shown later in this section.

Thirdly, it's accessibility and quality of the data. The Central Statistical Office data covers only enterprises with at least 10 employees. The rest, which does not keep full accounting records, is treated separately as a business activity of natural persons. It can be assumed that these microenterprises almost fully belong to the private sector. Their economic significance is not small at all. In 2018, almost 4.2 million persons worked in these enterprises (24.6% of the economically active population); they obtained 26.2% of total revenues (Central Statistical Office 2019, 2020).

The quite reasonable definition of the public sector elaborated by the Central Statistical office is not followed by its consistent implementation. The data published by this office is of limited usability because since 2013, it did not provide information on the identity of public owner (whether it is the central or a local government). And even when it did, it often omitted the category of mixed public–private ownership with a predominance of public capital; what is worse, there was usually no information on what exactly was meant by public sector enterprises. The extensive and hard work over identifying all the enterprises which are effectively state-owned is still not complete (only the largest enterprises have been thoroughly studied from this perspective so far), so there is still no possibility to portray the SOE sector in Poland in full.

The Central Statistical Office data is also inconsistent for a part of industry: since 2009, in line with the amended Polish Classification of Business Activities (PKD), the agency no longer uses the "electricity, gas and water supply" category replacing it with two: "electricity, gas, steam and air conditioning supply" and "water supply; sewerage, waste management and remediation activities." On the one hand, it made impossible to compare new data with that of the pre-2009 period; on the other hand, it is easier to distinguish between the central government and local governments ownership, because the category "electricity, gas, steam and air conditioning supply" includes energy enterprises controlled mostly by the central government, whereas "water supply; sewerage, waste management and remediation activities" category consists predominantly of enterprises owned by municipalities.

All this leads both to underestimation and over-estimation of the state-controlled enterprise sector with a quite substantial amount of unreliable data. Unfortunately, no other data is currently available for the whole enterprise sector in Poland. Therefore, in the next two sections (devoted to the scale and the extent of the SOE sector), only data of the Central Statistical Office is used. Despite its incomplete and sometimes inconsistent character, some conclusions can still be drawn, especially on the dynamics of the state ownership control. In the section devoted to the importance of the SOE sector, an attempt is made to assess the real role of the state in the enterprise sector making a closer look at the largest enterprises and the scope of the government's ownership control over them using the specially collected, revised and much more reliable data than those provided by the governmental sources.

5.3.1 The Scale of the SOE Sector

Formally, the de-statization of the enterprise sector in Poland during the transition has made a huge progress. At the beginning of the reforms, there were 8453 state-owned enterprises; since then, mainly due to privatization (but also to liquidation of insolvent entities, all in all there were about 1200 such cases), their number was radically reduced. Almost all SOEs have been corporatized; in 2019, only 55 uncorporatized enterprises left which still are the subject of the 1981 act in state-owned enterprises. Officially, according to the data provided by the Chancellery of the Prime Minister (2020), on June 30, 2020, the government possessed shares in 349 enterprises, including 254 active ones, i.e., not being shut down or under insolvency procedures. In 150 enterprises (43.0% of the whole set), the government possessed the majority, including 128 companies in which it had supermajority (more than 75% of shares) or was their 100% owner (sole shareholder companies of the Treasury, JSSP). The government was a minority owner with the blocking rights (between 25% plus one share and 50% of shares) in 61 companies (17.5% of the set), and formally was a "speechless" minority shareholder in as many as 138 enterprises (39.5%), including 31 companies, where it had less than 1% of shares.

Due to the reasons explained above, this number of state-controlled enterprises (211, if we set the threshold at 25%, given the fact that in almost all the cases of shareholdings within the 25–50% range, the government is the biggest investor so in fact it has the rights of the majority investor) is underestimated. According to an expert from Business Center Club business association (Szymański 2020), it is impossible to know the exact number of companies with the state participation, but in reality, in 2020, there was over 700 of them, mostly with the majority stake in the hands of the government, but in about 100 companies, the state share was below 10%. If we assume that the ownership structure of the whole set of companies with the government participation is similar to that of provided by the Prime Minister Office, one can assess the total number of SOEs at about 470 (which includes 55 uncorporatized firms).

To make the picture of the public enterprise sector complete, one should also mention over 4000 companies which belong to local governments or were they possess the controlling stake (both set up by local authorities and transferred from the central government through the "communalization" process). The exact number of these companies is also unknown, as the Central Statistical Office in this case does not provide any information on public ownership identity. It can be estimated by deducting the number of companies controlled by the central government from the total number of enterprises of the public sector provided by the Central Statistical Office (4839 in 2019). However, these enterprises, despite numerous, are usually small and their economic significance is not big at the whole economy's scale. In 2012, their share in gross output was 5.8%. Meanwhile, their share in gross value of fixed assets was much higher (19.8%, a half of all the assets of the public sector), mainly because local governments possessed a huge amount of infrastructure objects.

According to the Central Statistical Office, the share of the whole public sector in gross value of fixed assets was gradually contracting from 59.7% in 1995 (there is no data for the early years of the transition) to about 40% in the second half of the 2000s and since then has stabilized at this quite high level (Fig. 5.1). The share of public industrial enterprises was declining longer: from 80.2% in 1995 to 27.1% in 2013. Later, reflecting the growing statist trends in the economic policy, it started increasing and reached 28.6% in 2018. Relatively, high share of the state in gross value of fixed assets is explained by the fact that the central government keeps control of many very large enterprises with high value of assets which will be discussed further in this chapter.

It is not surprising that the public sector share in gross output was lower than that in the value of assets, as SOEs did not have achieving the highest return on investment among their top priorities. In 1995,

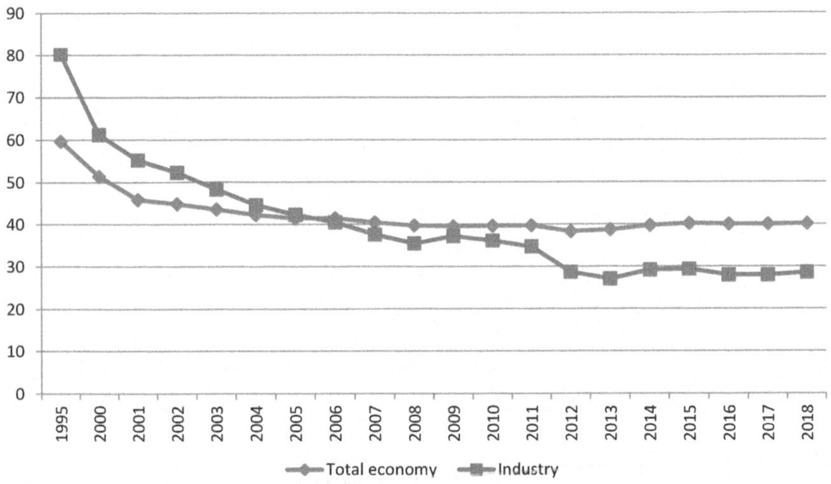

Fig. 5.1 SOEs' share in gross value of fixed assets (in %) (*Source* Central Statistical Office data, own calculations)

the privatization processes did not enter the advanced stage yet, so state share in industry was still high (51.3%), much higher than in the whole economy (38.5%). With privatization advancement, the public share in industry was decreasing in a faster pace than in the whole economy, so since late-2000s, the public sector's contribution to gross output became lower than the average (Fig. 5.2). The lowest level of the state share in both the whole economy and industry was achieved in 2016 (14.4 and 9.1% respectively). Since 2017, in line with the new statist development paradigm, they started to grow.

According to the Central Statistical Office data, the share of whole public sector of the economy in employment is still quite substantial and amounted to 21.3% in 2018. Comparing to mid-1990s, the number of employees shrank by 43%. Much deeper de-statization could be observed in the enterprise sector. In 1995–2018, the number of employees of state-owned enterprises controlled by the central government shrank 3.5 times; the share of employed in SOEs in the enterprise sector workforce shank from 32.3% to mere 9% (Fig. 5.3). Even deeper de-statization could be seen in industry, where in 1995, SOEs employed a half of the workforce; since then the number of employed in industrial SOEs has fallen 6.4 times

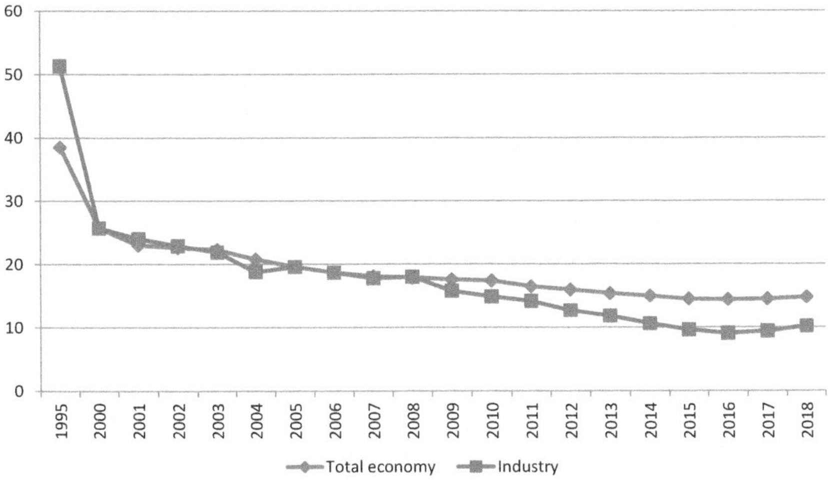

Fig. 5.2 SOEs' share in gross output (in %) (*Source* Central Statistical Office data, own calculations)

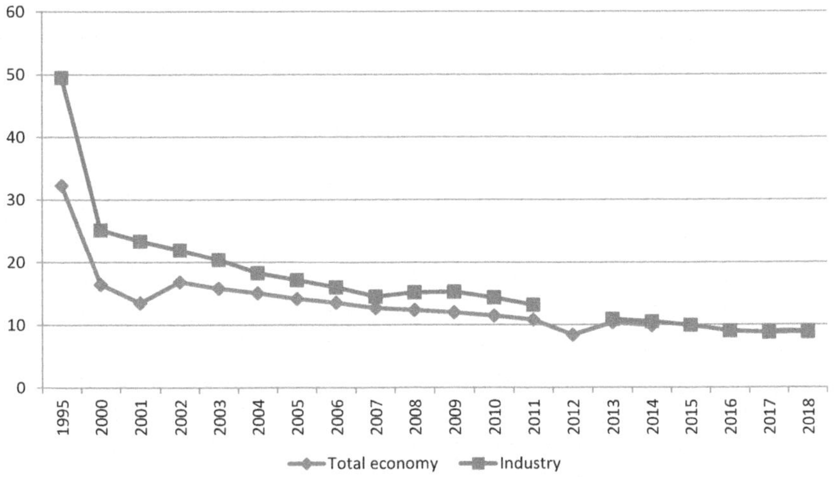

Fig. 5.3 SOEs' share in employment (in %). Gaps in the graph mean lack of data for this year (*Source* Central Statistical Office data, own calculations)

and now it amounts to 8.8% of the total employment in industry. It is worth noting, that the statist change in the economic policy, while being already reflected in official statistical data on the finances of the enterprises sector, still is not reflected in changes in the share of the SOEs in total employment. It kept gradually decreasing, albeit at a very slow pace. In absolute figures, however, we can see the growing number of employees of SOEs (1.8% in 2015–2018), but employment in the private sector grew faster (9.2%) which was mainly due to quite high pace of economic growth in Poland.

5.3.2 The Extent of the SOE Sector

In every sector of the Polish economy, and the enterprise sector in particular, the de-statization took place, although at a different pace and bringing much differentiated results. Unfortunately, the Central Statistical Office provides even more limited data breakdown on ownership for sectors of the sectors of the economy other than industry, only two sets of data being available: on employment and gross sales. As can be seen in Table 5.2, much progress has been made in all the main sectors, especially those which previously were the most state-dominated such as industry and transportation and storage. In 2018, the state share did not exceed 14.7% in sales and 26.8% in employment (both in transportation and storage, although in this sector, too, the advancement of de-statization was very significant). The most de-statized sectors were construction and trade and repairs, where state ownership became virtually inexistent. It should be noted, however, that they were among the least state-controlled areas of business activity even in the early years of the transition. In agriculture, which since the command economy times was predominantly privately owned, the state managed to keep relatively high share in sales while significantly reducing employment.

However, the data on the sectoral level do not show the whole picture, especially in industry, which at a first glance looks like a sector where the state involvement became quite marginal. In reality, the situation within industry is highly differentiated (Table 5.3).

On the one hand, it includes manufacturing, which was mostly private even in 1995, and was characterized with the lowest state involvement in 2018. At least according to the official data, the state share in the value of fixed assets, gross output, and employment amounted to just a few percent. On the other hand, in the rest of the industry, the state share

Table 5.2 The share of SOEs in selected sectors of the Polish economy in 1995 and 2018

	Gross sales (PLN bn current prices)		*Gross sales %*		*Employment (thou.)*		*Employment %*	
	1995	*2018*	*1995*	*2018*	*1995*	*2018*	*1995*	*2018*
Agriculture[a]	3.3	11.7	15.3	13.6	75.1	5.2	3.2	1.3
Industry	129.9	152.3	53.1	10	1485	286.1	49.5	8.8
Construction	4.7	3.8	12.4	1.1	827.8	10.5	19.1	1.1
Trade and repair[b]	33.8	10.3	9.2	0.5	1903.1	2.6	5.9	0.1
Transportation and storage	13.8	36.6	50.1	14.7	838.1	241.3	73.3	26.8
Accommodation and catering[c]	0.4	0.6	5.13	1.3	185.9	10.6	15.6	3.6
Total	185.9	215.3	26.3	4.8	5315	556.3	63.2	5.5
Total without trade	152.1	205.1	44.9	9.1	3411.9	553.7	41.1	7.2

[a]Market output instead of gross sales
[b]Gross sales: trade only
[c]Gross sales: catering only
Source Central Statistical Office data, own calculations

Table 5.3 The share of SOEs in industry in 1995 and 2018 (%)

	Gross output		*Gross value of fixed assets*		*Employment*	
	1995	*2018*	*1995*	*2018*	*1995*	*2018*
Mining and quarrying	97.6	46.2	98.7	42.5	96.9	58.7
Manufacturing	41.4	3.9	62.7	4.5	40.0	1.8
Electricity, gas, and water supply	97.6		98.3		96.3	
Electricity, gas, steam and air conditioning supply		49.9		46.1		43.1
Water supply; sewerage, waste management and remediation activities		50.0		92.6		62.8
Industry, total	51.3	10.2	80.2	28.6	49.5	8.8

Source Central Statistical Office data, own calculations

is still very high, especially in water supply, sewage, and similar municipal activities. In the latter branch, only 7.4% of the assets are controlled by private owners, the rest belongs predominantly to local governments. According to the Central Statistical Office data, in 2018 the state (mostly the central government) still controlled nearly half of the assets of mining and energy companies; they produced nearly half of these industries' gross output. In mining, SOEs employed almost 60% of the sector's workforce.

Looking at the dynamics of the state share in sectors of industry, one can see both common features and differences. As was noted before, the general trend which can be seen in the data before 2015 reflected gradual withdrawal of the state from ownership functions. The cases of regaining control over selected enterprises before the statist change of mid-2010s, sometimes quite spectacular, were still not numerous enough to become reflected in the aggregated data, except for the last year or two of the PO-PSL coalition rule. Later, the state share started gradually growing again, but this growth was different in different sectors of industry and reflected in different indicators.

The lowest value of the state share in gross output (Fig. 5.4) in industry as a whole was reached in 2016 (9.1%), the same was observed in manufacturing (3.2%) and energy (39.3), but in mining it happened two years earlier (42.1%) which may reflect intensification of the attempts to save this branch which was skidding into deep crisis. In water supply, sewerage and waste management, the lowest point was achieved only in 2017 (49.5%). From the lowest point to 2018, the state sector share re-growth in industry amounted to 1.1 p.p., being the highest in the energy sector, where it increased at 9.2 p.p., or more than a quarter, which reflected mainly the nationalization of power plants. In mining, the state share increased at 4.1 p.p., being a result of nationalizations and support for production provided by state-owned power plants. In manufacturing, the state sector re-growth was relatively modest (0.5 p.p.), as re-nationalization included only several companies, not being very large. At the same time not much was happening in the water supply, sewerage and waste management sector, as there were almost no ownership changes there, thus the share of local authorities' ownership remained intact.

The data on the dynamics of the value of total fixed assets and employment (Figs. 5.5 and 5.6) also generally show gradual de-etatization of sectors of industry followed by the signs of their re-statization since mid-2010s. But the picture is much less clear because of much higher impact

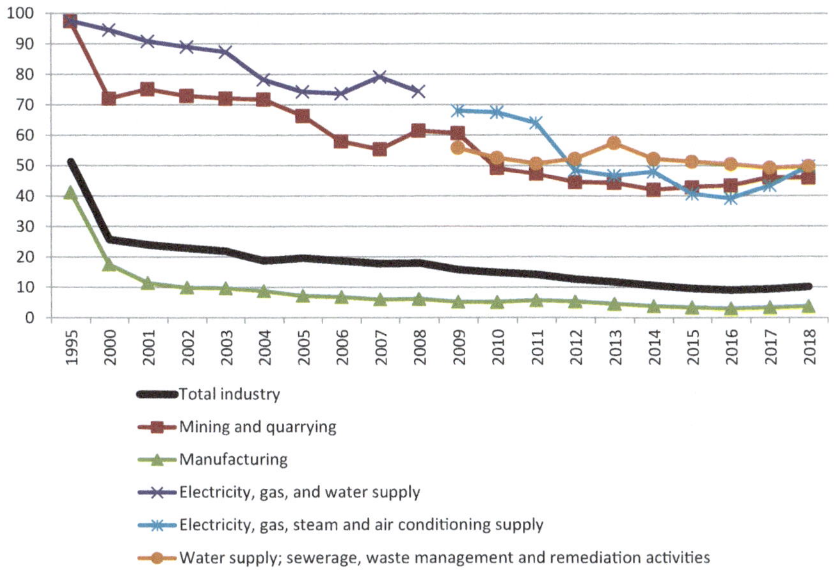

Fig. 5.4 SOEs' share in gross output in industry (in %) (*Source* Central Statistical Office data, own calculations)

of financial condition of enterprises on these two indicators. The deteriorating situation in many SOEs led to shrinking of their assets and employment reduction. In the industry as a whole, only in 2018, a slight increase in the share of the state in fixed assets can be seen (0.6 p.p.) and no sign of increase in the share in employment.

First of all, the effects of inferior condition of many SOEs can be seen in manufacturing and mining. Almost all nationalization cases in these sectors were directly or indirectly rescue investments, so the state property was replenished with badly functioning companies which made necessary write-offs of their assets and restructuring including getting rid of unnecessary assets and excessive employment (the latter was hard to perform due to political reasons, though). So generally speaking, the nationalized companies in these sectors were not able to significantly increase the state share in the value of global fixed assets and employment. In 2018, however, one can see a slight growth in fixed assets in mining which was apparently caused by the re-capitalization of coal mines by energy companies within capital groups. The situation in the energy sector was different:

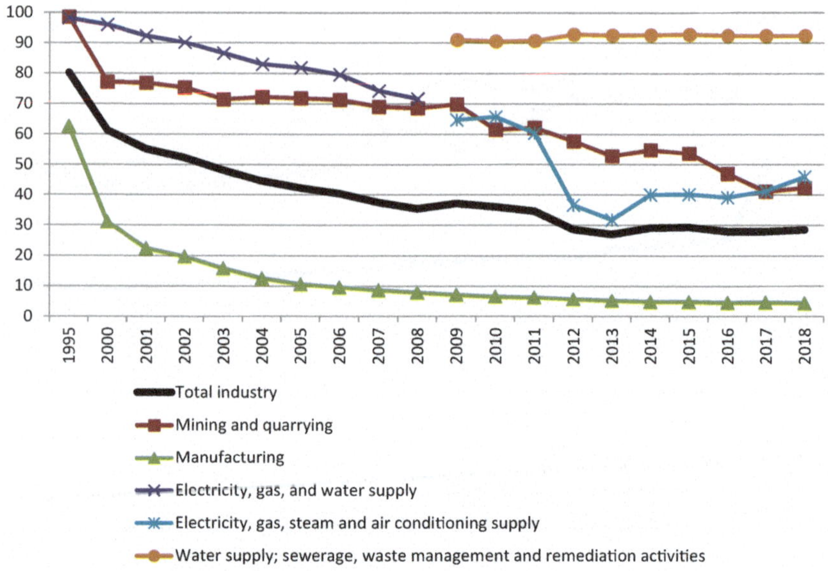

Fig. 5.5 SOEs' share in gross value of fixed assets in industry (in %) (*Source* Central Statistical Office data, own calculations)

the state acquired profitable power plants which were strong enough to withstand the burden of keeping the mines alive imposed on them by the government. Thus, even when they also had to do write-offs, the value of their fixed assets hasn't deteriorated this much; they were also able to evade reduction of employment for a longer perspective. Mostly municipal companies in the water supply, sewerage and waste management sector, as not being a subject of ownership policy of the central government, showed no dynamics in both areas in question.

The extent of SOE sector in Poland and its dynamics generally seem to fit paradigms of the economic policy pursued by the government in different periods of the post-communist era. However, also several dozen enterprises exist, where the reasons of keeping them in the hands of the government remain obscure. In 2020, on the official list of companies with state participation published by the Chancellery of the Prime Minister (2020), one can find, for example, Mors-Wola Sp. z o.o. and Chłodnia Szczecińska Sp. z o.o. cool stores (100 and 48.61% of shares respectively), Sklejka Orzechowo plywood producer (100%), Fabryka

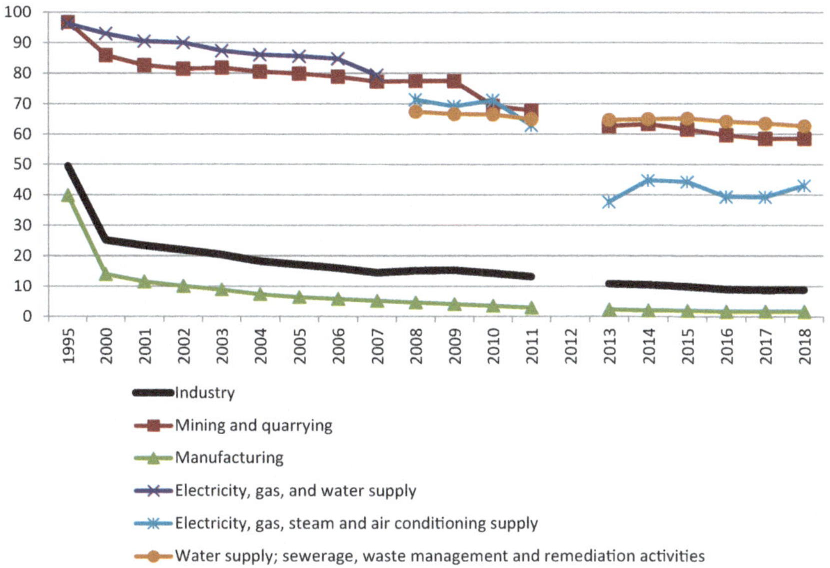

Fig. 5.6 SOEs' share in employment in industry (in %). No data for 2012 (*Source* Central Statistical Office data, own calculations)

Obrabiarek do Drewna Sp. z o.o. which produces wood machining tools (100%), CEZAS—a local supplier of school furniture, prints, and teaching aids (49.96), Chłodnia Białystok S.A.—a producer of frozen fruits and vegetables (49.15%), Meprozet Kościan S.A.—a manufacturer of slurry tankers (46.15%), and Bingo Centrum gaming room (15.13%). All these companies are fully operational and not subject for insolvency or liquidation procedures. The full list of such enterprises which for no apparent reason are still controlled by the state is probably much longer because the Prime Minister's one includes only enterprises directly owned by the government. Thus, it does not include, e.g., the case of re-nationalized PKL mountain cable operator which now belongs to the Polish Development Fund. However, all such enterprises are too small to influence the general statistics on ownership structure of the enterprise sector. Their importance being too small for the whole economy, they may still be of some value to someone who has prevented these companies from going to private hands, though.

5.3.3 The Importance of the SOE Sector

The importance of SOEs in the enterprise sector can be studied from two perspectives. The first one focuses on SOEs which the government regards as of significant importance to the economy. As it was discussed in Sect. 4.3, an official category of companies of significant importance for the national economy was introduced in 2017. These companies were to be treated in a special way by the state owner, e.g., through more strict requirements towards members of their boards and selling of any amount of their shares to private investors. The ownership structure of these enterprises was mostly "inherited" from the past, and in 17 out of 29 of them the state possessed less than 100% of shares, including 9 where the government holds a minority stake, at least formally. In fact, all of them directly or indirectly were controlled by the state. The list includes all the largest capital groups and single SOEs with sales in 2019 ranging from PLN 6.3 billion (USD 1.7 billion) up to PLN 111.2 billion (USD 29.3 billion), perhaps in order to keep access to their financial and other resources; in 2019, these companies accounted to about 10% of sales of the whole enterprise sector. There are also revenue-generating companies such as the Polish Real Estate Holding (Polski Holding Nieruchomości) which invests into commercial real estate projects. Finally, the list includes politically important companies which may have crucial importance in conducting the economic policy (e.g., Warsaw Stock Exchange, Industrial Development Agency) as well as providing control over the military sector (Polish Defense Holding) an information (public radio and television, and the largest news agency PAP).

The second perspective is the role of SOEs in the economy which can be measured by the share of state ownership among the largest enterprises. For this purpose, the last report on 500 largest enterprises (in terms of sales) prepared by Rzeczpospolita daily (Rzeczpospolita 2020) can be used. It's a thorough and detailed research based on data obtained directly from companies (through questionnaires and their websites) which includes quite reliable data on their ownership structure (central and local governments, domestic private, foreign), which is at least much better than that of provided by the government and the Central Statistical Office, as it really takes into account indirect state ownership. A good example is the case of the PGG which has been discussed before: instead of 0.000003% of the official state share, the Rzeczpospolita report rightfully marks this company as fully state-owned.

All in all, in 2019 the share of 500 largest Polish enterprises in the sales of the whole enterprise sector was about 44%, and about 41% in industry. On the 2020 list which has data on 2019, there were 48 enterprises with the state participation (9.6%); in 40 cases (in all but six it was the central government), the state was the largest shareholder, but in the rest of cases (8) it still had the capacity to control the company. In terms of the number of companies, the biggest number of SOEs was in mining (four out of five) and in energy and water supply, sewerage and waste management sectors (about a half of the whole number). At the same time, SOEs represented a minority of companies in other sectors, especially in manufacturing, construction, and trade (Table 5.4).

At the same time, the share of SOEs measured by economic indicators such as sales and number of employees is much bigger than their share in the number of companies. The share of volume of sales of these 9.6% of enterprises was disproportionally high (31.4%), the same goes to employment (33.2%). The largest disproportions could be seen in manufacturing, where the share of SOEs in sales was 5.5 times higher and in employment 2.3 times higher than their share in the number of companies; in financial and insurance sector, it was 2.6 and 3.8 times, respectively. In other

Table 5.4 Share of SOEs on the list of 500 largest enterprises in 2019

Sector	*No. of SOEs*	*Share of SOEs (%)*		
		In no. of enterprises	*In sales*	*In employment*
Industry	25	13.0	52.4	47.0
Mining and quarrying	4	80.0	95.2	...
Manufacturing	11	6.5	35.9	15.0
Electricity, gas, steam and air conditioning supply	8	53.3	90.1	92.7
Water supply; sewerage, waste management and remediation activities	2	50.0	57.1	80.2
Construction	1	3.1	3.6	1.9
Trade; repair of motor vehicles	6	3.7	6.2	8.9
Financial and insurance activities	6	12.5	35.6	47.2
Other	10	15.4	27.7	36.6
Total	48	9.6	31.4	33.2

Source Rzeczpospolita (2020), own calculations

sectors, as well the share of SOEs in sales and employment was much bigger than their share in the number of enterprises.

It meant that the larger was the enterprise on this list, the higher was the probability of it being state-owned (Table 5.5). Indeed, among 100 largest enterprises, already one quarter (25) was controlled by the state; among 50 largest—about 4/5 (19), exactly a half (10) among 20 largest companies and 7 out of 10 largest ones. Accordingly, in all but the smallest (top-10) groups of enterprises, the share of SOEs in sales and employment was substantially higher than their share in the number of companies.

It can be said that the state controls the top of companies in industry and finance: despite being formally a minority shareholder, the state has a corporate control over the largest Polish company (PKN Orlen—gas and oil) and the largest industrial company (KGHM PM—metals and mining). The government also controls four leading energy corporations and three dominant financial institutions: PKO PB and Pekao SA (both banks) and an insurance company PZU.

Paradoxically enough, for many years, no changes in the place of SOEs among the largest enterprises can be seen, despite apparent dynamics in the whole sector and changes in the role of SOEs in the economic policy. When the first such list of 500 largest enterprises was created, it contained data for 1995 and at those times, the share of the state among the largest enterprises was really big. In the whole set, the government had shares in 44% of them. In top-20 enterprises, the state-controlled companies really dominated: there were 17 of them (85%), their share in sales and employment was 89.2 and 97.1%, respectively. But already in

Table 5.5 Share of SOEs in groups of largest enterprises in 2019

Group of enterprises	*No. of SOEs*	*Share of SOEs (%)*		
		In no. of enterprises	*In sales*	*In employment*
10 largest enterprises	7	70.0	74.7	61.0
20 largest enterprises	10	50.0	63.2	57.8
50 largest enterprises	19	38.0	52.6	49.8
100 largest enterprises	25	25.0	43.3	45.3
Total 500 largest enterprises	48	9.6	31.4	33.2

Source Rzeczpospolita (2020), own calculations

1999, their share in top-20 fell to 10 firms, 63.8% in sales and 87.6% in employment. But still, the state had shares in 142 of 500 largest companies (28.4%). Since then, the share of the state in top-20 companies has stabilized at about half of the number of companies, 60% of sales and a bit more in employment, with some fluctuations from year to year, but without any visible trend. The share of enterprises with the state corporate control among 500 largest enterprises has stabilized by the end of 2010s at the level of 10–12% of the total number of enterprises and about 1/3 of sales and employment. Therefore, the importance of the state enterprise sector measured by its share among the enterprises with the highest output seems to just have petrified at a rather high level. Perhaps the growing statism in the ownership policy of the government (including crawling nationalization) did not led (yet) to substantial increase in economic importance of SOEs, the group of the largest private companies still outperforming them. Some of the enterprises on the top-500 list indeed get under control of the state, but at the same time other SOEs leave it.

However, there is an area where the dominance of large enterprises with state corporate control is very pronounced and was growing through the years. This is the Warsaw Stock Exchange (WSE). Until 2004, state-controlled companies' share in capitalization in the WSE WIG20 flagship index was 20–35%, which was comparable with the situation in stock exchanges in some developed countries that had an extensive SOE sector. After 2005, this share significantly increased to 40–45% and since 2010, it has been at a very high level of 60–70%, exceeding the 75% threshold in 2019 (Fig. 5.7). This is one of the highest values on the global stock markets. At the end of 2019, the government had corporate control over 11 out of the 20 largest Polish public listed companies. It is worth noting that only in 4 of them the state share was above 50%, in the remaining 8, it was 25–50% and various mechanisms of control leverage were used (from being the largest owner vis-à-vis dispersed other shareholders to special provisions in companies charter which favored the state owner). It was one state-controlled company less than in 2018, but the share of SOEs in the WIG20 index capitalization increased from 70.9 to 75.6%. It is also worth noting that since the second half of 2000s, the government increases its share among the largest listed companies as a formally minority investor; however, it effectively controls all these companies. At the same time, the share of companies where the state is a majority owner remains roughly at the same level. Therefore, perhaps such clearly visible

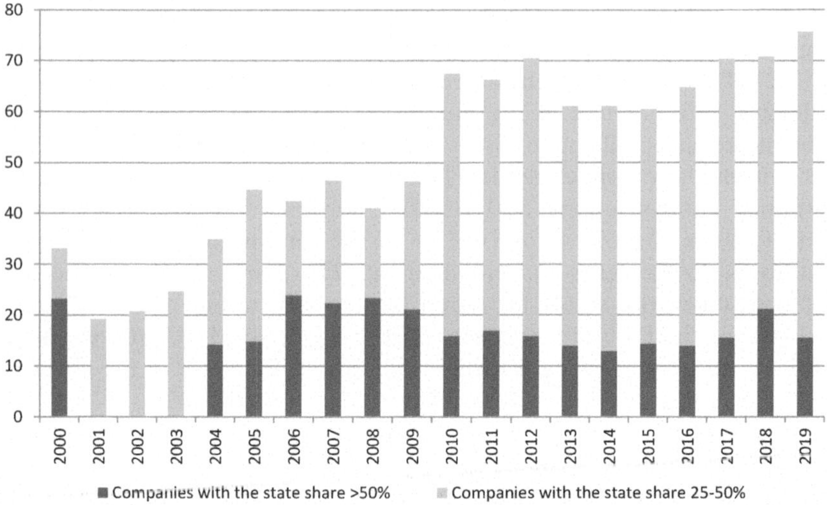

Fig. 5.7 The share of state-controlled companies in the WIG20 capitalization (in %) (*Source* Own calculations using the WSE data)

expansion of companies with the state corporate control on the WSE is rather a result of "reluctant privatization" with IPOs being a typical way of resolving the dilemma "to eat the cake and to have the cake," i.e., to have privatization proceedings and to keep corporate control, than of real expansion of the state sector in the Polish economy.

The importance of SOEs discussed above does not include ownership by foreign public or state-controlled entities. In fact, unlike in some other post-communist countries in Poland, its importance seems to be marginal because of the very limited scale (there are only several such cases in this country) and extent, as well as because of the identity of such foreign investors. In the group of 100 largest Polish enterprises from the Orbis database,[1] in 2018, only 4 were controlled by foreign public entities and their share in total assets and turnover was only 2.0 and 2.3%, respectively, showing no long-term growing trends. These companies were not the largest ones in the sectors of their activity (telecommunications, food, trade, and manufacturing) occupying places from 38 to 77 and very far from having dominant position on the market. In two cases, the investor was a governmental agency, in another two, a state-controlled corporation. In three cases, the foreign investor originated from a highly developed economy (Germany, France, and Japan), one was from an emerging economy (China). So at least in the first three cases, there was no ground for concerns about public investors from emerging markets which might behave in a harmful way for the host country's economic or political interests (Cuervo-Cazurra 2018). The fourth case, however, a greenfield investment in OEM electronics production, was rather not politically controversial as well.

Note

1. The data was kindly provided by Marlena Gołębiowska who collected it and made relevant calculations during preparation of her Ph.D. thesis on state-owned enterprises.

References

Aharoni, Yair. 1986. *The Evolution and Management of State-Owned Enterprises*. Cambridge, MA: Ballinger.

Bałtowski, Maciej, and Grzegorz Kwiatkowski. 2018. *Przedsiębiorstwa państwowe we współczesnej gospodarce*. Warsaw: PWN.

Bałtowski, Maciej, and Piotr Kozarzewski. 2014. *Zmiana własnościowa polskiej gospodarki 1989–2013*. Warsaw: PWE.

Bałtowski, Maciej, and Piotr Kozarzewski. 2016. "Formal and Real Ownership Structure of the Polish Economy: State-Owned Versus State-Controlled Enterprises." *Post-Communist Economies* 28 (3): 405–419.

Böwer, Uwe. 2017. State-Owned Enterprises in Emerging Europe: The Good, the Bad, and the Ugly. Working Paper 17/221. International Monetary Fund. Available online: https://www.imf.org/~/media/Files/Publications/WP/2017/wp17221.ashxAccessed July 27, 2020.

CEEP. 2000. *Development of Enterprises of Public Participation and of General Economic Interest in Europe since 1996. CEEP Statistical Review*. Brussels: European Centre of Employers and Enterprises Providing Public Services.

Central Statistical Office. 2019. *Statistical Yearbook of the Republic of Poland 2019*. Warsaw: GUS.

Central Statistical Office. 2020. *Activity of Enterprises with Up to 9 Persons Employed in 2018*. Warsaw: GUS.

Chancellery of the Prime Minister. 2020. *Spółki z udziałem Skarbu Państwa*. https://www.gov.pl/web/nadzor-kprm/wykaz-spolek. Accessed August 31, 2020.

Christiansen, Hans. 2011. The Size and Composition of the SOE Sector in OECD Countries. OECD Corporate Governance Working Papers 5. OECD, Paris.

Cuervo-Cazurra, Alvaro. 2018. "Three Logics of State Owned Firms." Paper presented at SMS Extension Conference, London, September 21.

EBRD Database. 2020. http://www.ebrd.com/what-we-do/economic-research-and-data/data.html. Accessed September 17, 2020.

Estrin, Saul, Zhixiang Liang, Daniel Shapiro, and Michael Carney. 2019. "State Capitalism, Economic Systems and the Performance of State Owned Firms." *Acta Oeconomica* 69 (1): 175–193.

Frączyk, Jacek. 2016. *Straty idą w dziesiątki miliardów złotych. Inwestycje zagraniczne państwowych firm wprawiają w osłupienie*. https://www.money.pl/gospodarka/wiadomosci/artykul/inwestycje-zagraniczne-straty-skarb-panstwa,71,0,2163783.html. Accessed November 1, 2018.

Frączyk, Jacek. 2020. "Miliardowa inwestycja państwowych spółek spisana na straty. Nowy blok Ostrołęki wyceniono na zero." *Business Insider*, May 20. https://businessinsider.com.pl/gielda/wiadomosci/inwestycja-w-elektrownie-ostroleka-c-spisana-na-straty-miliard-zlotych-odpisu/x6sh22v. Accessed September 28, 2020.

Gardawski, Juliusz. 2013. "Oczekiwany model kapitalizmu: ku etatyzmowi?" In *Rzemieślnicy i biznesmeni. Właściciele małych i średnich przedsiębiorstw prywatnych*, edited by Juliusz Gardawski. Warsaw: Scholar.

Grosman, Anna, Ilya Okhmatovskiy, and Mike Wright. 2016. "State Control and Corporate Governance in Transition Economies: 25 Years on from 1989." *Corporate Governance: An International Review* 24 (3): 200–221.

INSEE. 2019. *Tableaux de l'économie française. Édition 2019*. Paris: Institut national de la statistique et des études économiques.

Kowalski, Przemysław, Max Büge, Monika Sztajerowska, and Matias Egeland. 2013. State-Owned Enterprises: Trade Effects and Policy Implications. OECD Trade Policy Paper 147. OECD, Paris.

Kozarzewski, Piotr. 2016. "Zmiany w polityce własnościowej państwa polskiego." *Studia Ekonomiczne* 4 (XCI): 555–578.

Kozarzewski, Piotr. 2019. *Polityka właścicielska państwa w okresie transformacji systemowej. Próba syntezy*. Lublin: Wydawnictwo Uniwersytetu Marii Curie-Skłodowskiej.

Matuszak, Piotr, and Bartosz Kabaciński. 2019. "Non-commercial Goals and Financial Performance of State-Owned Enterprises—Evidence from the Electricity Sector in the EU Countries." Paper presented at Application of Empirical Methods in Modern Economics Workshop, Poznan University of Economics and Business, Poznań, June 27.

Matuszak, Piotr, and Katarzyna Szarzec. 2019. “The Scale and Financial Performance of State-Owned Enterprises in the CEE Region.” *Acta Oeconomica* 69 (4): 549–570.

Matuszak, Piotr, Sławomir Kuźmar, and Katarzyna Szarzec. 2020. Majority and Minority State-Owned Enterprises as State Aid Beneficiaries—Some Evidence Based on Micro-Data Analysis of Polish Enterprises. Working Paper. Poznan University of Economics and Business, Poznań. https://www.researchgate.net/publication/344154498_Majority_and_minority_state-owned_enterprises_as_state_aid_beneficiaries_-_some_evidence_based_on_micro-data_analysis_of_Polish_enterprises. Accessed September 22, 2020.

Mazur, Stanisław, Michał Możdżeń, and Marek Oramus. 2018. “The Instrumental and Ideological Politicisation of Senior Positions in Poland’s Civil Service and Its Selected Consequences.” *The NISPAcee Journal of Public Administration and Policy* XI (1): 63–90.

Ministry of the Treasury. 2003. *Program prywatyzacji majątku Skarbu Państwa do roku 2006*. Warsaw: Ministerstwo Skarbu Państwa.

Mühlenkamp, Hogler. 2015. “From State to Market Revisited: A Reassessment of the Empirical Evidence on the Efficiency of Public (and Privately-Owned) Enterprises.” *Annals of Public and Cooperative Economics* 86 (4): 535–557.

Office of Competition and Consumer Protection. 2002–2019. *Raport o pomocy publicznej w Polsce udzielonej przedsiębiorcom*. Warsaw: UOKiK.

Office of Competition and Consumer Protection. 2011. *Delegatury UOKiK – ochrona rynków lokalnych*. Warsaw: UOKIK. https://uokik.gov.pl/aktualnosci.php?news_id=2898. Accessed October 15, 2020.

Postuła, Igor. 2013. *Nadzór korporacyjny w spółkach Skarbu Państwa*. Warsaw: Wolters Kluwer Polska.

Postuła, Igor, and Aleksandra Wąsowska. 2018. “Managerial Discretion, Firm Performance, and CEOs’ Support for Privatisation of State-Owned Companies.” *Journal for East European Management Studies* 23 (1): 106–127.

Pula, Besnik. 2017. “Whither State Ownership? The Persistence of State-Owned Industry in Postsocialist Central and Eastern Europe.” *Journal of East-West Business* 23 (1): 309–336.

PwC. 2015. *State-Owned Enterprises: Catalysts for Public Value Creation?* Arlington: PwC.

Radygin, Alexander, Yury Simachev, and Revold Entov. 2015. “The State-Owned Company: ‘State Failure’ or ‘Market Failure’?” *Russian Journal of Economics* 1 (1): 55–80.

Rudke, Maciej. 2018. “Burzliwe lata spółek po objęciu rządów przez PiS.” *Rzeczpospolita*, November 13.

Rzeczpospolita. 2020.“XXI edycja rankingu Lista 500.” *Rzeczpospolita*, May 27.

Senderski, Marcin. 2015. “Inhibited Privatization: A Hurdle Race over Vested Interests.” *European Journal of Government and Economics* 4 (1): 46–66.

Szarzec, Katarzyna, Akos Dombi, and Piotr Matuszak. 2020. State-Owned Enterprises and Economic Growth: Evidence from the Post-Lehman Period. Working Paper, Poznan University of Economics and Business, Poznań; Eötvös Loránd University, Budapest.

Szarzec, Katarzyna, and Wanda Nowara. 2017. "The Economic Performance of State-Owned Enterprises in Central and Eastern Europe." *Post-Communist Economies* 29 (3): 375–391.

Szymański, David. 2020. "Spółek Skarbu Państwa jest więcej, niż się wydaje." *Business Insider*, January 17. https://businessinsider.com.pl/firmy/spolki-skarbu-panstwa-w-polsce-ile-ich-jest-jak-wygladaja-ich-finanse-opinia-dot/7m9szef. Accessed October 8, 2020.

Tihanyi, Laszlo, Ruth V. Aguilera, Marc van Essen, Steve Sauerwald, Patricio Duran, and Roxana Turturea. 2019. "State Ownership and Political Connections." *Journal of Management* 45 (6): 2293–2321.

CHAPTER 6

Sources of the State Corporate Control Policy in Poland and Its Evolution

In earlier parts of the book, it has already been shown that the ownership policy of the state after the beginning of the post-communist transition was characterized by two main features. The first feature is the continuous evolution, which nowadays appears in the form of an inverted and quite open letter U. Initially, there was a gradual expansion of the scope of ownership reform, introducing marked relationships in this area and private property one of the pillars of the emerging economic system. At those times, privatization was the main tool of ownership policy of the state and state corporate control policy was to a large extent neglected. Then, the reverse trend began to take on increasing importance, privatization slowed down more and more as the government and the political class started seeing the remaining state-owned enterprises as a valuable asset which had to be kept. Eventually, the state and state-owned businesses began being perceived as the locomotive of further social and economic development. The second feature is the generally highly gradual nature of the changes, a large degree of continuation of the ownership policy by successive governments regardless of their ideologies and programs. Rapid and spectacular changes rarely took place; new approaches usually gradually "matured" within the existing policy and were introduced gradually.

P. Kozarzewski, *State Corporate Control in Transition*,
https://doi.org/10.1007/978-3-030-78562-8_6

The factors determining the trajectory of corporate control policy (and ownership policy as a whole) can be analyzed from two perspectives formulated as two dichotomies. The first is the relationship between acting in good faith (i.e., in the public interest) by decision makers and the realization of private group interests, or rent-seeking. The second is the role of endogenous factors, having their source in Poland, and exogenous factors, coming from outside the country and being out of its control.

6.1 Acting in Good Faith vs. Pursuing Group Interests

6.1.1 *Hypotheses, Mutual Dependence and Compromises*

According to the official discourse of every government or ruling party, every policy was conducted in good faith, based on a sincere desire to ensure the country's development and prosperity of the population. Every change of policy was also explained by sincere intentions: the standard set of arguments here is the need to overcome the growing dysfunctions and to adjust policies to changing domestic and external challenges. But in the end, the main blame was with the predecessors who had not faced these threats. Elements of continuation, including in areas where predecessors were criticized, were usually neither announced nor explained during the course of a new better policy. The evolution of the government's ownership policy in Poland is a good example: both its initial formation and any changes have been explained with the public good: the need to carry out systemic transition, to take into account the social factor, to finance reforms and other socially crucial government actions, to prevent excessive growth of foreign influence, to counteract market failures, and to strengthen the factors of economic development; this is a far from complete list of arguments for changes that could be heard from the officials over the period of thirty years. The arguments gradually evolved from the need to build sound market institutions independent from political interference to the importance of the state as coordinator of economic life and creator of factors of economic development.

The opposite pole represented a view that ownership policy and its changes were followed mainly by rent-seeking group interests. Initially, when privatization of SOEs was the main agenda of this policy, it was criticized by opposition politicians and some researchers for being in fact a robbery of a national property behind which post-communist forces and foreign capital stood (Poznański 2000; Tittenbrun 2007; Kieżun 2012). Then, as state corporate control gained importance, especially after the statist turn of mid-2010s, critical opinions concentrated on politicization of SOEs and their attractiveness as sources of rent (Senderski 2015; Szarzec et al. 2020).

Therefore, it seems to make sense to include in the analysis of the factors determining the trajectory of the state policy towards enterprises, especially the statist paradigm change, verification of two broadly formulated hypotheses which offer alternative explanations. The first one claims that the main vehicle of the growing statization of state ownership policy, and state corporate control in particular, is a sincere Keynesian-type belief in the ability of the state to correct all the major market failures and to be the main vehicle of social and economic development through conducting an interventionist economic policy. The second one sees these processes as driven mainly by vested private interests of the ruling political class and its allies—because expanding state interventionism creates growing possibilities for discretionary decisions aimed at extraction of rents. In this case, the developmental rhetoric is no more than a smokescreen covering the real intentions of the rent-seekers. For the sake of brevity, those hypotheses will be called the good faith hypothesis and the vested interests hypothesis, respectively. The first, very limited attempt of such analysis was presented in Kozarzewski and Bałtowski (2017).

The hypotheses of good faith and rent-seeking are not fully dichotomous. They may be to a large extent interdependent and more often than not be the two sides of the same medal: mutually condition each other and result from each other.

The characteristic feature of the policy towards the enterprise sector in Poland, especially at the beginning of the transition and in the field of privatization, was its high degree of consensuality, i.e., striving to take into account the interests of a wide range of stakeholders and to obtain their consent. One can agree with Woodruff (2004) on the generally positive effects of such a policy (conducted in good faith), because it limited the possibilities to contest its results in the future. However, on the other hand, it probably contributed (although not being the only factor) to facilitating the articulation and realization of interests by various social groups whose objectives were not necessarily consistent with those of the state policy, including those opposing privatization. They could hinder privatization of some SOEs or at least distorting this process.

The second problem is the inability to separate these factors precisely. Due to the fact that periods of the "extraordinary politics," when the government is not the subject of external political pressure (Balcerowicz 1995, pp. 160–163) happen extremely rarely, the vast majority of decision-making processes takes place under the conditions of "normal politics" based on political competition and the necessity of compromises which take into account the interests of various social groups. And often these could inevitably be compromises between the goals set in good faith and someone's group interests.

Anyway, acting in good faith did not automatically prevent the policy from creating favorable conditions for the creation of the sources of rent and interest groups that benefit from them. Conversely, too broad realization of private group interests could become a catalyst for the policy of combating rent-seeking.

6.1.2 Good Faith

As for those who created the basics of the state ownership policy at the beginning of the transition, there is no reason to question their sincerity and disinterestedness, as evidenced by the fact that the vast majority of them were beneficiaries of neither privatization, nor keeping a large sector of state-owned enterprises. They did not become owners of the privatized assets, did not massively occupy seats on the SOEs boards, and did not build a lasting position in politics or in the economy. One can blame them for concentrating on privatization and neglecting the remaining SOEs, but such attitude can be understood from the liberal perspective; it should be remembered that during the first years, if the transition SOEs were formally deprived of all privileges. As it was noted earlier, the government was widely accused of leaving "its" enterprises to the mercy of fate. It is hard to find realization of some private interests here.

However, this did not mean a lack of political calculation in the actions of the government: the "extraordinary policy" carte blanche was neither absolute nor eternal being valid for a short period from autumn of 1989 till the end of 1990. This calculation, in contrast to later periods, was conducted primarily in the public interest, as understood by those in power, and was intended to ensure that reforms were carried out as quickly and deeply as possible, as long as this possibility existed. The reformers indeed feared losing power in the next parliamentary elections, but mainly because this could lead to the victory of opponents of the reforms who would stop or even reverse them.

The end of the period of "extraordinary politics" naturally limited the possibility of acting "in good faith," based only on the decision makers' own ideas of an optimal economic policy. It also encouraged various types of private interest groups, which under "extraordinary politics" were simply ignored. In the pro-reform activities of politicians and high-rank bureaucrats, the elements of opportunism, maneuvering, seeking the favors of various groups of voters and other influential social groups increased—which, by the way, could also take place within the framework of "good faith," the conviction that under the existing conditions it is worth sacrificing things less important to achieve the most important, and even choosing "lesser evil." This mainly took the form of refraining from privatization of some categories of state-owned enterprises and taking care of the most "sensitive" and still non-privatized sectors of the economy, where the opposition towards privatization and losing stare support was particularly strong. The escalation of economic opportunism and the shortening of the horizon of the state's ownership policy were also boosted by its fiscalization, when the main target first of privatization and later of the state corporate control became budget revenues.

Contracting area for "good faith" activities was also caused by the Ministry of the Treasury, which in order to build and preserve its political weight was very active in distributing political bounties in the state sector. The conditions of "good faith" policy also deteriorated because the successive governments more and more became oriented at realization of party interests. It hit badly the personnel policy in the governmental agencies, including in charge of state corporate control, where the staff started to be selected by the political loyalty key rather than their qualifications.

Nevertheless, the market reforms kept advancing and through the years the Polish economy was one of the fastest growing economies in Europe and was the only post-communist economy which was immune to financial crises and stagnation. A great deal of this success was contributed by the policy of the consecutive governments—and this meant that decision makers acted mainly in a good faith manner. However, there were areas, e.g., in the corporate control of the state, where rent-seeking behavior was increasingly obvious (which is discussed further in this chapter), but it still could not jeopardize the generally favorable course of events.

Besides, the drift of ownership policy of the state towards statism did not necessarily result solely from a reduction in the influence of the good faith factors in favor of factors associated with the increasing state economic policy capture by private interest groups. One of the indirect arguments supporting this hypothesis was the presence among the supporters of statist turn of many well-known researchers, experts and politicians who had contributed to the successes of the Polish transition and who were hardly suspected of pursuing their private political goals (Mączyńska 2012; Prusek and Bielecki 2012; Kawalec 2015). It may be argued that since early 2000s, the change of ownership policy with shifting attention from privatization to state corporate control was also influenced by the growing popularity of statist ideology. It should be noted however that until the end of 2015 it never meant an official radical denial of the policy pursued so far, which still could be called as largely liberal. In practice as well there were no sudden and radical changes of policy towards SOEs.

After the statist turn in the economic policy which in mid-2010s has been performed by the PiS coalition, the role of good faith in the policy towards the enterprise sector seems to be even more difficult to determine. First of all, because the period is not over yet, it is too "fresh" to be seen from a perspective. Besides, a large part of the facts necessary for such a credible assessment usually comes to light only after some time. Secondly, the corporate control in this period, like the whole social and economic policy, seems inconsistent, being the outcome of the interplay between various concepts and competing interests. It is characterized by an inconsistency both in ideological and practical dimension: among other things, a contradiction between the aspiration to build an efficient state and the broad (perhaps even more extensive than under previous governments) use of state ownership to generate rents. One can only guess how sincere were the official slogans of a strong state that would ensure both economic development and prosperity of the nation using a broad set of tools for top-down mobilization and the fight against pathologies, and to what extent it was just a populist demagogy. It seems, however, that there are some arguments in favor of the hypothesis that the factor of good faith played a significant role in the economic policy of PiS.

First of all, this is the fact that the authors of the concept of the statist change (especially Mateusz Morawiecki) directly referred to the anti-capitalist, anti-globalist autarkic development theories which became increasingly popular in recent years, assuming the key role of the state and national capital in achieving the objectives of social and economic development, as well as to the statist practice of some other countries.

These concepts may be attractive for many reasons, including offering seemingly easy solutions to complex development problems; they are an attractive offer for those who do not trust self-regulatory mechanisms (even if they are corrected by the state), who are afraid of globalization and for whom more isolation of the economy from the impact of the world market and far-reaching state control of economic processes seem to be an effective remedy. On the other hand, everything that weakens the direct state control over the economy and depletes the resources which the government can directly control, such as liberalization and especially privatization, might be regarded as an evil (perhaps sometimes necessary one). Such views, called by Balcerowicz (2018) "the presumption of the rightness of socialism," were and still are popular not only in Polish society as a whole, but also among politicians and academia. However, there are signs (discussed further in this chapter) that references to statist and isolationists theories (including them being often inaccurate) had also the hidden agenda of mobilization political support from transition losers and creating ground for state capture by private interest groups especially those seeking for rents in the state-controlled enterprise sector.

Secondly, there are symptoms of the attachment of the authorities to the attractive visions of great Poland: a dynamically developing country, occupying a dignified place on the economic (and political) map of the world. As Bałtowski (2019) points out, since 2016 very important economic decisions (or decisions which had economic effects) and state investments started being made in accordance with the political idea, regardless of the costs and economic consequences. One can imagine a sincere, although naive, fascination with the idea of modernization based on huge government projects, among others, referring to the economic policy of the Second Polish Republic in the inter-war period (with its ambitious projects of building the port in Gdynia or creating the Central Industrial Region). Some references were direct, such as the name of the Luxtorpeda 2.0 rapid rail transport development project, Luxtorpeda being a high-speed Polish train in the 1930s. The development traditions of pre-WW2 Poland had to be continued, e.g., in the plans of production of 1 million electric cars or the gigantomaniac Central Communication Port—which at the first stage was to serve 50 million passengers with the prospect of growth to as much as 180 million, i.e., 1.7 times more than the largest airport in the world in Atlanta, USA.

Thirdly, both the development vision and specific actions of the government often did not have direct beneficiaries who could derive private benefits from them, such as the projects mentioned above or plans of revision of some privatization transactions. It seems that these activities were not aimed at direct distribution of rents or bribing specific influential social groups, unlike many other actions of the government. They seem rather to result from a rather misunderstood state interest. What is more, as it was pointed out before, certain attempts were made, of doubtful effectiveness, to limit the rent-seeking on the state property: first of all in the personnel policy in the SOEs by cutting "excessive" salaries of CEOs and prosecuting the most drastic manifestations of the use of positions in these companies to achieve private benefits.

However, the question arises to what extent the influence of the good faith factor in the corporate control policy of the state was decisive and important. The answer to this question requires further research and is complicated, among other things, because it must take into account not only specific government actions and their effects, but also the intentions of the decision makers: whether they were motivated by the pursuit of effective actions for the benefit of the country or the realization of their group interests. Many such activities can be explained in both ways: for example, the consolidation of certain sectors of the economy mentioned in Sect. 4.2.2, which was officially intended to increase their competitiveness and improve their attractiveness for investors. In practice, one of its main effects was the emergence of strong interest groups, primarily at the industry level, which made further restructuring of this area of the economy difficult. Was it a deliberate effect or a "work accident"? At this moment, only a hypothesis may be formulated that the role of the good faith factor changed over time: it was the highest (perhaps playing a decisive role) at the beginning of the transition. Then, with the consolidation of interest groups in the economy, its role gradually declined until a certain rebound after 2015. It can be said with greater conviction, however, that the ideology of the good faith also evaluated, and radically: from a mostly liberal approach at the beginning of the transition to a predominantly statist one in the second half of the 2010s.

6.1.3 Rent-Seeking

The participants of rent-seeking are those interest groups that distribute rents it and those who receive them. In studies on Poland (Sztaba 2002, Wilkin 2012, Senderski 2015, Szarzec et al. 2020), first of all, widely understood authorities (politicians, decision makers, bureaucrats, etc.)

and the strongest interest groups capable of exerting effective pressure on decision makers are mentioned. It can be argued that other social groups (which did not constitute a political force with articulated interests) were also drawn into this "rent game." Moreover, in this game it is not always possible to make a precise distinction between those who generate rents and those who benefit from them.

To understand the issue of rent-seeking in Polish transition, and particularly in the shaping up and evolution of the state corporate control, one more addition seems to be needed which expands the notion of rent-seeking beyond generating revenue of a purely economic kind. Any kind of privileged position can be considered as a source of a specific rent, including the acquisition of resources for purposes other than monetization. For example, the redistribution of political influence, limiting political competition to a larger degree that it would result from the functioning of undistorted democratic mechanisms may be directed at satisfying other, non-existential needs. According to many observers, starting with Machiavelli (1532 [1961]), these needs may be striving for power and control over other people. Apart from that, there are also may be success and the sense of belonging (McClelland and Burnham 2003). In order to avoid terminological misunderstandings and confusion with the already existing terms, the "classical" type of rents (which bring financial benefits) will be referred to as a financial rent, while the latter (which satisfies non-existential needs) will be referred to as a non-financial rent. These types of rents are interrelated: obtaining a non-financial rent in the form of power may be necessary to obtain or distribute financial rents. On the other hand, the funds raised by extracting a financial rent may be used to obtain non-financial rents, for example, through attracting voters from a certain group in exchange for economic privileges for them. Both these rents are political ones in the sense that political power mechanisms are used to redistribute resources (Sztaba 2002; Wilkin 2012).

Within the ownership policy of the state in Poland state corporate control had much more rent-seeking possibilities than privatization policy. Firstly, because the rent-seeking potential of the state-owned sector of enterprises was high due to several "universal" reasons described in the literature such as rent-seeking potential of unfinished reform processes (Hellman 1998) and the immanent politicization of SOEs functioning because of the multiplicity of their goals set by the government (Tullock 1967; Fiorina and Noll 1978). Secondly, privatization procedures and mechanisms were characterized not only by a fairly high degree of transparency and the equivalent nature of the vast majority of transactions (when a buyer had to pay the price which reflected the value of the assets), but also by its consensual nature: the need to obtain consent from a wide range of stakeholders was conducive to the formation of stable ownership relations after privatization. Thirdly, it was the design of the reforms, which ensured consistent rules of the game in the economy, including a well-regulated and transparent Polish financial market, so it was much more difficult to extract rents from privatized assets than from state assets, where management processes were much less transparent and regulated. All in all, this made privatization an unattractive source of rents in comparison with other possibilities, including those provided by the state ownership policy (Kozarzewski 2019, pp. 297–298).

In general, the sector of private enterprises was a much less ample source of rents than the sector of SOEs. There were several reasons for that, one of the most important being, firstly, constant rotation of the political elite which made impossible long-term ties between private business and the government (Schoenman 2014); so domestic entrepreneurial class was interested in market reforms rather than in attempts to enter clientelist relationships with the government. Secondly, the FDI development path meant that the majority of big businesses were in the hands of multinationals which had fewer inclinations to collude with the political elites. Cronyism and oligarchy never reached significant proportions in Poland; throughout the whole period of transition, the levels of these phenomena were among the lowest among all post-communist countries (Bałtowski and Sękowski 2020; Bałtowski et al. 2021).

The groups of rent seekers in the area of state corporate control (see Table 6.1) can be divided into two large categories. The first is the groups associated with the exercise of power: representatives of the political elite and allied persons, as well as the members of government structures responsible for corporate control decisions. Apparently, the main objective of rent-seeking here is individual enrichment of the members of these groups and perhaps also the realization of certain non-financial ambitions. These rents are primarily of a direct nature: the initiators of their acquisition are at the same time their main beneficiaries.

Such rent-seeking was developing since mid-1990s, when, as it was shown in Sect. 4.2.2, the political parties and coalitions that took power began to treat state property as a kind of bounty for the winner. The

Table 6.1 Interest groups and rents received by them generated in the SOE sector

Interest group	*Type of rent*	*Redistributed resource*	*Main objectives*
1. Political elite and allies			
The ruling political class	FR, NFR	control over enterprises, including the expansion of the state sector	—creating sources of rents for themselves and their socio-political base —creating resources for the implementation of social and economic policy
Persons connected with the governing coalition	FR, NFR	positions in companies controlled by the state	—increasing control over the activity of companies —consolidation of power —personal enrichment
	FR	procurements, contracts	—personal enrichment
2. Supporting beneficiaries			
2.1. Within SOEs			
Employees of SOEs with dominant position on the market	FR	monopoly rent	—preservation of status quo —attracting voters
Employees of "strategically important" SOEs	FR	employment, wages, privileges (e.g. pension), investments (including rescue ones)	—preservation of their SOEs —solving social problems —attracting voters
Employees of enterprises which have been nationalized through rescue investments	FR	employment, wages	—solving social problems —attracting voters

(continued)

Table 6.1 (continued)

Interest group	*Type of rent*	*Redistributed resource*	*Main objectives*
Trade unions	ER, NFR	state support for enterprises and industries	—preservation of income —political weight
2.2. Outside SOEs			
Important groups of voters not related to the state: football fans, patriotic groups, etc	FR	sponsoring, hidden subsidies	—solving social problems —attracting voters
Propaganda entities: "friendly" media and support organizations (e.g. PFN)	FR	financing by SOEs through subscriptions, sponsorship etc	—political support for the ruling coalition

FR—financial rent, NFR—non-financial rent
Source own compilation

sources of rents included, among others, the positions of representatives of the State Treasury on supervisory boards, which were filled by the Ministry of the Treasury and other government agencies which held ownership functions. Each successive winning coalition tried to fill these positions with their trusted people, and the qualifications of these persons were not as important as their political identity. From the beginning of the new century, this practice became more and more all-encompassing and began to include the managing boards of SOEs. Apart from the adverse effect on the quality of management of these companies, they were also exposed to a loss of trust on the financial markets, which manifested itself in falling prices of their shares. But from the point of view of group interests, these losses could be seen as compensated by the amount of the rents received. Rents were extracted both by those who received lucrative jobs in companies controlled by the state and by the authority that held their distribution in its hands.

Until the end of 2016, the Ministry of the Treasury was the main such distributor. The ministry, and indeed the minister and his deputies, thus secured their political weight within the government. The ministry made efforts to strengthen its position through consolidation group interests related to state corporate control policy. In the 1990s and early 2000s, the influence of interest groups at the micro and mezzo levels (management of SOEs enterprises, trade unions, state-controlled industries, etc.)

was strong, and the State Treasury, often did not exercise effective control over state assets. Since the early years of the twenty-first century, the ministry has increased its real power in filling positions in SOEs not only by taking control over managing boards positions, but also by taking less account of the interests of the aforementioned groups (although, in the long run, the real impact of these activities on limiting the ability of these groups to receive rents was small). Such a situation lasted unchanged until the middle of the 2010s, regardless of the ideology and rhetoric of subsequent political forces gaining power in the country. Things began to change only after 2015: perhaps the excessive role of the Ministry of the Treasury as a distributor of rents was one of the reasons for the liquidation of this office by the government of the PiS coalition, because it could hinder both the implementation of statist policy based on ideological and pragmatic assumptions and the realization of group interests outside the ministry.

However, these positions apparently were still treated as the sources of rents, although in the conditions of their obtaining three significant changes took place. The first was the final elimination of privatization and its rent depleting effect. The second was intensified competition for state resources after the state ownership control had become scattered among several ministries which resulted in frequent personnel changes in the largest SOE boards' composition despite the high political stability of the ruling coalition. Re-centralization of control seems to slow down the personnel carousel a bit, but other factors which power it remained intact, such as nepotism, using the seats on the boards as loyalty award, personal competition for the seats on the SOEs boards, and attempts to fight the most drastic cases of corporate misbehavior. The third was the change of the paradigm of the role of the state in the economy itself, which objectively required elimination of the rent-seeking in SOEs as well as other forms of stripping these companies from their resources, because state enterprises now had to play the role of one of the key vehicles of economic and social development. In fact, the government managed to resign from treating SOEs as the direct source of budget revenues. However, new politically motivated burdens appeared and the meritocratization of the policy towards SOE boards' composition did not succeed at all, which can be explained by its capture by two interest groups described above. As a result, the current personnel policy of the state owner is more politicized than ever before.

The second most important category of rent seekers was social and professional groups, whose support was important for the political class. The specificity of the rents functioning here was their dual character resulting from the clientelist relationships between them and the political class. The groups in question received rents directly in a financial form (income, allowances, etc.). On the other hand, the political class, which distributed the rents, was also the beneficiary of a kind of a return rent, of a non-financial and indirect nature, creating for itself a political base that strengthened its power. The initiators of this kind of rents were both representatives of the political class and direct beneficiaries.

The "primary" beneficiaries of such rents, i.e., clients, were groups both within and outside SOEs. The SOE-related groups received rents both as a result of effective pressure on the patrons, i.e., authorities (using a wide range of tools from lobbying to open protests up to riots in the center of Warsaw) and on the initiative of rent seekers in the political class. The latter, in order to gain an advantage over political competition, often take the initiative of introducing various kinds of reliefs and privileges for selected social groups. The SOE-based groups of rent-receivers were mainly employees of large enterprises, especially in sectors with weak competition and dominance of state ownership, and trade unions which functioned in these companies. Apart from their statutory goals of defending interests of employees, trade unions had their own agenda related to institutional interests of these organizations (such as political weight) and personal interests of trade-union activists such of both financial and non-financial kind (income, career, etc.).These groups can be classified as active rent seekers, as they usually forced rents on subsequent governments in a more or less drastic manner.

One of the most privileged groups were coal miners, who benefited from numerous rents in the form of too high employment and wages, additional privileges in the form of, e.g., early retirement, as well as stability resulting not from the high competitiveness of this sector, but from the protective measures taken by the government. Rents transferred to this group have recently started to mean not only high costs for the economy, but also threaten the country's development prospects in the long term, e.g., by limiting the implementation of RES in order to ensure the rationale for the existence of coal-fired power generation. Besides, these clientelist relationships, i.e., the voices of the miners apparently are becoming too costly for the patrons themselves, because limiting the development prospects and potential problems with access to EU structural funds jeopardize the rents they receive. This may be one of the reasons why the government is gradually withdrawing from support for coal mining.

The category of SOE-based rent-seeking groups recently has expanded through rescue investments of the state in some troubled private companies, leading to the restoration of state control over them.

Groups not connected with the SOE sector were a relatively new category of receivers of rents, which started to grow during the late years of the PO-PSL coalition at the beginning of the 2010s and flourished under the PiS government. They were internally diversified, but had one common feature: they enjoyed support by SOEs. In this case, the rent-seeking initiative came rather from the political elite—with the acceptance of rent beneficiaries, of course. There were two groups of beneficiaries which differed not only in origin but also in the character of return rents generated by them for the political class. The first one was organized groups attractive as voters, such as football fans, member of patriotic and catholic organizations, etc. For them, the rents mainly took the form of various types of sports sponsorship and cultural patronage. After 2015, such activities become more and more politicized, and a new group of beneficiaries took the stage: those, whose task was to render propaganda support for the ruling coalition. Those were mostly "politically friendly" media, previously quite marginal, but which started getting a very substantial support by SOEs through subscriptions and placing advertisements. Besides, such political support functions started to be played the Polish National Foundation (PFN) which had been established by the group of the largest SOEs and initially had to promote Polish economy.

Despite the goals of the majority of the rent-seeking activities initiated by the political class were quite clear and were boiling down mostly to keeping the political power and receiving financial gains, the real objectives of quite many actions were obscure—especially when the direct beneficiaries were not the members of the political class and bureaucracy. For example, it is possible to imagine that support for unprofitable mines and other rescue investments at least partly resulted from the sincere belief that the state, while performing its social functions, should take care of the situation of endangered social groups, or, as it was claimed officially, this was the way to ensure the country's energy security or support social and economic development. Sports sponsorship and cultural patronage could have been supported by the government with the hands of SOEs as a form of promoting healthy lifestyle and national values, or simply resulted from the SOEs marketing strategy (as they usually claimed). At present, a hypothesis may be formulated that many of the activities in this area had the dual purpose of combining the public interest with the private one. According to it, the state usually either pursued social objectives with generating rents as a side effect, or vice versa: the implementation of social objectives was a pretext for (and a side effect of) creating and distributing rents.

Activities aimed at limiting the rent-seeking potential of the state policy in the enterprise sector, primarily through professionalization of state corporate governance and de-politicization of the state control, proved to be ineffective through the whole period of the transition. It can be assumed that in the past the cause was not only the advantage of private interest groups over pro-reform forces. Probably, the state sector, in the eyes of many reformers being generally disappearing (except for a few areas), was not perceived as posing an institutionally significant threat big enough to concentrate too much resources on fighting its dysfunctions. On the other hand, the implementation of the statist policy of PiS governments after 2015, whose success was impossible without increasing the scope of activities in good faith, extended the possibilities of extracting rents from the state domain to such a scale that even intensified counteractions were doomed to failure.

However, looking at Mihályi and Szelényi's (2017) typology of extracting rents in the CEE region (market capture by political elites, state capture by oligarchs, and capture of oligarchs by autocratic rulers) may lead to a somewhat paradoxical conclusion: although the role of group interests in the state's policy in the enterprise sector (and social and economic policy in this country as a whole) seems to be very important, none of the three mechanisms in Poland are still actually present, or they exist in trace quantities. There are neither real oligarchs in Poland, nor any significant bourgeoisie (especially of the communist descent) supporting the authorities in exchange for access to property. The Polish political regime, in the recent years becoming quite flawed by the Western standards, is still very far from autocracy. Hence the situation of deprivation of oligarchs (or some other strong rent-seeking groups) by an authoritarian political class seems to be impossible too.

Another characteristic feature of Poland is still low value of rents extracted from the SOEs. Apart from their intangible components (striving for power, prestige, etc.), they usually amounted to sums that could hardly be called dizzying. Monthly salaries for a supervisory board member usually amount to several thousand zlotys (a thousand Euros or so). CEOs earn more, but million-dollar payments, although occur, are extremely rare. According to the #samiswoi youth campaign of the PSL (Polskie Stronnictwo Ludowe, Polish People's Party), over 100 PiS politicians earned over PLN 11 million (about EUR 2.5 million) on lucrative positions in SOEs, central state administration and local governments (Gostkiewicz 2018) in an unspecified period of less than a year in 2017–2018. Assuming that on average it was a period of 9 months, the average earnings of the beneficiary amounted to slightly more than PLN 12 thousand (EUR 2800) per month gross which was 2.5 times more than an average salary in Poland but still not a breathtaking income. According to the study conducted two years later (Mikołajewska 2020), the total earnings of 84 persons connected with PiS which occupied the boards of 14 largest listed SOEs amounted so far to PLN 162.4 million (about USD 43 million). A high degree of inequality have been found: in two cases (both were CEO in the largest financial sector companies) the total income exceeded PLN 10 million (about USD 2.6 million) and annual income of these persons was about PLN 1.5–3.5 million (about USD 400–900 thousand). Income of other persons was much more modest, 41 of them receiving less than PLN 1 million (about USD 260 thousand).

Another source of rents was contracts signed by SOEs with private entities affiliated with these enterprises' CEOs and supervising bureaucrats. The exact scale of this practice is unknown, but anecdotal evidence, again, shows that the value of the rents was not extremely high. For example, the Central Anticorruption Bureau, in the framework of investigation devoted to nepotistic practices in SOEs (which eventually led to dismissal of David Jackiewicz, the first Minister of the Treasury in the PiS government—see Sect. 4.3.2), investigated a case of a PR agency established by Adam Hoffman, an ex-PiS press-secretary, and other members of the political elite, who used their political influence and personal contacts to sign contracts with the largest SOEs (Harłukowicz 2020). The total amount of questioned contracts was over PLN 1.2 million (about USD 340 thousand).

Thus, the total amount of rents of this kind apparently was an insignificant part of the country's GDP which in 2019 amounted to PLN 2.3 trillion (about USD 600 billion). Besides, in individual terms, firstly, even the highest earnings of the above-mentioned two CEOs, which might look very impressive in a country with one of the lowest personal income in the EU such as Poland, were still at least several times lower than those in comparable companies in the most developed market economies. Secondly, rents in Poland also did not give income comparable to those obtained in some other post-communist countries such as Russia, where the cream of rent-seekers was one of the richest people in the world, and the beneficiaries even of the middle-level state bureaucracy had a standard of living unimaginable in Poland with their expensive flats in metropolitan centers, magnificent villas and luxury cars.

The still relatively low value of rents in Poland probably results from both limited resources to be distributed (as opposed to countries where one can obtain a rent on natural resources, especially oil) and exogenous and endogenous institutional constraints for rent-seeking (discussed further in this chapter) which radically limit possibilities of breaking the law in obtaining them. Of course, it does not mean that they are not harmful for the economy and the society. What is harmful at a first place, it's the actual degree of state policy capture by interest groups which look for rents. However, due to the financial and institutional limitations existing in Poland, the degree of such capture is still lower than in many other post-communist countries, so the role of the good faith factor in the policy of the state, including towards enterprises, may be relatively greater.

6.1.4 *Impact of Good Faith and Rent-Seeking on the Evolution of the State Corporate Control*

Considering the corporate control policy of the state within the framework of this dichotomy, it is possible to formulate a hypothesis that both these factors and their mutual relations have contributed both to continuity and to change of this policy. They were beneficial for the relatively stable policy with a high degree of continuation, to a large extent, as it has been stressed several times in this book, making it independent of the official rhetoric of rival parties, especially during election campaigns. But they also contributed to the gradual drift of the whole ownership policy towards statism until, using Hegelian terminology, the transformation of quantity into quality in recent years took place in the form of a redefinition of the role of the state in the enterprise sector and the national economy as a whole.

During the transition, the good faith factor mainly played a stabilizing role, making an important contribution to the path dependency. Regardless of ideological differences, the basic political forces during the first 25 years of the Polish transition were united by a certain consensus on the main directions of reforms: a democratic state was to be built based on an efficiently functioning market economy which assumed the key role of the private sector; Poland was to open up to the world, join the club of the most developed countries by participating in economic, political and military arrangements. No major political grouping set the goal of rebuilding the planned economy and authoritarian regime, and stood in the position of isolationism. It was not until the coalition, which came to power in late 2015, that this consensus began to be undermined in practice, although the real government's actions were still much more moderate than the rhetoric of the officials announcing the great statist-isolationist change.

It also seems that the factor of good faith was at least in part responsible for the statist evolution of ownership policy. After the initial prevalence of liberal economists in public discourse and in decision-making circles, other options gradually came to light which, within the generally agreed framework described in the previous paragraph, promoted a more "pro-social" policy with greater state participation. Although this objectively fostered the growth of group interests and the politicization of the state's ownership functions, there is no reason to believe that these views could not have been expressed in good faith. Especially since the end of the 2000s, when the ideas of market failure, as a result of the global financial crisis, began to regain popularity all over the world. It was shown earlier in the chapter that the statist turn made by the PiS coalition, could be influenced by factors of good will, sincere conviction about the state's capabilities to face accumulated dysfunctions and developmental challenges. One of the ideological (or propaganda) assumptions of the "good change" was the necessity to break the previous state's incompetence.

Group interests could also play an important role in stabilizing the state's ownership policy. The coexistence of a quite efficient system of parliamentary democracy and attractive sources of rents, which the institutionally weak state was not able to eliminate, created a specific mechanism of rent-seeking. Its characteristic feature was the rotation of rent seekers, while the main source of the rents, the state enterprise sector, remained essentially unchanged. Not only did this mechanism counteract attempts to reduce rents, but it also prevented them from increasing rapidly or being extracted in a more drastic way, with open violation of the law because this could have been fatal for the existing beneficiaries after losing the elections. In this context it is understandable that the PiS coalition is trying to dismantle the existing public control mechanisms through limiting the rotation of political power in the future, ensuring a political monopoly for itself. If it succeeds, the political restrictions on rent-seeking in the state-controlled enterprise sector can be expected to weaken significantly.

Another stabilizing factor could have been, according to Lissowska (2008, p. 166), that all major interest groups (including those that benefited from the continuation of market reforms) demanded state support. This created conditions for strengthening the role of public administration, including as a distributor of rents and privileges. Under such conditions, it was not interested in changing the rules of the game.

The influence of interest groups on changing the state's ownership and corporate control policy towards a gradual rise in statism can also be seen. It results from the natural aspirations of interest groups to increase rents and the need to compensate for the shrinkage of its main source, i.e., the resources of SOEs. From this perspective, the acceleration of the statist drift since the beginning of the twenty-first century can be explained after Szanyi (2016) (who observed a similar phenomenon in Hungary) by the radical depletion of state property resources resulting from privatization in previous years. The interest groups extracting rents from state property felt threatened and began to block privatization more and more effectively. From this perspective, the Polish model of transparent and consensual privatization, with all its advantages in terms of the quality of the emerging private sector, could foster the consolidation of anti-privatization forces. Either way, the increased control of enterprises by the government, the possibility of obtaining profits from state assets decreased the attractiveness of their possible privatization for politicians, as it was already stated many years ago on the example of developed market economies (Shleifer and Vishny 1994). The consent of these interest groups to privatization appeared only when the state's finances turned out to be particularly threatened, which in itself could lead to the reduction of sources of rents.

6.2 Exogenous and Endogenous Factors

As in the case of the first dichotomy, the influence of these groups of factors seems to be complicated and ambiguous, and also variable over time. Moreover, there are diametrically divergent opinions on this subject among researchers and politicians, all of which determining the need for further, more in-depth research.

6.2.1 Exogenous Factors

There is an opinion in the literature that, in general, Poland's entire economic policy during the transition period was very much influenced by external factors—primarily of a subjective nature, in the form of activities of individuals and interest groups of foreign origin. They were supposed to trigger the transition process, starting from the concept of reforms not only borrowed without major changes from the Washington Consensus, but also developed with the decisive participation of Western experts, especially Jeffrey Sachs and David Lipton. An opinion is also popular that behind the reforms stood the interests of international financial circles headed by George Soros, and that the role of Leszek Balcerowicz and his team was to follow external instructions. In its purest form, such views were presented by Błasiak (2014) and Zyzak (2016).

Regardless of whether the reform policy including the state ownership policy was the result of a conspiracy or a deep conviction of the reformers as to its rightness, the most widespread accusation against it nowadays is that FDIs were one of its pillars. This view, previously known from the monograph by Kieżun (2012), was popularized after 2015 by Prime Minister Mateusz Morawiecki, who, among others, accused foreign capital of "colonizing" Poland, forcing Polish economy to function in the interest of foreign entities. He claimed that Poland paid out a multibillion dollar "neocolonial rent" of 5% of GDP every year (Gadomski 2016).

All these alarmist theses did not tackle the state corporate control policy in detail, their authors concentrated rather on privatization policy blaming all the governments since 1990 for neglecting the national interests of Poland through selling out the national property to foreigners. In their view, generally the enterprise sector would have been functioning much better if it remained in the state hands or was sold to domestic investors. But they also blamed the government for liquidation of allegedly strong Polish industries inherited from the communist past, such as electronics, machine building, or weaving—through lack of proper state support and opening the domestic market to international competition (which was done under pressure of some ideas and deliberate actions from outside). These claims resurfaced in mid-2010s and were used as a justification of increasing statism in the economic policy, including policy of the state corporate control.

Putting aside conspiracy theories, these theses point at two groups of exogenous factors that may have influenced the corporate control policy of the Polish state. The first one is drawing inspiration from the knowledge that emerged in other countries (primarily the Western developed economies) in the form of ideas, concepts and practical solutions. The second is the influence of world economic and political processes.

6.2.1.1 Knowledge Transfer

Polish economic thought has always been open to the ideas of Western economics, which has influenced the concepts of Polish transition. Indeed, the "Balcerowicz Plan" was based on the then existing state of knowledge on how to get economies out of the crisis, with its universalization of recipes and a total lack of experience in the effective transformation of command economies. No wonder that the core of the concept of Polish transition was based on ideas popular at that time, especially the Washington Consensus (Williamson 1989). They created hopes for reforms to be carried out quickly and effectively, which was credible due to the results of economic reform carried out according to these recipes in Bolivia or the success of liberal economic policy in Chile. Therefore, many Polish economists regarded gradualist concepts to be insufficiently effective. Moreover, unlike the liberal concept, the gradualist ones had never been successful in practice. Western experts also actively participated in the preparation of specific reforms in Poland and helped to monitor the economic situation by identifying emerging threats.

External knowledge sources helped Polish reformers to create a largely successful policy of post-communist transition indeed. On the other hand, they may be at least partly "blamed" for failures as well, particularly in the area of the corporate control of the state, the inability of creating an efficient policy towards enterprises that were to remain under the state control—because before the transition started and during its early stages SOEs were not on the agenda of the researchers and experts from developed economies.

Nevertheless, it seems unjustified to claim that the transition, including the state ownership policy, was formulated and conducted under the dictates of Western experts. Although the general idea of the transition paradigm and ownership policy was not original, these external recipes were significantly adapted to Polish reality and even own solutions were prepared, sometimes against the opinion of international advisers. This was the case, among other things, with the development of a non-standard, again contrary to the recommendations of Western experts, solution to the "bad debt" crisis of early 1990s in which state-owned banks and state-owned enterprises were involved. The domestically tailored solutions were implemented, which proved to be more effective than those proposed by foreign experts (see Sect. 4.2.1).

The successes of the first years of post-communist transition in Poland, which was quickly recognized as the leader of post-communist reforms (for stabilization of the economy and return to the path of growth, effective building of market economy institutions and the creation of a model regulated financial market), convinced the ruling political class to the fundamental rightness of the chosen path, which further weakened the importance of the external intellectual factor as a catalyst for reforms.

However, throughout the entire transition period, there was no consensus in the Polish expert and academia circles on many aspects of the reforms, including the policy towards the state enterprise sector. Discussions on the ultimate model of the system reforms referred to the experience of developed and emerging economies and to the current achievements of the most renowned foreign economists. Thus, the turn towards greater statism both in economic policy in other countries, and in world economic thought, which became particularly evident in times of the global financial crisis, could not go unnoticed. Especially if one considers the popularity of the market failure concept among a large part of Polish researchers and, to an even greater extent, politicians. The latter became increasingly eager to refer to the practice of developed market economies, especially their anti-crisis microeconomic policy as well as to the work of world-renowned economists. The justification for the statist turn by the experience of the West and Western economic thought was particularly intensified after the PiS coalition took power in 2015.

However, there are arguments in support of the claim that the statist drift in global economic policy was much shallower and less lasting than it is presented by supporters of statization of ownership policy in Poland. Firstly, the anti-crisis actions of governments in many developed economies did not boil down to an increase in statism, especially in the long run, and the nationalizations occurring at the end of the 2000s were usually of a rescue, transitional nature. In 2010, the EU launched the Europe 2020 growth strategy based, among others, on liberalization and privatization, limiting the state role in the enterprise sector. Concrete steps were taken especially in countries where statist policy started threatening the stability of public finances and the development prospects. Among other things, Greece and Portugal were persuaded to privatize the companies that came under state control as part of the rescue nationalizations. In fact, bailouts were by definition an extraordinary tool and not a part of a long-term economic strategy. So it may be argued that the global financial crisis has not led to the statization of economic policy in the long run, at least in selected developed Western countries (Artner 2017), or even liberalized it (in EU countries), including ownership policy (Farkas 2016, pp. 486–487).

Secondly, the increase in the role of the state in the economy, the increase in the importance of state ownership in the long term was primarily related to the global situation and resulted largely from the evolution of the balance of power in the global economy. The importance of the statised economies outside of the club of the world's most developed market countries was growing, especially of the Chinese economy; at the same time deep statization of the energy sector, again mainly in emerging economies, was seen (Bałtowski and Kwiatkowski 2018, Chapter 7). On the other hand, there was lack of signs of the skidding of developed Western economies towards state capitalism (Djankov 2015), so they could not become a role model of statization for decision makers in Poland and some other post-communist countries.

The question arises to what extent this reference to the West reflected the real influence of Western ideas and practices, and to what extent it was a more or less conscious attempt to justify the actions of the government, taken for other reasons, using the emerging pretexts. There is no clear answer to this question. On the one hand, looking from the perspective of the already presented analysis of the good faith vs. vested interests dichotomy, one can cautiously assume that the changes in the state's ownership policy in recent years (or proposals for change) could be to some extent inspired by these ideas. Inspirations with foreign economic thought experience can be seen, e.g., in the first proposals to domesticate the banking sector and a new development concept based on a strong state and domestic capital.

On the other hand, the first signs of statization of the Polish state's ownership policy (and economic policy as a whole) appeared as early as in the mid-1990s and gradually increased in importance during the first years of the twenty-first century, i.e., before the statist drift in theory and practice began to be noticeable in countries with developed market economies. What is more, the radical paradigm shift in Poland, presented as a defensive reaction to the emerging threats, took place only after the global financial crisis was over. The picture of some kind of de-synchronization of ownership policy in Poland and developed market economies is complemented by much less statist, than in many developed economies, policy towards the global financial crisis. In Poland, there were basically no rescue nationalizations in that period, and the financial sector, which was most affected in developed countries, in Poland went through the crisis without major losses.

Besides, the intellectual output of the West was often presented not in a balanced and reliable way. The statist discourse in world literature, indeed, has gained in importance, but has not appropriated the entire debate. Many publications were still being written, if not usually within a purely liberal discourse, but still far from the statist one. This applies, e.g., to the majority of valuable publications on the state policy in the enterprise sector and SOEs: Christiansen and Kim (2014), Musacchio and Lazzarini (2014), Mühlenkamp (2015), Szanyi (2016), Mihályi and Szelényi (2017), to name but few. Moreover, many such publications were positivist in nature and their authors described the observed phenomena and processes without evaluating them, let alone being apologetic towards them. International organizations such as the OECD, while appreciating the importance of the state sector, also did not postulate its extension or any preferential treatment. In Poland, in turn, the degree of domination of statist discourse in the literature on economics and economic policy at that time was much higher than in the West.

In any case, the supporters of the statist turn in Poland referred only to publications and ideas confirming their theses claiming that the statist stance was the current mainstream in the economics. Mateusz Morawiecki went the furthest in this respect, presenting one of his favorite authors—Thomas Piketty, a left-wing economist with an anti-capitalist stamina, as the representative of the "absolute economic mainstream" and the "highest-profile economist in the world" (Morawiecki 2016; Lis 2017).

Moreover, references to publications were not always reliable. An example is the pejorative use of the term "dependent market economy" contrary to the intentions of its authors Nölke and Vliegenthart (2009), for whom it was only the name of the model of capitalism based on FDIs, which was being developed in CEE countries and whose effectiveness they generally assessed positively. Another term abused by Prime Minister Morawiecki was "foreign-owned countries" allegedly coined for Poland by Piketty (Morawiecki 2016). In fact, it was used once in passing to refer to the CEE economies in an article by Novokmet et al. (2017) on inequalities in Russia. All this suggests that the intellectual output of Western economists has been used not only as a basis for formulating an economic strategy, but also (or perhaps mostly) to make this policy credible.

Given the fact that exogenous factors related to knowledge transfer were generally either weak or distorted, perhaps other factors, probably rather of endogenous character, played a greater role in the evolution of the Poland's policy towards the enterprise sector, especially since the end of the 2000s.

6.2.1.2 Impact of Global Economic and Political Processes

Poland was not isolated from the rest of the world either economically or politically. One of the main goals of the transition was to open up to the world in economic and political terms. This took the form of removing the barriers to the transfer of resources and integrating the Polish economy into world markets. Poland's openness to the world also meant joining the most important international organizations worldwide. The most important events in this respect were Poland's accession to the World Trade Organization (WTO) in 1995 and to the European Union in 2004. All this created not only new development opportunities for the Polish economy, but also challenges, increasing the country's dependence on global economic and sometimes political processes, and to some extent limiting sovereignty in decision-making at the government level.

In this respect, a crucial role was played by the need for Poland to comply with the EU *acquis communautaire*, which required the adjustment of Polish law and economic policy to the requirements of capital movements, public procurement, competition or public aid policies. The conditions of Poland's accession to the EU, and later—its membership in this organization, favored the demonopolization of a number of economic sectors (mainly infrastructure) and limited the state's ability to selectively support SOEs, as well as to create preferential conditions for domestic investors in relation to foreign ones. In general, it can be argued that the impact of Poland's entry into global institutional arrangements was conducive to limiting interventionism in Polish ownership policy, although it proved not strong enough to prevent it from growing. The fastest growth of statism, ending with a qualitative change in the role of the state in the business sector, happened during Poland's membership in the EU. It can be assumed that in the absence of restrictions resulting from membership in this organization (and the WTO) the pace of statization of ownership policy (and economic policy in general) would be even higher.

The second channel of influence of global processes, whose importance has been strengthened by the factors described above, was Poland's growing integration into the world economy—with its both positive and negative effects. One of the manifestations of this was the increasing influence of the economic situation on the world markets on the Polish economy; another—the FDI-led development path. Foreign capital, which actively participated in privatization of SOEs and creating new businesses in Poland, also influenced the ownership policy (and, more broadly, the economic policy) of the state as such: the policy towards FDIs (which was conducted with a number of goals in mind: systemic, economic and fiscal) required steps to be taken in order to attract them and to eliminate factors that could be repulsive for FDIs. This included broadly understood making the Polish investment offer more attractive by creating a favorable investment climate and opportunities for investments. In turn, foreign capital was interested in improving investment conditions and lobbied further reforms towards liberalization, transparency, and stable rules of the game. Among others, it limited the discretionary power of the government over the enterprise sector and possibilities of conducting statist policy in the enterprise sector. Thus the impact of FDIs on the corporate control policy of the state may be assessed as generally favorable. An additional factor here must be mentioned: favorable investment conditions not only made Poland attractive to FDIs in general, but also contributed to "positive selection" of foreign investors (Kozarzewski 2006, pp. 213–214) eliminating capital aimed at quick profits, the so-called secondhand investments (Papava 2002), and capital of domestic origin, which previously had escaped to "tax havens."

It seems, however, that the influence of foreign investors on Polish economic policy should not be overestimated and it would be a big exaggeration to say, following opponents of the FDI-led development path (Kieżun 2012) that the Polish government was captured by interests of multinational corporations. Moreover, the Polish economic policy was not always favorable to foreign capital and the possibilities for representatives of foreign capital to exert political influence on the authorities were limited in relation to domestic forces, among others because foreigners did not have such a powerful tool in their hands as the right to vote.

In a way, the real impact of FDIs on the Polish state corporate control policy in some aspects could be indirectly negative. Firstly, FDIs created threats for rent-seeking both through lobbying for transparency and limiting the government's interference, and through active participation in privatization thus limiting the amount of resources which could be redistributed among private interest groups. Secondly, through the fears within the political class and some part of the academia that the FDI-led development path created more threats than opportunities for the Polish economy. And the latter argument, as was mentioned before, was used for the official justification of the statist turn of the economic policy made in mid-2010s.

6.2.2 *Endogenous Factors*

It can be argued that the state's ownership policy has been substantially influenced by numerous objective and subjective internal factors. Some of the most significant of them have already been discussed earlier in this book, so here their synthesis is only presented.

6.2.2.1 State of the Economy

The first group of factors is the state of the economy and the resulting economic policy challenges. Before the start of the systemic reforms, the Polish economy was in a state of deep crisis caused by the ineptitude of the command system and the failure of attempts to streamline it through reforms that did not change its essence. The lack of possibility to repair the system objectively posed two tasks to the state: a short-term task to overcome the crisis and a long-term task of constructing a new sustainable social and economic system capable of development and resistant to systemic crises. Although the reformers' sources of inspiration were mainly of an exogenous nature (liberal anti-crisis policy, market economy based on private property, etc.), the need for these measures was completely endogenous: without crisis management policy, without reforms, the Polish economy was unable to function. At further stages of the transition, one can also see the impact of the economic situation in the country on the ownership policy: for example, fiscal problems, low efficiency of many SOEs or entire state-controlled industries, the need to ensure competitiveness of the Polish economy. All these problems had to be solved and could not be just ignored. Generally, the role of this group of factors in shaping the state corporate control policy seems to be decreasing over time from a very large one at the beginning of the transition to quite a secondary one nowadays. This evolution took place, firstly, because of the increase in ideological motivations of the policy in relation to pragmatic motivations; secondly, because of the most burning economic problems of the early stages of transition have been already solved. However, it did not prevent PiS politicians from using the allegedly bad state of the Polish economy (up to the blunt but untrue slogan "Poland is in ruin") as one of the main justifications of the statist turn in the economic policy and from proclaiming the need to make the state-controlled enterprise sector and public investments the main vehicles of the country's development.

6.2.2.2 Intellectual Potential

The second group of factors is the national intellectual potential, expressed, among others, in the ability to accumulate knowledge, process it and generate new knowledge in the form of assessment of existing challenges, tasks facing the state in the field of ownership policy and development of objectives and tools for its implementation. Before the transition, the Polish intellectual potential was unique among the countries of the Eastern bloc. Throughout almost the entire period of the communist rule, independent political and economic thought existed, and all the time unofficial or semi-official discussions on the need for reforms and their shape were conducted. Economists and representatives of other disciplines of knowledge were not isolated from world trends and were aware of the research achievements in developed capitalist countries. This contributed to the situation when, despite (especially at the beginning of the transition) the influence of exogenous factors was large (world literature, advisors, etc.), the Polish reforms, including the area of ownership and state corporate control, were to a large extent a national product. Their final shape (with all their drawbacks as well) was the work of Polish politicians and their intellectual supporters.

It seems that over time, the relative (vis-à-vis external ones) role of national factors in the generation and use of knowledge had been growing, as, e.g., reflected in the response to the global financial crisis of 2007–2008, which was different from that of many Western countries, and in the driving forces behind the statist turn which was based largely on ideological considerations developed mainly by Polish politicians. This does not mean, however, that this domestic knowledge was used by policymakers with increasing effectiveness—precisely because of this ideologization, which increasingly made knowledge a propaganda tool. Moreover, as Miszewski (2012, p. 11) rightly points out, neither at the beginning nor ever during the transition in Poland was it possible to develop a comprehensive vision of the target model of the economy, which can also be classified as an intellectual factor and which undoubtedly contributed to the drawbacks of the corporate control policy of the state (and its ownership policy in general). Here, the inability of local politicians and intellectuals to fill international knowledge gaps in the field of policy towards SOEs also must be mentioned.

6.2.2.3 Institutional Setup

The third group of internal factors is the institutional setup within which the state ownership policy functioned. Using Acemoğlu and Robinson's (2012) perspective, in general, there are two types of institutions. The first one is the extractive institutions which ensure getting rents at the expense of other social groups. The second is inclusive institutions, providing equal opportunities for all market participants and effective protection of their rights. One may argue that the extractive institution played important role in the corporate control policy of the Polish state because the state-owned enterprise sector was one of the major sources of rents generated by the economic policy. It seems that the real influence of the private interest groups which extracted rents from the state corporate control policy was steadily increasing. This contributed to the preservation of a substantial SOEs sector and even to the expansion of the ownership functions of the state. Of course, in an open economy such as Polish one, the possibilities of extracting rents from the state sector depended to some extent on external factors, but both the source of the rents and the groups involved in their extraction were domestic. Foreign rent seekers would be interested in privatization rather than in increasing the interventionism of the Polish state. Besides, the ownership policy of the Polish government after 2015 completely eliminated this external interest group and in general has significantly weakened the influence of foreign investors. On the other hand, the importance of domestic groups of rent seekers and state sector investments was growing.

Another element of the institutional system was the condition of the Polish state. It included several interrelated dimensions. The first one, the most concrete and directly influencing the corporate control policy, was the decision-making processes, not necessarily connected with the play of interests, i.e., the way of functioning of the state apparatus responsible for designing and implementing of this policy. Throughout the whole transition period, it was characterized, unlike in a number of other post-socialist countries, by a definite dominance of the executive branch of power. The majority of ownership functions were quickly centralized in the hands of one governmental agency, and the role of the parliament became quite formal. The whole system of conducting the state's ownership policy, and especially its corporate control pillar, which were never perfect, began to clearly deteriorate, starting from the first years of the new century—mainly due to the growing role of rent-seeking groups. After 2015 extractive institutions started to flourish even more, because the government through its statist policy created better conditions for them through expanding the major source of rents which were SOEs and public investments. Perhaps to a large extent, it was an unwelcome side effect, but it seems that since then the government lost control over its policy towards the SOE sector which started to drift being pushed by interest groups and the government's attempts to make it more steerable.

This dimension seems to be related to a very important institutional weakness of the Polish state, the general condition of the system of governance in Poland, which, according to some researchers, is constantly deteriorating, being characterized by increasing impotence at its highest level, which did not allow for a well-coordinated social and economic policy. Matyja (2018) called it entropy of the state, which in his view finally became apparent after 2005 (when the PiS coalition took power for the first time losing it in 2007). The main goal of the political activity became to win elections rather than a real change of the state for the better. The actions of the current PiS coalition, which took power again at the end of 2015, even if they were mostly based on good faith (which perhaps is an exaggeration), were unlikely to overcome this entropy because they did not touch the essence of the existing institutional shortcomings of the state, including in the field of ownership policy.

Last but not least, one of the most important institutional dimensions is the condition of democratic institutions. The permeability of democratic procedures, the quality of the political scene affect the quality of the state's functioning. They affect both the quality of functioning of public administration bodies directly or indirectly contributing to the ownership policy of the state, and the activities of various other stakeholder groups. In general, it can be said that well-functioning democratic institutions are conducive to ensuring that the state's ownership policy pursues the public interest, rather than private group interests. International comparative studies such as Democracy Index, Freedom in the World and Worldwide Governance Indicators show that while in this respect the situation in Poland before the statist change of mid-2010s was not fundamentally different from other CEE countries (being better than in the CIS countries but worse than in most developed economies), since then it started to deteriorate. On the other hand, throughout the whole period in question, the Polish political system and political practice retained a set of safeguards which made democratic mechanisms work relatively effectively: freedom of speech and independent mass-media existed, elections were held in a transparent way, separation of powers with independent courts existed. All this made possible political competition to function which ensured constant rotation of political elites. Besides, the rule of law was sufficiently efficient not to allow private interest groups for outright illegal activity. It did not eliminate, but strongly limited the voluntaristic policy of the government and constrained appetite of rent seekers.

6.2.2.4 Public Opinion

A fourth group of factors, which deserves to be discussed in a little more detail because it was not tackled in the earlier parts of this book, is the attitude of society towards the state's ownership policy. It is essential to identify to what extent shaping up and evolution of this policy was a reaction of politicians to the expectations of voters. In representative democracies political elites, and not the society, create concepts and visions, and society chooses those it finds most attractive. On the other hand, when making these concepts and visions public, politicians cannot fail to take into account the prevailing social preferences. This implies that if there have been no drastic changes in public opinion, it was rather the elites who played a decisive role in the evolution of state's policy.

Attitude towards state ownership started being studied (by the governmental Public Opinion Research Center—CBOS) only since 2015. At the same time, CBOS was the only one organization which since 1990 studied attitudes towards privatization on a regular basis, but stopped doing this in 2009. Other organizations sporadically conducted similar studies, but usually, they covered only one year and were based on different set of questions and samples. Thus we have no comparable data for the whole period of transition, but some observations on the specificity of public opinion on the state's ownership policy, its evolution and possible factors shaping it can still be made.

Throughout the transition period, in public opinion privatization was the least popular segment of reforms which did not reflect the real (quite small) extent of its dysfunctions (Kozarzewski 2019, pp. 321–323). The attitude towards the second pillar of ownership policy, corporate control of the state, was much more favorable, especially to the general idea of the state being an owner of enterprises. This was due to the great popularity of the idea of a welfare state; at the beginning of the transition, it was supported by the population's experience of the last period of the previous regime, when the state, despite the growing economic crisis, kept SOEs afloat, providing their employees with usually quite poor but still important certainty for tomorrow. Thus, at the beginning of the transition, dissatisfaction was aroused not only by privatization, but also by the policy aimed at eliminating the privileges of state-owned enterprises which was perceived as leaving them to their fate (Jarosz et al. 1991).

As a national public opinion poll shows, more than a quarter of a century later the majority of the population still advocated the existence of a large and strong state-controlled enterprise sector (CBOS 2019). Even among supporters of Nowoczesna, an opposition party with the most liberal economic agenda, 39% agreed with the statement in the questionnaire that a big number of enterprises must stay in the state hands. Among PiS supporters this opinion was shared by 79% of respondents. Moreover, in public opinion the differences between the state and private sectors began to blur. The SOEs started being attributed with advantages that had been previously perceived as mainly belonging to private companies: positive impact on the development of the country, quality products, high competitiveness and opportunities for personal development of employees (Ministry of the Treasury 2016).

Public opinion polls in Poland show a certain correlation between the state ownership policy and the society's attitude towards it. For the period before 2015 one can assume that support for large-scale privatization equals lack of support for preservation of the extensive SOE sector and vice versa. Studies show that periods of active privatization policy have been accompanied with an above-average positive attitude to privatization and conversely, in the periods when the government was slowing down privatization, public opinion was more skeptical towards privatization too. The general long-term trend was decreasing the share of privatization supporters in the society from above 40% at the beginning of the 1990s to about 30% by the end of the decade; in 2000s, the share of supporters usually was below 30% (CBOS 2009). The changes of public opinion were not abrupt or large, but they were clearly synchronized with changes in the privatization policy; there was no time gap between changes in the opinion and changes in the policy.

Analyzing these data, Bałtowski and Kozarzewski (2014, pp. 391–393) argue that there is a reason to believe that the privatization policy was independent from public opinion and it's public opinion which in fact was to some extent steered by the government's rhetoric which was to justify its policy. Other studies explain changing public attitudes towards privatization by the changes in the economic situation in the country: its deterioration increased the negative perception of privatization, while the improvement decreased it (Staniszewski 2013) or by population's learning to function in the market economy (when initial euphoria was replaced by disillusion and later by more balanced attitude) (Patena and Stawiarska 2016). In any case, there are no studies that would show the dependence of the state ownership policy on public expectations.

In the later period, the intensification of statist and anti-privatization trends in the governmental rhetoric and action was also unlikely to be an answer to the society's changing demand: at that time, or immediately before, there was no corresponding deterioration in the society's attitude to privatization, which roughly remained at the level of previous years or even improved slightly (Ministry of the Treasury 2016). Little can be said about changes in the public attitude towards SOEs: the polls conducted in 2015–2019 show gradually decreasing support for the idea of the state being one of the major owners of enterprises from 67 to 63%, but it is still too early to say whether it is a trend (perhaps reflecting the public reaction to persistent scandals in the SOE sector) or just a fluctuation.

All of this rather indicates that the changes in the corporate control policy of the state and its ownership policy as a whole are determined primarily by other factors than a response to public demand. It seems that one can at most speak of an indirect impact; in the case of growing statism, it would be the imminent attractiveness of a highly patronizing state to a significant part of society. Left-wing, statist and egalitarian, and even anti-market ideas were popular in the Polish public opinion in late communist times (Morawski and Kozek 1991; Mucha et al. 1991; Szacki

1994) and have not been radically overcome over the decades of the reforms.

The democratization of the Polish state was not accompanied by an adequate development of the society's awareness and knowledge about the functioning of the state and the economy. Among others, it makes the population prone to propaganda of any kind, but especially the populist one. In some respect, these are the processes similar to those described nearly 90 years ago by Ortega y Gasset (1932) on the example of democratizing Western European societies.

Due to the chronically narrow socio-political base of reforms, political parties in Poland were increasingly motivated to seek the support of social groups other than those who were natural reform allies. The 2015 and 2019 parliamentary elections in Poland were won by a grouping that was able, among other things, to take advantage of pro-paternalistic and statist sentiments. As one of the key PiS politicians put it, "this is the first government that really gives."

One more feature of Polish public opinion should be stressed: its low sensitivity to real dysfunctions of the authorities, including in the field of ownership policy. As noted by Gliniecki and Zaleska-Korziuk (2017), a significant part of the society considers completely normal that SOEs become, in a way, owned by the ruling party and may be used to pursue private interests of its members. Perhaps that's why none of the numerous scandals, revealed by journalists after the PiS coalition came to power in 2015 and which involved members of the current political elite, including their rent-seeking behavior towards SOEs, did not in any way affect the ruling party's ratings.

6.2.3 *Impact of Exogenous and Endogenous Factors on the Evolution of the State Corporate Control*

The factors analyzed in this dichotomy are much more diverse than those of good faith and group interests. Therefore, their synthesis is difficult. Nevertheless, it can be argued that, as with the previous dichotomy, both groups, i.e., exogenous and endogenous factors, played a role both in stabilizing the state's corporate control policy and in fostering its evolution.

External factors played a stabilizing role primarily in the long run. The transfer of knowledge in the form of reform experience in other countries, expert assistance, outcome of research, as well as the diffusion of corporate knowledge from foreign companies, etc., favored the creation of the foundations of ownership policy, the framework of which remained unchanged for a long time. The inclusion in the global economic and political processes increased Poland's dependence on factors of supranational character also in the strategic dimension. Basing the development paradigm on foreign direct investments and membership in international structures, especially in the European Union, made it difficult to introduce too radical changes in the area of ownership policy—due to commitments made or because it would bring no profit. Generally, the importance of this group of factors was gradually increasing in the 1990s, as the importance of FDIs in the economy grew and accession requirements were met more and more widely; in the twenty-first century, the importance of these factors started to gradually weaken as the elements of statism in Poland's economic policy were growing. Since then, a growing independence of the corporate control policy (and ownership policy as a whole) from external factors can be seen.

The exogenous factors also played the role of an initiator or catalyst of change: at the beginning of the transition it was mainly knowledge transfer that allowed for shaping and streamlining the ownership policy, but unfortunately only its privatization pillar. Then external economic and political factors gained importance, which, through the expectations of investors and the requirements of membership in international organizations, were conducive to the continuation and expansion of liberal reforms, including strengthening the ownership policy in terms not only of continued privatization, but also in the area of corporate governance of the state, such as reduction of monopolies and of state interference in the functioning of the enterprise sector. In the twenty-first century, however, not only the stabilizing but also the changing function of exogenous factors weakened. The growth of statism caused an increasing de-synchronization of Polish and most Western ownership policies. The experience of other countries was used more and more often just as a pretext to justify an increasing state interventionism.

Among the analyzed endogenous factors, institutional ones, primarily of an extractive nature, had the greatest stabilization potential. This was, first of all, the impact of interest groups related to the state sector of the economy on the ownership policy of the state, and more specifically, the institutional setup that ensured the unchangeability of sources of rents and the way they were extracted regardless of the personal composition of these groups. But these groups, as shown earlier, also became one of the most important catalysts for changing corporate control policy in the twenty-first century towards statism and creation additional possibilities for rent-seeking. On the other hand, institutional safeguards in the form of quite effective democratic mechanisms existed which, together with exogenous institutional anchors, limited the adverse effects of extractive institutions and had an overall stabilizing effect.

Secondly, the existing organizational structure for implementing the state corporate control policy, which was centralized, powerful, with a stiff organizational culture, was characterized by a high level of specific institutional inertia, resistance to change. Ruszkowski and Wójtowicz (2009, p. 100) draw attention to the rigidity of the rules of functioning of the Ministry of the Treasury despite the changes taking place on the political seats in this ministry. It can be said that the state's exercise of its ownership function has been captured in an institutional trap (Polterovich 2000). This is an equilibrium in which inefficient behavior is petrified because its change to a more (in the long run) effective one involves, in the opinion of decision makers, too high transaction costs. However, the decentralization of the state corporate control policy carried out by the PiS coalition government in early 2017 failed to break this institutional impasse and even worsened the ownership policy environment and expanded possibilities for rent-seeking. Deteriorating controllability of the system and growing capture of the state corporate policy by interest groups made the government recentralizing the state corporate control, but in fact, it was just a return to pre-2017 status quo without addressing its main faults.

For a long time, the role of a stabilizer could also be played by the broadly understood national intellectual capital, which together with the condition of the economy dictated the need to build a system based on private property and limited state interference in the economy, especially at the micro-level. At some moment the latter factor also started playing a role of a catalyst for change, since the state corporate control policy was more and more directed towards solving current or at most medium-term economic tasks: budget revenues, financing rescue or development investments, etc. The role of the intellectual potential was also ambivalent, contributing to the statist turn in ownership policy and economic policy in general.

In comparison with other factors, the role of public opinion, at least for most of the analyzed period, seems to be secondary as a factor of both change and especially stability. It played an important, albeit nor primary, role only twice: at the very beginning of the transition, giving a very short-term "credit of trust" to the reformers' team (which in the case of state corporate control was largely unused), as well as in the parliamentary elections of 2015, providing a political opportunity to complete the statist turn. Both were the factors of change (but essentially in the opposite direction), although the latter was, maybe paradoxically at first glance, largely dictated by the pursuit of stability, an attempt to return to the "good old days."

Summarizing the above considerations, it can be cautiously concluded that in the period after 1989 first a gradual increase in the importance of external internal factors could be observed, both in their stabilizing effect and a factor of evolution of the state corporate control policy. At the turn of the century, the trend began to reverse and selected internal factors began to come to the fore, which were increasingly conducive to the statization of this policy.

The importance of institutional factors was steadily increasing, especially those which have the adverse effect on the policy of the state corporate control and beyond. They also affect the private sector in the form of worsening of the investment climate, e.g., due to the introduction of restrictions on activity or violation of freedom of competition. Besides, the actions of the PiS coalition, even if they were carried out in only good faith (which is surely not true) and aimed at increasing the effectiveness of economic policy, including ownership one, in practice led to the weakening of safeguards against the realization of private group interests and the ability of these groups to capture the state. Politically motivated and expansionist state corporate control policy stood aside other destructive actions such as the dismantling of the mechanisms of the democratic rule of law, the weakening of the role of private capital, as well as the pursuit of isolationism and political independence from the EU.

References

Acemoğlu, Daron, and James A. Robinson. 2012. *Why Nations Fail: The Origins of Power, Prosperity, and Poverty.* New York: Crown Publishers.

Artner, Annamária. 2017. "Cycles of Nationalisation and Privatisation, and the Role of the State in Ireland." *Acta Oeconomica* 67 (4): 557–583.

Balcerowicz, Leszek. 1995. *Socialism, Capitalism, Transformation.* Budapest: CEU Press.

Balcerowicz, Leszek. 2018. "Domniemanie słuszności socjalizmu." *Rzeczpospolita*, February 15.

Bałtowski, Maciej. 2019. "Kapitalizm państwowy – próba konceptualizacji." In *Wokół teorii i polityki gospodarczej Grzegorza W. Kołodko*, edited by Elżbieta Mączyńska, 171–186. Warsaw: PWN.

Bałtowski, Maciej, and Grzegorz Kwiatkowski. 2018. *Przedsiębiorstwa państwowe we współczesnej gospodarce*. Warsaw: PWN.

Bałtowski, Maciej, and Piotr Kozarzewski. 2014. *Zmiana własnościowa polskiej gospodarki 1989–2013*. Warsaw: PWE.

Bałtowski, Maciej, and Stefan Sękowski. 2020. "Oligarchia w Polsce – dlaczego jej nie ma?" *Sprawy Międzynarodowe* 10 (forthcoming).

Bałtowski, Maciej, Piotr Kozarzewski, and Tomasz Mickiewicz. 2021. "State Capitalism in Poland and Hungary: Populist Varieties." In *Oxford Handbook of State Capitalism and the Firm*, edited by Mike Wright, Geoffrey Wood, Alvaro Cuervo-Cazurra, Pei Sun, Ilya Okhmatovskiy, and Anna Grosman. Oxford: Oxford University Press (forthcoming).

Błasiak, Wojciech. 2014. *Siedem dni ze Stanem Tymińskim. Codzienność z szokową transformacją w tle*. Dąbrowa Górnicza: Wojciech Błasiak.

CBOS. 2009. Prywatyzacja – oceny, skojarzenia, oczekiwania i obawy. Komunikat z badań 133, Centrum Badań Opinii Społecznej.

CBOS. 2019. Elektoraty 2019 – charakterystyka poglądów. Komunikat z badań 124, Centrum Badań Opinii Społecznej.

Christiansen, Hans, and Yunhee Kim. 2014. State-invested Enterprises in the Global Marketplace: Implications for a Level Playing Field, OECD Corporate Governance Working Papers 14, OECD.

Djankov, Simeon. 2015. Russia's Economy under Putin: From Crony Capitalism to State Capitalism. Policy Brief 15–18, Peterson Institute for International Economics. Available at: https://www.piie.com/publications/pb/pb15-18.pdf. Accessed November 2, 2020.

Farkas, Beáta. 2016. *Models of Capitalism in the European Union: Post-crisis Perspectives*. London: Palgrave Macmillan.

Fiorina, Morris P., and Roger G. Noll. 1978. "Voters, Bureaucrats, and Legislators." *Journal of Public Economics* 9 (2): 239–254.

Gadomski, Witold. 2016. "Mateusz Morawiecki. Partyzant śni o wielkiej Polsce." *Gazeta Wyborcza. Magazyn Świąteczny*, August 6.

Gliniecki, Bartłomiej, and Kaja Zaleska-Korziuk. 2017. "Report on Corporate Governance in State-owned Enterprises—the Polish Perspective." *Pro Publico Bono—Public Administration*, Special Edition 1: 98–115.

Gostkiewicz, Michał. 2018, "11 milionów złotych i to nie koniec. Ogromne zarobki polityków PiS w spółkach i samorządach." *Gazeta Wyborcza Weekend*, May 3. http://weekend.gazeta.pl/weekend/1,152121,23314951,11-mil

ionow-zlotych-i-to-nie-koniec-ogromne-zarobki-politykow.html. Accessed March 16, 2021.

Harłukowicz, Jacek. 2020. "Tajna operacja CBA przeciw Adamowi Hofmanowi. Odsłaniamy kulisy sukcesu słynnej agencji byłego rzecznika." *Gazeta Wyborcza*, December 14.

Hellman, Joel S. 1998. "Winners Take All: The Politics of Partial Reform in Postcommunist Transition." *World Politics* 50 (2): 203–234.

Jarosz, Maria, Marek Kozak, and Piotr Kozarzewski. 1991. Postawy pracowników wobec prywatyzacji przedsiębiorstw. Studia i Materiały 37, INE PAN.

Kawalec, Stefan. 2015. "Udomowienie banków uniezależni je od zagranicznych central." *Gazeta Prawna*, March 1.

Kieżun, Witold. 2012. *Patologia transformacji*. Warsaw: Difin.

Kozarzewski, Piotr, and Maciej Bałtowski. 2017. "Change in the Ownership Policy Paradigm in Poland: State Control vs. Privatisation." *Acta Oeconomica* 67 (1): 1–20.

Kozarzewski, Piotr. 2006. *Prywatyzacja w krajach postkomunistycznych*. Warsaw: ISP PAN.

Kozarzewski, Piotr. 2019. *Polityka właścicielska państwa w okresie transformacji systemowej. Próba syntezy*. Lublin: Wydawnictwo Uniwersytetu Marii Curie-Skłodowskiej.

Lis, Marcin. 2017. "Morawiecki podsumował 2 lata. 'Rzucamy wyzwanie skolonizowaniu Polski, stajemy się równorzędnym partnerem'." *Money.pl*, November 15. https://www.money.pl/gospodarka/wiadomosci/artykul/mateusz-morawiecki-podsumowanie-2-lata.106.0.2389098.html. Accessed November 2, 2020.

Lissowska, Maria. 2008. *Market Economy Institutions: The Case of Poland*. Warsaw: C.H. Beck.

Machiavelli, Niccolò. (1532) 1961. *The Prince*. London: Penguin.

Mączyńska, Elżbieta. 2012. "Uwaga na jednorękich ekonomistów!" *Nowy Obywatel*, October 12. http://nowyobywatel.pl/2012/10/12/uwaga-na-jednorekich-ekonomistow/. Accessed October 26, 2020.

Matyja, Rafał. 2018. *Wyjście awaryjne. O zmianie wyobraźni politycznej*. Kraków: Karakter.

McClelland, David, and David Burnham. 2003. *Power Is the Great Motivator*. Cambridge, MA: Harvard Business Review Classics.

Mihályi, Peter, and Iván Szelényi. 2017. "The Role of Rents in the Transition from Socialist Redistributive Economies to Market Capitalism." *Comparative Sociology* 16 (1): 13–38.

Mikołajewska, Bianka. 2020. "Rośnie klub milionerów związanych z PiS. 162,4 mln zł na 84 osoby w spółkach z udziałem państwa." *OKO.press*, July 11. https://oko.press/84-osoby-pis-zarobily-162-mln/. Accessed November 2, 2020.

Ministry of the Treasury. 2016. *Raport o ekonomicznych, finansowych i społecznych skutkach prywatyzacji w roku 2015*. Warsaw: Ministerstwo Skarbu Państwa.

Miszewski, Maciej. 2012. *Polska transformacja gospodarcza i jej uwarunkowania*. Katowice: UE w Katowicach.

Morawiecki, Mateusz. 2016. *Exposé premiera Mateusza Morawieckiego – stenogram*. https://www.premier.gov.pl/expose-premiera-mateusza-morawieckiego-stenogram.html. Accessed November 2, 2020.

Morawski, Witold, and Wiesława Kozek, eds. 1991. *Społeczeństwo wobec wyzwań gospodarki rynkowej*. Warsaw: Uniwersytet Warszawski, Instytut Socjologii.

Mucha, Janusz, Grażyna Skąpska, Jacek Szmatka, and Izabela Uhl, eds. 1991. *Społeczeństwo polskie u progu przemian*. Wrocław: Zakład Narodowy im. Ossolińskich.

Mühlenkamp, Hogler. 2015. "From State to Market Revisited: A Reassessment of the Empirical Evidence on the Efficiency of Public (and Privately-owned) Enterprises." *Annals of Public and Cooperative Economics* 86 (4): 535–557.

Musacchio, Aldo, and Sergio G. Lazzarini. 2014. *Reinventing State Capitalism: Leviathan in Business, Brazil and Beyond*. Cambridge: Harvard University Press.

Nölke, Andreas, and Arjan Vliegenthart. 2009. "Enlarging the Varieties of Capitalism: The Emergence of Dependent Market Economies in East Central Europe." *World Politics* 61 (4): 670–702.

Novokmet, Filip, Thomas Piketty, and Gabriel Zucman. 2017. From Soviets to Oligarchs: Inequality and Property in Russia 1905–2016. Working Paper 23712, National Bureau of Economic Research, Cambridge, MA.

Ortega y Gasset, José. 1932. *The Revolt of the Masses*. New York: W. W. Norton & Company.

Papava, Vladimer. 2002. "Necroeconomics—the Theory of Post-communist Transformation of an Economy." *International Journal of Social Economics* 29 (10): 796–805.

Patena, Wiktor, and Renata Stawiarska. 2016. "The Public Perception of Privatization in Poland from 1991–2014." *Finanse, Rynki Finansowe, Ubezpieczenia* 1 (79): 723–738.

Polterovich, Victor M. 2000. "Institutional Traps." In *The New Russia: Transition Gone Awry*, edited by Lawrence R. Klein and Marshall Pomer, 93–116. Stanford: Stanford University Press.

Poznański, Kazimierz. 2000. *Wielki przekręt. Klęska polskich reform*. Warsaw: TWiL.

Prusek, Tomasz, and Tomasz Bielecki. 2012. "Niech państwo zainwestuje, ale później sprzeda." *Gazeta Wyborcza*, October 27.

Ruszkowski, Paweł, and Andrzej Wójtowicz, eds. 2009. *Grupy interesów a prywatyzacja elektroenergetyki*. Warsaw: Wydawnictwo Naukowe Scholar.

Schoenman, Roger. 2014. *Networks and Institutions in Europe's Emerging Markets*. Cambridge: Cambridge University Press.

Senderski, Marcin. 2015. "Inhibited Privatization: A Hurdle Race over Vested Interests." *European Journal of Government and Economics* 4 (1): 46–66.

Shleifer, Andrei, and Robert W. Vishny. 1994. "Politicians and Firms." *Quarterly Journal of Economics* 109 (4): 995–1025.

Staniszewski, Robrt. 2013. "Społeczna percepcja prywatyzacji w okresie transformacji systemowej w Polsce." *Studia Politologiczne* 11 (3): 43–56.

Szacki, Jerzy. 1994. *Liberalizm po komunizmie*. Cracow: Znak.

Szanyi, Miklós. 2016. "The Reversal of the Privatisation Logic in Central European Transition Economies (An Essay)." *Acta Oeconomica* 66 (1): 33–65.

Szarzec, Katarzyna, Bartosz Totleben, and Dawid Piątek. 2020. "How Do Politicians Capture a State? Evidence from State-owned Enterprises." *East European Politics and Societies*. https://journals.sagepub.com/doi/10.1177/0888325420953485. Accessed September 22, 2020.

Sztaba, Sławomir. 2002. *Aktywne poszukiwanie renty, teoria, przykłady historyczne, przejawy w polskiej gospodarce lat dziewięćdziesiątych*. Warsaw: Szkoła Główna Handlowa Oficyna Wydawnicza.

Tittenbrun, Jacek. 2007. *Z deszczu pod rynnę. Meandry polskiej prywatyzacji*. Poznań: Zysk i S-ka.

Tullock, Gordon. 1967. "The Welfare Cost of Tariffs, Monopolies, and Theft." *Western Economic Journal* 5 (3): 224–232.

Wilkin, Jerzy. 2012. "Pogoń za rentą za pomocą mechanizmów politycznych." In *Teoria wyboru publicznego. Główne nurty i zastosowania*, edited by Jerzy Wilkin, 221–237. Warsaw: Scholar.

Williamson, John. 1989. "What Washington Means by Policy Reform." In *Latin American Readjustment: How Much Has Happened*, edited by John Williamson, 7–20. Washington, DC: Institute for International Economics.

Woodruff, David M. 2004. "Property Rights in Context: Privatization's Legacy for Corporate Legality in Poland and Russia." *Studies in Comparative International Development* 38 (4): 82–108.

Zyzak, Paweł. 2016. *Efekt Domina. Czy Ameryka obaliła komunizm w Polsce?* Warsaw: Fronda.

CHAPTER 7

Polish Experience in a Comparative Perspective

7.1 Introductory Remarks

The task of this chapter is to put the Polish experience in a comparative perspective of shaping up and evolution of the state corporate control in other countries of the former Eastern Bloc. The mostly qualitative character of the study makes the comparison of all former communist countries extremely difficult, firstly because of enormous quantity of (often inconsistent and incomplete) information to be processed and lack of possibility, due to a great variety of paths and factors which have formed them, to reduce analysis to very simple models with a limited number of easy to get parameters. To narrow down the set of countries to study, only those were considered where the role of the state-controlled sector was very significant and/or increasing. At the same time, state corporate control policy in each of these countries had to represent some specific pattern which might be archetypical for some variant of this policy. Additionally, several post-communist countries with very statist economic policy were not considered for analysis because they had not embarked upon any transition towards capitalist system (such as Turkmenistan and Tajikistan). Last but not least, there was a problem with access to information which was especially the case of many former USSR republics (i.e., which made Kazakhstan to be excluded from the study at the current stage of the research). Finally, three countries have been chosen:

P. Kozarzewski, *State Corporate Control in Transition*, https://doi.org/10.1007/978-3-030-78562-8_7

(1) Hungary, which till 2010 had been, as Poland, regarded as a transition leader and conducted a far-reaching de-statization of its economy (even more comprehensive than in Poland), experienced a radical change in economic policy towards state capitalism which included nationalizations, among others, in the financial sector, public utilities and some infrastructural sectors. This case is of additional interest because according to a widespread opinion (e.g., Szanyi 2016a; Sata and Karolewski 2020), Hungary and Poland follow some common pattern both in statist evolution of their economies and in deterioration of their political systems.
(2) Russia, where statist economic policy elements were present through the whole post-communist period and which has an extensive SOE sector. Nevertheless, by the end of the 1990s, its economy could be described as predominantly market one, based on private property; at the beginning of the 2000s, a trend towards consolidation of the state control over selected strategic industries started to unfold, together with limiting democratic mechanisms. Some features of this statist and antidemocratic turn were strikingly similar to those observed several years later in Poland (and Hungary) which even gave pretext to some researchers (Krekó et al. 2016; Kucharczyk 2017) to look for the "hand of the Kremlin" in these countries.
(3) Belarus, as a special case of "reluctant transition," to paraphrase Bortolotti and Faccio (2004), the reform outcast, where the state still keeps ownership control over the majority of the enterprise sector (and also exerting strong administrative pressure on private firms) and all the shallow and inconsistent market reforms were not aimed at building a market economy, but rather were an attempt to address the inefficiency of the existing administrative mechanisms. Despite all the dysfunctions, the Belarusian economic system which is characterized by a peculiar state-market duality so far managed to evolve without losing its long-term stability and no radical market reforms are planned.

In this chapter, similarly to the analysis of the Polish case, three groups of issues are studied: shaping up, evolution and the present situation in the state corporate control, the portrait of the SOE sector, and discussion on the factors that lay behind the identified processes and phenomena.

7.2 Hungary[I]

7.2.1 Situation Before the Transition

By the end of the communist era, some market reforms were already implemented in the Hungarian economy, and unlike Poland, the reform policy had a much longer history: it has been launched in 1968, when introduction of the New Economic Mechanism was proclaimed. Apart from Yugoslavia, it was probably the most comprehensive and long-lasting reform in the former Eastern bloc, which introduced a far-reaching liberalization and decentralization of the communist economy. Compulsory central planning was abolished and SOEs were granted high degree of autonomy: e.g., the right to choose what they wanted to produce and in what quantities, to freely choose suppliers and customers, to import and export, to use their profits for investments and to carry out their own personnel policy. Unlike in Poland, SOEs reform was of a managerial and not employee self-management kind (despite some extension of employees' rights in mid-1980s). Maximization of profits became the main goal for the SOEs (still dominant in the Hungarian economy). To make it possible, limited price liberalization was introduced.

Economic reforms helped to keep relatively high standard of living and lower shortages on the market than in most of the other countries of the bloc, yet they proved unable to prevent the Hungarian economy sliding into the crisis. Soft budget constraints of the SOEs (Kornai 1992), some restrictions on price setting and on several other aspects of their business activity, as well as incomplete property rights, did not allow SOEs, similar to the case of their Polish counterparts, to behave in a truly market manner. Shortages on the market still existed, inflation was growing, and foreign debt increased up to dangerous level; but even if at the end of the 1980s, the Hungarian economy was much less imbalanced than the Polish one.

Just before the transition started, the law on commercialization was passed which allowed SOEs to start their own transformation and to decide about their new ownership structure. It created grounds for "spontaneous privatization" through creation of companies by managers and employees. But still, comparing to the other states of the Eastern bloc, in Hungary by the end of the previous regime the share of the private sector was among the lowest: a mere 5% of the GDP in 1989 and the similar share in the total number of enterprises (Ludányi 1996, p. 123).

7.2.2 *Shaping Up and Evolution of the State Corporate Control During the Transition*

As in other countries in the region, the reforms in Hungary had to play a dual task of overcoming the crisis (albeit milder than in Poland) and to create a new, radically more crisis-proof economic system. Generally, Hungary has chosen the same transition path as Poland, which were three-pillar liberal market reforms with a key role of FDIs in privatization (although there were periods, when FDI participation in privatization was not encouraged). Hungary was even more consistent than Poland in avoiding wholesale methods of privatization and using solely equivalent methods of passing SOEs into private hands, as well as avoiding partial privatization which was regarded as causing problems with residual state ownership (Mihályi 1996). Privatization processes took off swiftly and the state share in the enterprise sector was declining in a faster pace than in Poland and any other transition country. Already in 1998, the share of the private sector in the Hungarian GDP reached 80% (EBRD 2020). Unlike in Poland and many other post-communist countries, many public service companies were also privatized, mainly to foreign investors. In 2008, privatization in Hungary was officially declared completed, even if some important companies were still owned by the state. Szanyi (2019a) argues that this was just a political declaration which created grounds for further nationalizations; in this respect, one can see similarities with official termination of privatization in Poland at the end of 2016. Despite this, privatization in Hungary may be regarded as highly successful because, according to Mihályi (2010, pp. 662–663), its all three main goals have been achieved: contribution to transition to capitalism and creation of the class of private owners, making the Hungarian economy integrated into the global business networks, and generating high privatization revenues. From this perspective, Polish privatization was quite a success as well.

Privatization was not the only path of transforming SOEs in Hungary. At the beginning of the transition, Hungarian SOEs accumulated huge debts due to growing competition combined with soft budget constraints which, among others, posed a serious threat to the banking system—the situation typical for early year of transition in post-communist countries. The Hungarian government, however, used different, extremely radical approach towards SOEs indebtedness comparing to that applied in Poland (conciliation agreements between SOEs and creditors) and the recipes popular among advisors for the post-communist governments (separation of debts in special funds). It decided that insolvent SOEs had to be simply liquidated and introduced a special bankruptcy procedure which, under the threat of legal punishment, had to be filed by the enterprises themselves. Later, bank portfolios were cleared from outstanding debts of these SOEs. Together with tightening budget constraints, it led to the bankruptcy of more than 500 SOEs which according to estimations (Szanyi 2019b, p. 221) decreased their total number by about 30%.

Unlike in Poland, at the very beginning of the transition, the Hungarian government effectively re-consolidated the property rights on SOEs in its hands creating in 1990 the State Property Agency (SPA) in charge of privatization and the Hungarian State Holding Company (HSHC) which was to manage enterprises which had to remain state-owned in a long-term perspective. In 1991, the Treasury Property Management Office (TPMO) was established which took control over assets which were regained by the state: property left by withdrawing Soviet military forces and by the liquidated political organizations. In 1995, the SPA and the TPMO were included in State Privatization and Property Management Plc. whose task was to privatize assets it controlled. At those times, the main task of state ownership managing agencies was first of all privatization so they were interested in keeping their assets attractive to possible investors and not interested in just keeping SOEs alive. Hence, such a radical attitude towards insolvent enterprises described above.

In 2008, further concentration of the state corporate control took place and the Hungarian National Asset Management Inc. (Magyar Nemzeti Vagyonkezelő Zrt., MNV) was established which collected under one roof all the major functions of state property management, which previously had been dispersed among three institutions (the third being the National Land Fund established in 2008), thus creating a superpower body even more omnipotent than the Polish Ministry of the Treasury. The MNV is a holding which keeps both majority and minority blocks of shares and is in charge of strategic planning for state-controlled companies which is in line with the economic policy of the government, elaborating guidelines on remunerating of managers and support for implementation of best practices of corporate governance. The Ministry of National Development is in charge of setting up the principles of the policy towards the state sector and the MNV is the main tool of implementation of this policy. Other organizations in charge of performing the ownership policy of the state are line ministries which supervise enterprises with no commercial goals and the Hungarian Development Bank (Magyar Fejlesztési Bank Zrt.) which is in charge of supervision of state-controlled financial institutions and also several enterprises in infrastructure and forestry.

Corporate governance of the SOEs has avoided the Polish legal duality: almost all SOEs which remained under the state control were commercialized and became the subject of the general corporate law. An exception is a dozen of statutory corporations which have no commercial goals.

For quite a long period, similarly as in Poland, there was no official document which would describe the goals of the state corporate control. In 2007, the Act on state property was passed which closed this gap. Since then, the main official rationale for keeping enterprises in the state hands is to perform social functions and implement the economic policy of the government. At the same time, the SOEs had to function in a financially efficient way. It is believed that the alternative solution, i.e., their regulation as private entities, would be too costly and inefficient (Christiansen 2013).

According to the 2007 CVI Act on State Ownership, the state may acquire (or dispose of) assets in order to: (1) execute state functions; (2) fulfill societal needs; and (3) achieve government economic policy goals. In practice, some rationales for state ownership that have been put forward, in addition to the "general public interest," have included energy security, delivering country-wide, affordable mail services (the Hungarian Postal Service Co.) or fulfilling cultural facilitation functions (the Hungarian National Film Fund) (Christiansen 2013, p. 17).

Therefore, it may be argued that in Hungary a much more consistent, than in Poland, system of state corporate control has been created with tight control over SOEs functioning. According to OECD (2005a) classification discussed in Sect. 3.3.6, it represents a centralized model which is regarded by this organization as the most effective one. However, very little is known about its real performance, especially before the statist turn initiated by the Fidesz government in 2010. One can expect that the high pace of privatization (which rapidly reduced the size of the state-controlled enterprise sector), the separation (before 2008) of the government's privatization and control functions, while keeping the latter in the hands of one body, setting concrete goals for SOEs and smaller size of the economy, may have contributed to more efficiency in the role of the state as an owner compared with Poland. Nevertheless, according to Mihályi (2020, p. 185), since late 1990s SOEs started being used by the government for short-term political gains. Quite similarly to Poland, it was rotation on the SOEs boards induced by changes of the ruling coalition and forcing SOEs to politically incurred expenditures.

It should be also noted that the system of the state corporate control had two sets of safeguards against undermining the role of the state in selected sectors and individual enterprises which were regarded as being of strategic importance for meeting the goals of social and economic policy. The first one is introduction in 2007 of the category of so-called permanent state-owned companies setting the minimum level of state participation in them. Currently, the list includes 63 SOEs, mainly from infrastructure sectors, with thresholds set mostly at 100% of state ownership; in the case of 12 companies, some private ownership is allowed, the state retaining minimum from 75% plus one share up to as low as a just blocking equity stake of 25% plus one share in the case of two firms.

In the same 2007, the second measure was introduced through the act on Undertakings of High Importance for the Security of Public Supply. It envisaged measures against takeovers of the strategically important companies in the energy sector regardless of their ownership structure. Among others, the boards of these companies got the instruments to nullify acquisition attempts, such as share buy-back programs or capital increases even after the announcement of a takeover bid. The restrictions limiting the number of own shares held by the company to 10% of its registered capital were removed, as well as restrictions on introducing a voting cap. Dismissal of members of boards of these companies required the supermajority of 75% of votes of the shareholders. The state got additional possibilities to control both acquisitions and the decisions of majority owners: the company planning the takeover bid had to submit a business plan for the company it wanted to acquire to the Hungarian regulator; the government got the right of using a "preference share" (a quasi-golden share) for blocking the most important decisions of the shareholders. Although never officially admitted, the main real purpose of this regulation was to prevent the hostile (in the opinion of the Hungarian authorities) takeover of the MOL, the largest Hungarian oil and gas company, by the Austrian oil company OMV—hence this act was widely known as "Lex MOL."

In 2010, the continuity of Hungarian economic policy was abruptly broken. The parliamentary elections were won by a national-conservative Fidesz party led by Viktor Orbán which got a supermajority of seats.

(Since then, Fidesz repeated this electoral success twice: in 2014 and 2018.) The new political leadership started a complex transformation of political and economic institutions towards authoritarianism and statism. The new Constitution was adopted in 2011, and a series of laws were passed, undermining the independence of the Constitutional Court and the Central Bank, weakening parliamentary control over the fiscal policy, increasing the government's control over media and shifting important functions from municipalities to the central government.

At the same time, the official discourse stressed the necessity to regain control over the economy for the sake of the national interests. This goal had to be reached mainly through transferring the ownership of strategically important industries from the hand of foreign investors into the hands of the state and domestic owners, in practice to those with political connections to Orbán.

A series of nationalizations has been carried out, first of all of the companies owned by foreign capital. They included financial sector (where also domestically owned savings cooperatives were nationalized), public services and some infrastructural sectors such as energy production and distribution. A wide array of pretexts was used, among others the need to decrease utility prices and guarantee deposits' security for the population. Several methods were used to "convince" the owners to sell their businesses to the state (Magyar 2016; Szanyi 2016b, 2019a). The first group of tools was regulatory pressure of the property-rights-restricting government intervention kind which was aimed at making these businesses unprofitable. Here, Magyar (2016, pp. 196–197) distinguishes "cold nationalization" which created unfavorable market environment (e.g., regulation of prices, introducing sector-specific taxes, introducing compulsory suppliers for public entities) and "market acquiring nationalization" (through monopolization of business activity in selected areas in state hands or introducing discriminating requirements towards the ownership structure of businesses). In some cases, pressure on foreign owners was supplemented with sweetheart deal offers—with the price well above the market level. Apart from making the deal more attractive for an owner to be expropriated, such "sweetness" could also serve the purpose of not scaring out capital from the respective countries (Mihályi 2020, p. 193). The second group of methods to facilitate expropriation was just using brute force: selective targeting by tax office, selective law enforcement, other forms of intimidation, etc.

In 2010–2014, a total number of 209 companies were bought out by the government for a total sum of EUR 5 billion (Szanyi 2016a). Between 2010 and 2013, the value of state property doubled (Voszka 2018), and in later years, it continued to grow. It is worth noting that these expenditures were a strong burden for the state finances given the very high public debt. Besides, as nationalizations in Poland, almost all of them were a part of the new economic policy and neither bailouts nor a part of crisis management tactics.

Ownership changes included also transfer of property from one private hand to another: either through so-called transit nationalization (Magyar 2016, p. 195) with subsequent re-privatization, or through forced buyouts, a form of corporate raiding (Sallai and Schnyder 2018). The beneficiaries of these practices were persons connected to the new political elite and the losers those entrepreneurs who didn't want to subdue and tried to behave independently or even exert political pressure on the government. According to Mihályi and Szelényi (2017), it marked entering the Hungarian rent-seeking model the new stage called "capture of oligarchs by autocratic rulers."

At the same time, these policies of Orbán were very selective. The foreign owners had been expelled only from several sectors which were attractive for the ruling elite in order, e.g., to get access to finance and to eliminate market competition in distribution of public funds through public procurements (Békesi 2017, p. 245). Thus, only parts of FDIs were targeted: banks and other financial institutions such as pension funds, trading companies including retail trade chains, companies in telecommunication, energy sector and crucially, media. Most of (quasi-) expropriations took place in these very areas. In other industries (e.g., automotive, pharmaceutical, electronics), FDIs remained untouched and even received various forms of support from the government such as strategic agreements and tax allowances which were quite outstanding in the EU context, and several times higher than those of Poland's (Szanyi 2016b; Sarnyai 2018). Despite the nationalistic rhetoric, FDIs remained the essential part of the Hungarian economy.

7.2.3 *Place of the SOE Sector in Hungarian Economy*

7.2.3.1 The Scale of the SOE Sector

No official statistics on the share of state-owned sector in Hungarian economy is provided by the authorities. Outdated EBRD estimations (the latest was from 2010) amounted to 20% of the country's GDP—along with Estonia, Czech Republic and Slovakia being the lowest among post-communist countries. Since then, this share has apparently increased, but it is hard to make any reliable estimation for the whole economy. Perhaps the closest to getting the idea of the scale (i.e., size) of the state-controlled sector in Hungary economy was the somewhat obscure "Government Enterprises and Investment" indicator calculated by the Fraser Institute for its Economic Freedom of the World annual reports. It is based on the estimations of the government's share in total investment and in an unclear way also its share in the enterprise sector (Gwartney et al. 2018, pp. 213–214), and the latest data available is for 2016. Since 2019, the Fraser Institute uses two indicators: the government's share in total investment and an ordinal indicator (State Ownership of Assets) which depicts the level of the state's involvement in the enterprise sector (Gwartney et al. 2019, p. 227). According to the value of the "Government Enterprises and Investment" indicator in 2016, the involvement of the state as an owner and investor was even higher than in Poland (30.5 and 18.6%, respectively). It represented a generally steadily growing trend since 2000 when it was as small as 14.0%. However observations of the state ownership policy rather make expecting the real share of the state in the Hungarian enterprise sector through the whole this period to be much lower that the Fraser Institute data suggested. Thus, the exact scale of the state-owned enterprise sector remains unknown.

The absolute size of the state sector measured by the number of enterprises is not fully known either. In 2012, the OECD (2014) estimated it at 371 with majority state shares. According to the MNV website (http://www.mnv.hu), in mid-2020 the state holding possessed shares of 165 companies including 20 under liquidation procedures. Out of 145 active companies, the Hungarian government had a majority stake in 79 of them and minority but still substantial stake (25% or more) in 23 companies. In 25 active companies, the state's share was less than 1%. The real control of the state over the enterprise sector is somewhat bigger because the MNV data does not take into account cases of indirect control and control by other state agencies. For example, the state controls 25.34% of the stock of the largest pharmaceutical and biotechnology company Gedeon Richter, while the MNV has only 5.25% of its shares. The same goes for the largest company in Hungary: MOL Group (oil and gas), where the MNV possesses 5.24% of its shares, but the state in fact controls 25.2% of the company.

7.2.3.2 The Extent of the SOE Sector

The last decade witnessed growing extent of the SOEs sector in Hungary, the government expanding its control over sectors of the economy through nationalizations. Apart from the above-mentioned Gedeon Richter and partly re-nationalized MOL group (which is practically a monopolist in the petrochemical sector), one can also mention MVM group being the largest electricity producer, distributor and seller, two big companies in railroad transport, and Magyar Posta which dominates the market of postal services. The state also controls the public utilities sector enterprises through the state holding company Nemzeti Közműszolgáltató Zrt which systematically buys out them from foreign owners. The state regained control over a part of the banking sector which previously was more than 90% foreign-owned; the state share can be estimated now at up to 20%. The state has regained also stakes in several manufacturing, transportation and services enterprises, even quite small (Voszka 2018).

The growing engagement of the state in different sectors of the Hungarian economy is statistically confirmed by the OECD's "Scope of SOEs" indicator which reflects the government's control of at least one enterprise in a number of sectors across the economy elaborated within the set of product market regulation (PMR) indicators (Vitale et al. 2020). The value of this indicator steadily decreased till 2008 and started to re-grow since then. In 2018, it amounted to 3.46 which was higher than the OECD economies' average (3.02), but much lower than in Poland (4.75) the latter having the second highest value (after France) among all OECD countries. Interestingly enough, despite growing engagement of the Hungarian government in infrastructure sectors, it's still lower (measured by "Government Involvement in Network Sectors" OECD PMR indicator) than the OECD average: 1.81 and 2.26, respectively. And it's a way lower than in Poland (2.96) (Vitale et al. 2020).

7.2.3.3 The Importance of the SOE Sector

It is not surprising therefore that the importance of the SOE sector in Hungary, i.e., the share of SOEs among the most important companies in the country, grew as well, albeit at the end of the 2010s still being at a significantly lower level than in Poland. Table 7.1 clearly shows the change of the ownership policy of the state after Fidesz came to power when some of the most important companies started being nationalized. Between

Table 7.1 SOEs among the largest Hungarian enterprises in 2009, 2013, and 2018

	10 largest enterprises			*50 largest enterprises*			*100 largest enterprises*		
	2009	*2013*	*2018*	*2009*	*2013*	*2018*	*2009*	*2013*	*2018*
Number of SOEs									
Majority ownership	1	2	2	6	5	5	8	8	10
Minority ownership[a]	–	1	1	2	4	3	4	5	3
Total	1	3	3	8	9	8	12	13	13
Share of SOEs (%)									
In no. of enterprises									
Majority ownership	10.0	20.0	20.0	12.0	10.0	10.0	8.0	8.0	10.0
Minority ownership[a]	–	10.0	10.0	4.0	8.0	6.0	4.0	5.0	3.0
Total	10.0	30.0	30.0	16.0	18.0	16.0	12.0	13.0	13.0
In operating revenues									
Majority ownership	7.4	12.9	16.9	9.9	10.1	12.9	8.7	9.5	12.6
Minority ownership[a]	–	41.6	34.2	3.2	25.0	20.0	3.4	20.4	15.7
Total	7.4	54.5	51.1	13.1	35.1	32.9	12.2	29.9	28.2
In assets									
Majority ownership	9.9	15.4	16.5	18.4	12.0	12.4	15.3	14.3	14.8
Minority ownership[a]	–	43.5	36.5	3.3	23.1	18.4	3.7	19.6	14.8
Total	9.9	58.9	52.9	21.7	35.1	30.7	19.1	33.9	29.6

[a]25–50% of shares

The data was gathered and processed by Maciej Bałtowski, Marlena Gołębiowska, and Grzegorz Kwiatkowski

Source Orbis database, companies' websites, own calculations

2009 and 2013, among 100 largest enterprises the total number of SOEs almost did not increase; however, their share in operating revenues more than doubled and the share in the value of assets increased about 1.8 times. This increase in importance of SOEs was achieved first of all through appearance of a few very big players controlled by the government. Whereas in 2009 there was only one SOE on the list of top-10 firms, there were already three in 2013, one of them with minority state's stake but big enough to effectively control the company. At the same time, the increase in the share in operating revenues and value of assets of these companies was disproportionally high: 7.4 and 5.9 times, respectively. It made them dominating among the 10 largest enterprises in the country.

In the recent years, there were only two state-controlled companies on the Budapest Stock Exchange BUX blue chip index (MOL and Gedeon Richter). At the end of 2019, when it included 15 companies, the share of these SOEs in capitalization of the whole set amounted to 24.3%. Being disproportionally big, it was still much smaller than the share of Polish SOEs in WIG20 index, where they absolutely dominated.

Finally, it should be noted that in Hungary SOEs which are controlled by foreign governments operate as well. However, according to Orbis data, among the 100 largest companies, in 2018 there was only four such companies (belonging to Austrian, Italian, Chinese and Japanese governments) and their role in the Hungarian economy is very modest: their share in top-100 companies' operating revenues and assets was 3.0 and 0.6%, respectively.

7.2.4 *Sources of the State Corporate Control Policy and Its Evolution in Hungary*

7.2.4.1 *Acting in Good Faith vs. Pursuing Group Interests*

Looking at the shaping up and evolution of state corporate control in Hungary during the post-communist transition from the perspective of good faith versus vested interests dichotomy, two periods can be seen: the first which lasted about 20 years and the second one that started in 2010, after radical paradigm change was introduced in the economic policy and, wider, goals and ways of functioning of the Hungarian state.

During the first period which was characterized by introducing deep and consistent market reforms, the Hungarian economic policy seems to be driven mostly by a sincere will of the greater part of political class and bureaucrats to build new, better economic system based on market institutions and rule of law. The SOEs were put under strict centralized corporate control, devoid of privileges they had enjoyed before transition started and subsequently undergone deep privatization. The quite radical policy towards SOEs when those enterprises that could be privatized were treated as assets and gradually sold, and the rest as a burden that had to be ridden off (among others, through bankruptcy procedures) radically restricted the possibilities of using SOEs for rent-seeking purposes. The reason was of rapid contracting of the resource base (withy slim chances to stop it) and limited possibilities of using the mechanisms of state corporate control for private gains. Thus, private interest groups' influence on this policy apparently was limited, at least there is much less evidence in the literature about abuses in the SOEs sector, than in Poland. In other words, not only the size of the SOEs sector, but the ability of SOEs to generate rents as well were much smaller in Hungary than in Poland.

Perhaps there was only one important area of rent-seeking related to state-owned assets and state corporate control policy—on the borderline with privatization. According to Szanyi (2019b), mass bankruptcies of SOEs together with creditors' passivity created favorable conditions for their managers and bankruptcy trustees to strip enterprises from their assets. The scale of this transfer of state assets into private hands was limited in scale, though. Besides, because these were insolvent enterprises with assets unattractive for potential investors, their market value could not be high. In general, privatization in Hungary, although contributed to generating wealth by some future oligarchs (Becker 2017), was not prone to wide-scale rent-seeking apparently due to the strong role of foreign investors in privatization processes (and they were hard to control in order to extract rents) and lack of rent-prone privatization schemes (like mass privatization in many other post-communist countries or "loans for shares" procedures in Yeltsin's Russia) which would allow to accumulate a large amount of assets in a non-equivalent and non-transparent way. In any case, in "pre-Orbán" Hungary, the bulk of rents in the enterprise sector (which indeed existed and eventually contributed to the emergence of oligarchs) were generated outside the ownership policy of the state, mostly through access of cronies to public finance.

The situation has radically changed since 2010, when the economic policy has been captured by private interest groups of Viktor Orbán's "family" (Magyar 2016, Chapter 5) and generating rents became one of the state's main tasks. Forced wealth redistribution began with nationalizations being one of the main tools. Part of the nationalized assets was appropriated by the cronies through transit nationalization, and another part strengthened the rent-generating potential of the SOEs sector. It started playing the role of one of the major suppliers of resources for the government's policy, both purely financial (for cronies, e.g., through access to financing by nationalized banks) and political: among others, the state-controlled sector in Hungary became an integral part of the populist policy of attracting voters through relieving financial burden on households, as one of the main SOEs task became providing population with affordable public services.

The general trends seem to be quite common with that of Poland's since 2015, like expanding the use of state-owned enterprises for milking resources for financial and non-financial rents. At the same time, several important differences can be seen as well. Firstly, in Hungary, unlike in Poland, the SOEs usually have not become rent-seekers themselves; the government treats them in a purely instrumental way and not like entities which deserve special political attention. Secondly, in Hungary, SOEs' boards are not used for gratifying political allies, as in Poland, perhaps because politically motivated nominations would jeopardize these enterprises' performance. The Hungarian rent-seeking mechanism seems to be oriented at fulfilling the needs of the quite limited number of the members of Orbán's "family" rather than satisfying the interests of an army of members of wider political elite. Thirdly, the Hungarian government expands its engagement in the enterprise sector through already existing enterprises, whereas in Poland the main tool for expansion is creation of new state-owned entities and investment projects, a technique that is hardly utilized in Hungary. What is more, many flagship governmental projects in Poland do not have clear and specific beneficiaries of a rent-seeking kind.

These dissimilarities seem to reflect the basic difference between the statist turns in these countries: in Hungary, the increasing role of the state in the economy apparently was much more focused on meeting the rent-seeking goals of a small circle of cronies and has much less ideological, strategic background than in Poland. Besides, in Hungary, the top decision-makers seemed to follow their objectives in much more effective way, whereas in Poland they apparently lost a substantial part of control over the situation because of too many interest groups engaged and too many often contradictory goals set.

The difference between the identity of the rent-seeking groups apparently lays behind the differences in the pattern of evolution of statism in both countries. In Poland, where the main rent-seeker groups were related to the SOEs and the state corporate control, they were able to gradually increase their influence on the economic policy, as many of them were very close to the top decision-making circles in the country. So the statization of the economic policy and its subduing to private interest groups was increasing in mostly evolutionary way. In Hungary, where during the first about 20 years of the transition the main rent-seeking interests concentrated in the new private sector, they were able to seize power only after the window of opportunity had opened. Hence the breach of continuity in 2010.

7.2.4.2 Exogenous and Endogenous Factors

Analyzing the second dichotomy, i.e., the importance of endogenous vs. exogenous factors of shaping up and evolution of the corporate control policy of the Hungarian government, one can find them mostly similar to that of Poland's. In both countries, the importance of the exogenous factors such as knowledge transfer, external economic and political factors was mostly secondary vis-à-vis endogenous ones: state of the economy, intellectual potential, national institutional setup and public opinion.

As in Poland, the importance of knowledge transfer varied with time: it was high at the beginning of transition because reforms were conducted mostly along the Washington Consensus principles. What is more, in Hungary, there were much less deviations from these recipes than in Poland, and there were much less original Hungarian solutions in tools and ways of reforming the economy. Nevertheless, Hungary managed to fully avoid mass privatization which was so insistently advised by international experts and had its own way in resolving the problem of insolvency of SOEs in the first half of the 1990s. Later, the importance of external knowledge was gradually decreasing. Unlike in Poland, the statist turn of the Orbán government was not related to the growing statist trends in the world debate and practice—even at a propaganda level. The revival of statist ideas was not the internal reason for changing the paradigm change of the economic policy in Hungary as well—because it lacked the good faith element present in Poland and was aimed solely at meeting private goals of a narrow circle of beneficiaries.

During the transition period, the importance of external factors of economic and political nature was growing and had quite similar trajectory as in Poland because of the similarity of transition paths which increased inclusion of both countries into global economic and political processes. Both countries entered the path of FDI-led development (here, the external impact was probably stronger in Hungary than in Poland because of the larger scale of FDIs in this country), both were building export-oriented economy, both simultaneously joined the World Trade Organization in 1995, NATO in 1999 and the European Union in 2004. But, despite growing exposure on the global economic trends, the statist turn in both countries was not directly induced by external shocks: nationalizations were seldom used as bailouts, especially as crisis management measures vis-à-vis the challenges of the global financial crisis of 2008–2009; in both countries, nationalizations intensified only after the crisis retracted. What is more, in both cases, the external political anchors could not prevent the countries' skidding into statism, populism and institutional deterioration.

Internal economic factors, as in Poland, played crucial role in starting the transition in Hungary and shaping up its course, although Hungary was among the countries which were relatively less affected by the crisis of the command economy in the late 1980s. But still, it became clear that in order to make the Hungarian economy competitive, deep reconstruction of the economic system was needed, including the ways the enterprise sector functioned. Hence the appreciation of the need to privatize most of the SOEs and the rest being put under the tight state corporate control. And, the same as in Poland, the condition of the economy was one of the main propaganda justifications for the statist turn of 2010 and all the same they were not based on the real economic situation.

From the point of view of the intellectual potential, Hungary was and still is among the leaders of post-communist countries. Before the transition, the intensity of free discussion on political and economic debate was perhaps more limited than in Poland (and USSR in the times of *perestroika*), but it existed and János Kornai was one of the most distinguished economists of the Soviet bloc. Although, as it was noted above, the Hungarian version of post-communist reforms did not differ much from the universal liberal recipes of late 1980s, the Hungarian reformers managed to make post-communist transition one of the most coherent and crisis-proofs, fine-tuned to the local conditions. They also avoided some mistakes made by the Polish government which, e.g., underestimated the need for effective state corporate control and allowed for its politicization.

After 2010, regardless of how one feels about the turn in the economic policy introduced by Victor Orbán, it is rather impossible not to agree that the state and business capture have been performed in a very effective and coherent manner. What is more, the Orbán's regime proved its exceptional stability and still enjoys the support of the vast majority of the Hungarian population, while the PiS regime has to constantly fight for voters. At the international scene, Viktor Orbán, while being perceived as *enfant terrible*, manages to fight for the interests of his "family" with much less political and reputational losses than PiS politicians do. To achieve such results, really clever and experienced persons are needed.

The same as in Poland, institutional setup was apparently among the most important factors that shaped the trajectory of the Hungarian post-communist transition as a whole and the evolution of the state corporate control. Here, the interplay of interest groups performed the key role, especially since the turn of the new century. Like in Poland, it had an inherently domestic character with foreign investors staying predominantly outside it as being interested rather in free market and rule of law than the possibilities of state capture. The only important difference between the two countries was that in Hungary rent-seeking groups concentrated mainly in the new private sector, whereas in Poland they were related mostly to the SOE sector and institutions of the state corporate control, and the differences in the trajectory pattern resulting from it.

Generally speaking, in both countries, the institutional safeguards, the system of checks and balances failed to prevent the development of Acemoğlu and Robinson's (2012) extractive institutions and to ensure expansion of the inclusive ones. In the Hungarian case, the manifestations of the former were first of all politicization of state institutions which were to be independent from the government, growing nepotism and vassal relationship, tolerance towards processes that were destroying the democratic and market rules of the game (Magyar 2016, Chapter 2).

In Hungary, as in Poland, broad public, its opinion and attitudes, apparently played certain secondary role in the trajectory of the evolution of the state corporate control and the state ownership policy as a whole. It can be argued that in Hungary, too, it was not the major factor of change, i.e., the policy was not shaped up to meet the expectations of voters, but the population's expectations made possible introducing changes which had main driving forces elsewhere. What is more, these attitudes could be shaped to make the changes even more easy to introduce.

The research on the Hungarians' attitude towards post-communist transition based on a numerous opinion polls conducted in 1989–2015 (Bíró-Nagy et al. 2016) shows that while the society found the ideas of democracy attractive, during all this period it generally did not share economic principles of capitalism and opted for strong paternalistic state which would ensure prosperity and equality. According to Eurobarometer (2009) survey, Hungarians were among the most skeptical European nations about positive impact of market mechanisms on the society's well-being. The reality of the transforming economy with growing inequalities, unemployment, areas of poverty and exclusion made them very critically assess the transition. From the early transition years, after the costs of the transition became evident, and through the whole analyzed period, the largest part of the respondents felt themselves as the regime change losers, although their attitude towards the effects of the transition was gradually becoming less critical. In any case, it reflected a deep disappointment in capitalism, because, as polls conducted in 1989 and 1990 show, the initial hopes were high but in fact not realistic enough. Accordingly, the Hungarian society generally negatively assessed the main directions of the economic policy, including the ownership one, opposed privatization, and was in favor of nationalization. Paradoxically enough, while being in favor of state interventionism, the Hungarian society is characterized by one of the lowest in Europe levels of trust towards the government and political parties (Bíró-Nagy et al. 2016).

These peculiarities of public attitudes apparently made the Hungarian society prone to the populist arguments of the Fidesz leaders and contributed to the very spectacular electoral successes three times in a row (2010, 2014 and 2018) getting the Fidesz (together with KNDP ally party) the supermajority of seats in the Hungarian parliament. It should be noted that during the previous 20 years of transition no populist party was even remotely close to such an electoral success despite the fact that the Hungarian society all the time presented anti-market and pro-paternalistic attitudes. It seems to corroborate the thesis that it was not the society that initiated the statist and populist change.

The role of the public attitudes in policy change in the case of Poland seems to be quite similar, although Poles show much higher level of acceptance of market economy principles presenting a mix of appreciation for economic freedom together with the active role of a welfare state. Perhaps much less decisive victory of populist forces at two recent parliamentary elections in Poland (PiS and allies had to try hard to get the votes) at least partly comes from the higher level of acceptance of market principles by the Polish society.

7.3 Russian Federation

7.3.1 Situation Before the Transition

Till the end of 1991, Russia was an integral part of the USSR in both political and economic dimensions, at the same time being the largest Soviet economy and having the decisive impact on the Soviet economic policy. Historically, the first command economy of communist type emerged in Russia after the 1917 Revolution as a part of the new economic and political order, which had to create a system devoid of real and imaginary failures of capitalism (such as cyclic crises, high income inequalities, lack of production of many pubic goods and exploitation of labor by capital) and ensure sustainable economic and social development, free of crises and other dysfunctions. It's in Soviet Russia and after 1922 in the USSR command economy based on state property and omnipotent state regulation shaped up after the World War II was "exported" to the countries within the Soviet sphere of influence.

Unlike in Poland and Hungary, up to the second half of the 1980s, the Soviet economy was one of the least reformed in the whole Eastern Bloc. All the previous attempts to address low efficiency of the economy, including reforms of the state corporate control, failed. It happened either due to the lack of desired results, as territorial decentralization introduced in 1957, or because of the resistance of party *apparatchiks* that blocked the so-called Kosygin reforms (after the name of Prime Minister who pushed it forward) of 1965 and 1979 which tried to expand autonomy of SOEs and introduce profit as one of the objectives of their functioning (Timoshina 2009, pp. 306–345).

At least formally, the economy still was strictly regulated by the state with the help of an enormous administrative machine: in mid-1980s at the USSR level, there were over 100 ministries among which 45 were directly or indirectly in charge of economic issues, of which 42 were line ministries. Two state committees should be mentioned as well: Gosplan

(The State Planning Committee) which was in charge of state planning and Gossnab (State Supplies) which was responsible for allocation of material resources to enterprises. In each republic, also the republican level of state administration existed, with their own councils of ministers, line ministries, system of state planning and supply. As a result, SOEs were subordinated either to the central government, or to a republican government. Since 1960s and 1970s, SOEs started being merged in industrial associations subdued to line ministries, thus creating intermediate levels of state corporate control. There were several types of such associations according to their geographic scope, administrative subordination and type of entities included: "all-union" associations (subordinated to the central government ministries and functioning in several republics) which included associations of lower level, "regular" associations (geographically concentrated companies of the same industry) subordinated to the central or a republican government, "scientific-production" associations (which also includes R&D entities), etc. In mid-1980s, there were about 50 "all-union" associations, as well as several hundreds of other associations.

Perestroika initiated by Mikhail Gorbachev in 1987 was the last attempt to reform the Soviet economy without embarking upon the systemic change. Perhaps at least partly it was inspired by some elements of the Yugoslavian, Hungarian and Polish experience of deregulation without democratization of the political system (albeit introducing some civil liberties) and resignation from keeping most of the economy in the state hands (albeit through using first of all indirect control tools). The Law on the State-owned Enterprise (Association) was passed in 1987; it increased the autonomy of SOEs, e.g., through formally liquidating production plans imposed by the ministries and direct orders issued by them. It also introduced elements of employee self-management.

In practice, the level of deregulation of SOEs' functioning was much more modest than declared. The governmental agencies were very reluctant to give up power over the enterprise sector. Directive planning was replaced with government orders set by the line ministries which were compulsory for SOEs and amounted to about 90% of their production (Samokhin 2001, pp. 308–309). Besides, Gosplan with the ministries set target performance standards for SOEs in the way to leave them as little room for autonomous functioning as possible. Material resources for SOEs were still distributed in a centralized way and enterprises in practice get no right to choose suppliers. Introduced in 1928, the five year planning was not abandoned as well.

However, other deregulation measures created new possibilities for evolution of the enterprise sector. The Law on Cooperatives of 1988 enabled the creation of new enterprises in the non-state sector, although private ownership was still not allowed. The Law on Leasing of 1989 allowed for partial ownership transformation through the leasing of state-owned enterprises' assets by employees. Finally, in 1990, the law "On Enterprises and Entrepreneurship" was passed by the Russian parliament (which canceled the relevant USSR regulations) which, among others, allowed for private entrepreneurship, introduced legal forms of companies which existed in market economies, and declared operational and financial independence of SOEs from the state. These regulations were widely used for asset transfer from SOEs first to quasi-private and then to fully private entities both on the initiative of SOEs' directors and, by the end of the Soviet era, governmental agencies after bureaucrats discovered the possibility to convert economic power of their organizations, especially distribution of resources, into private gains. Among others, it resulted in creation of nearly 3.5 thousand of various business associations, partnerships and consortiums with SOEs' and ministries' participation (Timoshina 2009, p. 358).

Being inefficient even before *perestroika*, at the turn of the 1990s the system of the state corporate control practically collapsed, the government losing the major tools of executing its role as the owner. SOEs managers got the real power over the enterprises, not being accountable to anybody and thus having "all incentives to steal 'their' state enterprises bare" (Åslund 2007, p. 18).

7.3.2 Shaping Up and Evolution of the State Corporate Control During the Transition

Starting January 1992, Russia formally embarked upon economic reforms which were to address the tasks of overcoming the economic crisis caused by the collapsing command system and creating the new economic system based on market principles. Generally, reforms were to be conducted along the Washington Consensus lines: they included measures aimed at macroeconomic stabilization, liberalization of prices and domestic market accompanied with liberalization of external relations in the market economy, de-concentration and demonopolization, privatization and building of market economy institutions such as financial market. However, in all these areas, unlike in Poland and Hungary, the reforms, especially at the beginning of the transition, were highly inconsistent and generally did not bring the desired results (Dąbrowski 1993, Chapters 5–11).

The economic problems of Russia caused by the inefficiency of the command economy of the late Soviet era were aggravated by the disestablishment of the USSR in December 1991. Apart from having nearly catastrophic effects at the macro-level, it severely affected the enterprise sector which apart from the macroeconomic instability was hit by the disintegrating inter-republican corporate control structures followed by broken linkages between enterprises which started being separated with state borders. Enterprises began massively losing both suppliers and customers. All this, and the lack of the credibility of the government's stabilization policy, led to numerous dysfunctions in the enterprise sector such as the explosion of inter-enterprise debt which in 1992 amounted to the country's GDP (Rostowski 1993). Instead of looking for the way out in consolidation of market reforms which would make market mechanisms work, SOEs' directors *en masse* started opposing reforms and especially austerity measures counting first of all on the state support. Directors' attitudes enjoyed support of the part of the government which opposed market reforms. As a result, the problem of inter-enterprise debts was resolved by fully administrative, non-market measures through balancing mutual obligations (*vzaimozachot*); the soft budget constraints were not lifted and even expanded through keeping state-owned banks interest rates way below the inflation level and issuing additional preferential credits in the second half of 1992.

The reform of the state corporate control was inconsistent and was to a large extent spontaneous. In 1992, line ministries were replaced by the Ministry of Industry with branch departments, a year later replaced with the Committee on Industrial Policy, also with branch departments. These structures lost most of the tools of control over SOEs and their role boiled down to distribution of resources mainly through government orders which was not performed by them efficiently enough. The reason was the deep financial crisis when the government was short of funds for such a policy, but after a brief period in 1992, SOEs still could enjoy certain level of soft budget constraints. In this situation, the complicated system of SOEs associations started to develop with various types of horizontal and vertical integration. These associations had more partnership relations with the governmental agencies than were subdued to them. The latter mainly rendered services for SOEs, such as providing resources and sales assistance. Also, the role of regional and local authorities increased in order to fill the void created by disintegrating command economy structure in both supplying SOEs with resources and controlling their activity (Samokhin 2001, pp. 336–337). Thus, SOEs got a lot of autonomy from the central government but at the same time retained some soft constraints and more often than not kept their monopolistic position in many sectors inherited from the Soviet past, albeit in a modified organizational form. The Russian Anti-Trust Committee had been established, but was very passive vis-à-vis monopolistic practices of SOEs (Fornalczyk and Hoffman 1993).

Another dysfunction of the SOEs-dominated market was barter. Initially, it developed as a response to the collapsing system of centralized resources distribution, hyperinflation and deep financial crisis when SOEs started creating a network of exchange of raw materials and goods. Economic reforms which, albeit inconsistently, were introducing market institutions, including monetary system and financial markets, did not lead to liquidation of barter. Firstly, because many SOEs still had no funds as they were regularly confiscated by the fiscal authorities to cover tax arrears; since 1995, SOEs also had problems with getting funds on the financial market because anti-inflation policy of the government severely limited money supply to the economy. Later, one of the main incentives of barter became tax and bank commission avoidance. Secondly, because of the institutional trap (Polterovich 2008) when short-term transaction costs of switching from barter relationships to monetary transactions seemed to many SOEs too high and risky despite possible long-term gains. At the end of the 1990s, about 80–90% of the total volume of industrial production was exchanged through barter (Makarov and Kleyner 1999). In the new century, along with development of market institutions and attempts of the government to tighten fiscal control over the enterprise sector, the role of the barter marginalized, especially among large enterprises (Kuvalin 2020).

During the first almost 10 years of transition, the government did not possess any coherent strategy towards the SOEs sector, especially its part which had to remain under the state control for a longer perspective. The Soviet system of control over enterprises had disintegrated, and the new network-based system could not be effectively controlled by the government. In fact, the government did not have full information about assets it possessed. Only in 1999, the government issued "The Concept of the

Management of State Property and Privatization in the Russian Federation" which contained the principles of the state's ownership policy and the ways of their realization. In the area of the state corporate control, the document postulated tightening the supervision over SOEs and making state-owned assets a tool for supporting the country's economic development. To achieve this, an effective system of state corporate governance had to be created and decisions made, whether particular SOEs had to remain under the state control or be privatized.

In the 1990s, the ownership policy of the government was focused on privatization. Initially, it was treated, as in Poland and Hungary, as a pillar of the transition and efforts for rapid change of the ownership structure of the economy were taken. By 1994, so-called small privatization was virtually completed; in 1992–1994, an ambitious mass privatization program was carried out. As a result, the vast majority of the small enterprises were sold to private hands for cash and a significant number of large industrial enterprises were sold for privatization vouchers. About 60% of the SOEs assets have been privatized and the share of the state in GDP shrank almost twofold from 95% before the transition to 50% by the end of the century (Jarosz and Kozarzewski 2002; EBRD 2008). The managers of privatized SOEs and employees became the largest group of owners (about 66% of shares obtained during mass privatization) (Radygin 1996). In reality, virtually all such enterprises were controlled by their managers—in an ownership (through the majority of shares) or non-ownership (by proxy from employees) way.

Then, the privatization had to enter its "monetary phase," i.e., case-by-case transactions of selling SOEs mainly through IPOs, but the government engaged in the "credit for shares" campaign of 1995 instead when selected private banks were asked for loans for the government and were offered shares of very attractive state enterprises (mainly in the steel and fuel and energy sectors) excluded from the previous stage of privatization as a collateral. Later, the state failed to repay the loans and the shares were transferred to the banks. There is much evidence (Black et al. 2000; Tarasov 2020) that this was a deliberate action by the Russian authorities, which badly needed both funds and political support from domestic wealthy capitalists, but could not conduct "straight" privatization due to political reasons: the Russian society was disappointed with reforms, especially privatization, and adepts of restoring the command economy became increasingly popular. The bankers saved the government and Boris Yeltsin was re-elected as a president in 1996, so the communist "counter-revolution" was prevented, but, among others, at the cost of emergence of strong oligarchy which had accumulated enormous capital in their hands and comprehensively controlled the actions of the government.

Since then, privatization lost its pace, and till the end of 1990s, only a few privatization deals were conducted. Despite a still large state-owned sector of the economy, its share shrunk to, according to different estimations, 25–30% of GDP (EBRD 2008; FAS 2019).

In 2000, the economic policy of the Russian state started radically changing. The team led by Vladimir Putin, which came to power after Boris Yeltsin's public "abdication" on the New Year eve of 2000, put forward the new paradigm of the economic policy (although never officially formulated in a concise form) and, wider, the role of the state in the economy. In his article published just before taking power, Putin (1999) denied the need to return to the command economy principles and declared the necessity of making the state "an efficient coordinator of the country's economic and social forces, balancing their interests, determining the optimal goals and parameters of social development and creating the conditions and mechanisms for their achievement" within market economy with the perspective of reducing the role of the state to formulating the rules of the game and controlling their observance. According to another article written by Putin (2000), the coordination role of the state should concentrate on resource extraction industry as the main factor of future Russian economy's growth via creation of powerful financial-industrial groups. Despite some analysts interpreted this statement as "a blueprint for his campaign to re-nationalize industry" (Anderson 2008, p. 29), Putin didn't mention nationalization, but stressed the need of "an organic combination" of market mechanisms with the state support.

Since the beginning of the century, the corporate control policy of the Russian government (and economic policy in whole), having a lot of features common for the whole period, has undergone certain evolution. Initially, in line with Putin's declarations, the new economic policy consisted of two pillars: restoring control of the government over the economic policy previously captured by the oligarchs and expanding the role of the state in the economy. Then, by the end of 2000s, the policy, at least formally, started to evolve towards reducing the state interventionism, strengthening property rights protection and creating knowledge-based economy with strong innovative private sector.

During the initial period of Putin's rule, the authorities very quickly forced the most prominent oligarchs to cooperate and withdraw from political activities. Those who didn't want to subdue were expropriated and jailed or forced to leave the country—Mikhail Khodorkovskiy, formerly the wealthiest man in Russia, being the most notable example (Goldman 2004). These expropriations, however, were not always nationalizations; in several cases, the property was transferred into the hands of businessmen connected to the new political elite.

At the same time, the government seemingly lost control over law enforcement and secret service structures (so-called *siloviki*) which started massively raiding profitable private businesses (Gans-Morse 2012). Bribed courts helped the riders to legalize their actions. The beneficiaries of such corporate raid were not only businessmen who used their political connections or outright bribery to use *siloviki* in taking over other businesses, but also *siloviki* themselves, including high officials of the FSB (Federal Security Service of the Russian Federation) and other law enforcement agencies (Viktorov 2019) which monetized their growing administrative resource in the times of the re-centralization efforts of the government. Probably because such pressure on business had a very strong impact on the country's investment climate and jeopardized economic growth, since the end of the 2000s the government started an anticorruption campaign. It significantly lessened the corruption burden on business and expropriative activity of *siloviki*. However, at the central level, the repressions of corrupted officials were only selective which could mean that this was at least partly just a tool of political struggle between the groups within the political elite (Rochlitz et al. 2020).

Under the new paradigm, privatization de facto seized to be a tool for market reforms, although it was never officially declared. On the contrary, since the end of the 2000s, in line with the official modification of the economic policy, the government kept stressing the need of reduction of the state-owned sector and appropriate privatization plans were adopted which remained largely unfulfilled.

In 2004, the government created the list of over 1000 enterprises "of strategic importance for the defense and security of the state, protection of morality, health, rights and legitimate interests of citizens of the Russian Federation." Ownership changes in these enterprises (even just corporatization) required a presidential decision. At the end of 2020, only 129 strategic enterprises remained on the list which does not mean that the rest was privatized. They were usually just corporatized or small blocks of shares were sold. Generally, since early 2000s, the government conducted mostly "reluctant privatization," mainly with fiscal objectives, when only minority state blocks of shares were sold in order not to lose corporate control over the enterprises.

At the same time, a few nationalizations of very large businesses took place. Some of them were "confiscations" (albeit formally conducted as buyouts) of companies which belonged to the "disobedient" oligarchs, like Yukos taken from Khodorkovskiy. However, most cases were just buyouts by companies controlled by the state of the previously privatized assets, including those which had been privatized via the "credits for shares" scheme. The state regained or gained control over Gazprom (which subsequently became used for further nationalizations), Sibneft, TNK-BP and several other companies in the oil and gas industry which made the state again the largest investor in this sector (Milov 2012). Mainly through consolidation procedures, the state regained control over the banking sector: in 2017, among the top-10 retail banks, only two were not state-controlled (Vedomosti 2017). Nationalizations also covered other sectors and included, e.g., Avtovaz vehicles manufacturer and United Heavy Machinery heavy industry and manufacturing conglomerate. Several largest nationalization transactions, as in Hungary, were sweetheart deals. There were numerous nationalizations of smaller companies in different sectors as well.

The government usually did not give the official explanations for these transactions, some of the largest ones having no apparent reason—political and especially economic, like the buyout of TNK-BP which in fact incurred heavy losses for the buyer—state-owned Rosneft (Sonin 2016). In this very case, perhaps the hidden reason was re-concentration of key industries in the state hands. Many other nationalizations could be attributed as rescue investments (Trudolyubov 2017). The studies on nationalizations present quite inconsistent conclusions: according to Chernykh (2011), in 2004–2008, i.e., when they were particularly widespread, the government first of all nationalized enterprises in strategically important sectors and rather was not driven by profitability or rescue concern: it did not take over the most profitable ones or largest loss-makers. Sprenger (2012) claims that in the same period larger and profitable companies were more likely to be nationalized and takeover by the state usually did not lead to improvement of their performance. According to Trudolyubov (2017), many nationalizations had a clear rescue character out of fear of social turmoil because of these companies' importance on the labor market or for their numerous clients among the population. The scope of nationalization and the factors which could stay behind it are discussed in more detail in the further parts of this chapter.

Apart from nationalizations, there were other ways of increasing the state presence in the enterprise sector. The state sector was expanding, among others, through generous recapitalization of SOEs (both those which were essential from the point of view of the country's wealth and military strength, and those which had to be rescued from insolvency). The role of the state was also expanding through increasing the role of state structures in the distribution of financial resources and control over formally private entities, expansion of the spheres of state regulation (Radygin et al. 2019, p. 16).

Since the late 2000s, the new area of state expansion shaped up, when the government started trying to shift the country's economic development from resource-based to knowledge- and innovation-based. In 2008, it adopted "The Concept of Long-term Socio-economic Development of the Russian Federation until 2020" which envisaged two stages of this change: until 2012, the already existing, traditional sources of growth were to be explored along with creation of institutional and technological conditions for switching to innovation economy. At the second stage, the transition had to be completed. According to the Concept, this had to be achieved mainly through market mechanisms with the state withdrawing from the direct management of economic processes. The new strategy resulted in setting up of huge projects of the state support for innovative businesses, the flagship ones being Rosnano Group and Skolkovo Innovation Center. The first one had to help in creating a nanotechnology-based industry in Russia through venture investments and preferential credits. The second one was a high technology business area near Moscow which was to host innovation business clusters. The state support consisted of the specific legal, administrative, tax and customs regulations for Skolkovo residents as well as grants for innovation projects.

According to several estimations (FAS 2019; Abramov et al. 2020, p. 5), these three factors, i.e., nationalization, support for SOEs and support for transition to knowledge-based economy, contributed to the gradual re-growth of the share of the state sector in the Russian economy.

From the organizational perspective, the present system of the state corporate in Russia is described by the OECD (2018, p. 26) as "centralized with exceptions": the Federal Agency for State Property Management (Rosimushchestvo), a subdivision of the Ministry of Economic

Development, is in charge of the design and implementation of the ownership policy, both state corporate control and privatization. In practice, it performs corporate control functions towards the majority, but not all SOEs. Selected enterprises of strategic importance are controlled by line ministries.

Presently, the SOE sector in Russia consists of several legal forms. Most of the SOEs are joint-stock companies with variable size of the state block of shares and formally are the subject of the general corporate law. Another form is so-called unitary enterprises, under direct administrative control of the central and local governments typical for post-communist economies, including Poland and Belarus. The third form is state corporations, a mixture of a governmental agency (i.e., they have regulatory power in the sector where they operate and cannot turn bankrupt) and of an enterprise. Each state corporation functions on the basis of a separate legal act. In 2020, there were 8 state corporations in Russia; the above-mentioned Rosnano being one of them. The state corporations were created for increasing the effectiveness of the state corporate control policy in the strategic sectors, strengthening the development policy of the state, but these goals largely were not met (Radygin et al. 2015).

Currently, there are no official goals and objectives of the state corporate control in Russia. Despite provisions of the 1999 Law "On General Principles of Organization of Legislative (Representative) and Executive Bodies of State Power of the Subjects of the Russian Federation," according to which the state may possess only the property necessary for the implementation of its functions, these functions were never explicitly enumerated. In 2013, the governmental program "Management of Federal Property" was adopted which included only general statements that ownership policy of the state and ownership structure of the economy must create conditions for sustainable economic development of the country and corporate control decisions must be justified in terms of economic efficiency and social responsibility. This document and its subsequent iterations were concentrated on the organizational and technical issues of state ownership policy, including privatization and exercising ownership functions in state-controlled companies. They seem to treat state corporate control function as similar to that of a private owner interested in the company's value and return on the invested capital—omitting the goals of SOEs that would justify their being in the hands of the state (Kozlova et al. 2019).

Lack of legal regulations, including both goals setting of the state corporate control other than economic efficiency and official tools for their achievement, contrasts with a wide-scale use of SOEs for meeting a wide range of goals which can be described as developmental, social and political. Developmental goals, as it was shown above, seem to be the core of the state corporate control policy in the twenty-first century. Enterprises, especially large ones, are also expected to meet social objectives such as keeping the employment level, limiting the prices increase or support for local community (Kozina 2005). Last but not least, some enterprises are also expected to realize strategic interests of the Russian state such as import substitution or using them (mainly in the energy sector) as a tool of foreign policy (Newnham 2011).

Peculiarity of the state corporate control in Russia is the fact that after the paradigm change at the turn of the new century the policy of the Russian state towards the enterprise sector largely did not distinguish any more between the state and private sector and expected that both ownership sectors would behave basically the same way. Not only SOEs, but also private businesses should actively contribute to the realization of the government's developmental and social goals. The state has consolidated control not only over SOEs (the most important of which being concentrated in huge financial-industrial groups), but also over the largest and most important private companies (Radygin 2008).

In order to achieve this, the government had a number of formal and informal ways of controlling behavior of enterprises (Grosman et al. 2016). Formally, it had only one legal instrument to leverage its control over companies: in 2001, the golden share was introduced which could be applied in enterprises that undergone privatization, regardless of the number of shares in state ownership left.

In practice, however, both the central government and regional governments had a number of tools of indirect control which were used to impose on enterprises the desired behavior. One of the main ones was state support for enterprises (at the federal, regional and local levels) in return for the provision of assistance by these companies to authorities in the resolving problems on the federal, regional and local levels, respectively. In the times of the global financial crisis of 2008–2009, large enterprises, including private ones, could receive financial support in return for keeping the employment and salary level, refraining from increase of prices, etc. Enterprises could also enjoy state support for contributing to regional and local development through investments in modernization, sponsorship, etc. In mid-2010s, selected enterprises, regardless of whether state- or privately-controlled, were expected to help the government standing against sanctions imposed by the EU, USA and other developed economies (Radygin et al. 2015). The largest private companies also had to help in overcoming the financial crisis of 2014–2015, e.g., through selling their foreign currency (OSW 2015, p. 8).

Yakovlev et al. (2020) called such arrangements an "exchange model" between the state and the business and described its gradual evolution towards support for more pro-developmental behavior of enterprises. According to their study, by the second half of the 2010s, this support became independent from the ownership structure of enterprises and their ability to lobby for it: in most cases, the sole reason for getting state support was pro-developmental activities of the enterprises, unlike in the previous periods, where SOEs and more influential private companies were likely to get aid. Another study (Simachev and Kyzyk 2020) points out that being a large SOE (or at least a large company which closely cooperates with the state sector) still matters partly because private players are less innovative and/or are afraid of the risks incurred by state aid; at the regional level, the aid goes first of all to enterprises that help resolving social issues and/or take part in implementation of public procurement projects.

Unlike in early 2000s, when entrepreneurs that did not want to follow the government's expectations were simply expropriated (especially oligarchs who wanted to play a role in politics, but also small businesses which did not want to pay bribes to officials), in 2010s this "exchange model" functioned on a largely voluntary basis. Still, the authorities also used methods of direct, albeit usually informal pressure on private enterprises in order to make them behave in a desired way: among others, to keep the employment level, to engage in charity or other forms of support for the local community. Radygin et al. (2015) even argue that privatization of an enterprise made it more likely to be a subject of informal pressure by the authorities. This pressure had features of property rights restriction because those opposing this "forced corporate social responsibility" risked sanctions such as numerous inspections by fiscal, fire and sanitary authorities, although the level of outright corruption, including bribes, has decreased significantly (Rochlitz et al. 2020).

Unlike in Belarus (see Sect. 7.4.2 in this chapter), the effectiveness of such pressure was differentiated and was high first of all in the case of businesses which broke law and regulations and/or had investment needs which they could not resolve by themselves (Kozina 2005). As studies show (Vasileva 2018), the practice of this informal exchange of subduing to the authorities' informal orders in return for access to resources or for just not being bothered was very widespread, especially in the SME sector because it was widely engaged in illegal activities (evading taxes, paying bribes, etc.) and therefore was an easy target for bureaucrats.

Among informal corporate control practices, appointment of high-rank bureaucrats on the companies' boards (mostly in SOEs, but in some cases also in private) should be mentioned which became especially widespread since the turn of the new century (Frye and Iwasaki 2011). This practice seems to meet several objectives: firstly, as "bounty" nominations similar to that in Poland; secondly, as an extra-ownership tool of tightening control over these companies functioning by the authorities; thirdly, having prominent persons on their boards helped the companies to get access to state-controlled resources.

7.3.3 Place of the SOE Sector in Russian Economy

As in the case of Poland and other analyzed countries, there is no easy way to get exact data on the size, extent and importance of the SOE sector. Formally, the Federal State Statistic Service (Rosstat) takes into account ownership of enterprises in data it gathers and publishes, but the categorization used is imprecise, inconsistent and misleading. Data on ownership is categorized according to the All-Russian Classifier of Forms of Ownership which includes as many as 33 categories of ownership taking into account not only ownership form, but also forms of legal entities. In its publications, Rosstat groups these categories in various manner; that is, in some tables one can find just two: state (which includes municipal ownership) and non-state (which includes, among others, state corporations), while in other tables other classifications are used. For example, a division into state, private and mixed (the latter including state corporations), or state, municipal, ownership of non-profit and religious organizations, and other ownership. Other divisions can also be found. Besides, separation of state and non-state forms of ownership is not clear. Firstly, Rosstat includes an enterprise in the state-owned category only when it is directly owned by the state, all so popular in Russia cases of cascade state ownership being treated as private sector. Generally, it leads to undervaluation of the size of the SOE sector. Secondly, in the case of mixed ownership, there is no information on the size of the state's stake.

Another problem with getting the reliable data on SOEs is incompleteness of the data. According to the report by the Accounts Chamber of the Russian Federation (Baturkin 2020), neither Rosstat, nor fiscal authorities, Rosimushchestvo and appropriate ministries have full information on the enterprises; sometimes they even don't know some of them exist. There are also problems with access to financial data from enterprises; many companies are reluctant to publish them while, for example, the Ministry of Economic Development passes to the government information only on about 1% of companies with the state share.

7.3.3.1 The Scale of the SOE Sector

According to Rosstat, among 3,827 thousand of business entities which operated in Russia in 2019, 298 thousand (7.8%) fully or partially belonged to the state. The official data shows that the Russian economy became mostly private property based long ago: measured by the value of the fixed assets, the state share dropped from 91.0% in 1991 to 25.7% in 1992 and during almost the whole transition period was characterized by very slow, but still downward trend reaching 15.1% in 2019 (Fig. 7.1). These figures seem to be too low and even absurdly low for the early transition period. Besides, most of the data looks like rough estimation because they are represented by round numbers.

In contrast, the state share in employment was unexpectedly high: from 46.8% in 2000 to 38.9% in 2019 (earlier data is not available), but here too, according to Rosstat, state share was gradually decreasing and private ownership prevailed (Table 7.2).

The official data is widely regarded as inaccurate and several independent estimations exist which vary greatly in the methods used. It leads to very different results and makes it difficult to compare them with each other. According to the Federal Antimonopoly Service (FAS 2019) which refers to some unidentified research, the share of the state in GDP already in 2013 exceeded 50% and was estimated at 60–70% in 2016 and 2017. This estimation became quite popular in the literature, although no details on how it had been calculated are available. Estimations with known methodology present more modest state share. The lowest one performed by the IMF experts (Di Bella et al. 2019) is based on the official Rosstat data; changes boil down mostly to expanding the state sector by the "mixed Russian" category. According to this research, in 2016 the

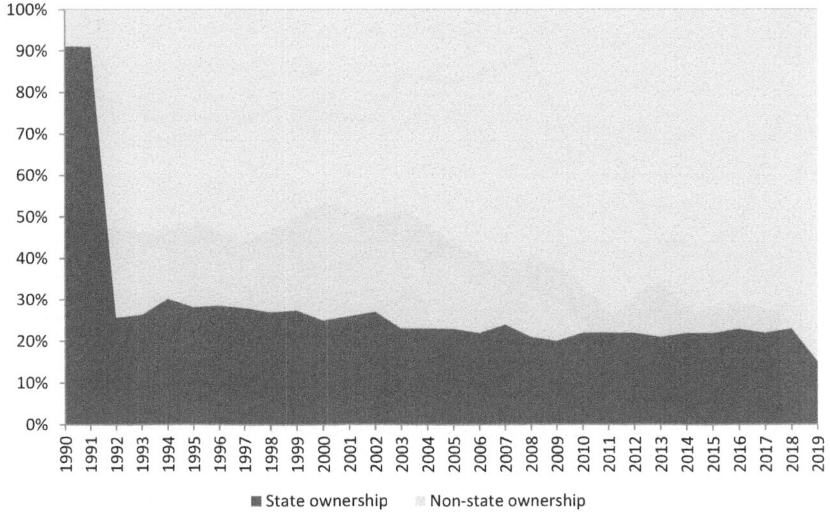

Fig. 7.1 Dynamics of the ownership structure of the fixed assets in Russia according to Rosstat (in %) (*Source* Rosstat)

Table 7.2 Ownership structure of fixed assets and employment in Russia according to Rosstat classification (in %)

	2000	*2010*	*2017*	*2018*	*2019*
Fixed assets					
State	25.0	22.0	22.0	23.0	15.1
Non-state	75.0	78.0	78.0	77.0	84.9
Employment					
State, municipal	46.8	43.3	39.1	38.9	38.9
Private	34.2	45.5	49.3	49.6	49.3
Public and religious organizations	0.8	0.4	0.4	0.4	0.3
Mixed Russian	15	5.1	4.6	4.5	4.4
Foreign, joint Russian and foreign	3.2	5.7	6.1	6.2	6.5

Source Rosstat

share of the state in gross value added amounted to about 33% which was only 1 p.p. more than in 2012—which, by the way, contradicts the popular opinion on substantially growing state involvement in the enterprise sector. Another research (Radygin et al. 2019; Abramov et al. 2020)

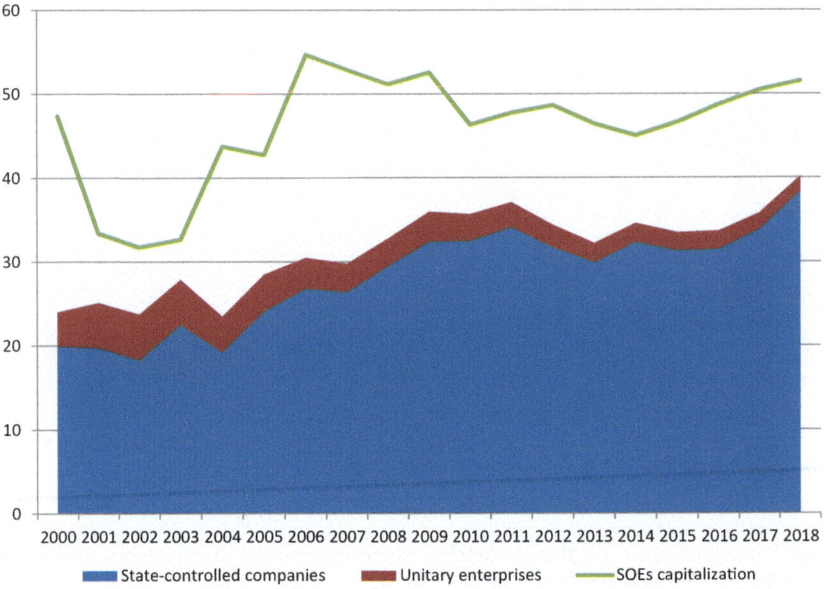

Fig. 7.2 Dynamics of the SOEs share in GDP and in capitalization in Russia (in %) (*Source* Abramov et al. 2020)

based estimations, among others, on the sample of 265 of Russia's largest private and state-owned companies which accounted for 96.1% of capitalization and 22.0% of total revenues in the Russian economy in 2017. According to it, since the turn of the century, the state share in GDP was steadily increasing—from 24.1% in 2000 to 40.2% in 2018 (Fig. 7.2). Whereas the IMF study may underestimate the size of the state sector, the latter one may overestimate it because it does not take into account smaller enterprises which can be predominantly private.

7.3.3.2 The Extent of the SOE Sector

The extent of the state ownership is uneven across sectors. According to the official Rosstat data on operating revenues (taking into account the "mixed Russian" category), the state participation was high only in the infrastructural sectors, but still less than 50% with the only exception of gas manufacture and supply where the state share was almost 2/3. In manufacturing, the state share amounted to modest 10.7% and was very low in extractive industries: 2.2% (Table 7.3). Especially the latter figure seems to be too low; the IMF research (Di Bella et al. 2019, p. 23) estimates state share in mining end extraction for 2016 as being 3.5 times higher (44%), than the official value for that year was (12.1%). What is more, there was a 10 pp. increase comparing to 2012 which meant continuation of the policy of consolidating of the state control over the extractive sector, contrary to official plans and declarations. Interestingly enough, in 2017–2019, there were no big privatizations which would explain the official over fivefold contraction of the state share in this sector. The rest of IMF estimations of the size of the state ownership across the sectors of the Russian economy for 2016 was much closer to the official ones, e.g., 21% in manufacturing (19.2% according to Rosstat) and 52% in electricity, gas and water supply (43.3% by Rosstat).

Outside industry, the most state-controlled sectors are the financial one and transport and communications. According to the IMF estimations (Di Bella et al. 2019, p. 23), in 2016, the state controlled as high as 59% of assets of the former sector and 48% of sales of the latter. Comparing to 2012, opposite trends could be seen: increasing state participation in the financial sector and decreasing in transport and communications. Within the financial sector, the largest state participation is in banking which kept increasing partly because factors being the bailout scheme launched by the Central Bank of Russia in 2017 which made it the owner of commercial banks in distress in return for providing them funds for recovery. However, according to the Association of the Banks of Russia (2020), the growth of the share of the state-owned banks both in the banking sector assets and in the total amount of credits and deposits of enterprises and population in 2018–2020 was very slow. The Association estimates the state controlled 74% of the assets of the banking sector in 2020 and 70–81% of credits and deposits. Similar results were presented in the FAS (2019) report.

At the same time, many sectors of the Russian economy can be regarded as almost fully private-controlled, at least formally. In agriculture, fishing, construction, hotels and restaurant business, and trade state participation amounts to single per cents (Di Bella et al. 2019, p. 23).

7.3.3.3 *The Importance of the SOE Sector*

It is not surprising that the importance of the SOE sector in Russia, i.e., the share of SOEs among the most important companies in the country, is high. As in many other post-communist countries, including

Table 7.3 Share of different forms of ownership in operating revenues in Russian industry in 2019 according to Rosstat (in %)

	With state participation[a]	*Domestic private*[b]	*With foreign participation*[c]
Mining and quarrying	2.2	78.1	19.7
Mining of coal and lignite	0.9	69.8	29.2
Extraction of petroleum and natural gas	1.3	80.9	17.8
Manufacturing	10.7	65.0	24.4
Manufacture of food products	2.8	75.7	21.5
Printing and reproduction of recorded media	20.4	65.3	14.3
Manufacture of coke and refined petroleum products	8.3	80.1	11.6
Manufacture of chemicals and chemical products	14.0	64.8	21.1
Manufacture of fabricated metal products, except machinery and equipment	38.1	54.7	7.2
Manufacture of computer, electronic and optical products	34.3	52.4	13.3
Manufacture of motor vehicles, trailers and semi-trailers	0.8	38.7	60.5
Manufacture of other transport equipment	39.7	48.5	11.8
Electricity, gas, steam and air conditioning supply	45.9	42.1	12.1
Electric power generation, transmission and distribution	45.6	39.8	14.5
Manufacture of gas; distribution of gaseous fuels through mains	63.2	31.8	5.0
Water supply; sewerage, waste management and remediation activities	33.5	64.2	2.4
Total	11.8	66.4	21.8

[a]Categories "state," "municipal" and "mixed Russian"
[b]Categories "private" and "public and religious organizations"
[c]Categories "foreign" and "joint Russian and foreign"
Source Rosstat, own calculations

those discussed in this book, SOEs are usually larger than private enterprises. According to the Orbis database, in 2018 almost one-third (31%) of 100 largest industrial enterprises in Russia were controlled by the state; they had nearly a half of the whole set's operating revenues (49.7%) and possessed over three-thirds of the top-100's assets (68.3%). As in Poland, the larger was an enterprise, the more likely it was state-controlled: in the top-10 group, a half were SOEs which controlled three-thirds of the revenues and over 80% of the assets. In the course of almost 10 years, since 2009, the share of SOEs in the top-100 list slightly decreased, but remained unchanged or even somewhat increased among the really large companies—from the top-10 (Table 7.4).

It should be noted that while the share of SOEs among the largest companies in Russia is quite similar to that in Poland, the share of SOEs in the whole economy in Russia is much higher. It can be explained by the fact that in Russia much smaller enterprises remained state-owned than in Poland, so proportionally less SOEs entered the lists of the largest enterprises.

But still, many Russian SOEs are really huge and contribute a fair amount to the country's GDP. In 2018, gross value added of two largest enterprises in Russia (in terms of sales), both being state owned (Rosneft and Gazprom), amounted to almost 11% of GDP; the top-10 SOEs gross value added amounted to 17.6% of Russia's GDP. What is more, in 2016–2018, there was a clear growing trend of the economic importance of the largest state-controlled companies (Abramov et al. 2020).

Companies with the state participation also play an important role on the financial markets, although perhaps more modest than could be expected given the role of SOEs in the Russian economy. In any case, since 2000, the share of SOEs in stock market capitalization was seldom considerably lower than a half, and in 2018 amounted to 51.6%. It should be noted that stock market in Russia is more developed than in Poland and Hungary: according to the World Bank data, in 2019 it amounted to 34.5% of GDP against 25.4 and 20.1% in those countries, respectively—and it reflects proportionally higher role of SOEs in the Russian economy. Besides, the Russian SOEs were steadily increasing their share in the value of corporate bonds on the market from a mere 9.9% in 2003 to 55.1% in 2018 (Abramov et al. 2020, p. 6).

At the end of 2020, on the Moscow Exchange MOEXBC blue chip index, only 6 out of 15 companies had state participation (which is much less than in Poland) and their share in the index capitalization was 50.3%.

Table 7.4 SOEs among the largest Russian enterprises in 2009, 2013 and 2018

	10 largest enterprises			*50 largest enterprises*			*100 largest enterprises*		
	2009	*2013*	*2018*	*2009*	*2013*	*2018*	*2009*	*2013*	*2018*
Number of SOEs									
Majority ownership	5	5	6	19	17	14	37	30	27
Minority ownership[a]	1	1	1	1	4	3	3	5	4
Total	6	6	7	20	21	17	40	35	31
Share of SOEs (%)									
In no. of enterprises									
Majority ownership	50.0	50.0	60.0	38.0	34.0	28.0	37.0	30.0	27.0
Minority ownership[a]	10.0	10.0	10.0	2.0	8.0	6.0	3.0	5.0	4.0
Total	60.0	60.0	70.0	40.0	42.0	34.0	40.0	35.0	31.0
In operating revenues									
Majority ownership	61.3	63.7	64.2	52.0	50.7	48.6	49.3	47.0	45.1
Minority ownership[a]	3.6	3.3	3.7	2.5	5.6	5.0	2.8	5.0	4.6
Total	64.9	66.9	68.0	54.4	56.3	53.6	52.1	52.0	49.7
In assets									
Majority ownership	77.9	79.2	79.6	71.5	70.0	67.9	69.1	67.2	65.4
Minority ownership[a]	2.3	1.5	1.1	1.7	3.5	3.2	2.1	3.4	3.0
Total	80.2	80.7	80.7	73.2	73.6	71.1	71.2	70.6	68.3

[a]25–50% of shares

The data was gathered and processed by Maciej Bałtowski, Marlena Gołębiowska, and Grzegorz Kwiatkowski

Source Orbis database, companies' websites, own calculations

It is still a bit less than could be expected given the fact that the three largest SOEs (in terms of sales), at the same time being the largest enterprises in the whole economy, were included in the index (Gazprom, Rosneft and Sberbank), but the Russian SOEs usually have much less proportion of shares traded on the market than companies without state participation.

7.3.4 Sources of the State Corporate Control Policy and Its Evolution in Russia

7.3.4.1 Acting in Good Faith vs. Pursuing Group Interests

Shaping up and evolution of the state corporate control in Russia seems to present a complicated interweaving of the factors of good faith and vested interests. It may be argued that since perestroika the economic policy of the Russian government, including ownership and corporate control policy, almost always included a fair portion of good faith, especially at turning points evoked by crises and lack of possibility of keeping the previous *modus operandi*. Economic reforms under Gorbachev were intended to return the Soviet economy on the growth path. However inefficient and even in some way destructive, they created ground for the post-communist transition in Russia and other Soviet republics through partial deregulation, introducing civil liberties, and evoking pro-market aspirations in some part of the society. Besides, the failure of perestroika to save the Soviet economy convinced a large part of the Soviet elite that market reforms had no reasonable alternative, that "state failure was greater than market failure" (Åslund 2009, p. 9). It made possible for Boris Yeltsin to form a team of liberal-minded young reformers, who started post-communist economic transition in Russia in January 1992.

There are no reasons to doubt in fairness of the key team members' intentions—as the Polish reformers, they were clearly devoted to the mission of saving their country from the catastrophe and creating sustainable mechanisms of its development. Within the state ownership policy, the mass privatization program, albeit accompanied with a deceiving propaganda of mass enrichment of the society, was aimed at rapid change of ownership structure of the Russian economy which was considered to be a pillar of the reforms. The tools chosen (wholesale non-equivalent transfer of ownership rights to mostly undefined group of beneficiaries) and the limited scope of privatization may be criticized from today's perspective, but at the beginning of the transition they were seen as the sole possible in the given economic and political conditions. Too narrow a window of opportunity, and not a lack of good will, may be at least partly the reason for the too incoherent reform of the state corporate control as well.

One can find signs of acting in good faith in all the other turning points that followed. The "loans for shares" scheme of 1995–1996 which led to creation of oligarchy was apparently aimed at not losing the political power by the Yeltsin's team. One of the reasons for this was to prevent the Communists from returning to power which would roll back the reforms and re-establish the command system. Regardless of how realistic were these fears (perhaps at that time the point of no return to the communist system had been already passed), they were really widespread among the reform supporters. The statist turn taken by Putin's administration could at least partly result from the sincere intentions to overcome negative factors in the economy's functioning, including the power of oligarchs over the economic policy, and to re-establish the ability of the government to steer the economic processes for public benefit. Here, basing the new policy on the state-led extractive industries and later on state-supported knowledge-based economy, as well as the pressure on enterprises and the "exchange model" of relationships between the administration and enterprises, could be regarded as the right tools. And they indeed provided some results that could be seen as positive for the society (especially those preserving employment and restricting price growth).

One of the Russia's peculiarities was that since the very beginning of the transition, no consensus existed among the elites and a large part of the society on the basic principles according to which the Russian economy had to function. This problem was rather marginal in Poland, Hungary and Belarus. In the first two cases (as well as in the rest of the CEE countries), there was a wide-scale belief about the necessity of building capitalism; in the latter case (as well as in some other countries which resigned from comprehensive market reforms), there was no mass disillusionment in the effectiveness of the command methods. In Russia, the reformers met strong resistance from a wide array of social groups that opposed dismantling of the command system and building market economy. They included not only groups whose interests were violated by the reforms, but also all those who sincerely did not believe in market mechanisms and saw the main cause of the crisis in the inability of the state administration to steer the economy in a strict enough way. Those "anti-reformers in good faith," called *gosudarstvenniki* (adepts of state interventionism), could be found everywhere: among politicians, SOEs directors and employees, academia, etc.

At the same time, it may be argued that the resistance towards comprehensive market reforms, including creation of the efficient system of the state corporate control, and pushing the *gosudarstvenniki's* agenda, was mostly motivated by vested interests. According to Åslund (2009), since perestroika, the economic policy of the Russian state was to a large extent driven by group interests; it started with Gorbachev's reforms, which "transformed the Soviet economic system into a rent-seeking machine" (Åslund 2009, p. 7) and were responsible for the final collapse of the Soviet economy. Indeed, the late USSR reforms of the enterprise sector created a strong interest group of "red directors"—directors of SOEs which gained a fair deal of independence from the state administration and used their power to keep the state supporting their enterprises, as well for asset stripping and tunneling. At the same time, a new area for business was shaping up at the peripheries of the state sector called by Kryshtanovskaya (2002) a "komsomol economy." It was based on commercial entities supervised by the party and komsomol apparatus which usually rendered not always legal services for SOEs, mostly of financial kind. Quite many managers of these entities, most of them being former komsomol *apparatchiks*, after the USSR collapse became wealthy businessmen, including a few financial tycoons. The latter managed to take over financing of many large SOEs and regional and local governments.

In 1990s, a decentralized system of rent-seeking formed which included many actors, the main rent-seekers being SOEs managers, new private entrepreneurs and state bureaucrats who gained from partial economic reforms (Hellman 1998). Here, an important role was played by privatization processes. Mass privatization of 1993–1994 led to emergency of a powerful rent-seeking group of the former SOEs' directors who took corporate control of their enterprises using voucher privatization schemes. Together with directors of large enterprises which remained under the state control they formed a so-called directors' party which forced on the government continuation of support of large enterprises under the slogans of preservation of the production potential of the country and keeping jobs. Already in 1992, the "party" managed to radically slowdown the economic reforms. But it was the "loans for shares" scheme which was described before and which in fact was a form of privatization that really put the state economic policy under the control of vested interests by creating a powerful group of oligarchs. This group also contributed to the gradual decline of the "directors' party" because oligarchs were interested in taking over enterprises headed by the members of the "party" and resources they were receiving from the state.

But just several years later, oligarchs started losing their power themselves. The first blow was inflicted by perhaps the most severe financial crisis in post-Soviet Russia in 1998 which strongly hit the banking sector. Many private financial businesses collapsed, although those oligarchs whose main businesses were in the non-financial sector, mostly survived. But they lost their political power, and some of them—also their property or even freedom in early 2000s, when Putin's administration, in line with the new statist and authoritarian approach—started consolidating the power of the government over the economic policy and, broader, over economic processes in the country. The period of "state capture by oligarchs" ended giving lace to the period of "capture of oligarchs by autocratic rulers" (Mihályi and Szelényi 2017), or, wider, "business capture by the state" (Yakovlev 2006). Only those former oligarchs were allowed to keep their businesses who resigned from any political activity and were ready to support the government; at the same time, the state administration strengthened its control over the enterprise sector as a whole. While SOEs managers and selected big private businesses still were able to receive rents in their relationships with the state administration, the amount of benefits contracted and, what is more important, they generally lost the ability to initiate rent-seeking arrangements. The state apparatus became the major beneficiary of rent-seeking capturing the control of rent generation and often forcing on enterprises transfer of their resources for the private benefit of the members of the state administration. What is more, perhaps deliberately (Åslund 2017, pp. 21, 31), the economic and political elite has been divided into competing clans which allowed the central authorities to stabilize their power through playing the role of an arbiter.

This period, which at the time this book was finished hasn't ended yet, consisted of two stages. The first one which lasted till the late 2000s was extremely chaotic and dysfunctional; attempts to eliminate the state capture by big business were accompanied with widespread corporate raid performed by *siloviki* and generally the wide scale of self-dealing by the state bureaucrats.

By the end of the decade, the government became aware of the destructive economic effects of these uncontrolled rent-seeking activities and violent pressure on business, especially when Russia was hit by the 2008–2009 global financial crisis. The second stage was characterized by the attempts to eliminate the most dysfunctional corruption schemes. Rochlitz et al. (2020) called the new policy "a move towards centralized corruption," as the main effort was put on fighting rent-seeking on the lower level of the state administration which left the higher levels mostly intact. In the area of state corporate control, the anticorruption attempts boiled down mostly to remove government officials from the SOEs' boards and replacing them with independent members, but this process, which started in 2011, was soon put on hold (Grosman et al. 2016). However, nowadays, many CEOs of the largest state-controlled companies are not current, but former state officials.

Thus, the government representatives on the SOEs boards remained one of the most important private interest groups within the system of the state corporate control in Russia being a part of a sophisticated rent-seeking network. Many wealthiest private businessmen still form an important part of it getting resources from public procurement and various means of state support for the enterprise sector. Another important rent-seeking group is members of public administration, MPs, local leaders and their families who own businesses and extract rents using their privileged position in distribution of state resources. Many enterprises, regardless of their ownership structures, as well as their management and employees, also enjoy transfers of rents from the state in the framework of the "exchange model" mentioned before or when the authorities want to save them from bankruptcy in order, e.g., to alleviate social problems.

Generally speaking, the specificity of rent-seeking in Russia which uses the resources of the state policy towards the enterprises sector (and the major channels of relationships between the state and the enterprise sector) is using all imaginable niches: state corporate control, privatization, public procurement, business support programs, etc. The more or less exact amount of these rents is unknown, especially those of corruption kind which involve members of the public administration and members of the federal and regional parliaments. But the value of the rents was probably very high from the very start of the transition (Åslund et al. 2001). Since 2015, within the anticorruption campaign, disclosure requirements were introduced for government officials and MPs showing that this group includes a lot of wealthy people. Basing on the disclosure declarations, in 2020 the total income of this group's top-100 (Forbes 2020) was RUR 65.8 billion (about USD 940 million), or about USD 9.4 million per capita. Among MPs and government officials, there were six "dollar billionaires" the wealthiest possessing the assets estimated at USD 6.3 billion and occupying the 19th place on the Forbes list of the wealthiest Russian businessmen (Lomskaya 2020). Virtually all this officially declared wealth originates from performing a dual role of an official/PM and an entrepreneur. Interestingly enough, no *silovik* entered the Forbes list of the wealthiest governmental officials and MPs.

The wealth of the members of the state administration may be dramatically underestimated. No synthetic studies have been conducted so far, but anecdotal evidence shows that quite a few Russian *chinovniks* are among the wealthiest persons in the country. The Anti-Corruption Foundation FBK created in 2012 by opposition politician and activist Alexei Navalny conducted about 80 investigations on the real wealth of high-rank government officials (including Putin and former Prime Minister Medvedev, and a lot of *siloviki*) and corruption schemes they used which included corporate raiding and preferential access to public procurement (FBK 2020). Using publicly available data, the investigations show that the assets which belonged to these people in Russia and abroad were many times higher than their official income. The reaction of the authorities on these investigations was repressions against the FBK and its investigators and deleting data on government officials' property from the state cadaster (Dolinina and Alykova 2021).

Large state-controlled companies were also the source of high income for their managers, virtually all of them originating from the state administration, including law enforcement and secret service agencies. In 2015, the government lifted the public disclosure requirements on their remuneration, but investigation journalists managed to access the data for 2018. For example, the Gazprom CEO Alexei Miller (former vice Minister of Energy) earned RUR 1.9 billion (about USD 30 million) and the general director of the biggest savings bank Sberbank German Gref (former deputy Prime Minister and Minister of Economic Development)—RUR 1 billion (ca. USD 16 million) (Baza 2021).

7.3.4.2 Exogenous and Endogenous Factors

Analysis of the second dichotomy shows a quite complicated nexus of different factors. It may be argued that the corporate control policy of the Russian government (and the economic policy as a whole) was more exposed to external influences than other economies discussed in this book, although their importance was still secondary vis-à-vis internal factors.

The role of knowledge transfer varied through the analyzed period and was the highest in the times of economic and financial crises, when the government looked for solutions outside the mainstream discourse imposed by the rent-seeking groups interested in preservation of the status quo. Thus, the knowledge transfer was high in perestroika and during the first years of the transition: partial liberalization of the late 1980s used the experience of other countries of the Eastern Bloc in "repairing the socialism," i.e., the reforms within the communist system, first of all Yugoslavia, Poland and Hungary. Not only the government was trying to adapt this experience to the challenges of the decaying Soviet economy; komsomol and party apparatus which was looking for the methods of monetization of their political status was also interested in the relevant experience of the "fraternal nations," especially that of official Polish youth organizations which started their businesses in the last years of the communist rule. (It may be better not to admit it, but I, in 1988 being a young researcher at the USSR Academy of Sciences, was personally involved in consultations for the *apparatchiks* from the district komsomol committee in Moscow on the possibilities of using the Polish experience for "komsomol entrepreneurship").

At the same time, political liberalization made easier for Russian researchers to get acquainted with the Western economic literature and for some of them to get attracted to the liberal ideas popular in that period, including the Washington Consensus concept. These ideas, which went beyond "repairing of socialism," were discussed in the circles of young Moscow and Leningrad economists, including those who later became in charge of creating the program of liberal reforms started to be implemented in January 1992 (Aven and Kokh 2013).

After the reforms started, the Russian government enjoyed a wide-scale support from foreign think tanks and international financial organizations, which assisted in elaboration reforms in the major areas of the Russian economy. Knowledge transfer included not only concepts elaborated by Western economists, but also the use of experience of post-communist CEE countries that started the reforms earlier, including Poland and Czechoslovakia. For example, the voucher privatization program used the experience of the Czechoslovakian mass privatization and experts from the Polish CASE Foundation contributed to the introduction of preferences for insiders in investing their vouchers in shares of the enterprises where they worked. However, foreign experts did nothing to help the Russian government to streamline the state corporate control and withstand the rent-seeking activity of the "directors' party" which colluded with the line ministries' *apparatchiks*. Perhaps neither the foreign experts, nor the Russian reformers were aware of the importance of this issue as the SOE sector was regarded as having soon to vanish; the SOEs directors who took over their enterprises in the course of the voucher privatization were expected to subdue to the forces of the market.

As time went by, the importance of the knowledge transfer was fading—until late 2000s, when the government started to look for the ways of increasing the efficiency of the enterprise sector and tried to turn the Russian economy to the knowledge-based growth path. In the area of the state corporate control, the government tried to introduce elements of best practices of corporate governance for SOEs that had been introduced in the developed marked economies and were also recommended by international organizations, e.g., the OECD (2005b). IPOs of several SOEs on Western stock exchanges also contributed to knowledge transfer on transparent and efficient corporate control. Besides, experience of the developed economies apparently had some importance in the plans (mostly unfulfilled) of the government to re-launch privatization and using bailouts as a tool of support for enterprises in distress.

External factors of political and especially of economic kind also played visible role in shaping up and evolution of the state corporate control in Russia. In the 1990s, their impact was mostly indirect. Although the Russian enterprise sector was hit severely by the economic crisis and during the first five years of the transition the industrial output shrank twofold, the reasons for these dysfunctions were of mostly domestic character. Some of them were "inherited" after the previous system, including perestroika, and another originated from the inability of the government to stabilize the economy and to return it on the growth path.

One of the most prominent exogenous factors, both political and economic, was foreign aid. Since the very beginning of transition, numerous international financial organizations, think tanks and private funds embarked upon the assistance for the Russian reformers. Apart from positive impact in the form of knowledge transfer, there were adverse effects caused by flaws in foreign aid concept and conditionality (Dąbrowski 1995; Cohen 1998; Wedel 1998, 1999; Åslund 2000), which, among others, led to too easy access of the Russian government to financial resources received from the international financial organizations. The latter captured the government in the "curse of aid" (Djankov et al.

2008) trap making it even less motivated for introducing deep reforms—especially that the donors quite soon relaxed their requirements, more interested in just preventing communists and populists from coming to power in Russia and keeping this country's behavior predictable.

The dissolution of the USSR, although formally initiated by the Russian authorities, also can be regarded as an exogenous factor for the corporate control, but perhaps its importance was quite limited, much less important than for most of other former Soviet republics. First, the central USSR administration was placed in Moscow and was mostly just taken over by the Russian government; there was no need to create new structures; the Russian economy was the largest in the USSR and much more self-sufficient; production and export capacities were not hit so severely by the USSR collapse as that of many other ex-Soviet states.

By the end of the 1990s, the external economic factors started playing more direct role, such as oil prices and the situation on the global financial markets. The first came the external shock of falling oil prices and the Asian financial crisis of 1997, which were among the main factors that triggered the 1998 financial crisis in Russia (Gaidar and Chubais 2011, p. 105)—so far the severest ever in this country. Next, the world prices of crude oil started growing since 1999 till the mid-2008. It could motivate the government to make the export-oriented oil and gas sector the main vehicle of the economic development and keep the state's grip on the relevant enterprises in order to ensure budget revenues and rents for interest groups. In 2008, the Russian economy got external shocks inflicted by both the global financial crisis and falling oil prices. The government started helping the enterprises most affected by them, but simultaneously it was forced to try increasing the efficiency of the enterprise sector as a whole through privatization and making state corporate control less dysfunctional. Besides, the government became motivated to look for new factors of growth such as development of innovative industries.

The reaction of the Russian authorities on the sanctions imposed in 2014 by the EU, USA, Canada and other developed economies for the Russian annexation of Crimea and military involvement in Eastern Ukraine was much more statist and included direct support for enterprises affected, both state-owned and private—among others, through preferences in public procurement and bailouts. The government also introduced counter-sanctions against the countries which joined the anti-Russian sanctions blocking import from them of selected agricultural goods which can also be regarded as a protectionist measure, first of all to protect the Russian agricultural sector from foreign competition (Åslund 2017).

At the same time, through the whole transition, period the state corporate control setup and policy was influenced by a number of endogenous factors.

The first group of the factors was the state of the Russian economy. It may be argued that not only corporate control policy (and ownership policy as a whole), but the economic policy in general was to a large extent driven by economic crises. The mere embarking upon reforms, first partial ones as in perestroika, and then more radical, system-changing, was toggled by the deep crisis of the command economy. Later, Russia experienced a series of financial crises, most of them having domestic origin. The banking crisis of 1995, caused by reckless behavior of young commercial banks and lack of proper state supervision over the financial market, broke out in an unfortunate time just before the presidential elections and when the popularity of the government and President Yeltsin was very low. In order not to lose power, as it was discussed earlier, the "loans to shares" scheme was launched. The overcoming of the crisis of 1998, which apart from external shocks also had roots in the erroneous macroeconomic policy of the Russian government (Gaidar 1999), led not only to tightening the macroeconomic policy, but also to consolidating the state control over the enterprise sector, including nationalizations of early 2000s and elimination of oligarchs. The 2008–2010 crisis which motivated the government to change its policy in the enterprise sector was triggered mostly by the external factors mentioned before, but it would not be so deep and long-lasting without internal factors such as structural weaknesses of the economy and dependence on export of gas and oil (Bogetic et al. 2008), as well as falling trust of investors in the Russian financial market because of the policy of the Russian state towards foreign investors in the energy sector and the war in Georgia (Radio Liberty 2008). The Russian financial crisis of 2014–2015 which also had an impact on the state corporate governance was also triggered by the external factors (falling oil prices and economic sanctions), but it would not be possible without internal factors such as dependence of the Russian economy on crude oil exports and the policy of the Russian authorities towards Ukraine (Tracey 2018).

It may be argued that in Russia the state corporate control policy, and the transition as a whole, despite importing economic ideas and some solutions, was mostly a domestic intellectual product. Before the transition, Russia possessed perhaps the largest intellectual potential in the USSR despite the fact that economic research free from ideological restrictions became possible on a wider scale (outside special units which worked for the party apparatus and the government) only in the times of perestroika. Studies on the crisis of the command economy started, but initially they were conducted within a somewhat liberalized communist doctrine and looked for the solutions in making the existing system viable through its modification, and not in the systemic transformation. This was partly due to the lack of faith in the possibility of a quick collapse of the communist system in the USSR, even when the post-communist transition had already begun in the CEE countries. To be fair, the Western kremlinology also regarded the dissolution of the USSR at most a some remote possibility (Brzezinski 1989, p. 245). On the other hand, this was a result of the deep indoctrination of the Soviet intellectual elite and the resulting resistance to revise certain axioms. It applied even to the most prominent critics of the communist regime, such as philosopher Alexander Zinoviev or political scientist Anatoly Butenko, who after the system had collapsed started to criticize the post-communist transition in Russia for being an attempt to overtake the course of history (Butenko 2000) or an outright conspiracy of the West (Zinoviev 1999).

In fact, the intellectual foundations of the market reforms in Russia were created only by the next generation of economists and political scientists who made use of the knowledge gathered in the West: Yegor Gaidar, Vladimir Mau, Alexander Ilarionov, Alexander Javlinskiy, Anatoly Chubais and others. Many of them took part in design and implementation of the reforms. However, which was also characteristic of most other CIS countries, liberal pro-market reform economic thought was not dominant in the Russia's discourse. Unlike in the post-communist countries of Central Europe, the ideas of restoration of the command economy were popular at least during the first years of the transition being supported by the Communist Party of the Russian Federation and a part of "red directors." Besides, there was a strong "centrist" option of the discourse which opted for restricted market economy with strong state interventionism which had to support domestic producers. It was put forward mainly by the lobby of managers of large SOEs and privatized enterprises.

In the twenty-first century, the outright anti-market stance almost disappeared from the economic debate; now the mainstream economic discourse stays mostly within the general principles of the market economy where discussions between supporters of more liberalism and more state interventionism take place. Liberal economists started being engaged in design and implementation of the economic policy, especially its macroeconomic part. So-called systemic liberals (liberal-minded economists which cooperate with the political class and are not concerned with violations of human rights and taking-down the democratic institutions) took positions in the economic ministries, the Central Bank and state agencies which were in charge of innovations. And indeed, they manage to conduct quite austere macroeconomic policy. The state corporate control policy also is clearly influenced by the liberal-minded part of the Russian economists which can be seen in the constant, however mostly rather unsuccessful attempts to limit the government involvement in the enterprise sector and to introduce equal treatment of SOEs and private enterprises.

The institutional setup of the Russian economy is extremely complicated and was a subject to constant evolution. Therefore, given the limited space in this book, the institutional aspects of the state corporate control can be presented only in a simplified and incomplete form. One of the main characteristics of the state corporate control policy, as well as the whole ownership policy of the state and its economic policy in general, is that they are captured by private interest groups. As it was discussed in the earlier part of this section, the composition of these groups evolved with time, although the main sources of rents remained basically the same. The captured state had limited capacities to restrict rent-seeking; the strongest efforts were made only when its destructive impact on the economy could lead to catastrophic results. At the beginning of the transition, mass privatization was supposed to limit the influence of the interest groups which extracted rents in the SOE sector. After the 1998 crisis, the government embarked upon the policy of not eliminating the rent-seeking at all (as the political class was one of the main rent-seekers), but of mitigation of the contradiction between private interest groups' behavior and the development prospects of the Russian economy. As Åslund (2017, p. 30) put it, since then "state corporations and cronies are allowed to tap the state on money, but not to destabilize the economy." One of the most notable results of this policy was the disappearance of oligarchy and transforming (some of) them into cronies.

Nevertheless, so far, the overall effectiveness of these efforts was very limited and the government failed to ensure sustainable growth of the Russian economy and make it less prone to exogenous and endogenous shocks. It may be argued that the invincibility of rent-seeking in Russia is caused by the mere foundations of the institutional setup based on the dominance of extractive institutions and top-down distribution of resources. The stability of this setup may originate from the national resource curse (Frankel 2012) which the government failed to overcome, strictly speaking the "oil & gas curse"—in the situation of flawed democratic mechanisms (Fish 2005; Åslund 2009) and even growing authoritarianism under Putin's rule. Russia has become a petrostate where energy rents are not only the source of wealth, they are also the source of power: "who owns the energy rents owns Russia" (Åslund 2017, p. 24). The authorities (apparently with the help of the "systemic liberals") are clearly aware of this curse, but so far failed to overcome it. Firstly, because even without the powerful oligarchs, the government couldn't counteract the numerous cronies' interests and the system's stability depends on the ability of the government to mutually reconcile them. Second, because the government itself is still a part of the extractive and redistributive system.

The latter may corroborate the view expressed by Bessonova (2006) and Kordonsky (2007) that in fact the current institutional setup in Russia to a great extent still is a continuation of the Soviet planned economy which conducted mass forced extraction and redistribution of resources in favor of interest groups and for achievement of social and political goals. In the post-Soviet times, these practices became less formalized and applied, apart from the SOEs sector, also to private enterprises (see Sect. 2.3.3). It seems, however, that the current economic institutional setup in Russia is much less centralized and omnipotent, at least in the enterprise sector. Firstly, it includes numerous clientelist arrangements at regional levels, where authorities and enterprises exchange resources for mutual benefit. Secondly, the areas excluded from forced or voluntary extraction (exchange) of resources seem to be much larger. After the government managed to overcome the uncontrolled corporate raids by *siloviki* and other state agencies, a large part of the enterprise sector, especially private companies, and many of those firms which do not break the law and/or create social problems, seized to become an object of the state pressure.

Unlike in the post-communist countries of Central and Eastern Europe, in Russia public opinion was generally unfavorable to market reforms. The communist indoctrination which has covered several generations of the Soviet population ban on any critical opinion on the communist system, blocking any unfavorable information on the internal life of the country, and the "iron curtain" which guarded the soviet society from getting information on how Western societies lived efficiently brainwashed a large part of the society. It had a kind axiomatic, black-or-white attitude towards economy and politics: socialism is good, capitalism is bad; in capitalism, there is unemployment and exploitation of workers by capitalists; in socialism, we have free education and medical care, full employment, etc.

In the second half of the 1980s, when perestroika started, the policy of *glasnost* became a real eye opener for many, and dethroned many personalities, starting with Lenin, Dzerzhinsky and other revolutionaries—although the belief that socialism has systemic (although unrealized) advantages over capitalism persisted. The society became aware of the necessity of reforms, especially vis-à-vis the deepening economic crisis and growing shortages on the consumer market; Gorbachev's reforms aimed at building of a kind of "market socialism" were generally supported by the society. They failed to bring immediate favorable effects and the economic situation kept worsening; but still, most of the society believed that transition to the market would improve their situation: in 1991, as many as 64% of the respondents supported market reforms and only 19% supported the consolidation of the planned economy (VTsIOM 1995). At the same time, only 10% were definite supporters of transition to capitalism and only 21% regarded the building of communism in the USSR as a historical mistake (Koval' 1997). It means that the society was in favor of liberalization, but without a radical system change.

Since the transition started in 1992, the public attitudes towards market reforms quickly changed into worse. Already in October 1992, 58% of the respondents were for return to the state price control. In the mid-1990s the situation has stabilized, the reform being supported (mostly cautious, only as a gradual change) by about 30% of the respondents and opposed by roughly the same part of the society; about 40% were disoriented and had no opinion (VTsIOM 1996). It means that the reformers had to function in the situation of the lack of public support and all the major reforms, including in the enterprise sector, more often than not were conducted not in line of the will of the majority of the society. And even if the society moderately positively treated some elements of the reforms, this support melted as time went by.

Due to flawed democratic institutions, the government usually could act not taking public opinion into account, though. However, in 1992–1999, two times the public support mattered and was needed. Both these cases were related to the ownership policy of the state. The first one was the need to engage the society in the voucher privatization program of 1992–1994 which was crucial for its success (and, as the experience of Belarus and several other former Soviet republics shows, the lack of public interest could lead to the mass privatization program failure). A massive propaganda campaign was launched which advertised taking part in mass privatization as a safe way to become wealthy and successful. At first, the society was fascinated with these perspectives; quite soon though it turned out that the market value of a voucher was very low (equivalent of about two half liter bottles of vodka) and the value of shares received for vouchers often even less or zero, and the main beneficiaries of the mass privatization were "red directors" and dubious investment funds where the population invested their vouchers. The society (quite rightfully) felt cheated, especially given the fact that the authors of the voucher privatization program deliberately deceived the population in order to get its support. The immediate effect was that the public opinion turned away from the reforms even more, starting to listen to slogans proclaimed by politicians like populist and nationalist Vladimir Zhirinovsky (his party won 1993 parliamentary elections) and communist leader Gennady Zyuganov.

The latter, being a consistent proponent of the return to a command economy (which included re-nationalization of the assets allegedly stolen from the society), embarked upon the presidential campaign of 1996 and for the most part of it was the most popular candidate. The government managed to save the situation through the beneficiaries of the "loans for shares" scheme supported Yeltsin's candidacy, among others, and through financing a fierce campaign "Vote or Lose" in the media which painted a black picture of Russia in the case communists returned to power.

This near-miss situation forced the Russian political class to modify the political mechanisms so *vox populi* would not really matter anymore. Firstly, from the very beginning of Putin's rule, the authorities started gradually blocking political competition; since then, no presidential and parliamentary elections were free from administrative pressure on voters, opposition candidates and outright falsifications of the election results. All civil society actions started being repressed. Secondly, a complex propaganda campaign through the captured mass media was launched to support the new statist course of the government. It included critics of the earlier period for allegedly ruining the Russian economy and the mere independence of the country together with the "rehabilitation" of the pre-perestroika USSR as a great successful country. The propaganda promised the recreation of a strong, omnipotent paternalistic state which would take care of a citizen (and in later years stressed the achievements on this way). All a citizen needed to do was to act along the rules imposed by the state. Thirdly, the authorities started showing that they really care about people. In the area of the state corporate control, it took the form, e.g., of imposing social obligations on businesses and saving some of them from closing down.

The authorities generally succeeded in their attempts to shape up public attitudes as they found a fertile ground in the population which was never too supportive to market reforms and was tired of the hardships of crises which came one after another and the unjust, in their view, distribution of income. In 2000, 71% of the respondents were in favor of re-nationalization of all the privatized property. In 2017, 73% of the respondents were still critical towards the privatization, but only 31% said that the state should return the property that it had lost in the 1990s, while another 31% supported the re-nationalization only in cases when privatization had occurred illegally (VTsIOM 2017). In 2018, although 48% of the respondents believed that private ownership was more efficient than the state one (and 38% presented the opposite view), at the same time 63% thought that the state engagement in the economy was too small (and only 11% that it was too big) and *en masse* supported state ownership of large enterprises. The authors of this study (Volkov and Kolesnikov 2018) explain this contradiction with economic ignorance of the population—among others, its lack of understanding of how else, than through direct state intervention, social and economic problems could be resolved.

Summarizing, it may be argued, that public opinion in Russia was never an important factor shaping the policy of the state corporate control; during the first decade of the reforms, there were episodes when it mattered for privatization policy; later, the whole economic policy was made to a large extent resistant to pressure from the broad public.

7.4 Belarus[2]

7.4.1 Situation Before the Transition

Till the collapse of the USSR at the end of 1991, the Belarusian economy was an integral part of the Soviet economy and shared all the features of the command economic system in its Soviet version. It was absolutely dominated by state ownership of the means of production and SOEs were under a strict control of the state administration. The same as in the rest of the USSR, the perestroika has brought some very limited liberalization in the enterprise sector of the republic, but the level of the turmoil caused by the deregulation measures was much lower than in many other USSR republics, especially in Russia, and the Belarusian authorities managed to keep a great deal of corporate control over the SOE sector.

Besides, although the Belarusian economy suffered the same faults of the Soviet economic system as the rest of the republics (low efficiency, numerous imbalances, etc.), by the end of the Communist era it occupied rather a special place on the economic map of the USSR. The republic benefited very much from the ambitious investment programs initiated for mostly political reasons (among others, because of the strategic geographic position of the republic) in the early 1960s which contributed to rapid industrialization and launching production in machine building, petrochemical and chemical industries, optics and electronics, and light industry. Already in mid-1970s these sectors contributed to about 2/3 of the republic's GDP (Papko 2017). The industrialization also included the agricultural sector where large state-owned farms have been equipped with modern (at the Soviet scale) facilities and dramatically increased production of meat and milk. The volume of industrial and agricultural production many times exceeded the domestic needs and the largest part of it was exported, mainly to other Soviet republics making Belarus an "assembly shop" of the USSR and one of the main suppliers of final investment and consumer goods for the rest of the Soviet Union. In 1980s, Belarus exported as much as about 80% of its GDP and was among the most export-oriented countries in the whole Soviet bloc (Yanchuk 2007). At the same time, Belarus was short of raw materials and spare parts and was dependent on deliveries from other republics.

Another feature of the Belarusian economy in late Soviet times was highly developed infrastructure because the geographical position of this country predestined its transit capabilities, being at the crossroad from East to West of the European continent and from North to South of the Western part of the USSR. Thus, the Soviet authorities heavily invested in road building, especially East–West and North–South highways. Belarus was also a transit country for the transport of oil and gas from Russia to the West.

The big economic importance of Belarus for the whole USSR resulted, among others, in relatively high level of economic development: in 1970s and 1980s, the republic's GDP grew faster that in the whole Soviet Union and at the end of the 1980s it had the highest level of the GDP per capita in the USSR and one of the highest in the whole Soviet bloc (Olechnowicz 2010). It contributed to the highest standards of living of the Belarusian population comparing with the rest of the Soviet Union. If we also take into account the quite high level of human development (UNDP 1993, p. 11) and well developed, comparing to other parts of the USSR and other countries of the Soviet bloc, social services, it may be argued that Soviet Belarus was one of the most developed socialist countries. What is more, when in the late 1980s most of the CEE countries were hit by the severe crisis of the decaying command economy and citizens of the larger part of the USSR suffered from growing shortages, Belarusians still enjoyed relatively stable and well-off life.

7.4.2 *Shaping Up and Evolution of the State Corporate Control During the Transition*

Given the fact that Belarusian economy was extremely dependent on supplies and customers from other republics, the more severe was the blow induced by the collapse of the Soviet Union which destroyed a great number of economic linkages within the former USSR (that had been created by the politically motivated locational decisions of the central planner). Belarusian enterprises were losing markets rapidly because of falling demand caused by liquidation of state investment programs in the newly independent states and growing competition from the world markets. They also lost many sources of subsidized raw materials and spare parts and could not afford buying them at market prices. Overnight, the stable world of Belarusian enterprises collapsed and they were absolutely unprepared to function in the market conditions and outside the territory of the USSR. The most prosperous Soviet republic swiftly became the most severely hit by the transition crisis among all the European post-Soviet countries (Antczak et al. 1995).

Not only SOEs were unprepared: the government of the newly independent Belarusian state was taken by surprise by this catastrophe and had no ideas what to do, how to reform the economy (Papko 2017, p. 62). It may be argued that the Belarusian government was one of least prepared for coping with the new situation on the post-communist space, especially compared with that of Poland, Hungary, Czechoslovakia and Russia which had substantive domestic intellectual potential and to a greater or lesser extent had been prepared for post-communist reforms. During the first years of the independence, only very cautious and partial reforms were initiated, including privatization which allowed selling a limited number of small and medium SOEs mainly through transferring ownership rights to their employees (and limiting these rights through restrictions on the circulation of shares). In 1993, a mass privatization program started which had a much less scope than had been anticipated. All in all, the scale of ownership transformation during the first years of independence was quite negligible: only 15% of the state assets undergone transformation of any kind, which most often than not it was only their commercialization (leaving full ownership control in the hands of the state). Till mid-1994, only 5% of the value of the state assets was transferred to private hands (Antczak et al. 1995). Green-field privatization was also very slow; new private businesses were mostly small enterprises in catering and services, although in the banking sector a few of quite powerful players emerged. Reforms in other areas also stalled which gave grounds to several researchers (Havrylyshyn 2007; Rovdo 2009; Olechnowicz 2010) to argue that a comprehensive process of market transition never started in Belarus. The government never fully liberalized prices and exchange rate; privatization was slow, hesitant and did not include large enterprises.

One of the unreformed areas was corporate control over SOEs which still was performed by line ministries. In 1992, officially in order to strengthen control over the state property, the State Property Management Committee of the Republic of Belarus was formed; in 1993, it was renamed to the State Committee of the Republic of Belarus on State Property Management and Privatization; and in 1994 becoming the Ministry of State Property Management and Privatization. Despite its name, it never was in charge of corporate control over SOEs.

Lack of reforms was apparently one of the causes of lack of adaptation of enterprises to the new conditions which in its turn contributed to continuing economic recession. In this situation, in July 1994, the first president elections were won by Alexander Lukashenko—an authoritarian politician with a strong anti-market rhetoric. Thus, instead of pushing forward market reforms, the Belarusian authorities have chosen the policy of strengthening the state control over the economy.

By November 1996, Lukashenko dismantled the separation of powers and consolidated the control over the state in his hands. He also managed to restore non-market exchange with Russia and re-launch a substantial part of production capacities remaining idle since the dissolution of the Soviet Union. In 1996–1999, the Belarusian authorities concluded a series of treaties whose goal was to establish a common state with Russia. It was never created; but these agreements guaranteed Belarus generous economic preferences from Russia for many years ahead. Belarus was given an unrestrained access to the Russian market; it was allowed to buy oil and gas at the same prices as Russian consumers which were twice below the market prices (Papko 2017).

By the end of 1996, the government finished the process of taking control over the economic system by re-introducing the main elements of central planning. The government adopted a program entitled "Main directions of the social and economic development for the years 1996–2000" which became the basis for setting targets for each state enterprise including, among others, the output exports and wage growth (EBRD 2008, p. 105).

There was no official document which would describe the objectives of SOEs and the principles of state corporate control. It can be deducted from the policy of the government towards SOEs that they had to be both the main vehicle of economic growth and the source of the well-being of the society (which also had to become a growth factor through stimulating internal demand). The latter made the government exerting strong pressure on the SOEs to increase wages, independently of their labor productivity and without stimulating their profitability. In this situation, SOEs looked for additional financial resources to meet the expectations of authorities and state-controlled commercial banks generously provided them with loans at the interest rates below the market level or even below the inflation rate (World Bank 2012, pp. 29, 36). Given the fact that worse performing SOEs were more active in looking for external financing and the banks did not reject such requests, the major bulk of loans was provided to the inefficient enterprises and this money was simply lost because the enterprises were not able to repay them. But in fact those loans were aimed rather at making SOEs alive than at helping them to improve their performance. To prevent a banking crisis caused by the growing number of non-payable loans in the banks' portfolios, the state just regularly re-capitalized commercial banks through money emission and, unlike the governments in other post-communist countries, did nothing to prevent re-emergence of the "bad debts."

Despite the lack of pro-efficiency incentives that would stimulate competitiveness of Belarusian enterprises (which remained predominantly state-owned), the government was able to conduct the highly statist Soviet-like economic policy for about 10 years. Very favorable terms of trade with Russia (Russian energy subsidies and extensive Russian market open for Belarusian goods) and, since early 2000s, rapidly growing global oil prices contributed to quite decent GDP growth rate and postponed the need for economic reforms, including restructuring of the enterprise sector and streamlining the state corporate control. However, in mid-2000s, most of these factors of growth started to deplete. The decisive blow at the "Belarusian economic model" (a term coined by pro-government economists who praised the alleged effectiveness of the return of "manual control" over the economy) was inflicted by the Russian government which significantly reduced its energy subsidies.

These subsidies were introduced in the framework of creation of the so-called Commonwealth of Belarus and Russia which was set up in 1996 and was to eventually end in creation of the unified Russian-Belarusian state. Quite soon, though, Lukashenko lost real interest in unification apparently because it would devoid him of political power (as the unification would effectively mean taking over Belarus by Russia), but the creation of the common state was never denounced. In its turn, Russia used energy subsidies as the element of political pressure on the Belarusian authorities. In mid-2000s, Lukashenko was faced the alternative to advance the "unification" with Russia or to try to improve the functioning of the Belarusian economy without Russia's assistance. In 2007, the Belarusian authorities decided for the second option through introducing some market elements into the economy, but simultaneously kept trying to restore the Russian economic preferences without too severe political costs such as losing independence.

The government partially re-launched market reforms: in 2007–2009, it liberalized all the prices except for limited number of "socially important goods," abolished wage control, simplified procedures for registration of small and medium enterprises (SMEs), corporatized several industrial giants, including a tractor producer MTZ and a truck factory MAZ, and declared privatization of 147 industrial and agribusiness enterprises. In 2011, the Belarusian government approved further plans for the privatization of 245 SOEs and corporatization of 134 SOEs (albeit most of them were middle-sized communal enterprises with low profitability). These reforms proved to be, firstly, inconsistent. Financial support for SOEs continued, albeit at a reduced scale; there was no liberalization of exchange rate policy and the government continued stimulation of internal demand. Secondly, the initial reform plans were implemented only very partially, especially in the field of structural reforms: privatization objectives were met only in a tiny part and the enterprise sector remained predominantly in the state hands.

These very reluctantly introduced reforms were finally abolished in 2012 after the Belarusian government partly succeeded in its efforts to restore the Russian economic preferences paying for them with transferring to the Russia's Gazprom of the ownership rights on the Belarusian national gas transporting company Beltransgaz and engaging in new economic integration projects initiated by Russia (which did not include integration into one state, though). In return, Russia abolished export duties on oil exported to Belarus, introduced a generous gas price discount and provided Belarus with a USD 3 billion stabilization loan. All this apparently made the Belarusian government losing motivation to continue the already hesitant and partial reforms. In 2012, it abolished the previous privatization plans and declared that new privatization deals would take place only on ad hoc basis. Privatization process was even reversed, two big previously privatized enterprises being taken over by the state. The Belarusian authorities returned to the practice of wide-scale support of internal demand by the increase in salaries in SOEs and the massive emission of credits to them.

Quite soon the "new" economic policy turned into disaster. Reckless monetary policy, continuing "depravation" of SOEs with generous support and protection from competition, restrictions on private entrepreneurship, falling global prices on goods exported by Belarus, shrinking Russian market because of falling income of the Russian population and the growing reluctance of the Russian government to support the Belarusian regime without substantial political profits contributed to deep economic crisis destructive to public finances and resulting in recession. For the first time since 1995, in 2015 the economy contracted (by 3.8%).

This made the Belarusian government turn to some sort of market reforms again. The major change in the economic policy occurred in 2015 consisting of the government's refusal to stimulate the GDP growth at any cost. The government has started prioritizing the macroeconomic stability over the increase in output and wages. Among others, the National Bank increased the interest rate well beyond the inflation level, liberalized the exchange rate regime and refrained from interventions in the market. In 2016, the government abolished price control on socially important goods and increased household tariffs for communal services, eventually phasing the subsidies out. The credit to the national economy was reduced, although its structure remained almost unchanged: mainly SOEs in construction, industry and services enjoyed support through the state-controlled commercial banks, despite the volume of this lending decreased by one-third (World Bank 2018, p. 23).

However, non-financial forms of SOEs support of a protectionist kind remained to exist which defended SOEs from competition from the domestic private sector and the world markets. At a local level, administrative obstacles were created for private firms which wanted to enter market segments already occupied by SOEs. The domestic market as a whole was protected with the set of protectionist measures: the volume of imports to Belarus was regulated by the decisions of the Council of Ministers and Presidential decrees; each year the government approved a long list of "import substituting goods." The Council of Ministers gave tax breaks to the Belarusian enterprises producing these goods and prevented foreign analogues from coming to the Belarusian market (Daneyko 2012).

Reduction of financial support for SOEs was accompanied with elimination of volume output targets for them and certain liberalization of the regulatory environment for small and medium businesses, although numerous formal and informal barriers for private enterprises continued to exist. At the same time, the Belarusian authorities demonstrated no interest in decreasing the share of state sector and reducing the role of large SOEs. Unlike in 2011, no plans of privatization have been declared and all very few privatization deals were carried out on ad hoc basis: the political elites were still trying to keep the enterprise sector under their "manual control." Unlike in many other post-communist countries, in Belarus privatization was not regarded even as a means of ensuring budget revenues, even in hard times as the Covid crisis of 2020–2021. The authorities keep using the quite common argument of "family silvers" here: as President Lukashenko put it in May 2020, it is not right to sell enterprises which have been created by the generations of working people. Unexpectedly enough, his another argument was impossibility of using privatization proceeds for financing socially important reforms: "I think (I am not the first year president): probably they will sell, but the money will not be used for reforms. We have already seen this in Russia. The money will be pocketed, you can be sure" (Belta 2020). It must be noted that in Belarus (as in other countries) privatization may be carried out only by the state agencies—so it sounded as an accusation against his own government. But perhaps aversion towards privatization comes not only from the lack of political will itself, but also from the fact that possible revenues from privatization of the largest SOEs would be quite modest and incapable to resolve the problems of Belarusian public finances (Adaskevich 2021).

Currently, the state-controlled sector of enterprises consists of two types of enterprises: joint-stock companies (JSC), where the government possesses all or the majority of shares, and performs (at least in theory) its ownership functions through the general corporate control mechanisms, and so-called unitary enterprises—a form very similar to that in Russia, when the enterprise has no ownership rights to its assets and is directly administered by the government. But in the case of the majority of state-controlled JSCs, functions of the board of directors have been significantly constrained by the regulations issued by the state administration. They do not act as independent supervisory and managing bodies, but as the channel through which the government's instructions are passed to the enterprises. Therefore, in practice, the majority of state-controlled JSCs are deprived of autonomy and the real decision-making is transferred directly to the state agencies (Avtushko-Sikorskiy et al. 2016, p. 37). Needless to say, the unitary enterprises have no autonomy at all.

A striking feature of the state corporate control in Belarus (given the dominant position of SOEs in the economy—see Sect. 7.4.3 of this chapter) is lack of the official concept of its objectives and the guidelines on the ways they could be achieved. The existing legal provisions which make the SOEs (and also to certain extent private enterprises) the part of the central planning system (albeit in much more relaxed form than in the Soviet times) are mostly concentrated on organizational issues, on how the control functions of the state are to be performed, reporting requirements, etc. The ultimate goals of the state corporate control remain mostly implicit. The same goes for the goals of SOEs—in Belarus, the functions of SOEs are set even wider than in developed market economies (such as addressing market failures and maximizing value for the society) and include direct provision of social services regardless of their main area of operation. Like in the Soviet times, SOEs maintain hospitals, child care and sport facilities, and even restaurants and museums (Ehrke et al. 2014).

Formally, the main owner of the state assets in Belarus is the governmental State Committee on Property (which was created in 2006 through merging the State Property Fund, the "heir" after the Ministry of State Property Management and Privatization, with the Committee on Land Resources, Geodesy and Cartography); local authorities are in charge of the municipal enterprises. In reality, the state exercises its ownership functions according to the decentralized or "sector ministry" model (OECD 2005a). At the central level, the ownership functions are given to 9 line ministries (such as Ministry of Transportation, Ministry of Healthcare, Ministry of Transport and Ministry of Communication). Other managers of state assets are five state consortiums whose origins can be traced back to the "branch ministries" of the Soviet times (Lavnikevich 2015). Each consortium includes several dozens of big enterprises from five different industries: petrochemical industry, light industry, food industry, timber and woodworking, and wholesale trade. State consortiums do not have the status of ministries, but perform very similar functions. They participate in the elaboration of the economic policy, issue legal acts and help to achieve the economic targets set up by the government. All enterprises being members of these consortiums have to report to the state authorities the results of their business activity and follow the government guidelines. In practice, it means that the government usually imposes on them the volume of output, prices, the level of salaries and several other targets.

It is worth noting that not only SOEs can be members of such consortiums: the membership of private enterprises which function in these sectors is not obligatory, but state authorities often force private companies to join (Avtushko-Sikorskiy et al. 2016, p. 20). Belonging to these structures are not only costs for private businesses, though; it creates a number of opportunities as well, such as access to public resources and being treated in a much less restricted way by the authorities comparing with fully independent private enterprises.

Despite the evidence that the decentralized model of the state corporate control is inferior towards more centralized solutions (OECD 2005a), the Belarusian government tried to facilitate the processes of state property management through its further decentralization. In 2010, it has established the second, lower level of the state ownership hierarchy gathering about 800 SOEs into 102 state holdings. These holdings were also used for improving the financial situation of the loss-making SOEs, although, unlike in Poland (see Sect. 4.3), it was not among the main objectives of the holdings' creation in Belarus.

Regardless of some efforts to improve functioning of the state-controlled enterprise sector, it is still characterized by long-term negative trends. Incoherent reduction of state support and deregulation measures even made things worse. SOEs generally made no use of somewhat relaxed grip on them on the part of the authorities and did not try to restructure and to look for market niches. In this situation, contracting subsidies was a strong blow at many of them. Besides, although private enterprises were not allowed to compete with SOEs on the goods markets, they started competing on the labor market and the attractiveness of employment in the private sector began to increase at the expense of the state-controlled one.

According to the World Bank (WB) estimations (Gayduk 2020), in 2012–2019 the profits of SOEs decreased from 8.3% of GDP to 4.2% of GDP, and the share of loss-making enterprises in the public rose from 4.8 to 11.4%. The government started admitting that the SOEs sector did not perform well. Belarusian experts and SOEs directors (Zayats 2020) first of all blame the inefficient system of the state corporate control, mainly lack of centralization of state corporate control agencies, direct interference of bureaucrats into managing SOEs and the practice of imposing on SOEs meeting objectives which are harmful for their microeconomic efficiency and often mutually contradictory, such as increasing wages with simultaneous cutting costs.

It is worth noting that not only the government, but also the expert community does not look for improvement of the Belarusian enterprise sector performance in privatization of SOEs. For example, the World Bank experts (Loyko 2019) blamed first of all the inefficient system of the state corporate control which did not allow to use the state-owned assets in a proper way, and the fact that SOEs were not fully the subject of market discipline—never mentioning that the SOE sector is just too big and includes enterprises which have no reason staying in the state's hands. In the roadmap prepared jointly with the Belarusian government, the World Bank proposed deep government-led restructuring of SOEs and their full exposure to the market. One can only assume that this organization sees no political window of opportunity for deeper economic reforms, including privatization, as it was previously known rather by putting forward liberal recipes for underperforming economies.

Having no plans to significantly reduce the sector of state-controlled enterprises, the government does not try to expand it either, although there was a case of buying out of 50% of shares of Belorusskaya Kaliinaya Kompaniya (wholesale trader of potassium fertilizers) from a Russian private owner by Belarusian state-controlled companies. The official narration combines the notion of keeping the "family silvers" in the hands of the nation with possible privatization of other objects on a case-by-case basis if it makes economic sense. In practice however, several attempts to attract private (foreign) investors to SOEs failed because of too high obligations of prospective owners of investment and social kind imposed by the seller. Perhaps in reality the policymakers are aware that expansion of the SOEs sector would impose more burden on the economy without any substantial profits. Which makes sense given the fact that in Belarus there are mass transfers of financial resources from the private to the public sector (Papko 2017) which help keeping the latter alive; expansion of the state sector at the expense of the private one would jeopardize this source of resources.

7.4.3 *Place of the SOE Sector in Belarusian Economy*

It must not be surprising that in one of the most unreformed post-communist economy the role of the state-controlled sector remains very important. However, the exact estimation of the quantitative characteristics of this sector is not possible—mainly because of the lack of the clear boundary between the state and the private sector.

Firstly, it's the ambiguity of definitions in Belarusian official statistics. According to the National Statistical Office (Belstat), only communal or state unitary enterprises belong to the state sector. All joint-stock companies are treated by the Belstat usually as one separate category, even those where the state remains the only shareholder. State-controlled JSCs are very common in Belarus, truck factory MAZ or MTZ tractor plant being the most prominent examples. In some sets of data, however, Belstat introduces categories "mixed ownership," "mixed ownership without foreign participation," "mixed ownership with foreign participation," "ownership of joint stock companies with a state share of more than 50%" and "ownership of joint stock companies with a state share of less than 50%." These categories are used in different combinations and not always in a coherent way, but still they give information that in these enterprises the state share exists. One also needs to keep in mind that the Belarusian authorities exercise a disproportionally strong power over the enterprises where they have only minority stakes which is leveraged mainly by the reporting requirements towards the relevant branch ministry and the right of the state shareholder to interfere into business decisions of the companies. Therefore, in this section, all the enterprises having public authorities among their shareholders are considered as state controlled, regardless of the size of the state share in them, and without division into majority and minority state ownership.

Secondly, the border between SOEs and privately owned enterprises is blurred because of the widespread property-rights-restricting government interventions in Belarus. There are strong doubts about the independence of many formally purely private companies subordinated to the Belarusian state institutions. For example, Amkodor JSC (a large producer of the road building, municipal, and forestry equipment) is directly subordinated to the Ministry of Industry, whereas Milavitsa JSC (the biggest Belarusian lingerie producer), alongside with other 85 private and state-owned enterprises, belongs to the Bellegprom state consortium this becoming a subject of direct state interference. However, I do not include these companies into the state-controlled enterprise sector because it is very difficult to set the exact threshold of the level of the state control, beyond which an enterprise can be regarded as a SOE. Besides, at least formally, such companies belong to the state structures voluntarily and at least a theoretical possibility exists that they may choose to become independent.

Another property-rights-restricting interventions are regulations imposed on businesses regardless of their ownership form concerning, among others, wages and prices setting. Although in the recent years the overall level of such restrictions is much lower than before, as the government generally eased it regulatory grip over enterprises, in the times of economic turmoil it at least partly reverts them. In 2020, different forms of price control on the selected socially important goods were reintroduced and direct price control over them was established in February 2021.

Last but not least, a problem of accessing the complete data exists. The official source—Belstat—often presents data on the enterprise sector in inconsistent way as regards time periods and indicators used. Disclosure requirements in Belarus are weak and companies often do not publish information about their ownership structure. The third source of quantitative information is the Orbis database which is highly incomplete apparently due to the problems with accessing the companies' data.

Therefore, in the analysis of the various aspects of the place of the SOEs sector in the Belarusian economy, different sets of data with different, not always coherent indicators had to be used.

7.4.3.1 The Scale of the SOE Sector

According the Belstat data and using the assumptions on the borders of the SOE sector described above, in 2019 the state still dominated the country's enterprise sector controlling almost 2/3 of the assets and employing just a little smaller portion of the workforce. In industry, in 2018, the state sector produced almost 70% of the output. Figure 7.3 shows that the share of the state measured with all these three indexes is characterized by a long-term gradually falling trend, regardless of practically lack of privatization of SOEs. Several factors apparently stay behind these dynamics. The first one is steadily worsening performance of SOEs which results not only in decreased output, but also in falling attractiveness of SOEs as an employer because wages in the public sector become less and less competitive with that of the private sector. The second one is the development, very slow but still existing despite all the restrictions

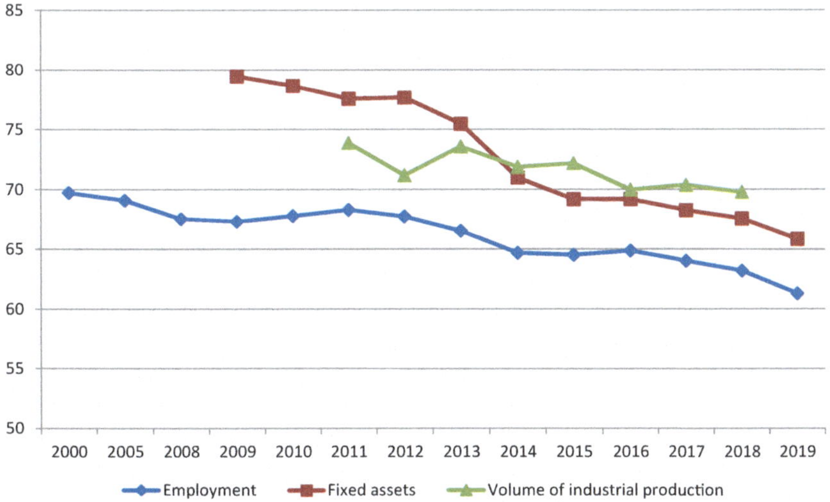

Fig. 7.3 Share of the SOEs in employment, fixed assets, and volume of industrial production in Belarus (in %) (*Source* Belstat, own calculations)

and administrative barriers, of the private sector (especially in selected industries, which is shown below), mainly of domestic origin, through green-field investments and expansion of already existing businesses.

From the perspective of the legal form of enterprises, unitary enterprises dominate: they possess about 2/3 of the fixed assets of the SOE sector and nearly as much of the employment. At the same time, these enterprises are the most responsible for gradual shrinking of the state sector, while joint-stock companies generally retained their share in fixed assets, employment and industrial output (Table 7.5). This issue needs further analysis, but a hypothesis may be formulated that commercialized enterprises, some of them with participation of private investors, in Belarusian conditions may be a less dysfunctional form of public entrepreneurship.

Apart from dominance of the state-owned sector, another peculiarity of the ownership structure of the Belarusian economy is very small role of FDIs which in 2018 contributed merely 3.5% of the country's gross value added. According to the National Bank of Belarus data, by the end of 2018 the total amount of FDIs was only USD 13.1 billon. The largest foreign investor in Belarus is Russia (USD 4.0 billion, 30.1% of total FDIs). The second largest investor is Cyprus (USD 2.3 billion, 17.6% of total FDIs); taking into account that this country is widely used as an off-shore investment platform for Russia (Repousis et al. 2019) and other former USSR republics, including Belarus (Chartyja'77, 2016), the Cyprian investments may be mainly of the Russian descent and some of them just domestic ones which have conducted a round trip for tax avoidance purposes.

7.4.3.2 The Extent of the SOE Sector

The extent of the state control of the Belarusian authorities over enterprises is very uneven across the sectors (Fig. 7.4). SOEs dominate in infrastructure sectors, mining, construction and manufacturing. At the same time, there is a big area of the Belarusian economy, where private entities dominate—first of all in real estate, retail trade, catering and accommodation, IT and communications. Even in the financial sector, private companies became a slight majority. Such ownership structure of the economy has formed as a result of the delayed privatization and discriminative policies applied against the private sector. Belarusian authorities have managed to keep control over the overwhelming

Table 7.5 Share of the SOEs in employment, fixed assets, and volume of industrial production in Belarus (in %)

	2000	*2005*	*2008*	*2009*	*2010*	*2011*	*2012*	*2013*	*2014*	*2015*	*2016*	*2017*	*2018*	*2019*
Employment														
Unitary enterprises	57.2	51.8	49.9	47.3	44.7	43.8	42.6	41.0	38.9	39.3	40.2	40.1	39.7	39.4
Joint-stock companies	12.6	17.3	17.7	20.0	23.1	24.5	25.1	25.5	25.7	25.3	24.7	24.0	23.5	21.9
Total	69.7	69.1	67.5	67.3	67.8	68.3	67.8	66.5	64.7	64.5	64.9	64.0	63.2	61.3
Value of fixed assets														
Unitary enterprises				54.6	54.3	54.5	52.6	50.7	47.0	45.2	45.5	45.0	44.6	44.5
Joint-stock companies				24.9	24.4	23.1	25.1	24.8	24.0	24.0	23.7	23.3	23.0	21.4
Total				79.5	78.7	77.6	77.7	75.5	71.0	69.2	69.2	68.3	67.6	65.9
Volume of industrial production														
Unitary enterprises						20.6	16.2	17.1	13.0	14.8	15.3	14.1	13.8	
Joint-stock companies						53.3	55.0	56.5	58.9	57.4	54.7	56.3	56.0	
Total						73.9	71.2	73.6	71.9	72.2	70.0	70.4	69.8	

Empty fields mean lack of data
Source Belstat, own calculations

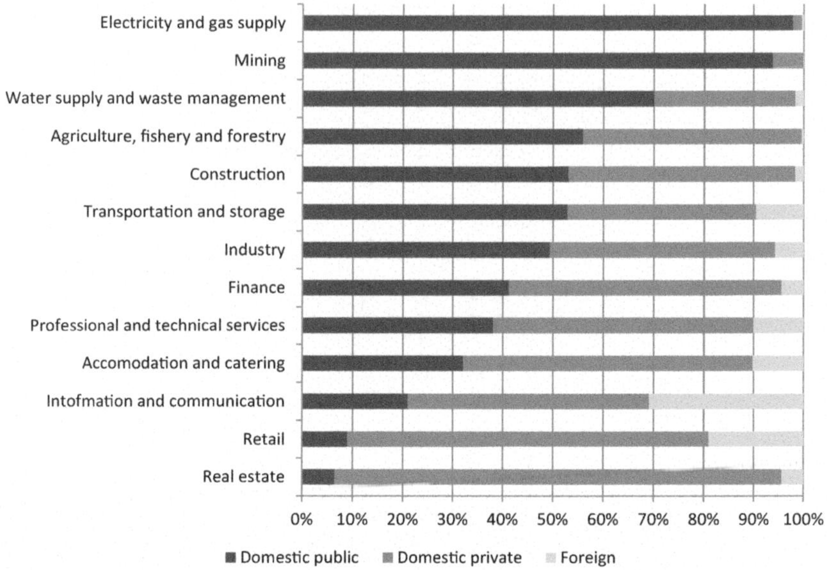

Fig. 7.4 Share of gross value added produced by different ownership sectors in various economic activities in Belarus in 2017 (in %) (The data was gathered and processed by Aliaksandr Papko. *Source* Belstat, own calculations)

majority of "old" enterprises inherited from the Soviet times. This domination of state ownership in industry, construction, transport, combined with hundreds of thousands people employed in public administration, state-owned education and healthcare system allowed the government to keep direct economic and political control over majority of population. Private enterprises, in their turn, had to develop in new niches, which emerged or started really developing after the fall of communism and were not occupied by the Soviet industrial giants (such as public catering, consulting, advertising and computer programming). Private business has also taken control over few spheres from which the state has withdrawn, most probably, due to the high control and maintenance costs, e.g., road transport and retail (Pelipas et al. 2014, p. 49). Private companies are mostly domestically owned, but there's a steadily growing foreign participation trend first of all in IT, communication (Belarus became popular for outsourcing IT services for European countries) and retail, with big chain stores entering the Belarusian market. However, the highest volume of FDIs was directed to industry (40.1% of the whole FDI inflow) (Mukha 2019).

7.4.3.3 The Importance of the SOE Sector

It must not be surprising that the importance of SOEs in the Belarusian economy (measured by the share of SOEs among the biggest enterprises in the country) is extremely high. On the list of 100 largest industrial enterprises (in terms of operating revenues) from the Orbs database, only 6 were not controlled by the Belarusian government, and in one case (Gefest, producer of kitchen household appliances), the authorities possessed a minority stake (31%), majority shareholder being a Russian state-controlled company Gazprom. In 2015, the share of the enterprises independent from the Belarusian state in operating revenues was 18.1 and 6.5% in employment. Such an overproportional share in turnover results from the existence of one very large foreign-owned company which is at the same time the largest industrial enterprise in the country: Gazprom Transgaz Belarus—former Beltransgaz fully sold in 2007–2011 to above-mentioned Gazprom. On the list of 10 largest industrial enterprises, its share in operating revenues was 23.4% in 2015. In this group of enterprises, there was only one another company not controlled by the Belarusian authorities: Savushkin Product, dairy products and juices producer owned by a private Belarusian national. It is a much smaller company, so in the top-10 group of companies (Table 7.6), the Belarusian state controlled 69.7% of turnover and as high as 89.5% of employment. If we take into account state control regardless its nationality, the SOEs absolutely dominated the top-10 group with 96.9% share both in turnover and in employment. But still, comparing with earlier data, the state share contracted: in 2009, in the group of 10 largest industrial enterprises (measured by volume of production), all the companies were fully controlled by the Belarusian state (Valex 2015).

All enterprises owned by the Belarusian authorities on the top-10 list have Soviet origin. They represent both oil refineries which operate in the country, four largest automotive manufacturers, one SOE operating in the food processing and one dealing with production of fertilizers. All of them are owned either directly by the government directly, or jointly by the government and other state entities—local authorities and/or other SOEs. In all cases but one, the government directly or indirectly possessed more than 98% of shares. In one case, 42.6% of shares belonged to a

Table 7.6 The top-10 industrial enterprises in Belarus in 2015

Company name	*Operating revenue, EUR million*	*Number of employees*	*Industry*	*State share, %*	*Owners of non-state shares*
Beltransgaz OAO	2751.5	6526	Transport via pipeline	0	Russian SOE
Naftan OAO	2397.0	10,730	Manufacture of refined petroleum products	99.8	Employees
Mozyrskii neftepererabatyvayushchii zavod	2063.0	4641	Manufacture of refined petroleum products	57.42	Russian POE
Grodno Azot OAO	642.5	7749	Manufacture of fertilizers	99.97	Employees
Glubokskii MKK OAO	538.2	930	Manufacture of dairy products	98.27	Employees
Minskii traktornyi zavod OAO	505.5	16,994	Vehicles manufacturing	100	
BELAZ OAO	326.0	10,059	Vehicles manufacturing	100	
Savushkin produkt OAO	317.1	2720	Manufacture of dairy products	0	Belarusian national
MAZ OAO	307.6	17,535	Vehicles manufacturing	100	
Belshina OAO	288.8	10,552	Vehicles parts manufacturing	100	
Share of domestically controlled SOEs, %	69.7	89.5			

Source Orbis database (data was gathered by Marlena Gołębiowska), companies' websites, own calculations

foreign (Russian) private investor, and only in this case, non-state investor was strong enough to be taken into account in corporate decisions.

Interestingly enough, the largest enterprise in Belarus in terms of number of employees and the fourth in the country in terms of turnover functions outside the industry and outside the SOE sector—it's a fully private Eurotorg retailer registered in Cyprus. According to the information on the company's website, in 2019 it employed 37.6 thousand, more than twice as many as the biggest state-owned employer MAZ truck factory (16.3 thousand) and had operation revenues almost four times higher.

This is an illustration of the specificity of the Belarusian enterprise sector which must be taken into account in the analysis of the importance of SOEs in Belarus. It is the fact that despite the SOE sector is dominant in the economy as a whole, big private players, mainly foreign, also exist, albeit usually in other sectors of the economy than SOEs so they do not compete directly with each other. Other examples of big private foreign investors who managed to "build into" the centralized and state-regulated economy of Belarus are the VMG Group—a Lithuanian woodwork company producing furniture for IKEA which opened its factory in Mogilev in 2013, and the Stadler Rail AG—a big Swiss manufacturer of trains which opened its factory near Minsk in 2014.

7.4.4 *Sources of the State Corporate Control Policy and Its Evolution in Belarus*

7.4.4.1 *Acting in Good Faith vs. Pursuing Group Interests*

In Belarus, the state corporate control shaping up and evolution analyzed from the perspective of good faith vs. vested interests dichotomy presents a peculiar picture, perhaps hardly to be met in any other post-communist country. Resignation from market reforms at the early stages of transition followed by the restoration of the command economy mechanisms apparently had a great deal of good faith in it. The concept of market-based development path was alien to the thinking of the Belarusian political class. It had no experience with self-regulating mechanisms and could not trust something that is not directly administered: all the experience the members of the Soviet elite had was related to the mechanisms of command economy. As Belarus was the "assembly shop" of the USSR and enjoyed relatively high standards of living, it could mean for them and for the general public that the Socialist economy was efficient enough. This maybe also is the reason for the fact that, unlike in other post-communist countries, there was no mass longing to convert power into private gains—neither among SOEs directors, nor among state bureaucrats. Perhaps they just did not feel the threat of depleting of their sources of income.

Besides, as the "assembly shop," Belarusian enterprises possessed relatively advanced technology and a wide array of customers (mostly in the USSR and COMECON countries, though) which could make them believe in a very high value and technical advancement of the Belarusian industrial assets. Opening markets for global competition, privatization, especially to foreign investors were perceived as a threat—not only for personal position, but also for all these "family silvers." Especially given the fact that most of the countries that to greater and lesser extent embarked upon market reforms suffered deep recession, growing problems for SOEs which resulted in their downsizing, rising unemployment, wages payment arrears, etc. Therefore, choosing tightening administrative control in order to overcome the crisis induced by the collapse of planned economy and the Soviet empire instead of market reforms could be seen as a beneficial for the whole Belarusian society. The unique Belarusian geopolitical position which allowed the country to have privileged access to the Russian market and enjoy Russian energy subsidies made the task of radical improvement of the enterprise sector performance less urgent. In the years that followed, the fact that Belarus managed to stop the recession, avoided mass unemployment, and for many years achieved quite descent rates of economic growth could be regarded as a confirmation of the correctness of the chosen statist path, the unique "Belarusian economic model."

The situation started changing when this model for various reason depleted its development potential and the government was forced to introduce some deregulation measures—but every time their reluctant character was obvious and the government kept trying to return the *modus operandi* of the economy to its initial state which was, simplifying, mostly administratively regulated economy with the key role of SOEs that performed not only economic, but also a wide array of social functions, and the private sector that was treated just as a major resource base for the economic policy.

However, quite surprisingly, in the system based on administrative steering the enterprise sector and transfer of resources, where Belarusian state officials had a vast power over economic agents, the relations between them and enterprises were never permeated with corruption and rent-seeking to a degree seen in many other post-communist countries, even with much less statised economies, as in Poland and Hungary. The study performed by Papko (2017) shows that the majority of resources extracted from the enterprises (both state-owned and private) was not going to the state officials' pockets. This does not mean that patron-client relationships did not exist, they were just of a quite unique kind: from the governmental side, they were fuelled mostly not by private interests (especially of financial kind) of bureaucrats, but by their search for resources for the realization of the goals defined by the state. At most, it can be said that members of the state administration extracted some kinds of non-financial rents such a career possibilities.

Of course it may be argued that the ultimate goal of the economic policy of the Belarusian government is not fully altruistic and has a lot of features of economic populism which helps to "bribe" the population and thus ensure the political stability in the absence of the democratic system of checks and balances. Till summer 2020, this strategy was quite successful, as Belarus was among the post-communist countries the least prone to change of ruling elite and political unrest. But it must be admitted that the state corporate control itself is not politicized, as in Poland, especially after PiS came to power, where SOEs finance political campaigns and support the allies of the ruling coalition, and seats on their boards are widely used as a bounty for the current political elite. Neither the policy towards the enterprise sector is used for personal enrichment of the members of Prime Minister's "family" and a wider circle of private sector cronies as in Hungary, nor fortunes are made on rents extracted from the SOE sector as in Russia.

In this situation, within the relationships between the authorities and enterprises, SOEs become the main rent-seeker. SOEs as such, as they are at the receiving end of the redistribution of the resources, and at a personal level, i.e., their employees and managers. According to Belarusian expert Aleksandr Chubrik (Zayats 2020), managers of SOEs are perfectly aware of the unique opportunities "to milk the state" (but in fact other economic agents) which are provided by the state-owned status of their companies and that they would be lost in the case of a change of the owner. Therefore, they oppose reforms and provide political support to the government. However, the rent-seeking potential of SOEs is deteriorating along with falling performance and contracting abilities of the government to keep SOEs alive through resources transfer. In a longer perspective, enterprise sector reform aimed at increasing of microeconomic efficiency will apparently lead to further deterioration of this source of rent.

7.4.4.2 Exogenous and Endogenous Factors

Analysis of the exogenous vs. endogenous factors dichotomy in shaping up and evolution of the state corporate control in Belarus also shows a peculiar picture.

Comparing with other analyzed countries, the role of external factors looked quite differently. The role of knowledge transfer was minimal. The "Belarusian economic model" and its evolution in a sort of a dual economy where the public and private sectors coexist is rather a purely "domestic" product to a large extent based on the model inherited from the Soviet past. Some elements of using external knowledge sources could be seen only in the attempts to improve the efficiency of the economy through introduction of some elements of market regulation; but the policy towards the SOE sector was based almost solely on attempts to tighten administrative control, i.e., the more strict realization of the principles of command economy. And currently there is no economy in the world, where such an approach proved its effectiveness. What is more, the adverse experience of other countries, especially from the former Soviet bloc, is often used by Lukashenko and his propaganda machine for justification of statist economic policy, including state control over the majority of the enterprise sector. According to them, this policy allows to avoid economic turbulence, selling out national property, growing poverty and losing independence.

At the same time, the role of the exogenous economic and political factors is much more prominent, albeit ambiguous. Collapse of the USSR and the Soviet bloc was one of the major factors of the deep economic crisis which forced Belarus into a largely involuntary transition with strong will of the authorities to keep as much of the old system as possible. Besides, through the whole analyzed period Belarus was strongly dependent on Russian energy subsidies and on the access to Russian market. It had strong impact on the trajectory of the Belarusian economic policy which was aimed at using these factors and at the same time avoiding their political consequences which threatened the independence of the Belarusian state (and losing power by Belarusian political elites and personally Lukashenko). In both cases, the role of the state corporate control policy apparently was first of all to withstand the pressure of external factors, to defend the state-owned enterprise sector and to be the stronghold of the independence of Belarus in the economic sphere vis-à-vis Russia's unification attempts. In the latter case, the only big concession was forced selling of Beltransgaz to Gazprom; during the whole period, Belarusian authorities opposed mass infiltration of Belarusian economy by Russian state and private capital. Limiting the access of non-Russian foreign capital to the Belarusian enterprise sector was limited too, but first of all in those sectors where it could jeopardize the position of domestic SOEs.

So, as in the case of knowledge transfer, economic and political exogenous factors caused rather petrifaction of the state corporate control policy rather than its evolution, especially towards deregulation.

The role of endogenous factors also had its specificity. The state of Belarusian economy and the state of the Belarusian SOE sector were among the main factors which shaped up the trajectory of the corporate control policy and the economic policy in general. Economy based on state ownership in the major sectors of the economy required a lot of effort to keep it afloat. Both actions aimed at partial deregulation (and privatization) and tightening the administrative control that followed one after another were taken under the pressure of circumstances, the need to overcome economic crises, ensure economic growth and a certain level of the society's well-being. As in the case if external economic factors, the changes in the corporate control policy of the state had a clearly reluctant character.

Domestic intellectual potential played rather a marginal role in shaping up and evolution of the state corporate control policy in Belarus—the same goes to the economic policy in the post-Soviet times as a whole. Unlike in many other post-communist countries, including those analyzed in this book, no renowned economist took part in preparation of these policies; at the beginning of the transition, there was no team of Belarusian economists which were ready to prepare the reform program; neither such experts were visible at the times of the *perestroika*. It may be argued that the deficiency of the local intellectual potential was one of the factors that prevented Belarus to embark upon market reforms (even at a relatively modest scale as in Russia or Ukraine). The situation started to improve in the second half of the 1990s, when a new generation of Belarusian economists emerged, affiliated, among others, to the IPM Research Center in Minsk. However, the authorities were not interested in making full use of their knowledge, as these economists presented liberal views and could not support the statist policy of the government—rather more or less openly criticizing it instead. Hostile attitude of the authorities towards this criticism made an open debate on economic issues difficult and many research activities and independent economists had to move abroad. Thus, the use of the economic domestic intellectual potential in Belarus remains low, and only economists loyal to the regime can have their say really freely and are used in shaping up the economic policy. Some other economists sometimes cooperate with the authorities, but mostly at the local level and in projects where such a cooperation is regarded by the government as ideologically "safe."

As in other analyzed countries, institutional setup seems to be one of the main factors which affect state corporate control in Belarus—again, at the same time possessing quite unique features. One of them is the extremely high role of extractive institutions and the way the Belarusian economy organizes and functions which fits the redistributional models created by Bessonova (2006) and Kordonsky (2007) even more than the Russian economy, for which they have been originally created. As Papko (2017) points out, the whole Belarusian economic system is characterized by centralized accumulation and distribution of resources with state planning being the main coordination mechanism. In this system, SOEs play a key role as both a recipient of resources (extracted from private sector, Russian subsidies, export proceeds, credits, etc.) and a tool for their further distribution (through wages, subsidized goods and services for the population, etc.). In several cases, SOEs perform a resource generation function themselves, if their profits are high enough.

Another feature is relatively weak rent-seeking: private interest groups, including those related to the SOE sector, are less influential and the value of rents is much more modest than in the rest of the analyzed countries. As it was discussed before, although SOEs are a strong interest group themselves and relationships between the state and enterprises it controls are of patron-client kind, they usually do not generate substantial private gains, especially financial, for people involved in the transactions; state corporate control policy is rather subdued to the political and economic needs of the government that particular private interests.

Both these factors made the SOEs sector one of the key elements of the system of checks and balances which apparently contributed to the very high degree of stability of the political regime (it has encountered serious problems only in 2020, after almost 30 years of existence), among the highest in the whole post-communist region.

The same as in all the other analyzed countries, public opinion and the system of values of the Belarusian society were not among the major factors which influenced the state corporate control policy (and the economic policy in general), but their features made the statist policy more feasible. Besides, the choice of such a policy itself seemed to be dependent, among others, on the system of values of the post-Soviet Belarusian political class which, as it was mentioned before, generally did not believe in market mechanisms and was in favor of keeping the command economy principles not only because it allowed to preserve power, but also out of sincere belief in their advantages.

At the beginning of the transition, the Belarusian society as a whole was perhaps one of the most indoctrinated societies in their negative attitude towards principles of capitalism and positive attitude towards state paternalism and interventionism. One of the reasons was the fact that before 1991 Belarusians had never had their national state, and their national identity was quite blurry (Daneyko 2017); thus to a large extent they identified themselves with the collapsed USSR rather than with the newly established Belarusian state; there was no common feeling that the nation must be independent. Because of relatively high standards of living of Belarusians in the Soviet times, they also did not feel that the principles of the command economy and highly paternalistic state had just exhausted their development potential, so most Belarusians did not see the need for economic reforms (as well as political) but longed to "good old" Soviet times. Therefore, the political class did not feel public pressure (which, e.g., was especially strong in Poland) towards economic and political reforms, building of independent state and democratic institutions. Besides, as Kuzio (2002) argues, societies with weak economic identity such as the Belarusian one have low tolerance for poor socio-economic conditions, so they are reluctant to support reforms with initial high costs. All this gave the Belarusian authorities, after Lukashenko came to power in 1994, freedom in conducting statist economic policy, arranging relationships with Russia and creating the political system not controllable by the society through exploration of the "Soviet" model of national identity based on nostalgia rhetoric (Kuzio 2001; Biketova and Chernyshov 2018). In the first years of the twenty-first century, when the political costs of Russia's support started do be perceived by Belarusian top authorities as a threat, Soviet-based rhetoric started to be substituted with a vague "Belarusian national idea" which apparently was to help in building national self-identification of Belarusians. Nostalgia after the Soviet past has been replaced with the idea of national paternalistic state with very similar characteristics: the only essential difference was adding a task to withstand the expansionist plans of Russia towards Belarus.

It is not surprising then that the attitude of the Belarusian population towards economic issues is still very pro-statist and pro-paternalistic. What is more, in the 2000s, when the above-mentioned rhetoric change took place, researchers (Rakova 2006) even identified growing popularity in the public opinion of paternalism and subsidiarity and increasingly negative attitude towards possible market reforms which were generally perceived as unnecessary and harmful. Later, as economic hardships increased and the government started quite reluctant, but still perceivable deregulation, public attitudes towards market principles started to improve. Comparing to 2008, in 2018, the share of strong supporters of market economy more than doubled (from 12.5 to 27.5%), and the share of strong supporters of state interventionism contracted from 31.4 to 27.3% (Urban 2019, p. 16). Attitudes towards private sector improved, but the society generally is still against privatization and still supports state ownership of enterprises, as well as state control over prices and wages. It may be argued that in the second half of the 2010s public opinion started to be characterized by the duality somewhat similar to that of the Polish society (see Sect. 6.2.2): simultaneous acceptance of some elements of market freedom with attractiveness of a paternalistic state which organizes life lets to privatize gains while taking over people's losses. However, the Belarusian society is of course still much less market-oriented and much more pro-paternalistic, than the Polish one. At the same time, many Belarusian respondents felt that the state did not sufficiently fulfill its duties—both in protection of the population and in support of private entrepreneurship and possibilities of people to earn money (Urban 2019, p. 13).

Thus, the system of values of the Belarusian society formed by its historical legacy, experience of post-Soviet times and the state propaganda is still favorable for the government. Its statist policy towards the enterprise sector, including many restrictions imposed on private entrepreneurs, is generally in line with public expectations, although it is not pre-determined by them.

Notes

1. In this section, some statements, research results and literature references from Bałtowski et al. (2021) were used.
2. In this section, some statements, research results and literature references from Papko and Kozarzewski (2020) were used.

References

Abramov, Aleksandr, Aleksandr Radygin, and Mariya Chernova. 2020. *Vliyanie gosudarstvennoy sobstvennosti na effektivnost' deyatel'nosti kompaniy i ikh aktivnosat' na rossiyskom fondovom rynke* [The Impact of State Ownership on Companies' Performance and Activity on the Russian Stock Market]. Moscow: RANEPA.

Acemoğlu, Daron, and James A. Robinson. 2012. *Why Nations Fail: The Origins of Power, Prosperity, and Poverty.* New York: Crown Publishers.

Adaskevich, Maksim. 2021. State-Owned Companies in Belarus: How Much Are They Worth and Will They Be Privatized any Time Soon? CASE Belarus Policy Brief, April. https://case-belarus.eu/wp-content/uploads/2021/05/policy-brief-soes.pdf. Accessed August 4, 2021.

Anderson, Richard J. 2008. *Putin's Campaign to Re-nationalize Industry and the Impact for Russian Reform and Foreign Policy.* Carlisle Barracks, PA: U.S. Army War College. https://apps.dtic.mil/dtic/tr/fulltext/u2/a493664.pdf. Accessed January 7, 2021.

Antczak, Rafał, Piotr Kozarzewski, and Krzysztof Połomski. 1995. Polityka gospodarcza Białorusi w latach 1992–1994. Studia i Analizy 48, CASE—Center for Social and Economic Research.

Åslund, Anders. 2000. *Russia and the International Financial Institutions.* Carnegie Endowment for International Peace. https://carnegieendowment.org/2000/01/18/russia-and-international-financial-institutions-pub-406. Accessed January 28, 2021.

Åslund, Anders. 2007. *How Capitalism Was Built: The Transformation of Central and Eastern Europe, Russia, and Central Asia.* Cambridge: Cambridge University Press.

Åslund, Anders. 2009. "Why Market Reform Succeeded and Democracy Failed in Russia." *Social Research* 76 (1): 1–28.

Åslund, Anders. 2017. Russia's Crony Capitalism: Stagnant but Stable. mBank—CASE Seminar Proceedings 148, mBank and CASE—Center for Social and Economic Research.

Åslund, Anders, Peter Boone, and Simon Johnson. 2001. Escaping the Under-Reform Trap. IMF Staff Papers 48, Special Issue, International Monetary Fund, Washington, DC.

Association of the Banks of Russia. 2020. *Bankovskaya sistema v tsifrakh i grafikakh. III kvartal 2020* [The Banking System in Figures and Graphs. 3Q2020]. Moscow: Association of the Banks of Russia.

Aven, Petr, and Alfred Kokh. 2013. *Revolutsiya Gaydara. Istoriya reform 90-kh iz pervykh ruk* [Gaidar's Revolution: A First-Hand Account of the Reforms of the 1990s]. Moscow: Alpina Publisher.

Avtushko-Sikorskiy, Alexandr, Ekaterina Burak, and Andrey Miroshnichenko. 2016. Mery, napravlennye na povyshenie effektivnosti upravleniia gosudarstvennoi sobstvennostiu [Measures to Improve the Efficiency of State Property Management]. Issledovanie SA#12/2016RU, Minsk: Belarusian Institute for Strategic Studies. https://belinstitute.com/sites/default/files/2020-05/BISS_SA12_2016ru_0.pdf. Accessed December 11, 2020.

Bałtowski, Maciej, Piotr Kozarzewski, and Tomasz Mickiewicz. 2021. "State Capitalism in Poland and Hungary: Populist Varieties." In *Oxford Handbook on State Capitalism and the Firm*, edited by Mike Wright, Geoffrey Wood, Alvaro Cuervo-Cazurra, Pei Sun, Ilya Okhmatovskiy, and Anna Grosman. Oxford: Oxford University Press (forthcoming).

Baturkin, Andrey. 2020. "Otchet o rezul'tatakh ekspertno-analiticheskogo meropriyatiya" [Report on the Results of the Expert Review]. *Byulleten' Schetnoy Palaty Palaty RF* 8 (273): 6–57.

Baza. 2021. "Alexei Miller poluchaet ₽1,9 mlrd, Gref – ₽1 mlrd" [Alexey Miller gets ₽1.9 Billion, Gref Gets ₽1 Billion]. *Baza*, January 12. https://baza.io/posts/40a7b78d-84f9-4d5a-a419-1f330b6faaa0. Accessed January 28, 2021.

Becker, András. 2017. "The Circulation of Oligarchs." In *Twenty-Five Sides of a Post-Communist Mafia State*, edited by Balint Magyar and Júlia Vásárhelyi, 111–128. Budapest: CEU Press.

Békesi, László. 2017. "The Economic Policy of the Mafia State." In *Twenty-Five Sides of a Post-Communist Mafia State*, edited by Balint Magyar and Júlia Vásárhelyi, 235–257. Budapest: CEU Press.

Belta. 2020. "Lukashenko o privatizatsii: kak my mozhem rasprodavat' zavody, kotorye sozdavalis' pololeniyami?" [Lukashenko on Privatization: How Can We Sell Out Factories That Were Created by Generations?], May 29. https://www.belta.by/president/view/lukashenko-o-privatizatsii-kak-my-mozhem-rasprodavat-zavody-kotorye-sozdavalis-pokolenijami-392771-2020/. Accessed December 11, 2020.

Bessonova, Olga. 2006. *Razdatochnaya ekonomika Rossii: evolyutsiya cherez transformatsii* [Russian Redistributive Economy: Evolution through Transformations]. Moscow: ROSSPEN. http://razdatok.narod.ru/BESSONOVA/b2006/Bessonova_RER_2006.pdf. Accessed December 23, 2020.

Biketova, Ekaterina, and Yuriy Chernyshov. 2018. "Natsiestroitel'stvo Respublik Belarus' i evropeyskiy komponent belorusskoy identichnosti" [Nation-Building in the Republic of Belarus and the European Component of Belarusian Identity]. *Mirovaya Ekonomika i Mezhdunarodnye Otnosheniya* 62 (2): 94–103.

Bíró-Nagy, András, Dalma Dobszai, Tibor Kadlót, and Annamária König. 2016. *Regime Change, Democracy and Hungarian Society*, edited by András Bíró-Nagy. Budapest: Friedrich-Ebert-Stiftung.

Black, Bernard, Reinier Kraakman, and Anna Tarassova. 2000. "Russian Privatization and Corporate Governance: What Went Wrong?" *Stanford Law Review* 52 (6): 1731–1808.

Bogetic, Zeljko, Karlis Smits, Sergey Ulatov, Olga Emelyanova, and Marco Hernandez. 2008. Russian Economic Report No. 17. MPRA Paper 12434, The World Bank.

Bortolotti, Bernardo, and Mara Faccio. 2004. Reluctant Privatization. Nota di Lavoro 130, Fondazione Eni Enrico Mattei (FEEM), Milano. https://www.econstor.eu/bitstream/10419/118014/1/NDL2004-130.pdf. Accessed July 30, 2020.

Brzezinski, Zbigniew. 1989. *The Grand Failure: The Birth and Death of Communism in the Twentieth Century*. New York: Charles Scribner's Sons.

Butenko, Anatoly. 2000. *Neravnomiernost' razvitiya i istoricheskoe zabeganie* [The Unevenness of Development and the Historical Forestalling]. Moscow: IMEPI RAN.

Chartyja'77. 2016. *Offshore Companies "Came to Light" in Belarus*. https://charter97.org/en/news/2016/4/6/198310/. Accessed December 16, 2020.

Chernykh, Lucy. 2011. "Profit or Politics? Understanding Renationalizations in Russia." *Journal of Corporate Finance* 17 (5): 1237–1253.

Christiansen, Hans. 2013. Balancing Commercial and Non-commercial Priorities of State-Owned Enterprises. OECD Corporate Governance Working Papers 6, OECD Publishing. https://www.oecd.org/corporate/OECDCorporateGovernanceWorkingPaper6.pdf. Accessed November 22, 2020.

Cohen, Ariel. 1998. Russia's Meltdown: Anatomy of the IMF Failure. The Heritage Foundation. https://www.heritage.org/europe/report/russias-meltdown-anatomy-the-imf-failure. Accessed January 29, 2021.

Dąbrowski, Marek, ed. 1993. *The Gaidar Programme: Lessons for Poland and Eastern Europe*. Warsaw: Friedrich Ebert Stiftung.

Dąbrowski, Marek. 1995. Western Aid Conditionality and the Post-Communist Transition. Studies and Analysis 37, CASE—Center for Social and Economic Research, Warsaw.

Daneyko, Elena. 2012. "Protektsionizm kak svyashchennaya korova belorusskoy ekonomiki" [Protectionism as a Sacred Cow of Belarusian Economy]. *Deutsche Welle*, November 9. http://www.dw.com/ru/a-16367838. Accessed December 16, 2020.

Daneyko, Elena. 2017. "Osobennosti belorusskoy natsional'noy identichnosti" [Peculiarities of the Belarusian National Identity]. *Deutsche Welle*, February 23. https://p.dw.com/p/2Y4nT. Accessed December 23, 2020.

Di Bella, Gabriel, Oksana Dynnikova, and Slavi Slavov. 2019. The Russian State's Size and Its Footprint: Have They Increased? IMF Working Paper WP/19/53, International Monetary Fund, Washington, DC.

Djankov, Simeon, Jose G. Montalvo, and Marta Reynal-Querol. 2008. "The Curse of Aid." *Journal of Economic Growth* 13 (3): 169–194.

Dolinina, Irina, and Yulia Alykova. 2021. "Pod prikrytiem Rossiyskoy Federatsll" [Under the Cover of the Russian Federation]. *Istories*, January 21. https://istories.media/investigations/2021/01/25/pod-prikritiem-rossiiskoi-federatsii/. Accessed January 20, 2021.

EBRD. 2008. *Transition Report 2008*. London: European Bank for Reconstruction and Development.

EBRD Database. 2020. http://www.ebrd.com/what-we-do/economic-research-and-data/data.html. Accessed September 17, 2020.

Ehrke, Jürgen, Gleb Shymanovich, and Robert Kirchner. 2014. Improving the Management of State-Owned Enterprises in Belarus. Policy Paper Series PP/023, IPM Research Center, Minsk.

Eurobarometer. 2009. EU Citizens' Perceptions about Competition Policy. Flash EB Series 264, Eurobarometer. https://ec.europa.eu/commfrontoffice/publicopinion/index.cfm/ResultDoc/download/DocumentKy/59146. Accessed December 4, 2020.

FAS. 2019. *Doklad o sostoyanii konkurentsii v Rossiyskoy Federatsii za 2018 god* [Report on the State of Competition in the Russian Federation in 2018]. Moscow: Federal Antimonopoly Service of the Russian Federation (FAS). https://fas.gov.ru/documents/685117. Accessed January 7, 2021.

FBK. 2020. "FBK: 79 rassledovaniy v odnom rolike" [FBK: 79 Investigations in One Video]. Uploaded on August 5, 2020. YouTube video, 16:46 min. https://youtu.be/s3-Us7eGTvk.

Fish, M. Steven. 2005. *Democracy Derailed in Russia: The Failure of Open Politics*. New York: Cambridge University Press.

Forbes. 2020. "Vlast' i den'gi. Reyting dokhodov gossluzhashchikh i deputatov 2020" [Power and Money: Rating of Incomes of Civil Servants and Deputies 2020]. https://www.forbes.ru/rating/409107-100-gossluzhashchih-s-samymi-vysokimi-dohodami-2020-reyting-forbes. Accessed January 27, 2021.

Fornalczyk, Anna, and Ryszard Hoffman. 1993. Demonopolisation and Deconcentration of Russia's Economy. In *The Gaidar Programme: Lessons for Poland and Eastern Europe*, edited by Marek Dąbrowski, 83–86. Warsaw: Friedrich Ebert Stiftung.

Frankel, Jeffrey. 2012. The Natural Resource Curse: A Survey of Diagnoses and Some Prescriptions. CID Working Paper 233, Center for Economic Development at Harvard University, Cambridge, MA. https://www.hks.harvard.edu/centers/cid/publications/faculty-working-papers/natural-resource-curse. Accessed February 2, 2021.

Frye, Timothy, and Ichiro Iwasaki. 2011. "Government Directors and Business-State Relations in Russia." *European Journal of Political Economy* 27 (4): 642–658.

Gaidar, Yegor. 1999. "Lessons of the Russian Crisis for Transition Economies." *Finance and Development* 36 (2): 6–8.

Gaidar, Yegor, and Anatoliy Chubais. 2011. *Razvilki noveyshey istorii Rossii* [Bifurcations of the Modern History of Russia]. Saint-Petersburg: Norma.

Gans-Morse, Jordan. 2012. "Threats to Property Rights in Russia: From Private Coercion to State Aggression." *Post-Soviet Affairs* 28 (3): 263–295.

Gayduk, Kirill. 2020. "Sektor gospredpriyatiy: strukturnye vyzovy" [Sector of State-Owned Enterprises: Structural Challenges]. *Bankauski Vestnik* 3: 26–30.

Goldman, Marshall I. 2004. "Putin and the Oligarchs." *Foreign Affairs* 83 (6): 33–44.

Grosman, Anna, Ilya Okhmatovskiy, and Mike Wright. 2016. "State Control and Corporate Governance in Transition Economies: 25 Years on from 1989." *Corporate Governance: An International Review* 24 (3): 200–221.

Gwartney, James, Robert Lawson, Joshua Hall, and Ryan Murphy. 2018. *Economic Freedom of the World: 2018 Annual Report*. Vancouver: Fraser Institute.

Gwartney, James, Robert Lawson, Joshua Hall, and Ryan Murphy. 2019. *Economic Freedom of the World: 2019 Annual Report*. Vancouver: Fraser Institute.

Havrylyshyn, Oleh. 2007. *Fifteen Years of Transformation in the Post-communist World. Rapid Reformers Outperformed Gradualists*. Washington, DC: Cato Institute.

Hellman, Joel. 1998. "Winners Take All: The Politics of Partial Reform in Postcommunist Transitions." *World Politics* 50 (2): 203–234.

Jarosz, Maria, and Piotr Kozarzewski. 2002. *Sukcesy i klęski prywatyzacji w krajach postkomunistycznych*. Warsaw: ISP PAN.

Kordonsky, Simon. 2007. *Resursnoe gosudarstvo* [Resource State], Moscow: Regnum. https://www.litmir.me/br/?b=415429. Accessed December 23, 2020.

Kornai, Janos. 1992. *The Socialist System: The Political Economy of Communism*. Oxford: Oxford University Press.

Koval', Tatyana. 1997. "Ekonomicheskaya reforma i obshchestvennoe mnenie" [Ekonomic Reform an Public Opinion]. In *Pyat' let reform* [Five Years of the Reforms], edited by Vladimir Mau and Nina Glavatskaya, 265–283. Moscow: IET.

Kozina, Irina. 2005. "Osobennosti 'sotsial'no otvetstvennogo biznesa' rossiyskikh predpriyatiy" [Features of "Socially Responsible Business" of Russian Enterprises]. *Zhurnal Issledovaniy Sotsial'noy Politiki* 3 (3): 367–377.

Kozlova, Svetlana, Svetlana Bratchenko, and Petr Zvyagintsev. 2019. *Upravlenie gosudarstvennym imushchestvom v sovermennoy Rossii: Evolutsiya kontseptsiy, instrumentov, mekhanizmov* [Management of State Property in Modern Russia: Evolution of Concepts, Instruments, Mechanisms]. Moscow: Institute of Economics, Russian Academy of Sciences.

Krekó, Péter, Lóránt Győri, Jekatyerina Dunajeva, Jakub Janda, Ondřej Kundra, Grigorij Mesežnikov, Juraj Mesík, Maciej Szylar, and Anton Shekhovtsov. 2016. *The Weaponization of Culture: Kremlin's Traditional Agenda and the Export of Values to Central Europe*. Budapest: Political Capital Policy Research and Consulting Institute. https://www.politicalcapital.hu/wp-content/uploads/PC_reactionary_values_CEE_20160727.pdf. Accessed November 13, 2020.

Kryshtanovskaya, Olga. 2002. "Biznes-elita i oligarkhi: itogi desyatiletiya" [Business Elite and Oligarchs: Results of the Decade]. *Mir Rossii* 4: 3–60.

Kucharczyk, Jacek. 2017. "Exploiting Political Polarization in Poland." In *Sharp Power: Rising Authoritarian Influence*, 94–123. National Endowment for Democracy Washington, DC: National Endowment for Democracy. https://www.ned.org/wp-content/uploads/2017/12/Sharp-Power-Rising-Authoritarian-Influence-Full-Report.pdf. Accessed November 13, 2020.

Kuvalin, Dmitriy. 2020. "Barter zhiv" [Barter Is Alive]. *Ogonyok* 19: 16.

Kuzio, Taras. 2001. "Transition in Post-Communist States: Triple or Quadruple?" *Politics* 21 (3): 168–177.

Kuzio, Taras. 2002. "National Identity and Democratic Transition in Post-Soviet Ukraine and Belarus: A Theoretical and Comparative Perspective (Part 1)." *RFE/RL East European Perspectives* 4 (15).

Lavnikevich, Denis. 2015. "Kholding i klaster: naydite 10 otlichiy" [Holding and Cluster: Find 10 Differences]. *BDG Delovaya Gazeta*, November 6. http://bdg.by/news/authors/holding-i-klaster-naydite-10-otlichiy. Accessed December 11, 2020.

Lomskaya, Tatyana. 2020. "Milliardy vo vlasti: uchastniki spiska Forbes sredi bogateyshikh gossluzhashchikh i deputatov" [Billions in Power: The Forbes List of the Richest Civil Servants and Deputies]. *Forbes*, September 18. https://www.forbes.ru/obshchestvo-photogallery/408835-milliardy-vo-vlasti-uchastniki-spiska-forbes-sredi-bogateyshih. Accessed January 27, 2021.

Loyko, Olga. 2019. "Glava Vsemirnogo Banka v RB: reformy neizbezhny i boleznenny" [The Head of the World Bank in Belarus: Reforms are Inevitable and Painful]. *Tut.by*, July 22. https://news.tut.by/economics/646057.html. Accessed December 15, 2020.

Ludányi, Arnold. 1996 "A Brief Overview of Hungarian Privatization (1990–1996)." In *Privatization in Post-Communist Countries*, edited by Barbara Błaszczyk and Richard Woodward, 123–152. Warsaw: CASE—Center for Social and Economic Research.

Magyar, Balint. 2016. *Post-Communist Mafia State: The Case of Hungary*. Budapest: CEU Press.

Makarov, Valeriy, and Georgiy Kleyner. 1999. "Barter v Rossii. Institutsional'nyi etap" [Barter in Russia: Institutional Stage]. *Voprosy Ekonomiki* 4: 79–101.

Mihályi, Péter. 1996. "Management and Sale of Residual State Shareholdings in Hungary." *Acta Oeconomica* 48 (3/4): 331–346.

Mihályi, Péter. 2010. *A magyar privatizáció enciklopédiája*. Veszprém: Pannon Egyetemi Kiadó – MTA Közgazdságtudományi Intézet.

Mihályi, Péter. 2020. "Votes, Ideology, and Self-Enrichment: The Campaign of Re-nationalization after 2010." In *Brave New Hungary: Mapping the "System of National Cooperation,"* edited by János Mátyás Kovács and Balázs Trencsényi, 185–209. Lanham, MD: Lexington Books.

Mihályi, Peter, and Iván Szelényi. 2017. "The Role of Rents in the Transition from Socialist Redistributive Economies to Market Capitalism." *Comparative Sociology* 16: 13–38.

Milov, Vladimir. 2012. "Natsionalizatsiya 'neftyanki' prodolzhaetsya" [Nationalization of the Oil Sector Goes On]. *Forbes*, July 25.

Mukha, Alekstandr. 2019. "Dvizhenie pryamykh inostrannykh investitsiy" [FDI Transfers]. *Nashe Mneniye*. https://nmnby.eu/news/analytics/6886.html. Accessed December 16, 2020.

Newnham, Randall. 2011. "Oil, Carrots, and Sticks: Russia's Energy Resources as a Foreign Policy Tool." *Journal of Eurasian Studies* 2 (2): 134–143. https://www.sciencedirect.com/science/article/pii/S187936651100011X. Accessed January 8, 2021.

OECD. 2005a. *Corporate Governance of State-Owned Enterprises: A Survey of OECD Countries*. Paris: OECD Publishing.

OECD. 2005b. *Guidelines on Corporate Governance of State-Owned Enterprises*. Paris: OECD Publishing.

OECD. 2014. *The Size and Sectoral Distribution of SOEs in OECD and Partner Countries*. Paris: OECD Publishing.

OECD. 2018. *Ownership and Governance of State-Owned Enterprises: A Compendium of National Practices*. Paris: OECD Publishing.

Olechnowicz, Aleksander. 2010. Białoruś straciła pokolenie. Analiza FOR 7, Fundacja Forum Obywatelsiego Rozwoju. http://case-belarus.eu/wp-content/uploads/2011/08/Analiza_FOR_7_2010_Bialorus_stracila_pokolenie.pdf. Accessed December 10, 2020.

OSW. 2015. *The Economic and Financial Crisis in Russia: Background, Symptoms and Prospects for the Future*. Warsaw: Ośrodek Studiów Wschodnich. https://www.osw.waw.pl/sites/default/files/raport_crisis_in_russia_net.pdf. Accessed January 29, 2021.

Papko, Aliaksandr. 2017. "Informal Barriers to the Development of Small and Medium Enterprises in Belarus." PhD diss., Institute of Philosophy and

Sociology of the Polish Academy of Sciences. https://www.academia.edu/41070896/Informal_Barriers_to_the_Development_of_Small_and_Medium_Enterprises_in_Belarus. Accessed December 10, 2020.

Papko, Aliaksandr, and Piotr Kozarzewski. 2020. The Evolution of Belarusian Public Sector: From Command Economy to State Capitalism? CASE Working Papers 12(136), CASE—Center for Social and Economic Research, Warsaw. https://www.case-research.eu/files/?id_plik=6381. Accessed December 10, 2020.

Pelipas, Igor, Anrdey Skriba, Irina Tochitskaya, Aleksandr Chubrik, and Gleb Shimanovich. 2014. *Belorusskiy biznes 2014: sostoyanie, tendentsii, perspektivy* [Belarusian Business in 2014: Situation, Tendencies, Perspectives]. Minsk: IPM Research Center.

Polterovich, Victor. 2008. "Institutional Trap." In *New Palgrave Dictionary of Economics*, 2008. https://ssrn.com/abstract=1751839. Accessed January 4, 2021.

Putin, Vladimir. 1999. "Rossiya na rubezhe tysyachiletiy" [Russia at the Turn of the Century]. *Nezavisimaya Gzaeta*, December 30.

Putin, Vladimir. 2000. "Mineral'no-syryevye resursy v strategii razvitiya rossiyskoy ekonomiki" [Mineral Natural Resources in the Strategy for Development of the Russian Economy]. In *Rossiya v okruzhayuschem mire: 2000 (Analiticheskiy ezhegodnik)* [Russia in the World Around: 2000 (Analytical Yearbook)], edited by Nikolay Marfenin, Nikita Moiseev, and Sergey Stepanov. Moscow: MNEPPU.

Radio Liberty. 2008. "Andrei Illarionov o finansovom krizise v Rossii [Andrei Illarionov on the Financial Crisis in Russia]." *Radio Liberty*, October 9. https://www.svoboda.org/a/468260.html. Accessed January 29, 2021.

Radygin, Alexander, Revold Entov, Alexander Abramov, Mariya Chernova, and Georgiy Malginov. 2019. *Privatizatsiya 30 let spustya. Masshtaby i effektovnost' gosudarstvennogo sektora* [Privatization 30 Years Later: Scale and Efficiency of the Public Sector]. Moscow: Delo.

Radygin, Alexander, Yury Simachev, and Revold Entov. 2015. "The State-Owned Company: 'State Failure' or 'Market Failure'?" *Russian Journal of Economics* 1: 55–80.

Radygin, Alexander. 1996. "Privatization in the Russian Federation." In *Privatization in Post-communist Countries*, edited by Barbara Błaszczyk and Richard Woodward, Vol. I, 207–237. Warsaw: CASE—Center for Social and Economic Research.

Radygin, Alexander. 2008. "Gosudarstvennyi kapitalizm i finansovyy krizis: faktory vzaimodeystviya, izderzhki, perspektivy" [State Capitalism and the Financial Crisis: Factors of Interrelations, Costs, and Perspectives]. *Ekonomicheskaya Politika* 6: 88–105.

Rakova, Elena. 2006. Vospriyatie naseleniem Belarusi tsennostey rynochnoy ekonomiki [The Perception by the Population of Belarus of the Values of Market Economy]. Working Paper 06/07, IPM Research Center, Minsk.

Repousis, Spyridon, Petros Lois, and Pavlos Kougioumtsidis. 2019. "Foreign Direct Investments and Round Tripping between Cyprus and Russia." *Journal of Money Laundering Control* 22 (3): 442–450.

Rochlitz, Michael, Anton Kazun, and Andrei Yakovlev. 2020. "Property Rights in Russia after 2009: From Business Capture to Centralized Corruption?" *Post-Soviet Affairs* 36 (5–6): 434–450.

Rostowski, Jacek. 1993. "Mutial Debt of Enterprises." In *The Gaidar Programme: Lessons for Poland and Eastern Europe*, edited by Marek Dąbrowski, 183–196. Warsaw: Friedrich Ebert Stiftung.

Rovdo, Vladimir. 2009. *Sravnitelnaya politologiya, chast' 3* [Comparative Political Science, vol. 3]. Vilnius: European Humanities University.

Sallai, Dorottya, and Gerhard Schnyder. 2018. The Transformation of Post-Socialist Capitalism—From Developmental State to Clan State? Greenwich Papers in Political Economy 18535, University of Greenwich, London. https://ideas.repec.org/p/gpe/wpaper/18535.html. Accessed November 30, 2020.

Samokhin, Yuriy. 2001. *Ekonomicheskaya istoriya Rossii* [Economic History of Russia]. Moscow: GU VShE.

Sarnyai, Gábor. 2018. "Is Hungary the New Tax Haven for International Companies?" *Hungary Today*, April 6. https://hungarytoday.hu/is-hungary-the-new-tax-haven-for-international-companies/. Accessed November 30, 2020.

Sata, Robert, and Ireneusz Pawel Karolewski. 2020. "Caesarean Politics in Hungary and Poland." *East European Politics* 36 (2): 206–225.

Simachev, Yuriy, and Mikhail Kyzyk. 2020. "Gosudarstvennaya podderzhka pred-priyatiy: benefitsiary i effekty" [State Support for Enterprises: Beneficiaries and Effects]. Voprosy Ekonomiki 3: 63–83.

Sonin, Konstantin. 2016. "Sud'ba ekonomicheskikh sovetov" [The Fate of Economic Advice]. *Vedomosti*, January 31.

Sprenger, Carsten. 2012. "Does Nationalization Work? Evidence from Russian State Takeovers." Paper presented at 21st Annual Meeting the European Financial Management Association, Barcelona, June 27–30.

Szanyi, Miklós. 2016a. "The Reversal of the Privatisation Logic in Central European Transition Economies (An Essay)." *Acta Oeconomica* 66 (1): 33–55.

Szanyi, Miklós. 2016b. The FDI-led Development Model Revisited? The Case of Hungary. IWE Working Papers 220, Centre for Economic and Regional Studies HAS, Budapest.

Szanyi, Miklós. 2019a. "The Emergence of Patronage and Changing Forms of Rent-Seeking in East Central Europe. Post-Communist Economies. https://doi.org/10.1080/14631377.2019.1693738.

Szanyi, Miklós. 2019b. "The Role of State Ownership in and after Hungary's Transition." In *Seeking the Best Master: State Ownership in the Varieties of Capitalism*, edited by Miklós Szanyi, 213–236. Budapest-New York: CEU Press.

Tarasov, Alexey. 2020. "Zalogovaya bomba" [Bail bomb]. *Novaya Gazeta*, December 5. https://novayagazeta.ru/articles/2020/12/05/88245-zalogovaya-bomba. Accessed January 4, 2021.

Timoshina, Tatyana. 2009. *Ekonomicheskaya istoriya Rossii* [Economic History of Russia]. Moscow: Yustitsinform.

Tracey, Gregory. 2018. "How the 2014 Economic Crisis Changed Russia's Economy." *Geohistory*, November 12. https://geohistory.today/2014-crisis-russia-economy/. Accessed January 29, 2021.

Trudolyubov, Maksim. 2017. "Kak Rossiya vernulas' v gossobstvennost'" [How Russia Returned to State Ownership]. *Vedomosti*, September 29.

UNDP. 1993. *Human Development Report 1993*. New York: Oxford University Press.

Urban, Dar'ya. 2019. Ekonomicheskie tsennosti naseleniya Belarusi v 2018 godu [Economic Values of the Population of Belarus in 2018]. Working Paper 19/01, IPM Research Center, Minsk.

Valex. 2015. *Krupneyshie promyshlennye predpriyatiya Belarusi* [The Largest Industrial Enterprises in Belarus]. Valex Management Consulting. https://valex.by/news/34-krupnejshie-promyshlennye-predpriyatiya-belarusi. Accessed December 16, 2020.

Vasileva, Alexandra. 2018. "Trapped in Informality: The Big Role of Small Firms in Russia's Statist-patrimonial Capitalism." *New Political Economy* 23 (3): 314–330.

Vedomosti. 2017. "Natsionalizatsiya krupnykh bankov" [Nationalization of Large Banks]. *Vedomosti*, December 20.

Viktorov, Ilja. 2019. "Russia's Network State and Reiderstvo Practices: The Roots to Weak Property Rights Protection after the Post-Communist Transition." In *Stubborn Structures: Reconceptualizing Post-Communist Regimes*, edited by Balint Magyar, 437–459. Budapest: CEU Press.

Vitale, Cristiana, Rosamaria Bitetti, Eszter Danitz, Carlotta Moiso, and Isabelle Wanner. 2020. The 2018 Edition of the OECD PMR Indicators AND Database—Methodological Improvements and Policy Insights. Economics Department Working Papers 1604, OECD. http://www.oecd.org/officialdocuments/publicdisplaydocumentpdf/?cote=ECO/WKP(2020)12&docLanguage=En. Accessed December 1, 2020.

Volkov, Denis, and Andrei Kolesnikov. 2018. *Novaya russkaya mechta: chastnaya sobstvennost' dla detey* [The New Russian Dream: Private Property for Children]. Moscow: Carnegie Moscow Center.

Voszka, Éva. 2018. "Nationalisation in Hungary in the Post-Crisis Years: A Specific Twist on a European Trend." *Europe Asia Studies* 70 (8): 1–22.

VTsIOM. 1995. Informatsionnyi byulleten' [Newsletter] 1, Russian Public Opinion Research Center (VTsIOM).

VTsIOM. 1996. Informatsionnyi byulleten' [Newsletter] 6, Russian Public Opinion Research Center (VTsIOM).

VTsIOM. 2017. Bol'shaya privatizatsiya: 25 let spustya [Large Privatization: 25 Tears After], Russian Public Opinion Research Center (VTsIOM). https://wciom.ru/analytical-reviews/analiticheskii-obzor/bolshaya-privatizacziya-25-let-spustya. Accessed February 3, 2021.

Wedel, Janine R. 1998. *Aid to Russia, Institute for Policy Studies*. https://ips-dc.org/aid_to_russia/. Accessed January 29, 2021.

Wedel, Janine R. 1999. U.S. Assistance for Market Reforms. Foreign Aid Failures in Russia and the Former Soviet Bloc. Policy Analysis 338, Cato Institute, Washington, DC.

World Bank. 2012. *Ekonomicheskaya transformatsiya dlya rosta. Stranovoy ekonomicheskiy memorandum dlya Respubliki Belarus'* [Economic Transformation for Growth: Country Economic Memorandum for the Republic of Belarus]. Washington, DC: The World Bank.

World Bank. 2018. *Belarus—Systematic Country Diagnostic: Towards a Competitive, Inclusive and Dynamic Belarus*. Washington, DC: The World Bank. http://documents1.worldbank.org/curated/en/602921520877070059/pdf/Belarus-SCD-03072018.pdf. Accessed December 11, 2020.

Yakovlev, Andrei, Nina Ershova, and Olga Uvarova. 2020. "Kakim firmam gosudarstvo okazyvaet podderzhku: analiz izmeneniya prioritetov v krizisnykh usloviyakh" [Which Firms Are Supported by the State: Analysis of Changes in Priorities under Crisis Conditions]. *Voprosy Ekonomiki* 3: 47–62.

Yakovlev, Andrei. 2006. "The Evolution of Business-State Interaction in Russia: From State Capture to Business Capture?" *Europe-Asia Studies* 58 (7): 1033–1056.

Yanchuk, Valeriy. 2007. Belorusskaya ekonomicheskaya model': ot liberal'nogo fundamentalizma k sotsial'no-ekonomicheskomu upravleniyu [Belarusian Economic Model: From Liberal Fundamentalism to Social and Economic Management]. Uchenye Zapiski 7, Vitebsk State University, Vitebsk.

Zayats, Dmitriy. 2020. "Byurokratiya tyanet gosudarstvennye prepriyatiya na dno" [Bureaucracy Drags State-Owned Enterprises to the Bottom].

Naviny.by, October 2. https://naviny.media/article/20201002/1601616082-byurokratiya-tyanet-gosudarstvennye-predpriyatiya-na-dno. Accessed December 15, 2020.

Zinoviev, Alexander. 1999. "Derniere entretien en terre d'Occident. Entretien réalisé par Victor Loupan." *Figaro Magazine*, July 24.

CHAPTER 8

Epilogue

8.1 Course and Effects of the Evolution of the State Corporate Control

State corporate control was one of the key issues of the post-communist economic transition in Poland because of its crucial role in the way the state performs its functions in the economy. In planned economy, the state was an owner of the most of the productive assets and omnipotent regulator of almost all economic activity. The new ownership role of the state was to be realized in the conditions of a mostly private economy, in a selective way, in order to achieve specific social and economic goals. The change could not be reduced only to abolishing mechanisms of administrative control over the enterprise sector and to downsizing the state ownership; the system of corporate control of the state over its property itself had to be deeply reformed. Firstly, effective control over SOEs had to be restored as being mostly lost during the decaying stage of the command economy system when highly flawed control mechanisms were dispersed among different ministries which entered bargaining games with management of autonomous SOEs. Secondly, this new system of the state corporate control had to correspond to the new objectives of the state in the reformed economy contributing to mitigation of market failures and performing other functions for the benefit of the society.

The reform of the state corporate control in Poland was only partially successful. On the one hand, the state indeed has radically reduced

P. Kozarzewski, *State Corporate Control in Transition*,
https://doi.org/10.1007/978-3-030-78562-8_8

its engagement in the enterprise sector comparing to the pre-transition times, nowadays controlling only a smaller part of it. On the other hand, the state's share in the enterprise sector is still much larger than the scope of the state's functions in a market economy would imply. It is especially visible in several sectors, including mining and infrastructure. Besides, the state corporate control also performs extended functions, among others engaging in rescuing inefficient enterprises, making SOEs perform extra social functions and supporting the political class and its allies. What is more, the SOE sector and governmental investments started being treated again as the main vehicle of economic development.

In some respect, presently the policy of state corporate control shows partial resignation from market economy principles and initial assumptions of the reformers about the optimal role of the state in the enterprise sector. The evolution path of the state corporate control in Poland in terms of state interventionism and politicization of the SOE sector was not linear and resembled letter U: during the first about 10 years of the transition, albeit not being in the center of reformers' attention, the state sector was contracting and losing its economic and political importance. Since the mid-1990s, however, the political class started appreciating its financial and rent-seeking potential, so re-politization of the state corporate control began. At the beginning of the twenty-first century, the contraction of the SOE sector started slowing down and was completely stopped by 2015. Finally, since mid-2010s, it became a part of a new statist development paradigm combined with a predatory use of SOEs for satisfying the needs of the members of the ruling coalition and their allies. This has contributed to the creation of a large state-controlled enclave in the Polish economy, which is a symbiosis of government agencies responsible for the implementation of economic policy (and perhaps more broadly: socio-economic policy) and state corporate control, on the one hand, and state-controlled enterprises on the other. The enclave is still expanding, largely closed to private (and especially foreign) capital and mostly fenced off from the influence of external economic conditions. It operates according to unclear, contradictory political and pragmatic goals, objectives and criteria. The unsatisfactory effectiveness of state corporate control forced the authorities to make quite chaotic and fully unsuccessful attempts at repairing it while maintaining and even expanding the features of the system that caused these dysfunctions. To paraphrase Polish writer and politician Stefan Kisielewski's words about communism, the government is trying to fight against the problems it had created itself.

Comparing to the Polish experience, in other countries studied in this book: Hungary, Russian Federation and Belarus, paths of state corporate control evolution and effects of the state control policy had both similarities and differences. All four countries are characterized with high dysfunctionality of the state corporate control, being inferior to that of in the developed market economies and to a large extent not complying with the recommendations of international organizations such as the World Bank (2014) and OECD (2015). SOEs are extensively used as a political tool in the interests of the political elites and violations of private property rights of non-public entities are common. In listed companies with state participation in Poland, Hungary and Russia and in virtually all Belarusian companies with any state participation, there are widespread processes of leveraging state control in relation to ownership stakes.

There are important differences between these countries, though, both in the shape of the path of evolution of the state corporate control policy and the specificity of the state corporate control itself (and, broader, in the role of state ownership in the economy). The paths were different in all the four countries. In Hungary, unlike Poland, deep de-statization of the economic policy took place at the beginning of the transition, and the statist turn of 2010 was a clear break of the previous trends—while in Poland there was a growing statist trend since mid-1990s, up to the paradigm change in mid-2010s. What is also important, Poland was the only country where this evolution was very gradual and its vector was always the same—towards statization of the economic policy, and there was an astonishingly high degree of policy continuity between the subsequent ruling coalitions, regardless of their ideological identity. The paradigm change was just some turn of quantity of state interventionism into new quality, rather than a radical change of the path. In Russia, the processes of cautious de-statization reversed at the turn of the new century and after a few years, attempts at limiting the state's involvement in the economy (mostly unsuccessful) started to be seen again. Belarus, unlike Poland, Hungary and Russia, never really embarked upon the market reforms; therefore, the changes in the state corporate control policy (towards deregulation) were periodically introduced only reluctantly, under the pressure of a deteriorating economic situation, and were mostly called back after the situation improved.

Nowadays, the Belarusian economy is the most statized among the four countries, with SOEs and the tight governmental grip over the economy still being the core of the economic system. Hungary is at the opposite end where, despite the nationalizations of the 2010s, the SOE sector is the smallest and plays much more modest systemic role among the four countries in question. In Poland and Russia, the role of the state-controlled enterprise sector is fairly important, although currently only the Polish authorities stress its crucial role in the country's development, whereas the rhetoric of the Russian decision-makers is much more liberal—although it does not fully correspond to the economic reality, where the role of the SOE sector is still high, the second highest among the four studied countries. This was one of the main, but not the only difference in the attitude of the governments towards the role of the state corporate control in the economic policy and its goals—where no common pattern can be seen (Table 8.1).

The table includes the goals of the state corporate control as can be deducted from the official declarations of the policymakers and the practice of its functioning. The first five may be regarded as realization of socially valuable functions; the last two are of a predatory kind, aimed at restricting market mechanisms and protecting the interests of selected entities—businesses and social groups—which is effectively harmful for the society and the economy. Despite especially in the case of the sixth goal the policymakers may argue to the contrary. In Poland, both "goodwill" (including pro-development) and "predatory" goals (which in many ways are mutually contradicting) seem to play an important role; in

Table 8.1 Goals of the state corporate control at the time of the study

	Poland	*Hungary*	*Russia*	*Belarus*
1. Provision of public goods	+++	++	++	++++
2. Improvement of labor relations	+++	+	++	++
3. Generation of public funds	+++	++	++	++
4. Increasing the availability of public services	++	+++	++	++++
5. Stimulating economic development	+++	+	+++	++++
6. Reducing the role of private and foreign investors	++++	+++	++	++++
7. Generating rents	++++	+++	++++	++

The importance of the given goal is shown by the number of pluses ranging from one (this feature does not exist or is of negligible importance) to four (this feature is very important)
Source PwC (2015); own assessment

Hungary the SOE sector is mainly used to clientelist purposes through supplying the population with cheap public services and securing access to resources for the members of the political and business elite. In Russia there seems to be a contradictory coexistence of the attempts to use the SOE sector and public investments as a major tool of economic development and a widespread use of both as a source of rents. In Belarus, according to the unwritten economic doctrine, the expectations about the abilities of the SOE sector to resolve social and economic problems are very high; at the same time, the level of outright rent-seeking activity seems to be the lowest among the analyzed countries.

8.2 Reasons and Driving Forces

The study tried to answer the questions on the reasons and driving forces of these paths and outcomes. One of the main questions was to what extent they are common for the four post-communist countries and probably also a wider question, whether they are a part of some more global trend. Another more question was to what degree these factors could be contextual—i.e., were individual for each country, or for post-communist countries (or some group of them) vis-à-vis other economies, first of all the most developed ones.

The analysis of factors which may lay behind the shaping up and evolution of the state corporate control policy, including its implicit and explicit goals, shows a very differentiated picture as well—especially when changes in the relative importance of these factors are to be taken into account (Table 8.2). Using the set of possible factors analyzed in Sects. 6.2, 7.2.4, 7.3.4 and 7.4.4 within two dichotomic perspectives (acting in public vs. private interest and exogenous vs. endogenous factors), it may be argued that at the beginning of the post-communist era the role of "good faith" factors was high enough in all countries, perhaps being the highest in Poland and Hungary, albeit in Belarus it meant adherence not to market reforms but to attempts to improve the command mechanisms. Later on, the importance of these factors started to deteriorate in all countries but Belarus, giving place to private interest groups. In Hungary, it ended in capture by them of the economic policy vis-à-vis very weak and ineffective resistance of social groups opposed to rent-seeking. However, it's in Poland where the state corporate control became the main source of rents within the ownership policy of the state and probably also within the whole Polish economy. In Hungary the rent-generating potential of

Table 8.2 Importance of the factors that influence the state corporate control

	Poland	Hungary	Russia	Belarus
Good faith	++++ / + / ++	++++ / +++ / +	+++ / + / ++	++ / ++ / ++
Interest groups	+ / ++ / ++++	+ / + / ++++	+++ / ++++ / +++	++ / ++ / ++
Knowledge transfer	++ / + / +	++ / + / +	++++ / + / ++	+ / + / +
Global economic and political processes	+++ / + / ++	+++ / + / ++	++++ / ++++ / ++++	++++ / ++++ / ++++
Domestic economic challenges	++++ / ++ / +	++++ / ++ / +	++++ / +++ / +++	++ / +++ / +++
Extractive institutions	+ / ++ / +++	+ / ++ / ++++	+++ / ++++ / ++++	+++ / +++ / +++
Inclusive institutions	+++ / +++ / ++	+++ / +++ / +	++ / ++ / +	++ / + / +
Public support	+ / + / ++	+ / + / ++	+ / ++ / +	+ / + / +

In each field, the left column is the situation at the beginning of the transition, the middle column is the middle of the transition period and the right column is current situation. The importance of the given factor is shown by the number of pluses ranging from one (this feature does not exist or is of negligible importance) to four (this feature is very important)
Source Own assessment

SOEs is much weaker, the main rent-seekers concentrating in the private sector; in Russia, both sectors are predominantly captured by rent-seekers. In Belarus the level of rent-seeking (in its common meaning) is quite low despite the prevalence of extractive institutions (Acemoğlu and Robinson 2012)—but they seldom have specific individuals as beneficiaries of the redistribution of resources.

The role of the exogenous factors in shaping up and evolution of the state corporate control in all four countries was smaller than of the endogenous ones, with a greater or lesser degree of specificity in each country. At the beginning of the transition, economic policy in Poland, Hungary and Russia was influenced by "imported" concepts of liberal market reforms which had a strong impact on the ownership policy in these countries. These concepts almost completely omitted corporate control of the state, though—and only Hungarian policymakers were aware of the importance of its comprehensive reforming. Later, from the knowledge transfer perspective, state corporate control policy in all the four countries, including its changes, was a predominantly domestic product. External political and economic factors were of indirect nature for the state corporate control affecting rather the economic policy and transition processes as a whole. For Hungary and Poland, it was a political window of opportunity created by the perestroika and the dissolution of the USSR—the latter was a kind of an external factor for Russia and Belarus as well. Later, the main external factors for Poland and Hungary became associated with increasing integration with the Western world; for Russia it was foreign assistance in the 1990s, situation on the world markets since the late 1990s and economic sanctions since mid-2010s. For Belarus, the main external economic and political factors originated from the specificity of relations with Russia—first of all Russia's policy towards Belarus and the situation on the Russian market. What is worth noting, however, that in none of these countries increasing statism in their economic policies apparently was connected with the growing statist trends in the world economic literature and policy practice of the second half of the 2000s, especially after the global financial crisis broke up—the trends which have even been baptized the "return of state-owned enterprises." All the measures, including rescue nationalizations in Poland and Russia, were clearly a response to current local problems and did not initiate any substantial paradigm shift. Although of course there could be some indirect impact of the fact that the most developed countries of the West also carried out rescue nationalizations: it could create an atmosphere of social consent to increased statism.

In all the four countries, endogenous factors were the most important in the shaping up and evolution of the state corporate control. Even when some strong external factors existed, as in the case of first of all Russia and Belarus, it may be argued that high exposure on them was pre-determined by internal ones, mainly the institutional setup which to a greater or lesser extent was (and still is) flawed in all countries in question. In Russia and Belarus, it was characterized by the high role of extractive institutions from the very beginning of the transition; in Hungary and Poland their role was quite marginal at the beginning; in Poland it seemed to be growing gradually since the mid-1990, while in Hungary its growth started to be really visible later, in the 2000s. In both Poland and Hungary, it led to significant institutional changes which included a high degree of state capture by interest groups and substantial destruction of democratic mechanisms.

What also distinguishes these two pairs of countries, it's the role of the domestic economic situation. In Russia and Belarus, the changes of the economic policy, including corporate control of the state, were largely crisis-driven (also, as was noted above, under the pressure of external economic factors), whereas in Poland and Hungary policy changes took place mostly independently of internal and external shocks, being driven by other factors, first of all institutional ones. Finally, the role of public expectations and public opinion differed as well and in all these four societies strong demand for paternalistic state existed. But in no country they apparently were among the major factors affecting the policy of the state (except for individual cases such as presidential elections of 1996 in Russia). Although in Poland and Hungary they at least had to be taken into account (and actively formed) to secure electoral success—which was not the case in Russia and especially Belarus.

However, despite similarities, especially within these two pairs of countries, essential differences exist. In Poland, comparing to Hungary, inclusive institutions are still stronger, as political competition, democratic institutions and civil society still function, albeit in a flawed way, which ensures a certain degree of public control over private interest groups. Besides, the current statist policy seems to have an essential "good faith" component which also creates a demand for limiting outright rent-seeking, although this factor seemingly loses importance in the recent years. Public attitude towards economic issues in Poland is still much more pro-market than that of the Hungarian society. In Belarus, comparing to Russia, extractive institutions seem to work differently, to much lesser extent excluding the broad public from income distribution. There is much more "good faith" in the economic policy of the Belarusian authorities aimed at meeting the economic needs of the population (abstracting from how effective this policy is and from the fact that it is conducted in the absence of basic civil liberties).

All this leads to repeating a somewhat banal conclusion that institutions matter—but probably its banality originates from it simply being in many cases accurate. It may be argued that it's the peculiarities of the institutional setup that lay behind a quite unique features of the state corporate control formation and evolution in Poland which, being highly prone to rent-seeking, at the same time assured a high degree of continuity of the policy (and the possibilities to generate rents) despite changes in the composition of the ruling political elite. And the fact that the state corporate control policy became—and remained—a kind of rent-seeking enclave in this country. Lack of proper attention to the SOEs sector reform (at that part of it that didn't undergo privatization) created favorable conditions for interest groups to flourish both at the enterprise and public administration levels. At the same time reforms in other areas created institutions with higher capacities to withstand group interests, including in privatization processes and the private part of the enterprise sector—with notable complete lack of oligarchy and still very limited number of crony businesses. It is very worrying therefore that the PiS coalition politicians which hold power since 2015 clearly try to destroy the existing system of checks and balances. They not only consolidate their power over the enterprise sector through changes in the rules and procedures of state corporate control; they also introduce overall institutional changes that destroy political competition, separation of powers and public control over the authorities—pushing the Polish political and institutional setup towards authoritarianism. At the same time the system of checks and balances (what was left of it), although being unable to prevent the crawling increase in dysfunctions in the state's policy towards the enterprise sector, still restricts skidding it into being fully captured by rent-seekers.

8.3 What May Happen Next?

A question arises, what are the future prospects of the clientelist equilibrium in the state corporate control in Poland that, despite all the evolution during the last 25 years or so, functioned according to certain common regularities—and even the official paradigm change of the role of the state in the economy proclaimed in mid-2010s did not radically break its continuity. Economists usually are not good in predicting future which at least partly is not their fault, though, if we look at the number of variables to be taken into account, many of them either difficult to obtain and/or to interpret, and lack of strict pre-determination of the ways the economy and the society functions. But economists must at least try to analyze future prospects of the studied subjects. At this stage (of the study and of the development of the situation) it may be cautiously stated that that this equilibrium will not be stable in a long run, at least in Poland, despite all the stabilization efforts of the ruling political elite. Its stability is based on the existence of resources which can be distributed as rents and in patron-client relationships. Popularity of the government and the ruling party has no ideological underpinnings, the large part of the population supports them just because they "give": money in the framework of generous social programs and paternalistic protection (or at least its illusion). Depletion of these transfers and decreased sense of social security would undermine this support.

It seems that sooner or later it will happen as there is no inexhaustible supply of the resources to be transferred. They are mostly "borrowed" from the future expanding the government's obligations in the following years. The coronavirus crisis which itself poses a heavy burden on public finances may only speed up this process of depletion of resources. It also destroys social trust in the government because its anti-crisis behavior is controversial and erratic and undermines the feeling of social security. Another potential factor is possible attractiveness of alternatives proposed by the opposition. So far it is dispersed and failed to put forward solutions that would be attractive enough to the society, a considerable part of which has been "spoiled" by populist rhetoric and actions of the government and the ruling coalition. In this situation, in order to attract voters who have chosen PiS, the opposition would need to offer even more clientelist agenda, which can't be done (and the opposition mostly does not want to do it). At the same time the opposition parties fail to find agenda attractive to the rest of the voters, who in fact are more numerous than PiS supporters, but they represent a wide array of preferences and never voted unanimously.

At the time the book was finished (summer 2021), two scenarios of future developments can be drawn: more pessimistic and more optimistic with some variants between them also being possible. The main variables which would affect the choice of the path seem to be (1) the level of resource-depleting potential of the coronavirus crisis and macroeconomically reckless expenditure policy of the government, (2) financial support from the EU funds, (3) the state of the democratic institutions and (4) the ability of the opposition to offer an attractive alternative for the majority of voters. Both scenarios assume that sooner or later the existing equilibrium will shift towards more institutional inclusiveness and that it will ultimately have a positive impact on the state corporate control (its depolitization and reduction of the state domain to the level necessary to meet its socially important goals)—but only at a limited scale. I see no possibility of switching to a neoliberal policy in the enterprise sector in the foreseeable future.

The most pessimistic scenario can be called "purgation through failure": the economic crisis is mitigated with EU funds which Poland receives in the framework of the COVID Recovery and Resilience Facility (RRF) and possible future programs, perhaps also with the help of financial aid from international financial organizations. These resources prove to be inadequate in a long run and the Polish economy skids into a deep crisis and social transfers radically lose their value. The dissatisfied society, however, have no legal possibilities to use their voices, as the ruling political elite has destroyed democratic institutions, including political competition, fair electoral process, separation of powers, independent media and civil liberties. The opposition is repressed and is unable to elaborate joint agenda. Public dissatisfaction takes extra-legal forms and the authorities start losing control over the economic and political situation. Thus, a sort of Lenin's (1915) "revolutionary situation" emerges when the society does not want to live in the old way, and the authorities cannot exercise power in the old way, so changes become imminent. But unlike towards the revolution, this situation will rather push the political class to initiate cautious economic and political reforms, including streamlining the state corporate control.

The most optimistic scenario envisages shorter time perspective for changes when the ruling coalition loses unity and splits into a "predatory" part sticking to short-term rent-seeking and a moderate wing which would include pragmatics who do not want to lose sources of rents in a longer perspective and try to secure the possibility of safe exit in the case of deep economic and political turmoil. The latter group may also include those "honest" statists who sincerely believe in the possibilities of the entrepreneurial state and are aware of the growing economic threats. Among others, this would limit the destructive potential of the ruling coalition for democratic institutions and the economy. The opposition finds the common agenda (or rather re-discovers it, since it has been discussed in 2019 before the domestic and European Parliament elections): a wide coalition whose short-term goal is to win elections; all the ideological differences may surface only after the PiS coalition is removed from power. This coalition wins elections, but one should not expect that it will withdraw the state from the enterprise sector because the idea of a strong state which combines developmental and social functions is very popular among opposition parties and only a minority holds liberal views. One can rather expect attempts to streamline the role of the state in the economy in a social democratic way, make it follow the interests of the whole society and not of private interest groups. Pressure from the EU structures in the form of sanctions over rule of law violations, especially if they include financial transfer cut-offs, may make this scenario more plausible.

Some elements of these scenarios can be seen in the political reality not only of Poland, but also Hungary, Russia and Belarus. In all these countries destruction of democratic institutions is used as a tool for preservation of power. However, in all these countries power is not based solely on oppression and suppression of political competition: in order to support authoritarian governments (or those moving towards authoritarianism), the population must not only be persuaded with ideological arguments (if not to say brain-washed) and fear of repressions, but also must receive some tangible benefits—in the forms of transfers, stability of their workplaces, price control, etc. All the countries in question to a larger or lesser extent conduct such a policy of "giving." But in order to "give" resources, the authorities must "have" them; therefore, they must try not to allow these resources to be depleted—not only through ineffective economic policy, but also through rent-seeking. Perhaps this is the main reason for the (mostly unsuccessful) attempts to limit rent-seeking in Poland and Russia, attempts in partial liberalization of the economies in times of crises in Russia and Belarus, and limiting the area of the economy controlled by private interest groups in Hungary to just a few sectors.

8.4 Things to Be Done

This book presents the outcomes of the ongoing study at its present state, so a lot of topics need further elaboration and several questions are to be answered. Firstly, this is the applicability of the existing research perspectives that study the issues of the role of the state in the economy and state ownership policy. Secondly, it's the need in better understanding to what extent the experience of Poland, described in this book in detail, is universal in relation to other post-communist countries and to market economies in general. The references and comparisons to Hungary, Russia and Belarus were not exhaustive, they only indicated some similarities and differences between the countries; a wider perspective was only tackled.

8.4.1 Fine-Tuning the Use of the Research Perspectives and Tools

As it was mentioned in Chapter 1, this book did not aim to create a universal approach unifying the existing research perspectives. Its intentions in this area were much more modest: an attempt was made to make the existing research tools more applicable to the subject under the study.

I believe that my book contributed at least to a modest extent to all the research streams discussed in Chapter 2. In both **transition and economic policy research** it was first of all drawing attention at the importance of proper state corporate control in economic policy in transition and in the post-communist transition in general. And that it was mostly neglected both in economic practice and among researchers. It had adverse effects for the transition course and outcomes and for our understanding of these phenomena. One of the items of the unfinished agenda here is discussed in the next section, which is the question of the universality and specificity of the Polish experience (and also other post-communist countries with high level of statism in their economic policies). Another item seems to be the question of effective corporate control policy and tools that would make possible to avoid the dysfunctions identified in this book. My study shows that this is more institutional than technical, organizational problem. We already have extensive knowledge about corporate control solutions and state policy in the enterprise sector that really work in developed market economies and my book contributes to showing what goes wrong in the studied countries. But the question is how to prepare feasible solutions, i.e., not only technically sound, but also implementable, i.e., first of all able to withstand the resistance of private interest that are violated by such a change.

What is more, the analysis conducted in this book shows that such interest groups are able not only to block reforms, but also to contribute to certain reform reversal—which is clearly seen in the cases of expansion of the state control over enterprises in Poland, Hungary and Russia performed under the pressure of interest groups. From this perspective, Hellman's (1998) model of "partial reform equilibrium trap" should be updated: "early winners" are able not only to stop reforms in order not to allow the sources their rents to be depleted, but also to reverse them in order to increase possibilities of rent-seeking. Among others it means that achievement of the critical mass that would overcome the resistance of early winners and transformation losers (Kozarzewski and Woodward 2006) is even much harder to obtain. There is still no good recipe how to do this, and I don't propose any either. But the better we know the mechanisms that stay behind the processes we observe, the closer we are to finding practical solutions.

Within the **capitalism research**, the study corroborates the opinion expressed in Sect. 2.3.1 that a model of capitalism applicable to post-communist countries, at least those analyzed in this book, must take into account the role of the state in the enterprises sector. At the same time, from this perspective post-communist capitalism cannot be regarded and studied as an internally homogenous category. The division into "varieties of post-communist capitalism" needs further analysis.

State capitalism (SC) concept (Sect. 2.3.2) in its updated form that concentrates on relationships between the state and enterprises (Wright et al. 2021) proved to be very fruitful for analysis of state corporate control. The research conducted in this book also adds arguments in favor of the variety of possible forms and manifestations of state capitalism. Out of these varieties, the "state capitalism with populist characteristics" (Bałtowski et al. 2021) seems to fit most in terms both of the set of features and tools used by governments—which is not surprising because this model was based on the cases of Poland and Hungary. However, additional research that included an expanded the set of countries shows that the proposed model is somewhat one-sided, concentrating predominantly on outright dysfunctions and realization of private interests. Therefore, I suggest adding one more feature which is treating SOEs as a key tool of economic development. Table 8.3 shows that this feature was virtually absent only in one case—Hungary, while being important in the rest of the studied countries. Further research on the specificity of SC in post-communist countries is needed though, on a larger set of cases in order to study in more depth common features and varieties within this group of economies. Perhaps also even wider approach is needed: to expand the analysis beyond the transition countries using a universal set of variables, which may help to understand what features of SC in selected groups of countries are of universal character and what are contextual.

Last but not least, an "unorthodox" approach claiming that the system which has shaped up in several post-communist countries cannot be described within capitalism concepts (Sect. 2.3.3) is worth further elaboration. Contrary to the claims of the authors of these theories, they seem to be applicable not only to descripting the whole economic "non-capitalist" models ("resource economy," "distributive economy"), but

Table 8.3 Features and tools of state capitalism

	Poland	*Hungary*	*Russia*	*Belarus*
Features				
SOEs as a key tool of development policy	+++	+	+++	++++
Politicization of SOEs	++++	+++	++++	++
Politicization of SOEs *à rebours*	+++	++	++	+++
Cronyism	+++	++++	++++	++
Oligarchy	+	+++	+++	+
Economic populism	++++	++++	++++	++++
Economic nationalism	+++	++	++++	++
Tools				
Impact through enterprises in which the state has more than 50% of shares	+++	+++	+++	++++
Impact through enterprises in which the state has 25–50% of shares (SCEs)	++++	++	+++	++++
Restricting ownership rights of private businesses	++	+++	+++	++++
Regulatory tools	++	++++	+++	++++
Persuasion, pressure, threats	++	+++	+++	+++

The importance of the given feature or tool is shown by the number of pluses ranging from one (this feature does not exist or is of negligible importance) to four (this feature is very important)
Source Bałtowski et al. (2021); own assessment

also features of specific capitalist models where the redistributive function of the state is especially pronounced and where SOEs are treated as a source of a variety of resources for such redistribution. And these features were identified in Poland, Hungary and Russia. At the same time there are strong doubts whether economies of Russia and even Belarus can be fully described with the help of this concept, because market relationships, especially in Russia (which was the case study for the initial research), are integral part of their economies as well. I believe that the concept of redistribution proposed in these theories needs further examination within capitalism studies (especially on SC), with a closer look at its manifestations and mechanisms.

8.4.2 Universality and Specificity

The study presented in this book tackles the problem of causality, the factors that stay behind the regularities of state corporate control in post-communist countries and the reasons of different paths and outcomes, in a limited way. It concentrated predominantly on mechanisms; besides, the fundamental causes of similarities were studied in more detail than the causes of the existing varieties. Plausible explanations of this variety within the studied group have been presented (which refer, among others, to historical, cultural and institutional differences). However, the question remains open what makes a post-communist country conduct a policy of state interventionism in the enterprise sector, especially to a large extent driven by private interests, in the situation when governments in a number of other post-communist countries, especially in Central and Eastern Europe, are much less interventionist and less captured by private interest groups. How come that Poland and Hungary, formerly the best transition performers (which allows to assume that they were generally the most capable institutionally), became probably the most captured states in this region?

Another question to be answered in future research is how universal is the character of the statist paths in these (and several other) post-communist countries. Is it a kind of a post-communist curse, a trap in which several transition countries have fallen? Or such developments reflect some global trend or at least share some universal regularities? Ten years ago, the most plausible answer to the second question would be "apparently, they do" because the "return of SOEs" looked like a part of a global trend. Indeed, since the global crisis of 2008–2009 state interventionism in the enterprise sector was included in the set of crisis management tools used in developed market economies, but after the crisis ended, their governments started withdrawing from performing ownership functions. So ultimately no "return of SOEs" in fact took place and there are little reasons to believe that the next crisis would change that, i.e., would change this temporary anti-crisis tool into a permanent tool used as a major factor for boosting economic development and welfare.

Therefore, maybe the case of Poland and several other post-communist countries are just isolated cases—not reflecting global trends or universal regularities. Is it just an outcome of certain specific circumstances—such as a combination of weak, not yet fully formed institutional system with a particular historical and cultural legacy?

References

Acemoğlu, Daron, and James A. Robinson. 2012. *Why Nations Fail: The Origins of Power, Prosperity, and Poverty*. New York: Crown Publishers.

Bałtowski, Maciej, Piotr Kozarzewski, and Tomasz Mickiewicz. 2021. "State Capitalism in Poland and Hungary: Populist Varieties." In *Oxford Handbook on State Capitalism and the Firm*, edited by Mike Wright, Geoffrey Wood, Alvaro Cuervo-Cazurra, Pei Sun, Ilya Okhmatovskiy, and Anna Grosman. Oxford: Oxford University Press (forthcoming).

Hellman, Joel S. 1998. "Winners Take All: The Politics of Partial Reform in Postcommunist Transition." *World Politics* 50 (2): 203–234.

Kozarzewski, Piotr, and Richard Woodward. 2006. "The Reform Process in Post-communist Transition: Understanding Reform in Eastern and Central Europe and the Commonwealth of Independent States." In *Understanding Market Reforms, Vol. 2, Motivation, Implementation and Sustainability*, edited by José MariaFanelli and Gary McMahon, 141–192. New York: Palgrave Macmillan.

Lenin, Vladimir. 1915. "Krakh II Internatsionala" [The Collapse of the Second International]. *Kommunist* 1–2.

OECD. 2015. *OECD Guidelines on Corporate Governance of State-Owned Enterprises*. 2015 ed. Paris: OECD Publishing.

PwC. 2015. *State-Owned Enterprises: Catalysts for Public Value Creation?* Arlington: PwC.

World Bank. 2014. *Corporate Governance of State-Owned Enterprises: A Toolkit*. Washington: The World Bank.

Wright, Mike, Geoffrey Wood, Alvaro Cuervo-Cazurra, Pei Sun, Ilya Okhmatovskiy, and Anna Grosman, eds. 2021. *Oxford Handbook on State Capitalism and the Firm*. Oxford: Oxford University Press (forthcoming).

Index

P. Kozarzewski, *State Corporate Control in Transition*,
https://doi.org/10.1007/978-3-030-78562-8

The manufacturer's authorised representative in the EU is Springer Nature Customer Service Centre GmbH, Europaplatz 3, 69115 Heidelberg, Germany. If you have any concerns regarding our products, please contact ProductSafety@springernature.com

Printed and bound by CPI Group (UK) Ltd, Croydon, CR0 4YY
30/09/2026
02225700-0012